KALAMBO FALLS
PREHISTORIC SITE

I

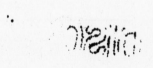

KALAMBO FALLS PREHISTORIC SITE

I
THE GEOLOGY, PALAEOECOLOGY AND DETAILED STRATIGRAPHY OF THE EXCAVATIONS

J. D. CLARK

Professor of Anthropology
University of California
Berkeley

WITH CONTRIBUTIONS BY
G. H. COLE
E. G. HALDEMANN
M. R. KLEINDIENST
E. M. VAN ZINDEREN BAKKER

CAMBRIDGE
AT THE UNIVERSITY PRESS
1969

Published by the Syndics of the Cambridge University Press
Bentley House, 200 Euston Road, London, N.W.1
American Branch: 32 East 57th Street, New York, N.Y.10022

© Cambridge University Press 1969

Library of Congress Catalogue Card Number: 68–25084

Standard Book Number: 521 06962 9

Printed in Great Britain
at the University Printing House, Cambridge
(Brooke Crutchley, University Printer)

To
JOHN HODGES
and
JIM CHAPLIN

CONTENTS

Acknowledgments   *page* xiv

1 The Prehistory of the Kalambo Falls: General Description   1
   by J. D. CLARK, *Professor of Anthropology, University of California, Berkeley*

2 Geology   20
   Part I: Geological and Physiographical Setting of the Kalambo
   Falls Prehistoric Site   20
   by E. G. HALDEMANN, *Chief Geologist European Division, Falconbridge Nickel
   Mines Limited, Toronto*

   Part II: Formal Nomenclature applied to Rock Stratigraphic Units
   recognized in the Quaternary Sediments of the Kalambo Falls   46
   Prehistoric Site
   by M. R. KLEINDIENST, *formerly Department of Anthropology, University of
   Chicago*

3 The Pleistocene Vegetation and Climate of the Basin   57
   by E. M. VAN ZINDEREN BAKKER, *Professor of Botany and Director of
   Palynological Research, University of the Orange Free State, Bloemfontein*

4 The Excavations: Site A   85
   by J. D. CLARK *and* M. R. KLEINDIENST

5 The Excavations: Sites B, C and D   153
   by J. D. CLARK *and* G. H. COLE, *Field Museum of Natural History, Chicago*

6 Correlation of Archaeological Sites in the Local Basin at the
   Kalambo Falls   190
   by J. D. CLARK

Appendices

A The Geology of the Kalambo Falls Prehistoric Site   197
   by GEOFFREY BOND, *Professor of Geology, University College of Rhodesia and
   Nyasaland*

vii

CONTENTS

B   Description of White Clay Band, Lower Clay Bank, Trench A 4,
    Site A, Kalambo Falls Prehistoric Site   *page* 215
    by D. R. C. KEMP, *Geologist, Tanganyika Ministry of Commerce and Industry*
    Geological Survey Division Laboratory Services

C   Identification of Fruits and Seeds from Site B, Kalambo Falls   216
    by F. WHITE, *Commonwealth Forestry Institute, Oxford*

D   Provisional Identifications of Charcoals and Wood Samples from
    the Kalambo Falls Prehistoric Site   218
    by L. CHALK, *Commonwealth Forestry Institute, Oxford*

E   Report on Bark and other Specimens from Site B, Kalambo Falls,
    Depositional Phase F 2, White Sands Beds, Mkamba Member   221
    by T. C. WHITMORE, *Department of Botany, University of Southampton*

F   Check List of eighty-two Botanical Specimens of Trees and Shrubs
    collected in the vicinity of the Kalambo Falls Local Basin   225
    by MRS MARY RICHARDS, *Abercorn, Zambia. Identified by* MARY RICHARDS,
    L. D. F. VESEY-FITZGERALD, *Principal Scientific Officer International Red*
    Locust Control Service (retired) and D. B. FANSHAWE, *Principal Scientific*
    Officer, Zambia Department of Forests

G   List of useful Plants, Trees and Shrubs collected in the immediate
    vicinity of the Kalambo Falls Local Basin in 1956   228
    by L. E. HODGES, *Rhodesian National Monuments Commission, and* J. D. CLARK

H   Heavy Mineral Analysis of Samples from Sites A, B and D, 1956
    Excavations   230
    by DEREK SEARLE, *Field Geologist, Anglo-American Corporation*

I   Summary of Analysed Pollen Samples: Kalambo Falls   232

J   Summary of Radiocarbon Dates from Excavated Samples,
    Kalambo Falls Prehistoric Site   236

K   Archaeological Horizons and aggregates from Archaeological
    Horizons, Kalambo Falls Prehistoric Site   238

    Bibliography   243

    Index   247

PLATES

(BETWEEN PAGES 240 AND 241)

Unless otherwise stated, photographs were taken by J. D. Clark

1   The Kalambo Falls from the air at the end of the dry season (October 1966). (*Photo. G. H. Cole.*)

2   Air photograph of the western end of the local basin at the Kalambo Falls showing the 1956 and 1959 excavations. (*Photo. Fairey Air Surveys of Rhodesia, Ltd, 1960.*)

3   The local basin at the Kalambo Falls looking east from the top of the 'Tanganyika Cliff' (Mkamba Member).

4   Eroded feature of Chitambala Gravel Beds with soil-covered Chisya Gravel Beds in foreground. (*Photo. G. Bond.*)

5   The lip of the falls from immediately upstream—end of the dry season, 1959.

6   The landslide between Sites D and B caused by the heavy rains of the 1961–2 season.

7   The Kalambo Falls during a period of very low water in October 1959 as seen from the Zambia (Northern Rhodesia) side. (*Photo. E. G. Haldemann.*)

8   The cliff on the southern side of the Kalambo Gorge as seen from the slope a little to the north above the Kalambo Falls (September 1959). (*Photo. E. G. Haldemann.*)

9   The Kalambo Gorge as seen from the hill to the north of the Kalambo Falls (August 1963). (*Photo. M. R. Kleindienst.*)

10   The Kalambo River in the Spillway Gorge during low water conditions (October 1959). (*Photo. E. G. Haldemann.*)

11   General view of Site A, excavation A 1, 1956. (*Photo. G. Bond.*)

12   A 1, 1956 (Chiungu Member) excavation, northeast wall section.

13   A 1, 1956 excavation. General view of Archaeological Horizon Rubble Ic.

14   A 1, 1956 excavation. Part of the east wall (northeast corner).

15   A 1, 1956 excavation, showing the lower part of the south wall.

16   A 1, 1956 excavation. The 'sump' in grid squares BC 8–9 dug to drain the remainder of the excavation.

17   A 2, 1956 excavation, the west end.

18   A 3, 1956 excavation, the southwest side.

19   Trench A 4, 1959, looking north to the Kalambo River. (*Photo. M. R. Kleindienst.*)

20 Trench A 4, looking south, cleared to the level of Archaeological Horizon Rubble I-composite, and showing the nature of this deposit (September 1959). (*Photo. E. G. Haldemann.*)

21 Trench A 4, Pit 1, 1963, south wall.

22 Trench A 4, 1959, river end north of grid line 21 (November 1959). (*Photo. B. Anthony.*)

23 The 1959 River Face Cliff clearance, looking toward the eroded Trench A 1 from near the mouth of Trench A 4. (*Photo. M. R. Kleindienst.*)

24 B 1, 1956 excavation, looking west to the river edge.

25 B 2, 1959 excavation, south wall excavated to a depth of 7 feet.

26 B 2, 1959 excavation, west and south walls.

27 B 2, 1959 excavation. General view looking northeast.

28 B 2, 1959 excavation, western end of north wall.

29 B 2, 1959 excavation, south wall showing the excavation carried to water level.

30 B 2, 1959 excavation, east and north walls showing the Acheulian Archaeological Horizon V surface.

31 View of Site C facing downstream (1966). (*Photo. G. H. Cole.*)

32 Site D in 1956.

FIGURES

1 The Kalambo Falls and surrounding country: locality maps.   *facing page* 1

2 The Kalambo Falls Prehistoric Site: contour map of part of the western end of the local basin showing the position of the sites.   *page* 14

3 Topographic sections (W. S. Chape) across the local basin at the Kalambo Falls.   15

4 Map of Kalambo drainage basin in Tanzania/Zambia showing the physiographical setting of the Kalambo Falls Prehistoric Site.   *facing page* 21

5 Provisional geological map of the local basin at the Kalambo Falls.   *page* 22

6 Profile of Augur Hole 2, opposite A 4 excavation, Kalambo Falls Prehistoric Site.   36

7 Geological section across the Kalambo valley at the Prehistoric Site.   *facing page* 38

8 Geological section across the Spillway Gorge at the Kalambo Falls Prehistoric Site.   *page* 39

9 Diagram showing frequency and orientation of long axes of 161 boulders in the Kalambo River in relation to the direction of flow.   40

FIGURES

10 Diagram showing frequency and orientation of long axes of 150 cobbles, boulders and artifacts in Rubble I-composite, A 4 excavation, Kalambo Falls Prehistoric Site. *page* 41

11 Cliff section at Site C, Kalambo Falls Prehistoric Site. 51

12 Locality map showing the area between Lake Mweru and Lake Malawi. 59

13 Schematic representation of the altitudinal distribution of the vegetation in the area. 60

14 The ecotone between montane forest and *Brachystegia* woodland near Sao Hill, Tanzania. (*After J. Proctor.*) 61

15 Schematic section of a valley with impeded drainage. 62

16 The position of the pollen samples collected in 1966, Site A, 1966 excavation. 66

17 Comparison of the temperature curve published by Wolstedt for the last 70,000 years in Europe with the results obtained at the Kalambo Falls. 72

18 Outlines of Site A excavations, showing grids. 89

19 Kalambo Falls Prehistoric Site: Plan of Site A, 1963. 91

20 Kalambo Falls Prehistoric Site at Site A: East Wall section of A 1 excavation, 1956. 94

21 Kalambo Falls Prehistoric Site at Site A: section at south wall of A 1 excavation, 1956. 96

22 Kalambo Falls Prehistoric Site at Site A: sections at west wall of A 1 excavation, 1956. 98

23 Kalambo Falls Prehistoric Site at Site A: section at north wall of A 1 excavation, 1956. 100

24 Kalambo Falls Prehistoric Site at Site A: section at north wall of A 2 excavation, 1956. 110

25 Kalambo Falls Prehistoric Site at Site A: sections at south and west walls of A 2 excavation, 1963. 111

26 Kalambo Falls Site A: sections at west and south walls of A 3 excavation, 1956. The deposits shown in the south wall section below Rubble Ib are those exposed in the 'River Face' cliff. 114

27 Kalambo Falls Prehistoric Site, Site A: section of A 6 excavation, 1966. 119

28 Kalambo Falls Prehistoric Site, Site A: west wall section of A 4 excavations, 1959 and 1963. *facing page* 124

29 Kalambo Falls Prehistoric Site, Site A: east wall section of A 4 excavations, 1959 and 1963. 124

30 Diagrams showing frequency and orientation of long axes of boulders in Rubbles IIa and IIb at A 4 excavation, 1963. *page* 134

31 Site A, Kalambo Falls: east, west and south wall sections, A 5 excavation, 1963. 139

32 Kalambo Falls Prehistoric Site, Site A: composite section of 'River Face' cliff based on excavations 1956–63. *facing page* 140

FIGURES

33 Kalambo Falls Prehistoric Site: Plan of Site B, 1963.   *page* 154

34 Site B excavations, showing grids.   155

35 Site B, Kalambo Falls: north and east (line 10) wall sections of B 1 excavation,
    1956.   *facing page* 156

36 Site B, Kalambo Falls: north section of B 2 excavation, 1959.   164

37 Site B, Kalambo Falls: south section of B 2 excavation, 1959.   164

38 Site B, Kalambo Falls: west wall section of B 2 excavation, 1959.   172

39 Site B, Kalambo Falls: east wall section of B 2 excavation, 1959 and sections in
    Pits B 3 and B 4, 1959.   172

40 Plan of excavations at Site C and generalized section of the Site C rubble lines as
    seen in excavations and cleared sections.   *page* 183

41 Site D, Kalambo Falls: east and south wall sections.   *facing page* 186

42 Drawings of seeds from Acheulian horizon VI at Site B, 1956, Kalambo Falls
    Prehistoric Site.   *page* 217

VOLUMES II AND III

Volumes II and III will cover the history and
ethnography of the Kalambo Falls area and
describe the archaeological industrial stages from
the Iron Age to the Acheulian with a general
discussion of the significance of the site

ACKNOWLEDGMENTS

Work at the Kalambo Falls Prehistoric Site has been spread over a period of fourteen years and it is not surprising, therefore, that there are many to be thanked for their help, which not only made possible the excavations but contributed materially to the extent of the evidence recovered from them.

Generous financial assistance for the 1956 season was received from the Wenner-Gren Foundation for Anthropological Research and for the 1959 work from the Boise Fund of Oxford University. The continued interest in the excavations taken by the late Dr Paul Fejos and the encouragement given to us by Sir Wilfrid LeGros Clark are most gratefully acknowledged. The National Science Foundation, Washington and the African Studies Program of the University of California, Los Angeles, made possible the analysis work during the summer of 1962 and the further laboratory and excavation programme undertaken during 1963. The Trustees of the Rhodes-Livingstone Museum were always most generous in their support of the Kalambo project while I served as Director of the Museum and gave me every facility when I returned to Northern Rhodesia in 1962 and 1963. The Northern Rhodesian Government and the Zambian Government, through their departmental officers, also rendered us much valuable assistance and advice. To all these I wish to record my sincere appreciation and thanks.

In the field we received help from many and varied quarters, but in particular I wish to thank the following for their invaluable collaboration which contributed so materially to the subject-matter of these volumes: J. W. Clayphan, W. S. Chape and the Surveyor-General of the Northern Rhodesian Department of Lands and Surveys for the topographic surveys of the Kalambo basin. Professor Geoffrey Bond and the Director of the National Museums of Southern Rhodesia and Dr E. G. Haldemann and the Director of the Geological Survey of Tanganyika for the geological mapping and morphological history of the basin. My colleagues and fellow archaeologists in the field—Dr Maxine Kleindienst and Mrs Lilian Hodges and all those mentioned by name in the following chapters—who gave so freely and uncomplainingly of their time and experience both on the excavations and in the laboratory. Similarly I must thank my colleagues in the Rhodes-Livingstone Museum (now the Livingstone Museum) and the National Monuments Commission of Zambia. The debt of Prehistory as well as my own debt to them all is immense and it is not only a duty but also a pleasure to acknowledge their help here. Some of them—Dr M. R. Kleindienst, Dr G. H. Cole, Dr B. M. Fagan and Mr Francis van Noten—are also contributors to these volumes.

When camped at Kalambo it was inevitable that we should on occasions seek help and advice from local officials and residents of Abercorn and their most generous response and friendship will always be remembered. In particular must be mentioned Miss Marian and Miss Hope Gamwell, Mr and Mrs John Carlin and Mr Colin Carlin, the District Commissioners and District Officers of the Provincial Administration, the Director and the Principal Scientific Officer, Mr L. D. F. Vesey-FitzGerald, of the International Red Locust Control Service. The interest and the many kindnesses of these people who became our friends not only smoothed our way but made our visits to Kalambo so completely unforgettable.

It was apparent from the wealth of vegetable remains found in the Pleistocene basin that it would be necessary to study the existing flora of the region. Accordingly, Mrs Mary Richards made a collection, now housed in the Botany School, Cambridge, of the flora of the Kalambo basin and vicinity, including the bark of many of the trees for comparison with the fossil bark (Appendix F). Mr D. B. Fanshawe, Principal Scientific Officer of the Northern Rhodesia Department of Forest Ecology, has kindly identified a collection of edible relishes, fruits and medicinal and other useful plants and trees collected by us in the basin. To both our grateful thanks are recorded here (Appendix G).

The pollens from the Pleistocene beds have been studied by Professor E. M. van Zinderen Bakker of the University of the Orange Free State, Bloemfontein, who has also contributed chapter 3. Drs L. Chalk, J. F. Hughes, and F. White of the Commonwealth Forestry Institute, Oxford, have studied and reported on the woods and seeds associated with the Acheulian and Sangoan occupation horizons, and Dr T. C. Whitmore has examined and reported on the bark recovered from these levels (Appendices C, D and E).

Dr Derek Searle carried out a heavy mineral analysis of sediments from the 1956 excavations (Appendix H). Dr Alex Muir of the Rothamsted Experimental Station, Harpenden, Herts, and Mr R. Webster of the Mount Mukulu Agricultural Station, Northern Rhodesia examined and reported on the organic muds and geophagous clays from the Acheulian horizons. Professor Sherburne F. Cook, of the Department of Physiology of the University of California at Berkeley, carried out the phosphorus and calcium analysis of the Iron Age midden and of Complex 11 on Site C.

To all of these experts our most grateful appreciation and thanks are due for their collaboration.

Dr K. P. Oakley, Keeper of the Sub-Department of Anthropology at the British Museum, assisted in many ways and in particular with the preservation and casting of the wooden artifacts. The actual preservative treatment was undertaken at the British Museum Research Laboratory through the kindness of Dr H. J. Plenderleith and by a new technique developed for wood of this antiquity by Mr R. M. Organ. To these three colleagues we gratefully acknowledge our indebtedness.

The dating of the radiocarbon samples has been carried out by Dr Wallace Broecker and Dr Edwin A. Olson of the Lamont Geochronological Laboratory, Columbia University, New York, and by Dr H. de Vries and Dr J. C. Vogel of the Natuurkundig Laboratorium der Rijksuniversiteit at Groningen, and the important results they have obtained put us all in their debt.

Of the many illustrations of the cultural material Mr Francis van Noten contributed those of the stone and iron objects found with the 'Later Stone Age' and Iron Age industries from the 1963 excavations at Site C; my son, John W. D. Clark, drew all the Iron Age pottery while my wife, Mrs B. C. Clark, is responsible for the drawings of the remaining cultural material, which is considerable. Mrs Eve Kemnitzer has redrawn the plans and sections of the excavation for publication. To each of them I wish to express my personal thanks and especially to my wife, whose encouragement and whose help in typing the manuscripts and in innumerable other ways has played such an important part in seeing this work through the press.

Other acknowledgments by those contributing the various special chapters will be made in the appropriate places.

I have reserved to the end the expression of thanks of myself and my colleagues in the Kalambo excavations to Mr Joseph Siantumbu. He served the Rhodes-Livingstone Museum for many years before 'retiring' to take up the duties of a village headman, from which he periodically 'returned to active life' to help us at Kalambo. We also owe a debt of gratitude to our labourers, most of whom have worked for us for three or more seasons. Their efforts—if not always willing, yet ever cheerful—were the practical means by which we were able to move vast areas of deposit and to recover 10–15 tons (10,160–15,240 kg) of artifacts. My colleagues and I think of them with affection and our thanks are gratefully recorded here.

J.D.C

CHAPTER 1

THE PREHISTORY OF THE KALAMBO FALLS: GENERAL DESCRIPTION

BY J. D. CLARK

The Kalambo Falls are situated at latitude 8° 30' S, longitude 31° 15' E on the edge of the Tanganyika Rift escarpment, near the southeastern corner of Lake Tanganyika, at an altitude of 3,772 feet (1,150 m). Twenty-one miles (33·5 km) to the south-southeast is the township of Abercorn, which was our centre for supplies. Abercorn is now connected with the falls by a good earth road so that the journey, which in 1953 took three and a half hours, can now be completed in three-quarters of an hour (Figure 1).

This approach road from Abercorn runs close to the side of two small swampy basins, filled with sediments, Ichianga and Siszya, but these contain no natural exposures like those at Kalambo. After this the road follows the summit of Siszya ridge, from which the country slopes steeply on the west to Lake Tanganyika. Through the *Brachystegia* woodland, carpeted with sparse grass, bracken and *Strophanthus*, occasional glimpses can be obtained of the lake itself. This ridge descends gradually, in two steps, and terminates at Polungu Hill. There is a superb view of the southern end of the lake, from Polungu Hill on a clear day, looking to Mpulungu and over to the western escarpment in the Congo Republic. To the east and north of this hill lie the Kalambo Gorge and the local basin, shut in, except at the northern end, by steep hills rising to heights of 600 feet (183 m) from the floor of the basin.

The road winds steeply down over quartzite and sandstone rock, a dolerite dyke or sill and then more quartzites, to the basin floor where the rich alluvial soils permit a few hundred Lungu villagers to make a permanent home by practising an effective but simple system of crop rotation. These are the only villages for several miles around and the absence of population—human and animal—in the surrounding poor woodland soils of the escarpment country is as noticeable a feature today as it was to Mrs Gordon Gallien's party in 1928 (Gordon-

Gallien, 1929). This is a country which is *traversed* but not occupied by the human and game populations moving from the lake to the higher, better watered parts of the plateau and *vice versa*, and for far back into the past it cannot have supported any appreciable population. The small but rich local basin above the Kalambo Falls must, therefore, have always served as an important stopping place in the movement of man and beast out of and into the Tanganyika Rift.

Today the vegetation at Kalambo Falls shows the effects of long years of cultivation and of cutting and burning. The Zambian side, however, has been a forest and game reserve for some years now so that the woodland has had a chance to recover. The upper slopes, down to the edge of the alluvial sediments, are populated by *Marquesia/Brachystegia* woodland forms among which the broad, shiny leaved *musuku* (*Uapaca pilosa*), the evergreen *mpundu* (*Parinarium curatellifolia*) and the *kapele* (*Ziziphus abysinica*) bear edible fruits. Although the buttress-rooted *Marquesia* itself does not occur in the valley today it is present on the hills and on the plateau not many miles distant.

Today the alluvium is covered every year by a nearly impenetrable growth of 'elephant' grass of the genus *Hyparrhenia* but this is, no doubt, largely the result of cultivation. Where, however, erosion or poor soil restricts grass growth it is not uncommon to find a dense mass of thorny thicket and nearer the river groups of *Borassus* palm and an occasional *Ficus* and *Acacia*. *Phragmites* reeds grow thickly in the swamp.

In spite of annual burning the *Hyparrhenia* grass is just as thick and tall every year—no doubt as a result of the comparatively high rainfall which brings the river down in flood from January to March and renders the clean and regular excavations of the previous year almost unrecognizable.

This part of the great elevated Central African shield of ancient rocks, mostly Plateau Series sandstones, is known as the Tanganyika Plateau. It is reasonably well watered and lies at an average elevation of between 4,000 and 5,000 feet (1,220 and 1,525 m) above sea level. On the Zambian side of the border for the most part the country is flat and undulating and above it rise occasional ridges or isolated hills of up to 5,500 or 6,000 feet (1,677–1,830 m) (Figure 1).

The rocks are mostly sandstones, quartzites and shales belonging to the Katanga/Kundelungu System of Precambrian age through which have been intruded sandstones, dolerites and porphyries (Reeve, 1961), all of which have suffered, first, extensive folding and then pene- and pedeplanation, during earlier Miocene and older times (Haughton, 1963). Rifting, cutting across this ancient peneplain, perhaps beginning in the Tertiary but most extensively in the Pleistocene, has produced the deep, precipitous, scarped and lake-filled troughs of Tanganyika, Rukwa and Malawi, sunk some 2,000 feet (610 m) and more below the plateau. This earth movement was accompanied by volcanic activity at the north end of Lake Malawi (formerly Nyasa) where the Rungwe volcanic intrusions reach a height of 9,713 feet (2,962 m).

This tectonic activity has raised up the plateau surface that flanks the rift and so produced the elevated horst known as the Ufipa Highlands, lying between the southeast side of Lake Tanganyika and the Rukwa rift; and a similar block of high country between the Kipengere and Odzungene ranges to the north and north-northeast end of Lake Malawi.

The country at the southeast end of Lake Tanganyika is, therefore, a terrain of sharp changes in relief—of humid highland ridges and plateaux, dry sunken troughs, steep, dissected escarpments and deeply incised river valleys. From the highlands forming the watershed between three drainage basins streams flow westward and southward to Lake Tanganyika, the Congo and the Atlantic Ocean. To the eastward they flow to Lake Malawi and the Indian Ocean and northward to the basin of internal drainage that contains Lake Rukwa.

The high ridge country is shaped like a Y with Lake Rukwa near the centre. It forms a natural access route from East Africa into the southern parts of the central plateau. This 'Tanganyika–Nyasa corridor' country, as it has been called, between Lakes Tanganyika and Malawi must always have been a most important, if not the main highway for movement between the interior of southern Africa and the northeast. It was probably the route down which the earliest food-producing peoples entered southern Africa. It was the route used twice by the Ngoni in the earlier part of the nineteenth century and Arab trade routes from the coast passed down both arms of the Y to converge in northeastern Zambia on the way to Katanga.

Abercorn at 5,400 feet (1,647 m) and the surrounding area of the plateau receive a mean annual rainfall of between 40 and 48 inches (1,000 and 1,200 mm), though in exceptional years, such as 1962, as much as 72 inches (1,800 mm) has been recorded. The Kalambo Falls lie just within the rain shadow of Lake Tanganyika, however, and the mean annual rainfall is between 48 and 56 inches (1,200 and 1,400 mm). This is the total rainfall, likely to be reached or exceeded one year in five, but in four years out of five the total likely to be reached lies between 40 and 48 inches (1,000 and 1,200 mm). Rainfall variability is calculated at not more than 15 per cent. Mean seasonal effective rainfall for the Abercorn and Kalambo Falls region is shown at between 24 and 28 inches (600 and 700 mm), where effective rainfall is the amount that goes to replenish ground-water and so is available for plant growth. The remaining rainfall is surplus run-off which, however, contributes to stream flow. This surplus is spread over the greater part of the rainy season from December to March. This is, of course, an

3

area of summer rains which commence in late October and continue until early April. There is, therefore, a six months dry season. (*Atlas of Fed. Rhod. and Nyld.*, 1961, maps 12A and 12B; Jackson, 1961, map 4.)

The mean annual temperatures at Kalambo Falls lie close to the 72·5° F (22·5° C) isotherm and are higher than those on the plateau, which average between 63·5° and 68° F (17·5° and 20° C) at Abercorn, some 1,900 feet (579·5 m) higher. The mean maximum temperature for Kalambo is about 82° F (28° C). The mean maximum for the hottest month—October—at the end of the dry season is 90·5°–95° F (32·5°–35° C) and for January, about the height of the rains, is 77°–81·5° F (25°–27·5° C). The local basin above the Kalambo Falls is also relatively more humid, lying within the 70–75 per cent range. The prevailing winds and those that bring the rain come from the southeast and blow from the Indian Ocean. (*Atlas of Fed. Rhod. and Nyld.*, 1961, maps 14 and 15; Jackson, 1961, map 10.)

These altitudinal and meteorological differences have produced considerable variation in the vegetation patterns as between the plateau, the low-lying lake basins of internal drainage and the highlands above 5,500 feet (1,677 m). The sandstone and quartzites which form the solid geology of the greater part of the plateau produce light brown to buff sandy soils, quickly drained, heavily leached and often grey in colour in the lower lying parts. The fertility of these soils is low and they are locally underlain by massive ferricrete.

In places, however, as over much of the Abercorn plateau, arkose and intrusive igneous rocks have developed red earths with a clay-loam texture, and in deep sections it can be seen that they overlie much weathered and reddened rock which recalls the laterites of the Congo basin. The fertility yield of these soils is high and they support woodland of the very extensive *Brachystegia* and *Julbernardia* type (sometimes known as *miombo* woodland) that forms part of the woodland savannah which covers so much of the continent south of the Sahara outside the region of Equatorial lowland forest. The main trees are deciduous and grow close together but never form a closed canopy so that grasses and low scrub are always present.

On alluvial soils and on the watersheds a type of woodland known as *chipya* ('fierce fire') is found in which *Marquesia* and *Entandrophragma* are two of the dominants. This is sometimes associated with evergreen thicket and Lawton suggests that it may be a degraded form of dry, evergreen, tropical forest now nearly destroyed by man (Lawton, 1963, p. 53). The *miombo* and *chipya* woodland is the type of vegetation on which the indigenous population largely practises the *chitimene* (slash and burn) type of agriculture.

Running through this plateau woodland are wide, shallow, grass-filled valleys known as *dambos* some of which combine in the headwaters to form major rivers such as the Chambeshi, one of the sources of the Congo River, or the Luangwa, one of the major tributaries of the Zambezi. These *dambos* are seasonally or perennially swampy with a stream at the centre which may support relict or edaphic patches of evergreen forest known as *mushitu* along its banks. These *mushitu* are of considerable interest for interpreting the past vegetational history of the local Kalambo basin. They preserve a closed tropical forest habitat, a closed canopy, protection from fire, a high humidity and a permanent water supply. They have been described as 'an ecological retreat which provides favourable habitat conditions for moisture-loving tropical forest tree species' (Lawton, 1963, p. 57).

In composition the *mushitu* contains other species besides true swamp forest trees, which belong with the lowland forests of the Congo and west Africa, and others again that are typical of the wet, cool, montane forests of east and central Africa. Both have found refuge in the riverine forests and are confirmatory evidence for the belief, which the pollen evidence from Kalambo does much to substantiate, that at one or more periods in the past the climate was favourable to the spread of lowland moist forest of the Congo type, while at other periods cooler and wetter conditions permitted the montane forests, now growing at 6,000 feet (1,830 m) and upwards in some of the higher country of the Ufipa and Poroto Mountains, the Muchinga Escarpment or the Nyika Plateau, to spread down on to the main parts of the plateau.

Any *mushitu* that may once have existed in the valley above Kalambo Falls has long since been destroyed by cultivation, but two can still be seen occupying sheltered niches half-way up the slopes of what the 1928 Expedition called Burnt Ridge on the Tanzania side of the valley. A thick growth, largely of evergreen trees and bush in which the *Parinarii* is prominent, still makes any mapping of the Spillway Gorge a surveyor's nightmare. There is a fairly continuous growth of *Syzygium guineense* along the river banks with sometimes *Diospyros*, *Kigelia* (or 'sausage tree') or *Parkia*. Two groves of oil palm (*Elaeis guineensis*) are growing in the sheltered mouths of two tributary streams on the Tanzania side but it is not known whether they are indigenous or imported. The oil palm is a valuable food source and its growth in favoured localities in the corridor country is a further indicator of the former wider extent of lowland moist forest in the past.

One of the most interesting of the *mushitu* is that of Siszya, some 14 miles (22·4 km) southeast of Kalambo. This is a 'dry' forest and is not associated with a stream but is able to survive because it is ecologically complete. It contains predominantly moist tropical forest species though some montane species are also present.

5

In addition to the large synclinal basin that contains Lake Bangweulu, to the southwest, there are a number of small lakes and swamps which, in the vicinity of the Rift, owe their origin to the tilting that has uplifted these marginal areas. There are many such small basins in the Abercorn and Sumbawanga districts today and some of them contain open water lakes such as Chila at Abercorn. Others, as the Ichianga basin about 10 miles (16 km) south-southeast of Kalambo, are now swampy while others, like the Umgini pans south of Abercorn, are mostly dry. The heavy rains of 1961–2 followed by another good season in 1962–3 transformed many of those that were dry or swampy into open sheets of water.

Much of the highlands over 6,000 feet (1,830 m) and the volcanic soils in the Mbeya section of the Rift are grass covered and excellent cattle country. Tsetse is absent from the highlands and main part of the plateau in the Tanzania–Malawi corridor country, being confined to the hotter lowlands north and west of Lake Rukwa. Tsetse today is not found east of the Kapembwa mountain at the south end of Lake Tanganyika, but, in the early years of the century it had spread along the lake shore to cover the southeast corner also. These high grasslands are probably in great part man induced at the expense of montane forest and result from the firing and cutting of the trees for cultivation for, once the forest has been destroyed, it is replaced by grass and is incapable of reconstituting itself. One of the most significant wood and forest trees for the Kalambo Falls study is *Podocarpus milanjianus*, since pollen of this species has been found in the Upper Pleistocene deposits in the basin.

In the low-lying drier country surrounding the Rift lakes *Brachystegia* and other *miombo* species grow on the steep, indurated and skeletal soils of the escarpments but on the alluvial soils the *itegi* type of thicket, widespread in the drier regions of southern and central Tanzania, is dominant. Lake Rukwa lies in the centre of an extensive area of grassland which still supports large herds of game and gives an indication of what the richness of the fauna of the corridor region generally must have been before the use of firearms. Not so much the *miombo* woodland itself but the *dambos* and grasslands adjacent to them, when first observed by Europeans, supported large herds of elephant, buffalo, eland, sable, roan, kudu, waterbuck and zebra, to mention but a few. Hippo were plentiful in the lakes and rivers of the Rift and Plateau and in 1928 were still to be found in the lower reaches of the Kalambo River adjacent to the lake. Eland, zebra, reedbuck and oribi are still to be found on some of the high grasslands such as the Nyika Plateau, while the *mushitu* are the home of several West African forms such as the yellow backed duiker, blue monkey and smaller game (Ansell, 1960, pp. xxi–xxiii).

Although there is no tsetse fly in the valley today no cattle, sheep or goats are to be found there since the fly occurs only some 10 miles (16 km) to the east. The only wild animals are baboons and monkeys occupying the Spillway Gorge and the flanks of the main gorge; cane rats and other small game to be found along the river and an occasional visitor in the shape of leopard, wild pig or antelope. Lions are sometimes to be met with on Siszya Ridge but not in the valley itself, which is, however, an excellent breeding place for snakes, particularly puff adders and mambas.

This, then, is what the local basin above the Kalambo Falls is like today and, except where man has taken a hand, it is not unlike what it must have been at the beginning of the prehistoric record here in late Acheulian times.

In this country live a number of Bantu tribal groups whose associations lie with southern Tanzania rather than with Zambia or Malawi. The country round the southern and southeastern end of Lake Tanganyika is inhabited by the Lungu, who are culturally and linguistically related to the Mambwe and Inamwanga living further to the southeast in the corridor country. They were at one time a people without chiefs who were cultivators but, nevertheless, subsisted largely by hunting. The Lungu at the Kalambo Falls, as elsewhere, claim relationship with the Fipa in the highlands of Sumbawanga. They are among the few cattle-owning tribes in the Northern Province of Zambia. In the past their crops of finger millet and sorghum suffered periodic devastation by the red locust, the breeding grounds of which lie in the Rukwa and Mweru Wantipa Rifts.

The Kalambo River in its lower and middle reaches forms the boundary between Zambia and Tanzania (Figure 4). Its source is in the Ufipa highlands whence it flows southwards or south-southwestwards for some 55 miles (90 km) and then turns nearly a right angle to flow westwards for another 13 miles (19 km) after plunging more than 700 feet (213 m) over the escarpment into Lake Tanganyika. In its westward course the river flows in a wide valley cut some 600 feet (183 m) below the surrounding plateau and supporting riparian forest, *mushitu* and groves of raffia palm in favourable localities. At Sansia, 7 miles upstream from the falls itself the river, having emerged from one of these swampy *mushitu* areas, drops approximately 100 feet (30·5 m) over an outcrop of Plateau Series and runs swiftly on, to turn again northwards and enter the local Kalambo basin where the valley narrows and the flanks of the outlying ridges of the plateau crowd in upon it.

The local basin at Kalambo Falls is a mature but small one, being approximately 2½ miles (4 km) long by a mile (1·8 km) wide. It is contained between two quartzite ridges running in a northwest/southeasterly direction parallel to the rift scarp. At first when it enters the valley the stream is running swiftly over coarse gravel beds but as it passes Headman Dominico's village, Chiungu, its course is slowed and it enters a swampy area of *Phragmites* reeds. From here on instead of flowing directly to the falls it meanders sluggishly, its banks often fringed by stands of attractive, grey-barked *Zyzigium* trees. It has here cut deeply through a series of fine-grained sediments of Pleistocene and later age and at one point is actually flowing in the opposite direction from which it came before turning again to enter a short narrow gorge cut through the uptilted quartzite ridge that forms the edge of the Tanganyika Rift and so over the falls. It is these sediments that contain the unique succession of cultural stages that have enabled us to trace the story of man from the end of the Acheulian up to the present day. This uniqueness lies, however, not so much in the existence of this strati-graphic record, for comparable successions must surely exist in many such tropical basins, but in the exposure of the beds that enables them to be studied.

The Kalambo Falls are one of the unforgettable sights of Africa. Not in the same way as their, rightly, more famous and much more extensive counterpart on Zambia's southern boundary—the Victoria Falls—but because they con-stitute a single, perfect, example of the beauty that is to be found in falling water, in a setting of unsurpassed grandeur. As is so often the case in Africa, places like the Kalambo Falls are so well hidden that their presence is quite unsuspected until one suddenly comes upon them. The falls and the gorge are effectively obscured from the local Kalambo basin by the ridge of hills forming its western boundary and the falls cannot be seen to advantage except from the flanks of the gorge. The water falls 726 feet (221 m)[1] over a bar of hard quartzite rock in a single unbroken drop into the gorge below. Kalambo is thus over twice as high as the Victoria Falls and is the second highest in the African continent. In the dry season the width of the river at the top of the falls is rarely more than 12 feet (3·6 m) but at flood time it must be as much as 60 feet (18·3 m) wide or more.

The beauty of the fall itself is offset by the awe-inspiring grandeur of the Kalambo Gorge with its steeply sloping sides rising over 1,000 feet (305 m) above the river. In the immediate vicinity of the falls the walls are vertical and the innumerable ledges formed by the jointing of the quartzites provide nesting places for the marabou stork. These are birds that appear ungainly and repulsive

[1] The height was measured as 705 feet (215 m) by the 1928 party (see below) but on remeasurement by J. W. Clayphan of the Department of Surveys and Lands, Northern Rhodesia in 1956, the height was found to be 726 feet (221 m). In 1927 A. D. Combe of the Uganda Geological Survey computed the height of the Falls by aneroid to be between 675 and 725 feet (205·8 and 221 m) and he also remarked upon the bed-rock geology. (Combe, A. D. 1927. 'Summary of investigations carried out between Entebbe and Cape Town', Uganda Protectorate, *Annual Report of the Geology Department for the year ended 31st December, 1926*, pp. 28–32.)

when on the ground but graceful in the extreme when seen gliding effortlessly back and forth over the gorge making full use of the turbulence of the air over the chasm, the river at the bottom looking no larger than a thin thread of water.

It is not known who was the first European to visit the Kalambo Falls. In 1898 the British and German Boundary Commission parties found the gorge but though they heard of the existence of the falls were unable to find them. The first definite record dates to 1913 when they were visited and photographed by the Rev. W. E. M. Owen, a missionary from Zambia (Rose, 1929, p. 44) and by a German party from Kasanga.[1] The same year they were measured by Messrs Lionel Smith and Chris Draper from Abercorn. 'Lionel climbed down into the gorge by crossing the lip at the falls and scrambling down the cliff face on the northern side. Draper, at the top, tied a piece of calico on to a stone and lowered the stone on a long string held over the gorge with a *chiwale* (raphia) palm pole. Lionel, at water level at the bottom of the gorge, fired a shot from his rifle as the stone and calico touched water. The string measured 701 feet' (Brelsford, 1952, p. 73).

The first accurate description of the falls is given by J. W. Cornwall and Colin Rose while on an expedition organized by Mrs E. Gordon-Gallien in July 1928. They spent about six weeks there in July and August and made topographical and geological maps of the area (Cornwall, 1929; Rose, 1929).

They approached Kalambo from the former German *boma* or administrative post of Kasanga 10 miles to the northwest on Lake Tanganyika. It took them a day to walk with porters up the valley of the Kawa to the top of the falls. Their survey of the gorge is probably the only one to have been made and is thus particularly interesting. They calculated that the Kalambo fell 1,050 feet (320 m) in about 7 miles (11 km) between the Sansia Falls and the main fall at Kalambo and a further 525 feet (160 m) in approximately 5 miles (8 km) from the foot of this fall to the lake. Rose records the presence of two further falls within the gorge itself, the first of about 50 feet (15 m) and the second about 30 feet (9 m). The river here flows in a vertical-sided secondary gorge 'whose walls rise sheer for 100 feet and which is only about three yards wide' (Rose, 1929), a phenomenon that Rose rightly judged to be the result of uplift subsequent to the formation of the main gorge.

Our own first acquaintance with the falls was made on 10 October 1953 during what we had intended to be a quick visit after completing excavations at Mpulungu at the south end of Lake Tanganyika. The party consisted of John

[1] Prints of photographs of the bottom of the falls taken by this German party are preserved in the Livingstone Museum and one of Mr Owen's photographs was published in the *Geographical Journal* for 1926.

and Lilian Hodges, the former as Inspector of National Monuments, Dr N. J. van Warmelo, Government Ethnologist, Pretoria, and the writer.

In October 1943 a collection of 'Later Stone Age' artifacts, including certain hollow scraper forms and a bored stone (Clark, 1958), had been made by D. Gordon Lancaster near the south shoulder of the valley above the falls. In 1950 J. C. McNaughton of the Northern Rhodesia Geological Survey had collected further specimens including some of 'Middle Stone Age' form. Our objective was to locate this surface site and to see the falls. The artifacts in question came from the exposed area of the road and round the rondavel on the south side where the steps descend to the top of the falls. They lay on bedrock in a few inches of sandy loam mixed with rock rubble and it was soon obvious that little further was to be obtained there.

The following day John Hodges and the writer, in the course of a traverse of the Spillway Gorge and of the western end of the Kalambo basin, after twice nearly falling into old pit traps dug for wild pig, concealed by the tall, thick *Hyparrhenia* grass, came out upon an area on the south side of the river about a quarter of a mile ($\frac{1}{2}$ km) upstream from the falls where the grass had been burned. Here the ground sloped down to the river, which we could see had cut back the bank into a small cliff. On investigation this proved to be a near vertical section some 25–30 feet (7·6–9·1 m) high. By falling rather than climbing we managed to negotiate the descent.

The cliff contained a well-marked horizon half-way up the section and we spent some time collecting artifacts of Lupemban type from this before dropping the whole of the way to the bottom of the cliff. Here we found the bank to be composed of fine-grained sediments—clays and sands—from which were washing out a number of beautifully made Acheulian hand-axes and cleavers many of which were in a quite fresh condition. This was a discovery of the greatest interest for African archaeology but what was of even greater significance was the presence of several cracked, blackened and partially carbonized tree-trunks that were sticking out from the bank, where they had been exposed by the falling level of the water in the river. We found it hard to believe that these trunks could be of the same age as the Acheulian hand-axes. It was, however, obvious that the short time that remained to us of the field season must be spent in investigating a site of such great potential interest. For Sunday, 11 October, my notebook records: 'Found most important Pleistocene lake deposits exposed in section in the Kalambo River. Collected numerous surface specimens.' Thus we obtained our first knowledge of the area we later called Site A and which is one of the most important in the basin.

From 12–17 October, when the rains had already begun to break and we had to leave, we excavated a step trench in the lower half of the river bank where the later A 1 excavation was situated and explored the western end of the basin, finding four horizons with stone tools. These horizons were separated by fine-grained sediments, and deposits of the same kind continued below water level. The two lower horizons contained many finely made and quite fresh Acheulian tools associated with tree-trunks and smaller pieces of wood and clearly represented camping places. The third floor, the next above, also contained Acheulian tools but less finely finished while the uppermost horizon contained a mixture of Lupemban, Sangoan and older artifacts associated with water rolled and sub-angular rubble—the horizon that was later to be known as Rubble I.

The river banks further upstream preserved other sections where tools were eroding, and what were later known as Sites B and C were also located on this initial visit and marked down for future investigation.

A preliminary account of the site and its contents was published in 1954 (Clark, 1954), and in 1955, on the occasion of the Third Pan-African Congress on Prehistory which met in Livingstone in July and August of that year, delegates who took part in the excursion to Zambian sites were able to see further excavated sections at Sites A and B, where at the latter site the Acheulian surfaces with wood and associated tools were overlain by black peaty banded clays (Clark, 1955).

In 1956, with the help of a generous grant from the Wenner-Gren Foundation for Anthropological Research, New York, and funds voted by the Trustees of the Rhodes-Livingstone Museum, we were enabled to carry out the first full-scale investigation of the local Kalambo basin and spent four months in the field from 7 July to 28 October. During this time three areas, one large and two smaller, were excavated at Site A and one area was excavated at each of Sites B and D. The results far exceeded expectations and a large quantity of artifacts was obtained from stratified, sealed levels. The fineness of the raw materials and the richness of the seven horizons ranging in time from the Acheulian up to the 'Magosian' made Kalambo a unique site for studying the technical development of prehistoric culture in the southern tropics. These excavations also revealed the presence of an early Iron Age showing undoubted affinities with the Dimple Based Pottery tradition of the lakes region of East Africa.

The lower horizons containing the artifacts showed little evidence of disturbance by water action before burial and it was apparent that the lithic and other material lying on them represented debris from human occupation sites. We developed, therefore, a technique for excavating these 'floors', and the later disturbed surfaces, first cleaning off the overlying sterile sands and clays and exposing the floor, or section of floor, so that the relationship of everything on it could be clearly seen and plotted. In this way we were able to obtain details of the relationships of the tools, factory waste, natural stones and wood and so of relationships between classes of shaped tools, thus supplementing the information to be obtained from a study of the artifacts themselves. In this way part of an extremely rich Acheulian floor was uncovered on Site B.

The comparatively high rainfall and the fairly high clay content of the Pleistocene and later sediments in the basin, together with the acid nature of the deposits and groundwater, have destroyed all but the most recent bone; yet they provide ideal conditions for the preservation of vegetable remains. Only at the river or stream banks do the deposits ever dry out sufficiently to destroy these organic remains completely and in the excavations the beds are always damp enough from the surface down to preserve charcoal and, in the lower portions, for wood and other plant remains to have survived in an excellent state of preservation. Thus we obtained samples for pollen analysis by Professor E. M. van Zinderen Bakker at Bloemfontein and wood samples, seeds and other remains for study at the Commonwealth Forestry Institute, Oxford. Charcoals and wood were sent for radiocarbon dating to the Lamont Observatory Geochronological Laboratory of Columbia University and to the Groningen Radiocarbon Laboratory. Besides the stone artifacts we were in 1956 fortunate enough to find a number of pieces of wood that showed signs of utilization and shaping by Acheulian man.

My companions during the 1956 excavations were Mrs Lilian Hodges of the Rhodes-Livingstone Museum and Mr Joseph Siantumbu, the Museum's trained field assistant, who were there for the full four months. For shorter periods, Mr Brian Williams, who had become Inspector of Monuments in Zambia after the untimely death of John Hodges, Mrs Florence Anderson and Miss Patricia Anderson helped with the work. The rest of our labour force was recruited locally from the few small villages of BaLungu on the Zambian and Tanzanian sides of the river. During my enforced absences in Livingstone to attend to Museum affairs Mrs Lilian Hodges supervised the excavation of both sites and her careful and methodical fieldwork during 1956 and again in 1959 was a major contribution to the success of the excavations.

A topographical survey of the immediate area of our excavations at the western end of the basin was undertaken by Mr J. W. Clayphan of the Department of Lands and Surveys, Northern Rhodesia. Dr (now Professor) Geoffrey Bond, then of the National Museum of Southern Rhodesia in Bulawayo, completed a geological survey of the basin and showed that the water level there had fluctuated in relation to the blocking and unblocking of the Spillway Gorge.

Excavations were resumed at Kalambo in the dry season of 1959 with the help of a grant from the Boise Fund of Oxford University and funds from the

Rhodes-Livingstone Museum. The aim was to uncover as wide an area as possible of the Acheulian living floors on Site B, to investigate the depth of deposit buried below low-water level and to obtain as deep and long a section as possible through the deposits of Site A in order to find undisturbed the sedimentary series overlying the Ochreous Sands which had been cut out by the main erosion surface.

Fieldwork began on 29 May and ended on 11 November—a period of nearly five and a half months. The work was concentrated on two sites. A trench 250 feet (76 m) long, named A 4, was put in up the hillside at right angles to the river bank on Site A and a 'paddock' area was dug on Site B adjacent to that excavated in 1956. In addition, two pits were sunk in the edge of the swamp area close to Site B and other surface sites were also collected. Until 25 September Mrs Hodges was again in charge of the excavations whenever the writer was away. On 21 September Dr M. R. Kleindienst of the University of Chicago arrived at Kalambo and took over the excavation of the long trench on Site A. In addition we were fortunate in having the help of several assistants for varying periods—Mrs Florence Anderson, Miss Barbara Anthony from Harvard University, Mrs Peggy Tindall, Mr B. M. Fagan, Keeper of Prehistory, and Mr C. S. Holliday, Chief Technical Officer, both of the Rhodes-Livingstone Museum, Mr J. H. Chaplin, then Inspector of Monuments, Northern Rhodesia and Mr Mario Bick from Columbia University. We were pleased to welcome Mr Neville Chittick, Commissioner of Antiquities in Tanzania, for a brief visit towards the end of the season. Mr Joseph Siantumbu again worked for the full season and our local labour force varied between fifteen and thirty men.

Dr Bond was unable to join us in 1959 but Dr E. G. Haldemann, then of the Tanganyika Geological Survey, spent two weeks at Kalambo continuing the geological fieldwork and running sections across the basin. A detailed topographical survey of the basin (excluding the Spillway Gorge) and sections were completed by Mr W. S. Chape of the Northern Rhodesian Department of Lands and Surveys (Figures 2 and 3).

The 1959 season provided knowledge of the sediments overlying the Acheulian layers in the lower and earlier part of the sediments of the 60 feet (18·3 m) terrace, which surprised us by being capped by a compacted rubble bed locally indurated and most difficult to dig through. The Sangoan was found *in situ* overlying the deposits with the Acheulian but the Lupemban was found, as in 1956, only in geological context on the main Rubble I-composite and its subdivisions. At Site B we uncovered the southern end of the Acheulian living floors found in 1956 and overlain by sands cut out by channelling before the deposition of the Ochreous Sands containing Sangoan tools.

Further pollen and radiocarbon samples and additional wooden implements were recovered as well as large numbers of artifacts of all types except the 'Later Stone Age'.

CONTOUR MAP OF PART OF THE KALAMBO BASIN

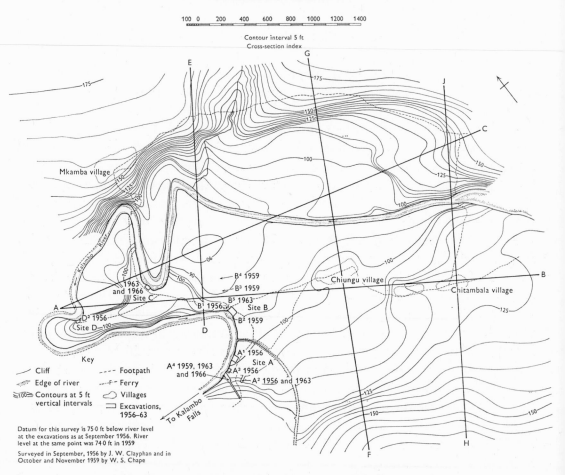

Fig. 2. The Kalambo Falls Prehistoric Site: contour map of part of the western end of the local basin showing the position of the sites.

In 1962 analysis of the cultural material in the Rhodes-Livingstone Museum in Livingstone showed that it was impossible to separate the different phases of the Lupemban thought to be represented on the main erosion surface on the basis of typology and technical differences alone. It was apparent that at least three stages existed judging from the typology and size range of the various artifacts—a lower, a main, and an upper or final—and it was therefore desirable

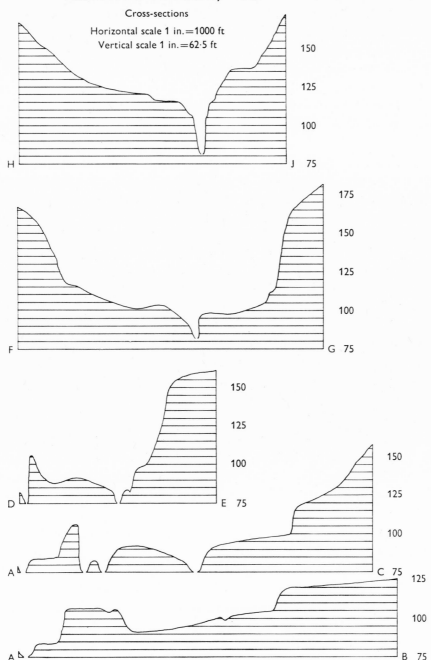

Kalambo River Basin Survey 1959

Cross-sections

Horizontal scale 1 in.=1000 ft
Vertical scale 1 in.=62·5 ft

Fig. 3. Topographic sections (W. S. Chape) across the local basin at the Kalambo Falls.

15

to undertake further fieldwork with the specific object of isolating these phases stratigraphically.

With financial support from the National Science Foundation, Washington, and the African Studies Program of the University of California at Los Angeles, the months of July and August 1963 were spent at Kalambo. Dr M. R. Kleindienst was co-director with the writer and we were assisted for varying periods by Miss Sue Bucklin of Northwestern University, Miss Barbara Anthony of Harvard, Mr Charles M. Keller of the University of California at Berkeley, Mr Francis van Noten of the Musée royal de l'Afrique centrale at Tervuren, Belgium, Mr David Phillipson of Cambridge University, Mr J. W. D. Clark of Durham University and by Mrs B. C. Clark who ran the commissariat and illustrated selected finds. Once again Mr Joseph Siantumbu, now retired, came with the party as foreman and field assistant.

Fortunately the rains had not seriously damaged the walls of the uphill half of Trench A 4 and we were able to deepen and extend the pits dug through the Red Rubble in 1959. We were able to isolate the lower Lupemban horizon, to show that the upper final phase is contemporary with the formation of the Red Rubble and that the 'Magosian' stage is later than this bed.

The high floods of 1961–2 and other seasons had cut back the bank at Site A some 30 feet (9 m) since 1959 and thus gave us clearer sections than before. We were also able, therefore, to correlate more exactly the different river face sections at Site A and to uncover partial Acheulian floors in the uppermost White Sands.

On Site B part of the small area of the main Acheulian floor that lay behind and between the 1956 and 1959 excavations was excavated and plotted.

At Site C the foot of the cliff face cut into the 30 feet (9 m) terrace was littered with much pottery and microlithic flakes that had come from the top levels where it seemed possible that the pottery was associated with burials. Accordingly an area on top of the 30 feet (9 m) terrace next to the cliff was excavated by Francis van Noten. This formed part of a settlement area of the early Iron Age and a very rich collection of Channelled Ware pottery was recovered. Under the Iron Age occupation was found a small living area with microlithic artifacts and this gave us our first proper knowledge of this cultural material at Kalambo Falls.

In the floods of 1961–2 a landslide had occurred in the vicinity of Site D, on the right side of the Kalambo River a little south of the mouth of the Kaposwa, where the slope is quite steep. Over a distance of about 300 feet (91 m) the foot of the slope slumped into the river as a result of undercutting of the weathered bedrock and water saturation of the colluvium. This led to a narrowing of the river channel, which is bridged by a mass of tangled tree-trunks and brushwood that could form the basis for a natural dam. This affords a practical and visible explanation of a manner in which the entrance to the Spillway Gorge may have been blocked in the past.

In 1963 we climbed down to the bottom of the Kalambo Gorge, the descent route being from the Tanzania side. It is cold at the bottom and the spray from the falls forms a fine mist that supports a lush green vegetation of ferns, elephant ear (*Colocasia antiquorum*) and wild banana clinging to the black shale rock that underlies the quartzites in the lower 100 feet (30·5 m) of the gorge. With the exception of a swift or two and a large troop of baboons on the upper slopes we saw no sign of life, though the droppings of dassies (hyrax) show that they live close to the spray line. We found no sign of human habitation either other than some late potsherds near the top. There was too much water in the swiftly flowing river for us to be able to approach right to the foot of the falls but the view of the falling water amply compensated for the climb and it was of interest to know that the archaeological importance of Kalambo lies solely in the basin at the top and not in the gorge at the bottom of the falls.

In 1966 a further two weeks' work, between 14 and 29 October, was carried out at the Kalambo Falls. On this occasion the writer and his wife were accompanied by Dr Glen H. Cole of the Field Museum of Natural History, Chicago. At Site A an excavation, using pre-cast concrete rings as casing, was successfully carried out to a depth of 9 feet 2 inches below the low water level of the Kalambo River, without reaching bedrock. This resulted in the discovery of three further archaeological horizons of Acheulian age, and a number of clay and sand samples was also obtained for pollen analysis. At Site C Dr Cole excavated in the lower part of the cliff exposure and, at the northern end of the section, found that Rubble I was subdivided into four artifact-bearing horizons, from a sand between two of which he recovered charcoals for radiocarbon dating. Adjacent to the camp site south of the river, excavation in the red soil and clay sand slope wash deposits overlying the Mkamba Member provided evidence of a pottery ware younger than the early Iron Age Channelled Ware and thus intermediate in age between the latter and modern Lungu pottery. The new ware overlay a horizon with microlithic artifacts similar to those excavated from the Site C occupation floor in 1963.

During the last four field seasons our camp was conveniently situated on the southern slopes of the local basin just east of the Spillway Gorge and a little to the south of Site A.

Summarizing, therefore, sediments that belong to four separate aggradation phases, including the present phase of river action, can be identified and each of these, except the last, contains cultural material in abundance. These sediments are exposed in terrace-like features that occur in the local basin at heights of about 60 feet, 30 feet and 6–12 feet above the present river level.

As a result of the work at Kalambo between 1956 and 1966, we now have the most complete, uninterrupted, stratified sequence of culture history from any site in southern Africa and a continuous record stretching from approximately 60,000 years ago up to the present day. Professor van Zinderen Bakker has also obtained a unique though still incomplete record of climatic and vegetational changes taking place in the basin during the same period. The absolute ages of most of the culture stages represented have been obtained by the radiocarbon method so that only the lowest deposits lying below water level now remain to be investigated.

This book brings together the results of fourteen years' work at what was for the writer, and, I think, for most of those who have worked there, one of the most interesting and fascinating sites we have experienced. The surroundings, the people, the finds and our personal relations all made the Kalambo Falls an unforgettable site and many are the memories that we carry with us. If the temptation to record some of the more unforgettable incidents here is irresistible it may perhaps serve to help encourage others to search for more such sites in what is undoubtedly one of the most interesting and probably least known parts of the African continent. Some of our most vivid recollections are of the unsurpassable colours of the *miombo* woodland at the close of the dry season with the sun shining on the reds and russets and transparent greens of the new foliage and vying with the browns, buffs and yellows of the old, viewed against the deep purple background of the gorge; the delicate mauve of the 'bush crocus' (*Kampheria*, sp.) just before the first rains; of the wind that persistently gets up at about 10.00 p.m. and blows for a full twelve hours as the hot air of the Rift rises and the cooler air of the plateau is sucked down to take its place at the level of the lake; the angry chatter of monkeys at sundown, the cough of a leopard and the ensuing barking and gesturing of the baboons in the Spillway Gorge; dinner in camp and the arrival of an unwanted visitor in the shape of a large cobra falling on to the table from the fig tree above; the heat of the day and the welcome arrival of the cook at the dig with hot tea to quench a raging thirst; the efficacy of clay figurines in promoting work or in ensuring the privacy of the tents; the evening sick parade, and the imaginary complaints of the camp hypochondriac; diplomacy stretched to its limit when arranging compensation for an additional foot of cassava garden to include in our excavations; the cheerful call 'Piet-my-vrou' of the red-chested cuckoo; the vervet monkeys—and others besides—who spent so much time watching us at work; the rare congregations of a hundred or more marabous wheeling and turning in the sky; the chimpanzee that helped to build the new road to Kalambo in 1959; the nightly bush fires on 'Burnt Ridge' as the dry season closes, diminishing and expanding until the whole top of the ridge seems to be on fire; and the onset of the rains that brought the 1959 season to a close and inspired the telegram 'Genesis, 7, 7'. These are but a few of the memories that remain with us of our first fourteen years at an unforgettable site.

REFERENCES

Ansell, W. F. H. (1960). *Mammals of Northern Rhodesia*. Government Printer, Lusaka, Zambia.

Atlas of the Federation of Rhodesia and Nyasaland (1961). Federal Department of Trigonometrical and Topographical Surveys, Government Printer, Salisbury, Rhodesia.

Brelsford, W. V. (ed.) (1952). Measuring the Kalambo Falls. *Nth. Rhod. J.* **1**, 6, p. 73.

Clark, J. D. (1954). An early Upper Pleistocene site at the Kalambo Falls on the Northern Rhodesia/Tanganyika border. *S. Afr. Archaeol. Bull.* **9**, no. 34, pp. 51–6.

(1955). *Northern Rhodesia Excursion Handbook for the Pan-African Congress*. Rhodes-Livingstone Museum, Government Printer, Lusaka.

(1958). Certain industries of notched and strangulated scrapers in Rhodesia, their time range and possible use. *S. Afr. Archaeol. Bull.* **13**, no. 50, pp. 56–66.

Combe, A. D. (1927). *Annual Report of the Geological Department for the year ended 31 December 1926*. Uganda Protectorate, Government Printer, Entebbe.

Cornwall, J. W. (1929). The survey of the Kalambo Gorge. *Geogrl J.* **74**, no. 1, pp. 33–8.

Gordon-Gallien, Mrs Enid (1929). The Kalambo Falls. *Geogrl J.* **74**, no. 1, pp. 28–32.

Haughton, S. H. (1963). *Stratigraphic Geology of Africa South of the Sahara*. Oliver and Boyd, Edinburgh and London.

Jackson, S. P. (1961). *Climatological Atlas of Africa*. CCTA/CSA, Government Printer, Pretoria.

Lawton, R. M. (1963). Palaeoecological and ecological studies in the northern province of Northern Rhodesia. *Kirkia*, **3**, Salisbury, Rhodesia, pp. 46–77.

Reeve, W. H. (1961). Geological map of Northern Rhodesia (scale 1 : 1,000,000). Geological Survey, Lusaka, Zambia.

Rose, C. (1929). The geology of the Kalambo Gorge. *Geogrl J.* **74**, no. 1, pp. 38–46.

2-2

CHAPTER 2

GEOLOGY

Part I: Geological and Physiographical Setting of the Kalambo Falls Prehistoric Site

BY EDUARD G. HALDEMANN

1. INTRODUCTION

The Kalambo Falls Prehistoric Site is situated in an open stretch or small, local basin of the Kalambo valley, a little upstream from the lip of the Kalambo Falls, near the southeastern end of Lake Tanganyika. The Kalambo River marks the boundary between Zambia and Tanzania for about 20 miles (32 km) eastwards of its small delta in the lake. The site can be reached by car from Abercorn, 21 miles (33·5 km) to the south, along a good road to the Kalambo Falls Protected Forest Area and National Monument. The geographical position of the site is shown on the map of the Kalambo drainage basin (Figure 4).

A. D. Combe, who visited the area in August 1926, was probably the first geologist to descend into the gorge at the bottom of the Kalambo Falls. His aneroid readings demonstrated that the height of the falls was between 675 feet and 725 feet (205·8 and 221 m) and not of the order of 1,200 feet (366 m) as had been previously believed. Combe (1927) briefly described the various rock types found at the falls.

Survey work by E. Gordon-Gallien's expedition, in 1928, led to the publication, in the *Geographical Journal*, of the first detailed maps of the Kalambo Falls area (Cornwall, 1929). A paper on the geology of the vicinity of the falls and two geological maps were presented by C. Rose (1929), the geologist of the expedition. The Quaternary sediments of the local basin are shown as alluvium on Rose's maps.

During October 1956, Professor G. Bond mapped the Quaternary deposits of the local basin and examined sections then exposed by the archaeological excavations. In his report (Appendix A) he gave an account of the Quaternary sediments and their stratigraphic relationships. Bond also described the 'solid geology and raw materials of artifacts', using Rose's work as a base, and outlined the geomorphological history of the site area.

While working for the Geological Survey of Tanganyika, I first visited the Kalambo Falls in 1952 when travelling through Ufipa to the Karema area. From 23 September to 5 October 1959, at the invitation of Professor Clark,[1] I carried out geological and geomorphological investigations at the Kalambo Falls Prehistoric Site and neighbouring areas. This included the surveying of sections across the Kalambo valley and some other work in the local basin. The Quaternary sediments of the site area had already been mapped and subdivided by Bond, thus I did not consider questions relating to stratigraphy to be my concern. In 1961, I did two months of geological survey work in southern Ufipa (Haldemann, 1964) during which time I briefly revisited the Kalambo Prehistoric Site with Dr M. R. Kleindienst.

While the present report was finished early in 1965, the geomorphological studies essentially date back to 1961 when I was still with the Geological Survey of Tanganyika. Consequently, the terminology used with regard to geomorphological features is the one which was then in common use by the Geological Survey.

2. GENERAL GEOLOGICAL SETTING

The hard rocks in the vicinity of the Prehistoric Site essentially belong to the Plateau Series of Zambia. The Kalambo drainage basin, however, extends far to the north into the Ufipa area of Tanzania where older Precambrian rocks such as migmatitic gneisses and granulites of the Ubendian occur. In the area under consideration there is a belt of quartz porphyry (Kate Porphyry) and porphyritic granite (Kate Granite) between the sediments of the Plateau Series and the Ubendian rocks (see map of Kalambo drainage basin, Figure 4).

Although the full westerly extent of the Ubendian rocks is not known they are believed to represent the basement on which all the later rocks of the area were deposited. The Ubendian of Tanzania is referred to as Basement Complex in Zambia, and it is equivalent to the rocks of the Ruzizi Group of the eastern Congo.

Rocks of the Plateau Series rest unconformably on the Kate Porphyry and form an escarpment above the latter which, for many miles, coincides with the watershed of the Kalambo drainage basin to the north and south of the Sansia

[1] This invitation was accepted with the permission of Messrs A. M. Quennell and W. H. Reeve, then Directors of the Geological Surveys of Tanganyika and Northern Rhodesia, respectively.

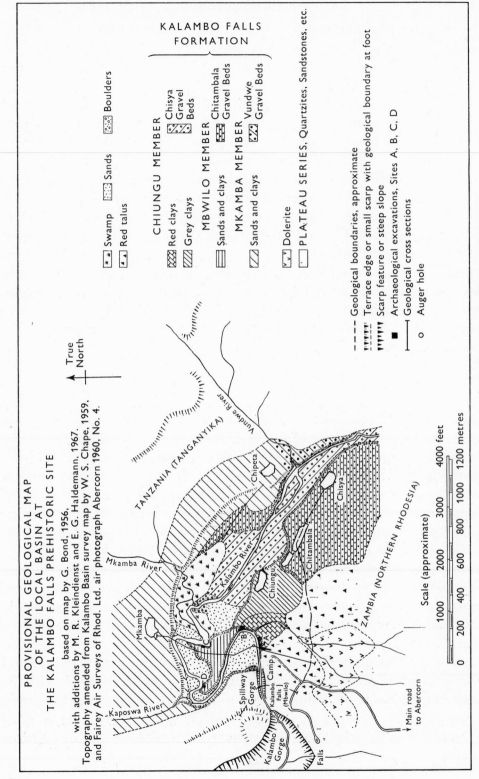

KALAMBO FALLS FORMATION

CHIUNGU MEMBER
- Red clays
- Grey clays
- Chisya Gravel Beds

MBWILO MEMBER
- Sands and clays
- Chitambala Gravel Beds

MKAMBA MEMBER
- Sands and clays
- Vundwe Gravel Beds

- Swamp
- Red talus
- Sands
- Boulders

- Dolerite
- PLATEAU SERIES, Quartzites, Sandstones, etc.

--- Geological boundaries, approximate
ᴠᴠᴠᴠ Terrace edge or small scarp with geological boundary at foot
ᴠᴠᴠᴠ Scarp feature or steep slope
■ Archaeological excavations, Sites A, B, C, D
— Geological cross sections
○ Auger hole

PROVISIONAL GEOLOGICAL MAP
OF THE LOCAL BASIN AT
THE KALAMBO FALLS PREHISTORIC SITE

based on map by G. Bond, 1956,
with additions by M. R. Kleindienst and E. G. Haldemann, 1967.
Topography amended from Kalambo Basin survey map by W. S. Chape, 1959,
and Fairey Air Surveys of Rhod. Ltd. air photograph Abercorn 1960, No. 4.

True North

TANZANIA (TANGANYIKA)

Vundwe River

Chipeta

Chisya

Chitambala

ZAMBIA (NORTHERN RHODESIA)

Mkamba River

Mkamba

Kalambo River

Chiungu

Kaposwa River

Spillway Gorge

Kalambo Camp Falls (Mbwilo)

Kalambo Gorge

Falls

Main road to Abercorn

Scale (approximate)

1000   1000   2000   3000   4000 feet
0   200   400   600   800   1000   1200 metres

Fig. 5. Provisional geological map of the local basin at the Kalambo Falls.

Falls. The field evidence shows that the Kate Granite post-dates the Kate Porphyry.

On his maps of the Kalambo Gorge, Rose (1929, pp. 39 and 43) gives the following subdivision and distribution of the sedimentary rocks:

TOP   Upper Sandstone Series:
> Not subdivided. The outcrop is shown in a NW–SE direction along the coast of Lake Tanganyika and to as far east as the ridge followed by the Abercorn–Kalambo Falls road.

Lower Quartzite Series:
> Brown and white massive sandstones;
> Chert beds;
> Quartzites, etc. The quartzites of this series are shown to form the lip and face of the Kalambo Falls; cherts occur to the west and southeast above the Prehistoric Site. The whole series extends over the area of the local basin and along the Kalambo River as far east as the Sansia Falls.

Clay-slates and 'Schists':
> Green clay-slates and 'schists';
> Brown clay-slates and 'schists';
> False bedded sandstones;

BOTTOM   Red brown, hard sandy shales. All these rocks are exposed only at the base of the Kalambo Falls and in the gorge downstream of it (see Plates 7 and 8).

A study of the rocks grouped together as Lower Quartzite Series has revealed the following: The purer quartzites, or orthoquartzites, are very resistant to weathering. In thin-sections they show sub-rounded to rounded quartz grains (0·3–0·6 mm), normally with chert, and interstitial sericite or sericite and carbonaceous material. Other specimens show fine- to coarse-grained particles of quartz and quartzite cemented by quartz in optical continuity with the clastic grains. The feldspathic quartzites and feldspathic quartz-sandstones consist of sub-angular to rounded quartz grains with microcline feldspar, chert and sericite, and some accessory muscovite and zircon in places. The 'cherts' or silicified mudstones in thin-sections are seen to contain quartz, albite, chert, sericite and chlorite grains in a fine siliceous groundmass; some specimens also contain limonite and carbonaceous material and/or a little epidote.

Rose observed that the various layers of sandstone and quartzite dip gently to WSW. He did not record any unconformity between layers of the sequence. At the time of Rose's work these sediments were referred to by various stratigraphical terms, i.e. 'Tanganyika Sandstones', 'Tanganyika Formation', 'Tanganyika System', 'Abercorn Beds', 'Abercorn and Kasanga sediments', 'Katanga System', 'Kundelungu beds of the Katanga System', etc. Wallace (1907, p. 391) described the Tanganyika Sandstones and said that they 'face the

23

south end of (Lake) Tanganyika in cliffs and steep slopes, altogether amounting to over 3,000 feet in thickness'. Rose (p. 41) only observed that 'their age, as far as can be stated definitely, is probably Pre-Devonian'.

The age of the Plateau Series and Kate Granite remains rather controversial. The rocks of the Plateau Series of the Abercorn area and eastern shore of Lake Tanganyika were named 'Abercorn Sandstones' by McConnell. He stated (1950, p. 17) that 'the formation consists chiefly of massive yellow, grey, or purplish hard quartzitic false-bedded, fine- to medium-grained sandstones with beds of grits and conglomerates containing well-rolled quartz pebbles. The sandstones may become soft, micaceous and shaly and pass to an olive shale.' The 'Abercorn Sandstones' were included in the Bukoban System of Tanganyika.

Page (1959, 1960) describes the Plateau Series of the Abercorn area as a 6,000 feet (1,830 m) thick formation 'of a distal molasse facies' which he sub-divided into Lower and Upper Plateau Series separated by an unconformity. The lower division consists of 1,000 feet (305 m) of shales and medium-grained sandstones metamorphosed by the Kate Granite. The Upper Plateau Series is a 5,000 feet (1,525 m) thick, rhythmical succession of unmetamorphosed arenites and shales with notable beds of chert, and extensive greywackes and slumped beds at the top of the series. 'Resting with strong unconformity upon the Plateau Series are the flat-lying Abercorn Sandstones, the lower 2,000 feet of which have been mapped. They consist of medium-grained current-bedded clean sandstones which are interrupted a few hundred feet above the basal un-conformity by a cherty and argillaceous horizon.' Page correlated his 'Plateau Series' with the Roan System and his 'Abercorn Sandstones' with the Kunde-lungu System of the Katanga.

In his review on the Proterozoic rocks of Western Tanzania, Halligan (1963) accepts Page's differentiation between Plateau Series and Abercorn Sandstones and correlates the latter with the Upper Kundelungu of the Katanga. Halligan does not query the Proterozoic age of the Abercorn Sandstones and with refer-ence to his correlations he adds that the final solution of the stratigraphic prob-lems hinges on the age of the Kate Granite. However, the correct interpretation of the age relationships of Precambrian successions based on absolute age deter-minations of magmatic intrusions is difficult, to say the least. This is demon-strated by the fact that a recent age determination for the Kate Granite gave $1,726 \pm 70$ million years (Pallister, Geological Survey, Tanganyika; personal communication 30 December 1963). While this date is questionable *per se* it makes it impossible to accept Page's 'Lower Plateau Series' which is said to ante-date the Kate Granite. But there are other points in Page's description of the stratigraphy, lithology and structure which do not seem to fit the visible facts. Therefore, for the purpose of the present account, the reviewed sediments are referred to as undifferentiated Plateau Series in accordance with the Geological Map of Northern Rhodesia (Reeve, 1961) and the map of the Mambwe area (Haldemann, 1964). Thus, the Abercorn Sandstones are not differentiated from the Plateau Series. The age of the Plateau Series of the region around the southern end of Lake Tanganyika depends on the age finally given to the Upper Kundelungu of the Katanga and may not rule out an early Palaeozoic age for the upper members of the Plateau Series.

Intrusions of dolerites in the form of dykes and sills are quite numerous in the Plateau Series and are also present on the slope to the south above the Prehistoric Site. In thin sections these dolerites generally show fresh labradorite, augite, pigeonite and iron ore; some specimens contain a little interstitial quartz and/or micropegmatite. They can therefore be termed 'pigeonite dolerite', 'quartz dolerite' and 'micropegmatite dolerite'. These dolerites post-date the Plateau Series and could be Palaeozoic in age.

Apart from the 'Kasanga breccia', discovered at the bottom of the escarpment road near Kasanga, which consists of angular to sub-angular, pebble- to boulder-sized fragments of quartzite cemented by a red matrix of limonite and hematite, the only other hard rocks in the area are well cemented breccias related to faulting in the Plateau Series, and some quartz veins.

3. GEOMORPHOLOGY AND STRUCTURAL FEATURES

Generally speaking the Kalambo Falls and Prehistoric Site are situated on the southeastern edge of the Lake Tanganyika rift valley where the shore rises steeply from the graben to the uplifted area of the Ufipa horst block, which is bounded on its eastern side by the Rukwa rift valley. McConnell (1950) and Dixey (1956) observed that the NW to NNW striking rift valley faults on either side of the Ufipa block show a relation to, and parallel, Precambrian structural trends, including the general strike of the Plateau Series sediments, and metamorphic zones of the Ubendian. One could add that although the direction of dolerite intrusions is variable, the majority of the dykes in Ufipa tend to conform to a NNW direction. Dixey (1956, p. 20) concluded 'that, prior to the Tertiary and later rifting, there existed in this region an ancient strong topography with a relief of several thousand feet' and he thought it unlikely that the Ufipa block is due to upthrust in post-Tertiary time alone. There are obvious signs of downfaulting in Pleistocene to Recent times in the Rukwa trough but its overall structural pattern is quite complex and involved various stages of block-faulting as well as trough-faulting since post-Karroo times (James, 1956). Because of the absence of Karroo and Cretaceous sediments in the southern area of Lake Tanganyika it would appear, however, that this part of the Tanganyika trough is probably a post-Cretaceous feature, and its present form may have been produced entirely in end-Tertiary to Recent times.

There is quite an abundance of published accounts on the rift structures and erosion surfaces of eastern Africa, but only a few authors have actually covered the whole region from the southern end of Lake Tanganyika across the Kalambo drainage basin on the Ufipa block down into the Rukwa trough. Published maps showing the faults related to the rift episode in detail and on a reliable topographic background are non-existent. These faults and the geological boundary of Plateau Series sediments are shown on the 'map of Kalambo drainage basin' (Figure 4) which also portrays the relevant physiographical features including bathymetric contours of the southeastern part of Lake Tanganyika. The history of the Kalambo Falls Prehistoric Site poses many problems which cannot be disentangled without a knowledge of the regional geomorphological history and structural features. This study, however, must include the whole Kalambo drainage basin as well as Lake Tanganyika. The published results of the Belgian hydrobiological exploration work 1946–7 provided the necessary information on Lake Tanganyika. The bathymetric contours are shown in feet and not in fathoms for easy comparison with other elevations; they were constructed by the writer from the metre soundings, sections and the bathymetric map (Capart, 1949), and adjusted to the new topographic map and known fault features.

The middle and upper portions of the Kalambo drainage basin extend over a flat surface which continues to the north across the partly ill-defined watershed into the Mfuizi drainage basin, and links up with the wide valley floor of the Sumbawanga corridor to the east. This flat ground represents the most conspicuous surface of the so-called Ufipa Plateau. On the Kalambo–Luiche divide it stands at 6,000±50 feet (1,830±15 m), at Sumbawanga at 5,650–5,850 feet (1,722–1,783 m), and on the Luiche–Naluzi valley watershed, in the Sumbawanga corridor, its elevation is about 6,000 feet (1,830 m). The same surface is present in the eastern (Lake Sundu–Kanyele River) and western part of the Kalambo drainage basin where it drops from approximately 5,400 feet (1,646 m) at the Ipeta Swamp to about 5,100 feet (1,555 m) at the bottom of the erosion scarp formed by quartzitic sandstones of the Plateau Series above the Kate Porphyry near the Kasanga road. Over the outcrop of the Plateau Series the surface is recognized in the level of the interfluves which is tilted in a SW to WSW direction. The inclination of this tilted portion of the surface between the watershed and the top of the escarpment above Kasanga and Kirambo is roughly 160 feet per mile (48·8 m per 1·6 km). The described surface pertains to the 'mid-Tertiary surface' or 'sub-Miocene erosion bevel' (Pulfrey, 1960). This is the most extensive and best preserved surface in East Africa and Zambia but, in the area under consideration, it has been uplifted in relation to the plateau country of Zambia and Central Tanzania which stands at an average general level of about 4,000 feet (1,220 m). Moreover, it has been much disturbed by later block-faulting. In the Abercorn area and to the south of it, it has been up-warped to elevations ranging from 5,000 to 5,500 feet (1,524–1,676 m). There are no indications that the 'mid-Tertiary erosion surface' has been related to an already existing Lake Tanganyika basin which would have presented a local base level.

On either side of the Sumbawanga corridor there are ridges and mountains which represent remnants on the 'mid-Tertiary surface'. The high ground to the east is formed by mountains and ridges showing concordant bevels over a considerable distance. From the south, below Malonje Mountain, the old Sumbawanga–Abercorn road leads over an undulating, high-level residual plateau with red earths and murram, at an elevation of 6,900–7,100 feet (2,103–2,164 m), for a distance of over 15 miles (24 km). Above this surface there are residuals of yet an older surface, notably Mbizi Mountain (8,074 feet (2,461 m)) with its rain forest, and Malonje (7,933 feet (2,418 m)). This high ground or remnant block is bounded by a series of faults believed to be of late-Tertiary to Recent age from the Rukwa trough, but its western boundary would appear to be essentially an erosion scarp. On the known evidence the high ground to the east of the Sumbawanga corridor cannot be interpreted simply as a differentially uplifted portion of the 'mid-Tertiary surface' of the Ufipa Plateau. Concordant ridges and summit levels also occur on the west side of the Sumbawanga corridor and the more conspicuous ones are at 1,000–1,100 feet (305–335·5 m) above the valley floor. Again, residuals of an older surface are present, e.g. Mongali (7,613 feet (2,320 m)) and Vimbwe (7,443 feet (2,269 m)). The residual plateaux and concordant summit levels, which stand at 800–1,100 feet (244–335·5 m) above the 'mid-Tertiary surface', are referred to as the 'late-Cretaceous surface'. Therefore, the highest residuals represent remnants of the 'end-Jurassic' or 'Gondwanaland surface' (King, 1957, p. 102; Haldemann, 1962, p. 2). However, these residuals in Ufipa appear in various stages of erosion, little above the 'late-Cretaceous surface' in places, and the vertical interval between the 'end-Jurassic' and 'mid-Tertiary' surfaces can only be approximately determined. It would appear to be of the order of 1,800–2,400 feet (549–732 m). Detailed mapping in the Sumbawanga area will presumably reveal that the 'late-

Cretaceous surface' is composite and can be subdivided into two, if not three stages. The recognized range of vertical intervals at which the 'late-Cretaceous' and 'end-Jurassic' surfaces stand above the 'mid-Tertiary surface' enables the interpretation of the various high points of the local topography.

Before the disturbance of the 'mid-Tertiary surface' the Atlantic–Indian Ocean divide passed through the Southern Highlands of Tanzania whence to the western side of the Kenya Rift Valley zone or, according to Pulfrey (1960, p. 15), to the vicinity of the western rift. The general inclination towards the Atlantic was approximately one foot per mile, in which case the elevation of the divide would have been 1,800 to 2,200 feet (549–671 m). A comparison with present elevations indicates that the vertical movements, to which the East African region has been subjected since mid-Tertiary times, were of the order of 2,000–3,500 feet (610–1,067 m), but in some special cases (e.g. Ruwenzori and Kungwe) the uplift was much greater.

In his evaluation of the known evidence, Cooke (1958, p. 20) concluded that: '(1) The lower-Miocene lake beds in East Africa were deposited on a very little warped mid-Tertiary peneplain of fairly low initial relief except for the presence of block-like residuals of an earlier erosion cycle rising above it; (2) the distribution of these lower-Miocene lake beds agrees broadly with the outlines of the rift valleys...'

In Kenya, Uganda and in the Congo the sequence of events could be elucidated by fossil evidence and datable volcanics. Moreover, the existence there of a conspicuous 'end-Tertiary' or 'Pliocene surface' approximately parallel to and a few hundred feet below the 'mid-Tertiary surface' further helped in picturing the sequence of events. Unfortunately, such evidence is missing on the Ufipa Plateau and in the Abercorn area.

On the 'mid-Tertiary surface' the ancient Kalambo River must have had a completely different drainage basin. This ancient Kalambo can be viewed as part of a river system which was directed from the southern part of the Ufipa Plateau towards Sumbu and Lake Mweru, whence towards Lake Upemba, the Kasai and the Ogooué in Gabon (cf. King, 1957, p. 106). Regional vertical movements and local faulting which disturbed the 'mid-Tertiary surface' produced a basin of internal drainage somewhere in the area occupied by the present Lake Tanganyika, and the Ufipa Plateau emerged as a local watershed. It is believed that such a basin already represented a local base level during the 'end-Tertiary cycle', i.e. in Miocene and lower Pliocene times. There is some geomorphological evidence in support of this interpretation but no fossil evidence. Cooke (1958, p. 26), on the other hand, suggested that the establishment of a basin of internal drainage in Lake Tanganyika probably did not occur before the late Pliocene. He based this suggestion on the distribution of fish faunas and the balance to be struck between the 'maximum period of unchanged survival and the minimum time demanded to account for the extensive speciation which has occurred in the fish and molluscan fauna of Lake Tanganyika' (Cooke, pp. 24, 26). However, the Belgian hydrobiological exploration work produced evidence that the level of Lake Tanganyika was subjected to repeated, very considerable, lowering in Quaternary times (see Section 4 below). This must have been accompanied by changes in the salinity which, undoubtedly, influenced the evolution of the specific fauna of the lake very significantly. Thus, the faunal evidence used by Cooke may at best give a minimum age for the existence of Lake Tanganyika, but not the much earlier time range during which the first basin was formed (cf. also Moore, 1903).

Lake Tanganyika is divided into a northern and a southern basin separated by a drowned ridge in the continuation of Kungwe Mountain. The northern basin has been subdivided by Capart (1949) into the Usumbura and Kigoma basins, the latter representing a most spectacular example of trough-faulting with the bottom of the trough being at 4,100–4,300 feet (1,249–1,311m) below lake level. The southern basin has been subdivided into the Albertville and Zongwe basins, separated from each other by the wide sublacustrine swell of Marungu, on the opposite side of Karema. The Albertville basin is a one-sided feature, essentially produced by block-faulting, with an enormous scarp rising from an elevation of −300 feet (−91·5 m) at the bottom of the lake towards Kungwe Mountain (8,450 feet (2,576 m)) on the eastern side of the lake. The sections produced by the Belgian exploration work show a drowned topography with two or three U-shaped valleys on the western side of the Albertville basin and several deeply cut V-shaped valleys between Utinta and Cape Kibwesa on the eastern side of the Marungu swell. The Zongwe basin appears to be a composite trough with step-faulting and block-faulting developed on its long-drawn eastern side, trough-faulting in the deepest section, and a near vertical fault bounding its western side. The deepest point of Lake Tanganyika was located in the Zongwe trough on the Congo side, about 7 miles (11·2 km) off the shore; it is 4,843 feet (1,470 m) below the present lake level (773 m) or about 2,300 feet (700 m) below sea level. The fact that alluvial cones of present-day rivers draining the Marungu Plateau could readily be detected at the bottom of this deep trough can be taken as proof for the very young age of this feature. Capart (1952, p. 26) reported that the soundings revealed many sublacustrine, V-shaped valleys to a depth of 1,700–1,800 feet (518–549 m) below the present lake level. He thought that they could only be explained by the great variations of the lake level during Quaternary times. In some areas, however, the connection between the present rivers and the drowned valleys has been obscured by very young faulting and Capart's explanation should be amended accordingly. In any case it can be taken for certain that the different parts of Lake Tanganyika have been formed at different times. It is assumed that the Albertville basin, and probably also part of the Zongwe basin, represent the oldest part of the lake and already formed the local base level to which erosion on the Ufipa Plateau proceeded during the 'end-Tertiary cycle'.

The wide, NNW directed valley, partly occupied by the present Kalambo River at the Prehistoric Site, is interpreted as a remnant of the 'end-Tertiary surface'. This valley follows the strike of the quartzites of the Plateau Series. To the south it lines up with flat ground now occupied by *dambos*, close to the Abercorn–Kalambo Falls road, and to the north over a valley watershed with the lower Kawa River before it disappears in the lake. At the Prehistoric Site this old valley is one to two miles wide and about 600 feet (183 m) below the level of the 'mid-Tertiary surface'. There are other river alignments in the Abercorn area and on the Ufipa Plateau which could have pertained to a NW to NNW directed drainage during the 'end-Tertiary cycle', but later faulting, uplift and tilting have obscured much of the evidence. The wide valley encountered at a depth of 2,600–2,750 feet (793–838 m) below the present lake level between Moliro and Msamba, to the west of Kala, may represent a down-faulted portion of the 'end-Tertiary surface'. It is by way of this drowned valley that the rivers from the Abercorn and Sumbu areas could have reached the Zongwe or Albertville basin of the early lake. However, it is the phase of diastrophic events which disrupted the drainage on the 'end-Tertiary surface' and continued from end-Pliocene to Recent times that produced the modern shape of Lake Tanganyika and led to the present drainage system of the Kalambo.

The remarkable, asymmetrical shape of the Kalambo drainage basin is shown on the map (Figure 4). Apart from the shape it is the size of the basin which deserves attention. None of the other rivers of the eastern shore of the lake to as far north as Karema have captured such a large drainage area as has the Kalambo. Any, or all, of the following points seem to have given the Kalambo an advantage over the other rivers and influenced the development of this drainage basin:

(1) The Kalambo existed as a larger river, albeit with a different drainage basin, on the 'end-Tertiary surface'. One of its contributing drainage areas of individual stream segments was favourably located to capture streams from the area to the east and north of the Sansia Falls.

(2) The lower Kalambo is situated at a point on the lake where northwesterly striking faults as well as easterly directed faults occur along which erosion could proceed more rapidly.

(3) The lower Kalambo coincides with a low area in the topography in the boundary zone between the upwarped Abercorn area and the southwesterly directed regional tilt of the southern Ufipa Plateau. In fact it may belong to one of the cross-structures which can be traced as highs and lows across Ufipa. The upwarping of the Abercorn area, which pushed the Kalambo divide northwards and caused the upper Lumi River to flow into the Saisi, probably preceded the local faulting.

As a result of its composite nature, the asymmetrical Kalambo basin shows significant differences in the density of the drainage net between the lower and upper reaches. The longitudinal profile of the Kalambo is very complex and includes swampy, reversed sections; immature narrow, steeply graded gorges; and interruptions by nickpoints (waterfalls). Thus, there are several local base levels and with regard to run-off and sediment transport into Lake Tanganyika, the Kalambo does not truly reflect the size of its drainage area. Nevertheless, each addition to the drainage area must have led to changes in the hydraulic characteristics of the lower Kalambo. These changes have a bearing on the nature of the Quaternary deposits at the Prehistoric Site and the evolution of the Kalambo Falls, as well as the changes brought about by faulting in the lake area.

The Sumbawanga–Kanda fault, which runs in a SSE direction through the Sumbawanga corridor, has displaced ferricrete layers of the red soil profile. In the Naluzi valley, near Mpuwi, the throw of the fault measured on fresh facets is 70 feet (21·34 m). The scarp is little incised. On the road to Kaengeza Mission, where the throw is over 70 feet (21·34 m), the fault can be seen to parallel old structures of the amphibolitic country rock. In the Mtembwa valley, further to the south, the alignment of the fault is at an angle to the northwesterly Ubendian foliation. To the north of Sumbawanga, before the fault disappears, the facets are still 20–25 feet (6·1–7·6 m) high. Here, some microlithic artifacts, believed to have derived from the ferricrete horizon, were noted at the bottom of the small scarp. The Sumbawanga–Kanda fault is interpreted as very young, probably of post-Pleistocene age.

Another very conspicuous feature of the Ufipa Plateau is the fault which runs from near Msunya on the Kalambo-Mfuizi divide, in a SSE direction, reappears in the Kanyele River, and marks the boundary between the Kate Granite and the Ubendian rocks (Mwimbi fault) to beyond Ulumi Mission. On its downthrow side is a large *mbuga*-corridor with most of the *mbugas* below the fault showing little or no incision by the present cycle of erosion. Although it is very likely to be a rejuvenation of an older fault, the last movements must have taken place in comparatively recent times. The tilting effects on either side of this block-fault have led to the capture by the Kalambo of the northern and eastern area previously drained by the Mfuizi. The points where the Kalambo and Kanyele cross the fault still act as local base levels.

The Lake Sundu fault on the eastern side of the Kalambo drainage basin is another example of very young faulting. This fault probably had a throw of the order of 15–25 feet (4·5–7·6 m) only, but enough to interfere with the present *mbuga* system, and to produce Lake Sundu as a small, temporarily discharge-less basin. The sandbanks in the swamp to the west of Lake Sundu must have been produced by wave action when the lake was at a slightly higher level. There is no effective drainage from the present swamp into the next tributary of the Kalambo; nor are there any noteworthy streams which would have caused a silting-up of the lake. Therefore, the shrinkage of Lake Sundu must essentially relate to a change in climate from wetter than present day to present-day climate. Judging by the overall setting the Lake Sundu fault is unlikely to be older than end-Pleistocene in age and the change in climate must have occurred afterwards. In 1961, a site with microlithic artifacts was discovered by Dr M. R. Kleindienst to the west above Lake Sundu (see Haldemann, 1964). The effect of tectonic disturbances in Quaternary times can be noted in many river systems outside the Kalambo drainage basin; the upper stretch of the Saisi is a typical example of an impeded drainage.

The different parts of Lake Tanganyika have not only been formed at different times but also involved an interplay of systems of block-faulting and tilting, and trough-faulting. From the unilateral, easterly tilted block structure of the Albert-ville basin the lake continues over the Marungu swell into the Zongwe basin, which shows a bilateral trough in its deepest portion. To the south of the Zongwe basin the typical trough gives way to long-drawn westerly and southwesterly dip-slopes produced by unilateral block structures and submerged valleys. Only at the southeastern end of the lake, between Mpulungu and Kasanga has a small trough-fault been recognized by soundings. This local trough feature is close enough to the Kalambo Falls to have borne on its evolution. On the whole, how-ever, it was the downwarping of a series of tilted blocks that determined the morphology of the southern end of Lake Tanganyika. This had already been recognized by Gillman (1935, p. 32). References in the literature to 'Lake Tanganyika Rift' implying a simple down-faulted trough have, therefore, to be read critically. Attention has already been drawn to the sublacustrine V-shaped valleys which relate to much lower lake levels in Quaternary times (Capart, 1952, p. 26). Reasons other than structural ones which have caused repeated, very considerable vertical changes in the lake level are discussed below (Section 4).

It is apparent from the above review that the diastrophic events during end-Tertiary to Recent times which led to the formation of the modern Lake Tanganyika and to the present Kalambo drainage basin must have had a very significant bearing on the formation of the Kalambo Falls and on the local basin filled with Quaternary sediments at the Prehistoric Site.

4. HYDROLOGICAL CONSIDERATIONS

The following notes on the hydrology of the lake are largely based on the results of the Belgian hydrobiological exploration of Lake Tanganyika in 1946–7 (Capart, 1949 and 1952).

It is certain that, at present, the evaporation from the free water surface almost compensates the intake from precipitation over the lake and inflow from its drainage area. The run-off through the Lukuga represents only a very minor fraction of the water losses. Capart (1952, p. 26) calculated that with its discharge of 100–200 cubic metres per second, the Lukuga is evacuating a 10–20 centimetres thick layer of water from the lake each year. The evaporation on the other hand accounts for the annual loss of a 160–200 centimetres thick layer, if one applies the evaporation rate of 158·3 centimetres per year determined at the 'Chutes Cornet' in Katanga. There, the daily mean air temperature is 25·5° C and the daily mean moisture content 82·66 per cent. In another area with a drier and colder climate, where these figures were 21·3° C and 64·75 per cent, the evaporation reached 206·7 centimetres. It is interesting to compare the figures used by Capart with two examples of the corrected mean annual evaporation rate determined by pan evaporimeters in Kenya (Sanson, 1954):

Magadi (Rift Valley, altitude 2,010 feet (613 m):98 inches (248·9 cm);
Kisumu (Lake Victoria, altitude 3,760 feet (1,146 m):64 inches (162·5 cm).

The evaporation rate of 158·3 centimetres would, therefore, appear to represent a minimum for Lake Tanganyika, and during the dry season the evaporation rate must be considerably higher. With an outflow of 100–200 cubic metres per second, a reduction of the intake by 20 centimetres per year can produce a deficit in the water regime which can quickly lead to a lowering of the lake level below the rock bench at the outflow of the Lukuga. According to Capart such a situation has occurred several times in the history of the lake. The sublacustrine V-shaped valleys found by soundings in the continuation of most of the present rivers to a depth of 1,700–1,800 feet (518–549 m) below the present lake level are taken as proof for the existence of much lower lake levels in Quaternary times. Capart (1949, p. 11) observed the existence of several sedimentary layers which indicate that the lake level was repeatedly 1,800–1,950 feet (549–595 m) below the present level. He said that, perhaps, the lake level even reached a depth of 2,790 feet (850 m) below the present level on one or two occasions.

Capart (1952, p. 27) has tried to throw some light on the relationship between the major changes of lake level and the discharge of the Ruzizi. The Pliocene to Recent volcanic activity of the western rift area produced, amongst others, the Virunga volcanoes which interrupted the connection between Lake Kivu and Lake Edward and caused the waters of Lake Kivu to flow into Lake Tanganyika by way of the Ruzizi. During the dry season in 1947, the discharge of the Ruzizi into Lake Tanganyika reached 222 cubic metres per second. At the same time the Lukuga was flowing at a rate of 97–109 cubic metres per second. The lake thus gained from the Ruzizi roughly double the amount of water evacuated by the Lukuga.

The above hydrological observations demonstrate how precarious the present equilibrium of Lake Tanganyika is. A small diminution in precipitation or increase in evaporation alone can produce a lowering of the lake level. The discharge of the Ruzizi would appear to have been the controlling factor and it is believed that the lake, or the individual sub-basins which form the present lake, was a dischargeless basin prior to the addition of the Ruzizi. Lava fields also occur south of Lake Kivu. In the upper Ruzizi valley, alluvial gravels were found between separate lava flows and three phases of eruptions, the oldest being assigned to the Lower Pleistocene or earlier, were recognized. If these eruptions have interrupted the flow of the Ruzizi for any extended period, changes in the level of Lake Tanganyika could be related to them in time. An accurate dating of the late Pliocene and Quaternary volcanic events in the Kivu area would certainly throw some light on the history of Lake Tanganyika and, consequently, assist in the interpretation of the Kalambo Falls Prehistoric Site.

In the absence of any reliable dates one can at least conclude that several changes in the level of Lake Tanganyika occurred during the Pleistocene. Lower lake levels must have affected the local climate and the vegetation. Today, the Prehistoric Site is just over three miles from the lake shore measured in a straight line. Judging by the present environment there is no straightforward answer why this site was favoured by the prehistoric people over other places on the Kalambo, the Kawa River, Lake Chila at Abercorn, or the lake shore for that matter, except perhaps for the fact that it was a convenient place to cross the Kalambo. However, at the time the lake level was 1,800 feet (549 m) below the present-day one, the shore was at a distance of 34 miles (54·7 km) from the site, and if the level was indeed lowered once or twice by 2,790 feet (850 m) as suggested by Capart, the distance would have been 48 miles (77 km). The water of these lower lakes must have been considerably more saline and, on account of the drier climate, the Kalambo was very likely the only permanent river and source of fresh water in the southeastern area of the lake. Without taking into consideration the changes produced by tectonic activities, the repeated lowering of the lake level by hydrological factors alone would make the choice of the site by prehistoric man more understandable.

Cooke (1958, p. 61) has drawn attention to the fact that topographic changes produced by substantial faulting have had a significant effect on the climate. This is undoubtedly so in the Lake Tanganyika region, but here the situation is even more complex because the hydrological observations show that other causes led to changes in the lake level as well. One of these causes is the evaporation from the free water surface of the lake. Evaporation is controlled by many factors, the temperature of the air being only one of them. However, changes in the temperature during the Upper Pleistocene, inferred from palynological evidence (see Chapter 3), must have affected the evaporation rate and oscillations of the lake level.

Changes in the lake level which took place in the last century are well known from observations by the early European explorers. In 1874, Stanley found no water flowing out of Lake Tanganyika through the Lukuga gap. In those days the Lukuga was filled up by vegetation and sand. Hore reported that the waters had risen to the lowest point in the Lukuga gap in 1877 or the early part of 1878, when the Lukuga River again became a permanent outlet (Hore, 1892, p. 147; Thompson, 1888, vol. II, pp. 54–72). The breaching of the bar at the mouth of the Lukuga caused the lake level to fall in subsequent years. In 1882, von Wissmann saw the Lukuga as a wide, rapid effluent of Lake Tanganyika, forcibly breaking open the old discharge channel (1891, pp. 255–6). He observed that the constantly falling lake was lower by 16 feet (4·8 m) than the highest watermark. Sandy, largely unconsolidated lake beds laid down when the lake was at a higher level and of somewhat larger extent were uncovered in many places. Such lake beds occur for instance in the curve of Kungwe Bay, in the lower reaches of the Ifume near Karema, at Kasanga, and at the mouth of the Kalambo.

In this connection it is perhaps interesting to draw attention to a story believed to persist in the folklore of the Holoholo or Sowa who inhabit the shore in the area of Kungwe Mountain. According to this story, the ancestors of the Holoholo, who came from the Congo side, made use of a long island which existed in the continuation of Kungwe Mountain, i.e. on the now drowned divide between the northern and the southern basins of Lake Tanganyika (cf. Section 3 above). Soundings have proved the existence of a steep drowned ridge the highest point of which is 100 feet below the present lake level. There would appear to be a grain of truth in this old story, indicating that the ancestors of the Holoholo witnessed the existence of a lake level say about 300–400 feet (91·5–122 m) below the present-day one.

Unfortunately, there are no data on the precipitation in the Kalambo drainage basin, evaporation, discharge of the Kalambo, absorption into the ground, subterranean condensation and transpiration. In other words, none of the factors which determine the hydrological cycle are known. All we have are some general observations concerning the climate and vegetation of the region. The mean annual rainfall over the basin appears to vary between 30 inches (762 mm) and

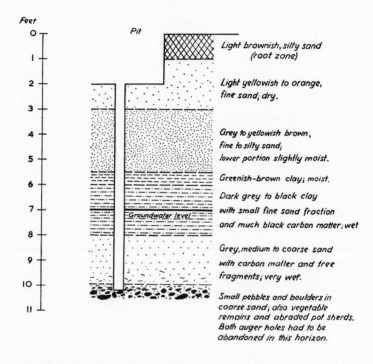

Fig. 6. Profile of Auger Hole 2, opposite A 4 excavation, Kalambo Falls Prehistoric Site.

48 inches (1,219 mm) and the mean annual temperature between 65° and 75° F (18·3° and 23·9° C). Considering the relative run-off effectiveness as a function of precipitation and temperature the area appears as a hypothetical morphogenic region in which the possible relative importance of specific weathering and erosional processes, in decreasing order of importance, is as follows: Chemical weathering—mass movement—running water (Leopold, Wolmand & Miller, 1964, p. 45). A slightly cooler climate, only a reduction in the range of the mean

36

annual temperature by 10° F (5·5° C), would change the order to: mechanical and chemical weathering—running water—mass movement.

Mean velocity, mean depth, width of flowing water, and sediment load are variable functions of the river discharge. It is known that changes in the discharge of the Kalambo have occurred during different climatic stages and changes in the size of the drainage basin. Changes in discharge in sand-bed rivers, which apply to some present sections and earlier phases of the Kalambo at the Prehistoric Site, result in complex changes in the configuration of the river bed. Cross-bedding and other depositional features observed in the Quaternary sediments of the local basin at the Prehistoric Site relate to such changes. With regard to degradation and aggradation, channel scour and fill, Leopold *et al.* (p. 227) have drawn attention to a time connotation which also applies to the Kalambo site: 'Scour and fill involve times measured in minutes, hours, days, perhaps even seasons, whereas aggradation and degradation apply to persistent mean changes over periods of time measured in years.'

The backscour in the bedrock behind the lip of the Kalambo Falls and the Spillway Gorge is certainly more than two feet (see Figure 6, Profile of Auger Hole 2, and Figure 27) and possibly over 10 feet (3 m). It was also observed that the elevation of the bed above the arbitrary datum of the Kalambo during rising stages of floods and maximum sediment load can be as much as 7 feet (2·1 m). Water in excess of channel capacity must flow overbank and examples of overbank deposits are numerous at the Prehistoric Site. Thus, it is apparent that the recognition of hydraulic characteristics is of considerable importance in the interpretation of the artifact-bearing sediments of the local basin.

5. THE LOCAL BASIN AND ITS EVOLUTION

The local basin at the Prehistoric Site is an erosion feature in the valley floor of the 'end-Tertiary cycle' in which sediments were deposited during Pleistocene to Recent times. In places, the bedrock subsurface of this basin must be lower than the lip of the Kalambo Falls (altitude 3,785 feet (1,154 m)) because of scouring effects. The difference in elevation between the subsurface of the local basin and the 'end-Tertiary valley floor' is estimated at about 300 feet (91·5 m). The northern, broader end of the local basin is obscured in the direction of the Kalambo-Kawa divide by soil creep and hill wash over the Pleistocene deposits. In the so-called 'Tanganyika Cliff' section on the north side of the Kalambo the thickness of Pleistocene sediments from the river level to the base of the murram layer is 56 feet (17 m); allowing for the depth of the river and a few feet of sediments below the river bed, the maximum thickness of the Pleistocene deposits would appear to have been about 70 feet (21·3 m) (see Figure 7, Geological Section across Kalambo Valley). Some control must have existed to prevent the sedimentation in the local basin from building up to the level of the 'end-Tertiary valley floor'. At its southern end the local basin narrows and merges with the V-shaped section the Kalambo has cut into the old valley floor, which is practically no longer recognizable.

The altitude of the valley watershed between the Kalambo and Kawa drainage is about 4,100 feet (1,250 m), or 225 feet (68·6 m) higher than Mkamba, the village above the 'Tanganyika Cliff'. On the south side of the divide, the Kaposwa, a tributary less than a mile long, flows into the Kalambo. Running north is the Simwela (or Katindisi), a small tributary of the Kawa, which enters the lake in the direction of the old valley floor at Kasanga. Faulting below the confluence of the Simwela and Kawa has produced a lowering of the last section of the Kawa valley, and backward erosion by the Simwela is progressing much more rapidly than that of the Kaposwa. Near its source on the valley watershed the Simwela has cut a small V-notch into the thick soil profile and its bed is on bedrock. The bedrock was found to be a quartzitic sandstone which dips at 20° to NE (50°) and there is some jointing parallel to the NNW direction of the stream. The outcrops are much less than 100 feet (30·5 m) below the divide and thus seem to prove that the local basin of the Kalambo never extended this far north towards the Kawa drainage area. At the divide the cross-section of the old valley is broad and shallow; although some creep and hill wash from the sides has occurred, this valley represents a unique remnant of the 'end-Tertiary surface' in the southeastern area of Lake Tanganyika.

About 100 yards (91·5 m) above the Kalambo Falls the river emerges from a WSW directed gorge, about 150 yards (137 m) long, cut in hard quartzitic rocks. The north wall is near vertical up to 42 feet (12·8 m) above the river level, but debris of a rock-fall lies at the foot of it near the lower end of the gorge (Plate 10). The blocks of this rock-fall mask bedrock of the north wall up to 16 feet (4·8 m) above the river and are found in the river bed right across to the south wall. They are impeding the river which is only transporting fine sediments through the gorge. In places the fine sandy river bed above the rock-fall is 6–7 feet (1·8–2·1 m) deep. Judging by the river gradient to the lip of the falls this depth indicates a scouring effect behind the lip of the falls.

In the thick-bedded, massive quartzite of the north wall of the Spillway Gorge occur thin layers or bands of a sheared rock which was found, in a thin-section, to be a sericite schist composed of finely divided sericite and coarse muscovite, and biotite, with scattered grains of limonite and hematite. The quartzite and

38

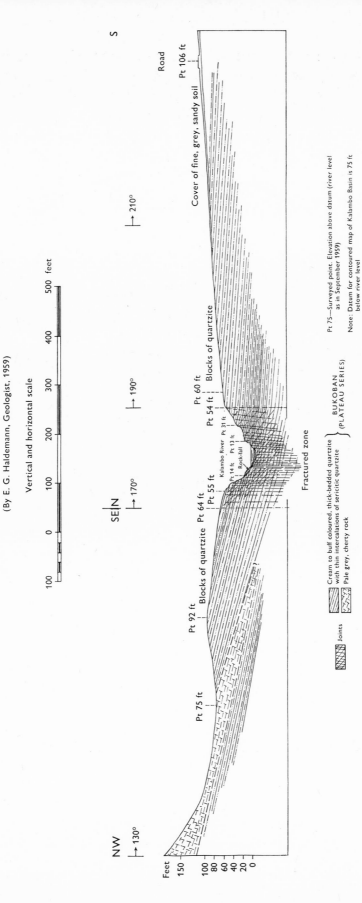

Fig. 8. Geological section across the Spillway Gorge at the Kalambo Falls Prehistoric Site.

these schists dip at 30–40° to E (102–110°). The very pronounced set of vertical joints which strikes to WSW (245–250°) determines the direction of the gorge. The joints of this set represent an important fracture zone which coincides with

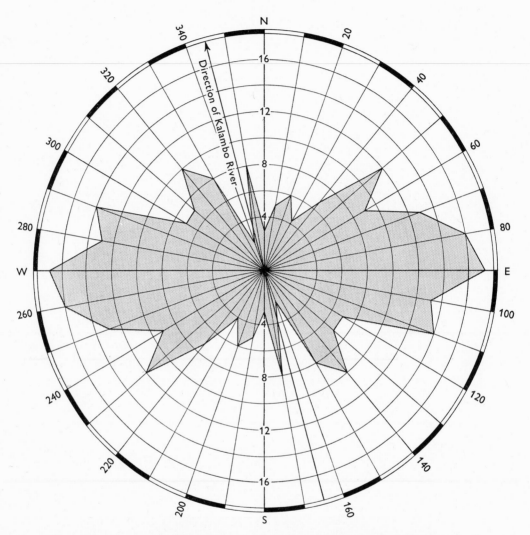

Fig. 9. Diagram showing frequency and orientation of long axes of 161 boulders in the Kalambo River in relation to the direction of flow.

the cross-fault of the face on the south side of the Kalambo Falls (Plate 8). A second set of joints dips at 65–70° to 235°; corrected to the direction perpendicular to the gorge this set dips at about 35° into the gorge. The attitude of the jointing readily explains why rock-falls occur on the north and not on the south side of the Spillway Gorge (see Figure 8, Geological Section across Spillway Gorge).

The survey of the south side of the Spillway Gorge revealed a nickpoint at

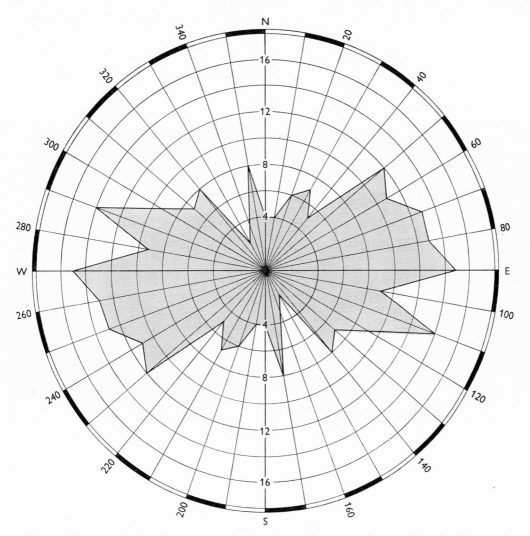

Fig. 10. Diagram showing frequency and orientation of long axes of 150 cobbles, boulders and artifacts in Rubble I-composite, A 4 excavation, Kalambo Falls Prehistoric Site.

13 feet (4 m) above the river. At this point the vertical wall changes to a slope which rises by 6½ feet (2 m) over a distance of 28 feet (8·5 m), whence another steep wall follows to a nickpoint at 31 feet (9·5 m) above the river. The next change in the slope angle occurs at 54 feet (16·5 m) above the river. It was noted

that the quartzites on the south side of the gorge only dip at 23–25° to E (102°) while the jointing is practically identical to the one on the north side.

The elevation reached by Quaternary sediments in the local basin is approximately level with the floor of the wide valley section into which the Spillway Gorge is cut. The local base level of the Kalambo is the river bed at the entrance to the Spillway Gorge and/or the lip of the falls. The various stages of cut-and-fill in the sedimentary sequence however indicate that the base level has fluctuated markedly. Bond (see Appendix A) suggested that periodic damming of the gorge was the mechanism responsible and that sediments which could have caused the damming are likely to have been brought down by the tributary stream from the south. On occasions, this tributary, which enters the Kalambo between Site A and Site B, formed an outwash fan across the upper end of the Spillway Gorge, thereby raising the local base level and impeding the Kalambo.

I observed that remnants of a boulder bed with boulders up to more than 2 feet (60 cm) in diameter, mixed with angular blocks, occur on the north side of the Kalambo above the flat ground opposite trench A 4 and at the entrance of the Spillway Gorge. The top of this boulder bed is 22 feet (6·7 m) above the river level and a well-marked bench is present at 7½ feet (2·3 m) above the river, i.e. at the present-day flood mark. This remnant could relate to a damming produced by the mentioned tributary from the south, but more likely it represents a deposit by the Kalambo.

Today, the Kalambo remains a fast-flowing river from where it enters the local basin to a point about 400 yards (366 m) SSE of Mkamba village. Here, it changes its straight northwesterly course and starts to meander until it reaches the Site A area whence it takes a westerly course through the Spillway Gorge. At the point where it changes to a slow running, meandering river it is depositing its coarse bed load which consists largely of quartzite boulders and pebbles (see Figures 9 and 10, orientation diagrams). No Ubendian rocks were noted. Below this point, the river carries practically only fine-grained sediments.

6. SUMMARY OF LOCAL GEOMORPHOLOGICAL DEVELOPMENTS

From the observations and suggestions made above, the history of the local basin and the Kalambo Falls can be summarized as follows:

1. On the 'mid-Tertiary surface' an ancient Kalambo was part of a westerly directed river system. This ancient Kalambo occupied a wide valley several hundred feet above the top of the walls of the Spillway Gorge.

2. Regional vertical movements and early faulting, which produced a basin of internal drainage somewhere in the present Lake Tanganyika region, initiated the 'end-Tertiary cycle' of erosion. During this cycle a new river system developed which was related to the local base level of this basin. The Kalambo formed a NNW directed valley parallel to existing structural alignments. Towards the close of the 'end-Tertiary cycle', the wide valley floor was about 600 feet (183 m) below the level of the 'mid-Tertiary surface'. On the ridges on either side of the 'end-Tertiary valley floor', remnants of the earlier, westerly directed drainage remained in the form of wide wind-gaps, notably one above the Spillway Gorge.

3. Diastrophic events in end-Pliocene times which brought the 'end-Tertiary cycle' to a close, included block-faulting and related tilting effects which disrupted the NNW directed drainage of the Kalambo. The various sub-basins of the present Lake Tanganyika were established and the new base level or levels led to a new drainage system. From the shape of the present Kalambo drainage basin and the southeastern end of Lake Tanganyika it is apparent that the uplift of the Ufipa Plateau and the tilting of the blocks had produced a southerly directed component. This led to a reversal of a portion of the NNW directed Kalambo valley, and since the present Kawa valley is a much younger feature the old valley may have been occupied by a tributary which flowed from some distance to the NNW in a SSE direction towards the area now occupied by the local basin. Such a situation would also help to explain the later developments on the northern side of the local Kalambo basin. Backward erosion of a stream, situated on the west side of the old wind-gap, captured the Kalambo and thus gained a much larger drainage area than the ones of other streams of the then existing shore zone. In consequence the wide valley cross-section 60–75 feet (18·3–22·8 m) above the present river level in the Spillway Gorge was formed at the site of the ancient wind-gap. It is thought that this new valley developed in end-Pliocene times before the beginning of the Pleistocene Epoch. The U-shaped upper portion of the Kalambo Gorge below the falls is correlated with this wide valley section above the Spillway Gorge; both are interpreted as remnant features of the end-Pliocene valley which was probably linked with similar valleys on the western shore (Sumbu area) of the lake, and together with these it drained into the Zongwe basin of the lake.

4. Renewed tectonic activity at the beginning of the Pleistocene resulted in further uplift and faulting. On account of these tectonic events, and the addition of an effective drainage of the Kivu area, Lake Tanganyika probably attained much of its present shape. The cross-faulting at the Kalambo Falls and Sansia Falls, and in intermediate valley stretches, is believed to have taken place at this

43

stage. The same presumably applies to the large fault along the Lufubu River which strikes out into the lake to the north of Chilingala Mountain, opposite the mouth of the Kalambo. This faulting also affected the Kawa drainage and eventually led to the present position of the Kalambo–Kawa divide. Vigorous erosion cut a narrow, steep gorge along faults and fractures which now determine the cliff on the south side of the Kalambo Falls and the Spillway Gorge (Plate 8). The cutting of the Spillway Gorge and the formation of the basin behind it was accompanied downstream by the rapid deepening of a long and very steep cascade from a point to the west of the present falls. After this deepening had reached the softer clay-slates which underlie the thick-bedded and well-jointed quartzitic rocks, the cascade rapidly collapsed. Because of these peculiar geological conditions the formation of the Kalambo Falls could well have taken place in early Pleistocene times or say during a time range of about one million years (reckoning with a duration of about two million years for the Pleistocene Epoch). It may be mentioned here that the clay-slates, which actually still further the backward migration of the Kalambo Falls, have only been exposed in the Kalambo gorge and nowhere else in the region because they are situated on a local anticline (Rose, p. 41) produced by folding of the Plateau Series in the late Precambrian or perhaps early Palaeozoic times. The cutting of the Spillway Gorge, the deepening of the local basin, the formation of the Kalambo Falls, the V-shaped portion of the gorge below the falls, and the V-shaped valleys found in Lake Tanganyika by soundings can all be explained as having largely been the result of erosion during the early and Middle Pleistocene.

5. The establishment of a local base level at the entrance of the Spillway Gorge had a very important bearing on later developments: The history of the local basin became independent from subsequent changes in the lake level except for climatic variations influenced by different lake levels. Since the Kalambo loses a great proportion of its sediment load in the local basin, its erosional capacity below the Spillway Gorge is considerably increased. This is a factor by which the Kalambo differs from the other rivers in the area and which bears very significantly on the rapid formation of the falls. Below the falls, the valley first shows a U-shape, then a V-shape as mentioned, and in its deepest portion there is a narrow, inaccessible gorge with walls about 100 feet (30·5 m) high. Several falls occur in this gorge which must look very much like the narrow cascade which preceded the formation of the falls. This deepest gorge is a young feature which must relate to a late stage of uplift in the area, probably the one accompanying the trough-faulting which produced the small graben at the southeastern end of the lake (see Plates 7, 8 and 9).

6. The deposition of sediments containing the earliest artifacts which started

in the late-Middle Pleistocene, or later, coincides with a comparatively slow damming of the Spillway Gorge. This can be explained by a collapse of a wall in the then much narrower Spillway Gorge caused, for instance, by earthquakes related to tectonic movements in the area of the lake (Plate 10). However, the Kalambo kept flowing through the blocks barring the gorge but, as it filled up the basin, it also gradually filled up the space between the rock debris and impeded itself to higher levels. Thus, the gorge became a barrier until the level of the wide valley section above was reached. A substantial change in the discharge of the Kalambo, whether produced by a change in climate and/or by the addition of a new area to the drainage basin and/or tectonic events, then led to a gradual clearance of the Spillway Gorge to its previous floor. Other, subsequent fluctuations, stages of downcutting and aggradation in the local basin can be readily accounted for by the damming of the gorge by the above-described tributary stream from the south, and by changes in the hydraulic characteristics of the Kalambo River.

REFERENCES

Capart, A. (1949). Sondages et carte bathymétrique. *Inst. Roy. Sci. Nat. Belgique*. Exploration hydrobiologique du Lac Tanganika (1946–7). *Résultats scientifiques*, **2**, fasc. 2.

(1952). Le milieu géographique et géophysique. *Inst. Roy. Sci. Nat. Belgique*. Exploration hydrobiologique du Lac Tanganika (1946–7). *Résultats scientifiques*, **1**.

Combe, A. D. (1927). Summary of investigations carried out between Entebbe and Cape Town. *Annual Report of the Geological Survey of Uganda* (1926), pp. 28–32.

Cooke, H. B. S. (1958). Observations relating to Quaternary environments in East and Southern Africa. *Trans. Proc. geol. Soc. S. Afr.* Annexure to **60** (Alex. du Toit Memorial Lecture, 5).

Cornwall, J. W. (1929). The survey of the Kalambo Gorge. *Geogrl J.* **74**, 33–8.

Dixey, F. (1956). The East African Rift System. *Colon. Geol. Miner. Resour.* Suppl. 1.

Gillman, C. (1935). Geomorphological notes. *Annual Report Geological Survey Tanganyika* (1934), pp. 31–3.

Haldemann, E. G. (1962). The geology of the Rufiji Basin with reference to proposed dam sites. *Bull. geol. Surv. Tanganyika*, **33**.

(1964). Mambwe (Mwimbi). Brief explanation of the geology. *Geol. Surv. Tanganyika*, Quarter Degree Sheet 241 (with part of 241 S).

Halligan, R. (1963). The Proterozoic rocks of Western Tanganyika. *Bull. geol. Surv. Tanganyika*, **34**.

Hore, E. C. (1892). *Tanganyika: Eleven Years in Central Africa*. Edward Stanford, London. 2nd edn.

James, T. C. (1956). The nature of rift faulting in Tanganyika. *C.C.T.A. East-Central Regional Committee for Geology*, 1st meeting, Dar-es-Salaam, pp. 81–94.

King, B. C. (1957). The geomorphology of Africa. *Sci. Prog. Lond.* **15**, 672–81; **16**, 97–107.

Leopold, L. B., Wolman, M. G. & Miller, J. P. (1964). *Fluvial Processes in Geomorphology.* W. H. Freeman & Co, San Francisco and London.

McConnell, R. B. (1950). Outline of the geology of Ufipa and Ubende. *Bull. geol. Surv. Tanganyika,* **19**.

Moore, J. E. S. (1903). *The Tanganyika Problem.* Hurst and Blackett Ltd, London.

Page, B. G. N. (1959). The Plateau Series and associated formations in the Abercorn District. *Annu. Rep. Research Inst. Afr. Geol., Univ. of Leeds,* **4**.

—— (1960). The stratigraphical and structural relationship of the Abercorn Sandstones, the Plateau Series and Basement rocks of the Kawimbe area, Abercorn District, Northern Rhodesia. *Annu. Rep. Research Inst. Afr. Geol., Univ. of Leeds,* **5**.

Pulfrey, W. (1960). Shape of the sub-Miocene erosion bevel in Kenya. *Bull. geol. Surv. Kenya,* **3**.

Reeve, W. H. (1961). Geological map of Northern Rhodesia, scale 1:1,000,000. Geol. Surv. Northern Rhodesia.

Rose, C. (1929). The geology of the Kalambo Gorge. *Geogrl J.* **74**, 38–46.

Sanson, H. W. (1954). The measurement of evaporation in East Africa. *East Afr. Meteorological Dept., Techn. Memorandum,* **5**.

Thompson, J. (1888). *To the Central African Lakes and Back.* Sampson Low, Marston, Searle and Rivington, cheaper edn, London.

Wallace, L. A. (1907). North-Eastern Rhodesia. *Geogrl J.* **29**, 391.

Wissmann, H. von (1891). *My second journey through Equatorial Africa from the Congo to the Zambezi in the years 1886 and 1887.* Chatto and Windus, London.

Part II: Formal Nomenclature applied to Rock Stratigraphic Units recognized in the Quaternary Sediments of the Kalambo Falls Prehistoric Site

BY MAXINE R. KLEINDIENST

1. INTRODUCTION

The Quaternary sediments in the local basin upstream from the Kalambo (Mbwilo) Falls were mentioned by Rose (1929, p. 41), who regarded them as lacustrine deposits laid down in a basin formed by earth movements. He mapped the sediments as 'Alluvium' (Figures, pp. 38 and 41). In 1954 and 1962 the Quaternary geology of the basin was briefly described by Clark (1954, 1962) in preliminary papers on the archaeology of the prehistoric site, and a third outline was published in 1963 (Howell & Clark, pp. 484–8). The section cleared at Site

A for the Third Pan-African Congress on Prehistory in 1955 was given by Mortelmans (1956, pp. 86–8). In these papers the sediments were regarded as lacustrine. After excavations had been completed in 1963, a summary of the evidence and a schematic section were published (Clark & van Zinderen Bakker, 1964). Detailed work in 1959 and 1963 had shown that the sediments were largely fluviatile in origin.

In 1956, Professor G. Bond made a geological survey and described the Quaternary deposits (Appendix A); some additional observations were made by Dr E. G. Haldemann in 1959 (Chapter 2, Part I). The detailed observations of the archaeologists are mainly limited to the areas of the excavations, and extensive use has been made here of the report by Bond. The map accompanying his report has been amended to include additional information, to correct details of topography, to show the section lines surveyed by Haldemann, and to conform to the formal nomenclature defined below (see Figure 5).

Following the recommendations of the geological section of the July 1965 conference, sponsored by the Wenner-Gren Foundation for Anthropological Research (Bishop & Clark, 1966, 1967),[1] the geological evidence has been re-

TABLE I. *The Kalambo Falls Prehistoric Site: Rock stratigraphic units*

Formation	Member		alluvial facies	colluvial facies
Kalambo Falls Formation	Chiungu Member	?	predominantly red sandy clays and clays	Red sandy clay
		Chisya Gravel Beds	predominantly grey sandy clays and clays	
		?		
	Mbwilo Member	?	Sandy clay	
		Chitambala Gravel Beds	Sands or sands and clays interstratified with rubbles	
			Rubble Bed[a]	Red Rubble Bed
		?		
	Mkamba Member	?	Pits Channel Fill sands	
		Vundwe Gravel Beds	Rubble Bed[b]	
			Ochreous Sands and Grey Clay Beds	
			White Sands and Dark Clay Beds	
		?	?	?

[a] Rubble I or its subdivision in the archaeological nomenclature.
[b] Rubble II or its subdivision in the archaeological nomenclature.

[1] Note that any geological terminology given for the Quaternary sediments of the Kalambo Falls Prehistoric Site in Bishop & Clark (1967) is to be regarded as an exercise in how formal terminology might be applied to such sediments, and not as the terms intended to have actual priority of usage.

assessed in terms of the codes of stratigraphical nomenclature given in Quennell (1960) and Hedberg (1961). Accordingly, the bulk of the Quaternary sediments are here described as the Kalambo Falls Formation, with appropriate subdivisions (Table 1).[1]

2. DEFINITION: THE KALAMBO FALLS FORMATION

The type section for the Kalambo Falls Formation is designated as that exposed by Trenches A 4/A 6, the excavations along the River Face Cliff, and Trench A 1 at Site A. Detailed descriptions of lithology, sections (Figures 20–3, 27–9, 31–2; Plates 11–23), and a summary of the geological evidence are given in chapter 4, and will not be repeated here (see also Chapter 2, Part 1, Chapter 5, and Appendix A). In the Site A area, located just upstream of the outlet from the local basin, a more complete geological record is preserved than in other sections of the basin.

The Kalambo Falls Formation is subdivided into the Mkamba Member, the Mbwilo Member, and the Chiungu Member, all of which occur in the type section and at Site B. At Site A, the sections exposed in the steep south bank of the Kalambo River, and in the excavations, show a complex succession of cutting and filling in fluviatile deposits. In such a geological environment, the sediments cannot be expected to be reproduced in detail at the other archaeological sites. However, although the sequence cannot be traced directly, the deposits at Sites B, C, and D can be correlated on the bases of lithology, organic remains, C14 dating, elevation and artifact content (Chapter 5).

In general, the deposits are interbedded sands, silts, and clays with more clayey sediments at the top. The sands frequently show current bedding, and there are numerous minor discordances representing either breaks in deposition or local erosion, marked by abrupt changes in lithology, and/or the presence of pebbles, angular rubble, larger cobbles or boulders, organic remains, and in places, artifacts. These nonconformities are more noticeable near the base of the exposed sequence, in the Mkamba Member, and in the Mbwilo Member where its basal Rubble Bed is low in elevation. Other discordances are eroded surfaces representing breaks of greater magnitude, some of which can be identified in several of the excavations. Some fillings of relatively small channels have also been sectioned in the trenches, the fillings usually being made up of coarser sediments at base overlain by sands or clayey sediments. Channel fills at the base of the Ochreous Sands and Grey Clay Beds of the Mkamba Member, the

[1] Because of the paucity of suitable local geographical names, it has been necessary to depart from the International Code (Hedberg, 1961) in that most beds are named only from their lithology.

48

Pits Channel Fill containing the uppermost identified deposits of the Mkamba Member in Trench A 4, and the 'Older' and 'Younger Channel Fills' in the Chiungu Member at Site A are examples. The degree of sorting, current bedding, channelling and rapid lithological changes both vertically and horizontally are all characteristic of river deposition.

Rubble layers interstratified with fine bedded sediments are well exposed in Trench A 4 (beds nos. 15 and 18, Figures 28 and 29) and in the Site A River Face Cliff (Figure 32). Although much or most of the coarse material in these rubbles was undoubtedly contributed by such processes as slopewash and creep, some also came from the eroded older sediments as these were cut through and the fines removed. In the excavations rubbles are, in places, demonstrably lag deposits, and most have also been affected by river action (Chapter 4, pp. 127–8). These rubble layers occur in the upper part of the Mkamba Member (Rubble II and its subdivisions in the archaeological nomenclature), and in the Mbwilo Member (Rubble I and its subdivisions).[1] The only beds in the type section which retain the primary characteristics of colluvial deposits are the red soil capping the section which exhibits evidence of transport by slopewash, and the Red Rubble Bed in Trench A 4, which is similar to slope deposits on Polungu Hill to the south (beds nos. 1, 2, 3 in places, and 14, Figures 28 and 29).

The strongly contrasting facies presently being deposited by the Kalambo River in separate areas along its course in the local basin were noted by Bond (p. 201). On the east, after entering the basin, the river is depositing boulder gravels, and to the north, at the beginning of its meander stretch, fine material causing a swamp to form. Further downstream to the west and southwest it is depositing sands on the inside of its major bends. A pit and auger holes were sunk into the overbank deposits on the north side of the Kalambo River opposite Trench A 4 in 1959 (Figure 6). The sediments are similar to some of those found in the excavations, being fine sands and clays, overlying coarser sand with a pebble horizon at base containing mixed cultural remains including potsherds. There, the area is covered by a riverine forest behind a sandbank relating to the present river regimen.

Bond identified coarse gravels belonging to at least three successive cut and fill cycles, and noted that in the oldest sediments (the Mkamba Member) three facies occurred (pp. 203–4): Boulder gravels in the lower Vundwe valley to the east, fine silt or clay deposits in the 'Tanganyika Cliff' to the north and northeast, and

---

[1] The use of the same cipher for subdivisions of Rubble I at the different archaeological sites does not necessarily imply that the rubbles in different trenches are correlated. Even where a correlation is suggested, in a fluviatile environment this can mean no more than a rough equivalence in time of formation. The archaeological nomenclature is a convenient form of reference (Appendix K).

sands to the south and west in the archaeological excavations. It is to be expected that the sorted fluviatile deposits interfinger with and grade into colluvial (hill-slope) deposits on the flanks of the basin, but this has only been seen just west of the mouth of the Kaposwa. Soils and talus mask the boundary zone. The base of the Kalambo Falls Formation, and the underlying Plateau Series on which it rests, have not been seen since the White Sands and Dark Clay Beds of the Mkamba Member pass below river level (Chapter 4, Trench A 6, Figure 27).

The long section surveyed by Haldemann (Figure 7) gives the altitudinal relationships of progressively younger river deposits. Those belonging to the Mkamba Member reach an elevation of about 60 feet (18·3 m) above the Kalambo River (although the top few feet may be redeposited soils—the section at top was masked by native cultivation in the 'Tanganyika Cliff'); those of the Mbwilo Member at Site C, about 30 feet (9 m) (see Figure 11), as do those of the Chiungu Member which rest on sediments of the Mbwilo Member at Trench A 4. The lowest sand fill varies from about 6–15 feet (1·8–4·5 m), but probably belongs to several local shortlived periods of filling by the Kalambo.

The Kalambo Falls Formation is confined to the local basin, with a maximum lateral extent of about $1\frac{3}{4} \times \frac{3}{4}$ miles (2·8 × 1·2 km). The total measured thickness of sediments in composite section is 115 feet (35 m). The exposed deposits of the Formation as defined here cover a known time range from at least 60,000 years B.P.[1] to about 350 years B.P. (Upper Pleistocene and Recent) (Appendix J). A wider correlation based on C14 dates and climatic events indicated by the palynological evidence is given in chapter 3 (Figure 17; see also Clark and van Zinderen Bakker, 1964: Figure 2).

3. THE MKAMBA MEMBER

Deposits belonging to the Mkamba Member have been previously called 'Lake Beds Series' (Clark, 1962, p. 201), and 'Lake Beds' (Howell & Clark, 1963, p. 486) following Bond (p. 203). The name is taken from Mkamba village.

Bond (p. 204) describes a boulder gravel facies, here termed the Vundwe Gravel Beds. In the Site A type section, sands predominate and are somewhat coarser in grain size than in exposures on the northern side of the basin. Although no excavations have been made on the north side of the Kalambo, the discussion by Bond and Haldemann's lithological description on the long section (Figure 7) indicate that the sequence belongs to the middle and upper parts of the Mkamba

---

[1] C14 dates are given in counted elapsed 'C14' years, regarded as 'B.P.'. (1965. Half Life of Radio-carbon (C14). *Geochronicle*, **5**, 1.)

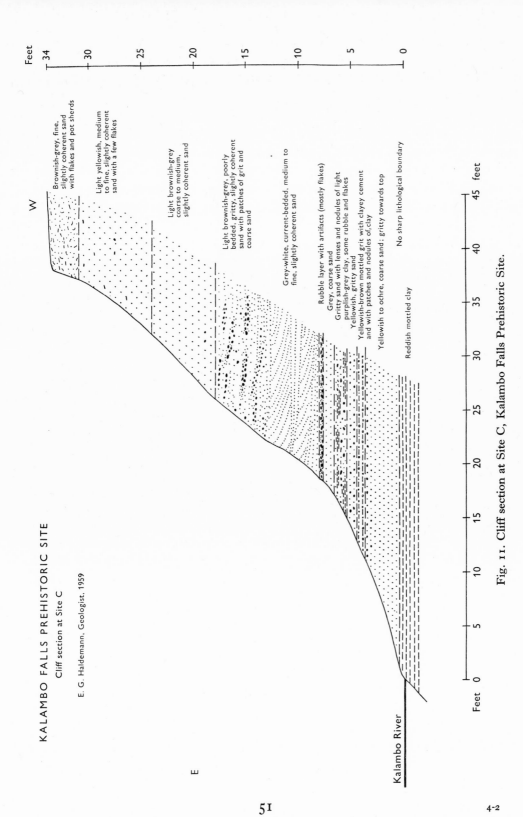

KALAMBO FALLS PREHISTORIC SITE

Cliff section at Site C

E. G. Haldemann, Geologist, 1959

Feet
34
30
25
20
15
10
5
0

W

Brownish-grey, fine,
slightly coherent sand
with flakes and pot sherds

Light yellowish, medium
to fine, slightly coherent
sand with a few flakes

Light brownish-grey
coarse to medium,
slightly coherent sand

Light brownish-grey,
poorly
bedded, gritty, slightly coherent
sand with patches of grit and
coarse sand

Grey-white, current-bedded, medium to
fine, slightly coherent sand

Rubble layer with artifacts (mostly flakes)

Grey, coarse sand

Gritty sand with lenses and nodules of light
purplish-grey clay, some rubble and flakes

Yellowish, gritty sand

Yellowish-brown mottled grit with clayey cement
and with patches and nodules of clay

Yellowish to ochre, coarse sand: gritty towards top

No sharp lithological boundary

Reddish mottled clay

E

Kalambo River

Feet 0   5   10   15   20   25   30   35   40   45   feet

Fig. 11. Cliff section at Site C, Kalambo Falls Prehistoric Site.

51

4-2

Member, as defined at Site A. The clay at the base of the high 'Tanganyika Cliff' section is lithologically similar to that exposed at river level at Site C (Figure 11), and to beds filling a channel at Site D (Chapter 5, beds nos. 5, 6, 7 and 8 on Figure 41), which from their stratigraphic position and elevation are correlated with more sandy deposits in a channel at Site B (Chapter 5, Figure 37), and with the lower part of the interstratified ochreous sands and grey to brown clay beds in Trench A 4 (beds nos. 19–25, Figures 28 and 29). The unit is called the Ochreous Sands and Grey Clay Beds from its characteristics in the type section. The correlation is supported by the fact that artifacts of Sangoan type, found *in situ* at both Sites A and B, have also been found weathering out near river level at Site C and along the base of the 'Tanganyika Cliff'.

The lower part of the Member is named the White Sands and Dark Clay Beds, according to its lithological characteristics. Two enriched C14 dates from Site A (GrN-2644 and GrN-4896, Appendix J) indicate a minimum age of 60,000 years B.P. for these sediments exposed just above present river level. They are separated from the overlying Ochreous Sands by an unconformity, best seen in the type section at Trench A 1 (Chapter 4, Figure 22) and at Sites B and D. Overlying the Ochreous Sands and Grey Clay Beds in Trench A 4, a Rubble Bed (II) rests on an eroded surface, followed by further sand deposition, and then a filled channel cut—the Pits Channel Fill. The magnitude of these breaks is not yet well enough understood to justify the naming of these units as additional members, and they are all included within the Mkamba Member. A C14 date from just above the Rubble Bed (II) gave about 31,000 years B.P. (GrN-4648, Appendix J) but by how much time this antedates the top of the Pits Channel Fill and the top of the Mkamba Member in Trench A 4 is unknown. Palynological evidence of former environments (Chapter 3; Appendix I) was obtained from the White Sands and Dark Clay Beds and from the basal Ochreous Sands in the excavations, but little pollen was found to be preserved in sediments exposed higher above the present water table. Samples taken from the exposed face of the 'Tanganyika Cliff' were barren.

Acheulian artifacts are found in the White Sands Beds, Sangoan artifacts in the Ochreous Sands Beds, and some artifacts of lower Lupemban type in the Rubble Bed (II). A few artifacts, possibly belonging to the Lupemban cultural stratigraphic unit, were found at the base of the Pits Channel Fill (see Chapter 4, Table 2, and Appendix K).

The measured section at the 'Tanganyika Cliff' is 60·8 feet (18·5 m) high, the upper 5 feet (1·5 m) being a soil which may in part be redeposited colluvium. The height of the type section is 40 feet (12·2 m). The maximum measured thickness of sediments preserved in the type section is 61 feet (18·6 m), base not seen. The remnants preserved on the north, and near the entrance to the Spillway Gorge, suggest that the sediments of the Mkamba Member once filled a large part of the local basin.

4. THE MBWILO MEMBER

The name Mbwilo is taken from the Lungu name for the Kalambo Falls. The deposits of the Mbwilo Member overlie those of the Mkamba Member unconformably in the area of the excavations. They rest on a well-developed erosion surface, traceable from Trench A 4 at about 22 feet (6·7 m) above the present river level, to just above river level east of Trench A 1 (Figure 32). On this surface is a Rubble Bed (I-composite or Ic in the archaeological nomenclature) that characteristically is composed of sub-angular to sub-rounded rubble and cobbles (Chapter 4, Table 1), including mainly derived artifacts of types belonging to most of the cultural stratigraphic units provisionally distinguished at the Kalambo Falls Prehistoric Site (Appendix K). The history of this accumulation is undoubtedly complex, and its time range is not fixed. The artifact content has been observed to vary with elevation, depending upon what older sediments have been cut through at progressively lower altitudes, but also because higher slopes were habitable surfaces while the overlying loose or slightly consolidated current-bedded sands and clays were deposited in the deeper cuts.

In Trench A 4, the Rubble Bed lying at the bottom of a broad channel cut, was traced upslope to the Red Rubble Bed, a colluvial deposit. Two thin rubble layers separate from the Rubble Bed in the River Face Cliff section, and are interstratified with the sands and clays overlying it (Rubbles Ia and Ib in the archaeological nomenclature, beds nos. 18 and 20, Figure 32). A buff sandy clay overlying the Red Rubble Bed is not superimposed on the current-bedded sands, but appears to be the uppermost bed of the Mbwilo Member in Trench A 4.[1]

A similar well-developed erosion surface overlain by the Rubble Bed and slightly consolidated to loose current-bedded sands interstratified with rubble horizons is exposed at Sites B, C, and D (Chapter 5). It cannot be identified in the 'Tanganyika Cliff' and presumably a cliff face was already being cut on the north at that time.

Important pollen evidence comes from clays overlying the Rubble Bed in Trench A 1 (Chapter 3, Appendix I). A single C14 date of about 30,000 years

---

[1] Alternatively, it may once have overlain the Rubble Bed as well, and have subsequently been removed by erosion. The sandy clay contains artifacts of 'Magosian' type.

53

B.P. (L-3991, Appendix J) exists for the Rubble Bed at a low elevation in Trench A 1, but is suspect in view of the date from above the Rubble Bed in the Mkamba Member. A further date of about 9,500 years B.P. (L-395D) comes from over the rubble layer (Ia) in Trench A 3 at about 16 feet (4·8 m) above river level, a horizon which includes artifacts of 'Magosian' type. When deposition ceased is unknown, but it probably pre-dates about 3,900 years B.P. (GrN-4224, 4225) when people making microlithic artifacts lived at Site C, where, therefore, a surface must already have existed.

The 'Older Boulder Beds' mapped by Bond (p. 204) are considered to be the coarse facies of the Mbwilo Member although this has not been verified by excavations. The correlation is based upon their apparent discordant relationship with sediments of the Mkamba Member on the northeast, their elevation of about 25–30 feet (7·6–9 m) above present river level, and their mapped extent. In addition, microlithic tools and associated artifact types can be found in the thin soil resting on the surface of these gravels near Chitambala's village. The boulder gravels are termed the Chitambala Gravel Beds (Plate 4).

In the type section, the thickness of the sands, clays and rubble horizons of the Mbwilo Member is 22 feet (6·7 m). The thickness of the Red Rubble Bed and overlying sandy clay upslope adds about 12 feet (3·6 m). The thickness of the basal Rubble Bed and overlying sands and rubbles at Site C is approximately 23 feet (7 m). Sediments of the Mbwilo Member apparently originally filled only the excavated central part of the local basin, banked against a steep cliff on the north and overlapping a more gentle slope on the southwest side of the local basin.

5. THE CHIUNGU MEMBER

The clayey sediments of the Chiungu Member rest unconformably on deposits of the underlying Mbwilo Member in the type section, filling channels cut into the latter. Predominantly grey sandy clays and clays at base give way to predominantly red sandy clays, clays and redeposited soil at top (Figures 21, 22 and 32). At Site B (Chapter 5, pp. 164–5) the deposits are banked against a spur in which both the Mbwilo and Mkamba Members occur. Although the sediments of the Chiungu Member are found in the main excavations, and the upper red deposits can be traced from Site A to Site B, their relationship to the gravels called the 'Younger Boulder Beds' by Bond (here named the Chisya Gravel Beds) and to his 'Swamp beds of an intermediate age' (pp. 205–6) in the area of Chiungu village has not been proved by trenching. These two units appear to be in unconformable relationship with the Chitambala Gravel Beds of the Mbwilo

Member, however, and are therefore provisionally included in the Chiungu Member.[1]

C14 dates (Appendix J) indicate an age greater than approximately 1,500 years B.P. (L-395C) for the basal deposits in Trench A 1, and an age of less than 350 years B.P. (GrN-3189) for the top of the Member at Site B. The deposits at both Sites A and B contain Iron Age remains (Kalambo Industry); the time-span of the Iron Age occupation may only equate with that of the lower part of the Chiungu Member, however. A few vertebrate bones have been found, but no pollen.

The composite thickness of the Chiungu Member in the type section is at least 20 feet (6·1 m). At Site B it is about 16 feet (4·8 m), base not seen on the east. The original extent of the deposits appears to have been less than that of the Mbwilo Member, filling only the axis of the local basin.

6. OTHER DEPOSITS IN THE LOCAL BASIN

Until further work is done on the regimen of the Kalambo River, and soil formations in the area, the latest fluviatile deposits and present-day soil cover in the basin cannot be included in the formal terminology. Hillslope deposits have also been little studied.

Bond noted (p. 205) that the present gravel 'delta' of the Kalambo was not definitely seen to pertain to a separate cycle of erosion and deposition from that of the Chisya Gravel Beds, and that the 'delta' appeared to be encroaching on the presently forming swamp deposits. Two pits, B 3 and B 4 (Chapter 5, pp. 175–6) were sunk in the area mapped by Bond as containing swamp deposits and sands related to the present river. These showed clays and sands (swamp or overbank deposits) overlying a gravel which may be the Chisya Gravel Beds as suggested by Clark, but which looks equally likely to be in continuation with the gravels of the 'delta'. In B 3, the upper 3 feet of the gravel contained potsherds and slag pertaining to the Kalambo Industry, so that it is either in part contemporary with or post-dates the time of the deposition of sediments of the Chiungu Member in the main Site B trenches, as do the overbank deposits opposite Site A. The upper part of the sections in the Site B pits are lithologically similar, in some respects, to the upper clays and sands of the Chiungu Member at Site B, but this may only reflect a similar geological environment. It seems likely that all the fluviatile sediments in the local basin, which post-date the Mbwilo Member, and

[1] The 'midden' deposit which overlies the sands of the Mbwilo Member between Site B and Sites C and D is regarded as a soil formation and is not now included in the Chiungu Member (Figure 11; Appendix A, p. 205).

which reach elevations of 6–20+ feet (1·8–6·1 m) above the adjacent river—including those of the Chiungu Member—may relate to the same, continuing, cycle of river action; it may well be that eventually these can all be included in the Chiungu Member.

REFERENCES

Bishop, W. W. & Clark, J. D. (1966). Systematic investigation of the African Later Tertiary and Quaternary. *Curr. Anthrop.* **7**, 2, 253–6.

(1967). *Background to Evolution in Africa.* University of Chicago Press, Chicago.

Clark, J. D. (1954). An early Upper Pleistocene site at the Kalambo Falls on the Northern Rhodesia/Tanganyika border. *S. Afr. Archaeol. Bull.* **9**, 34, 51–6.

(1962). The Kalambo Falls Prehistoric Site: an interim report. In G. Mortelmans and J. Nenquin (eds.), *Actes du IVᵉ Congrès Pan-africain de Préhistoire et de l'Étude du Quaternaire*, Musée royal de l'Afrique centrale, Annales, Série in 8°, Sciences humaines, 40: Section III, pp. 195–201.

Clark, J. D. & Zinderen Bakker, E. M. van (1964). Prehistoric culture and Pleistocene vegetation at the Kalambo Falls, Northern Rhodesia. *Nature, Lond.* **201** (4923), 971–5.

Hedberg, H. D. (1961). Stratigraphic classification and terminology. *International Geological Congress, Report of the Twenty-first Session, Norden, 1960*, part xxv.

Howell, F. C. & Clark, J. D. (1963). Acheulian hunter-gatherers of sub-Saharan Africa. In F. C. Howell and F. Bourlière (eds.), *African Ecology and Human Evolution.* Aldine, Chicago. Pp. 458–533.

Mortelmans, G. (1956). Le troisième congrès pan-africain de préhistoire (Livingstone, juillet 1955). *Académie royale des Sciences coloniales*, Classe des sciences naturelles et médicales, *Mémoires* in 8°, nouvelle série, vol. IV, fasc. 3, pp. 1–128.

Quennell, A. M. (1960). Report of the East-Central Regional Committee for Geology, Subcommittee on Stratigraphical Nomenclature. Joint Meeting, Leopoldville, 1958, *C.C.T.A.* **44**, 11–26.

Rose, C. (1929). The geology of the Kalambo Gorge. *Geogrl J.* **74**, 38–44.

CHAPTER 3

THE PLEISTOCENE VEGETATION AND CLIMATE OF THE BASIN[1]

BY E. M. VAN ZINDEREN BAKKER

THE VEGETATION

The vegetation of the area around the Kalambo Falls is very varied as great differences exist in altitude, exposure and humidity in the different biotopes. Under natural conditions the shores of Lake Tanganyika, the rocky slopes of the Rift Valley, the ravines, the plateau and the higher mountains would practically all be covered by different types of woody vegetation. The only exception would be the swamps, which occur in the valleys with impeded drainage, and the mountain areas above the altitude of about 2,700 metres, where the woody vegetation gives way to open grassland. This natural vegetation pattern has, however, been disturbed by man in nearly every plant community, so that forest and woodlands have often been replaced by extensive grasslands, impenetrable thickets, and degraded types of woodland. The general vegetation pattern of this area has been described by B. Gilchrist (1952), C. G. Trapnell (1953), D. B. Fanshawe (1961), J. M. Rattray and H. Wild (1962), R. M. Lawton (1963) and M. Streel (1963). The *Forest Flora of Northern Rhodesia* by F. White (1962) contains a wealth of data on the distribution of the forest species. Much useful information on the composition of certain vegetation types has been obtained from Mr D. P. Bands.

In considering the vegetation we shall pay attention only to the natural vegetation types which have existed in this area where Tanzania, Zambia and the Congo Republic meet. This description will facilitate the evaluation of the fossil pollen spectra. We can postulate that, until recent prehistoric times, the influence of man on the vegetation was not strong enough to disturb the

[1] The South African Council for Scientific and Industrial Research, the Nuffield Foundation and the Wenner-Gren Foundation for Anthropological Research gave financial assistance for the pollen research and deserve deep gratitude.

Sincere thanks are also due to Mr D. P. Bands from the Department of Forestry of Northern Rhodesia for his valuable information on forest ecology and for assessing the climatic interpretation of the fossil pollen spectra.

natural pattern of distribution. The extensive ridge and slope grasslands, such for example as those which cover the Ufipa plateau, are of fairly recent origin.

Besides man, climate is the most important factor responsible for the distribution of the plant communities. The plateau, which in this area has an altitude of 1,000–1,500 metres, receives no measurable rainfall from June to August. The area with this pronounced dry climate in winter reaches from the coast of South West Africa and Angola and stretches right across the continent, where it penetrates the equatorial rain belt as far as northern Tanzania. The plateau north and south of the Kalambo Falls Prehistoric Site receives an annual precipitation which diminishes towards the north from 120–100 centimetres on the Zambian side to 100–70 centimetres on the central Tanzania plateau. The southern end of Lake Tanganyika has at present one rainy period in summer and does not fall in the equatorial zone with double rainfall periods.

The elevated areas such as the Ufipa plateau, the Kipengere and the Muchinga Ranges, receive progressively more rain in proportion to their altitude and extent (Ufipa 100–125 centimetres; Muchinga Range more than 125 centimetres; Rungwe Mountain, altitude 2,950 metres, more than 200 centimetres) (Figure 12).

We begin our description of the vegetation at the altitude of Lake Tanganyika (770 metres) where we find a tall open woodland in the embayments of the lake. Some of the important trees in these warm and dry biotopes are: *Pterocarpus*, *Combretum*, *Ricinodendron*, *Sclerocarya* and *Tamarindus*.

The vast plateau of the northern part of Zambia and southern Tanzania is at present covered with extensive deciduous woodlands (*miombo*) in which different species of *Brachystegia* and *Julbernardia* play an important part. This woodland can be divided into many different types and occurs between the altitudes of 900 and 2,000 metres. Many different trees occur scattered in these woodlands, such as *Afrormosia angolensis*, *Albizzia antunesiana*, *Erythrophleum africanum*, *Monotes* sp., *Protea angolensis* and several species of *Uapaca*. Grasses are not found in large numbers, while *Cyperaceae* occur sparsely.

Streel (1963) discussed the ecology and origin of these deciduous woodlands and points out that they are well adapted to a heterothermic climatic regime. It is only in the Lufira valley (Katanga) that these woodlands at present form the natural climax. The vast deciduous *Brachystegia* woodland of the plateau has mostly originated through bush fires and developed out of homothermic semi-deciduous dry forest, of which relics are still found in many areas (*muulu* in Katanga). Streel points out that these woodlands may have had a much wider distribution in former times when the rainfall was relatively abundant (80 cm at least) and the dry period in winter lasted at least five months, while the variations in extreme summer temperature were great (in the range of 25° C). The semi-deciduous and evergreen guinean and montane forests cannot withstand these extremes of temperature and humidity.

It is very likely that under present-day climatic conditions the dry evergreen and semi-deciduous forest would cover vast areas had it not been exterminated by the age-long bush fires. Half a dozen patches of relics of the old forest type still exist at present in the Kalambo Falls area.

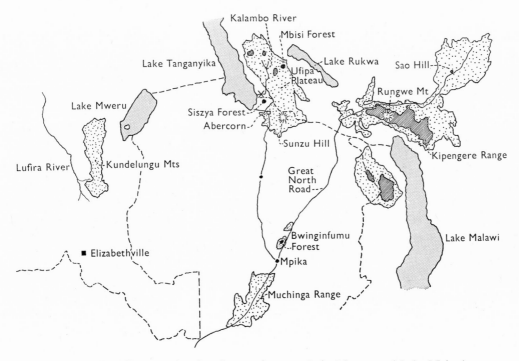

Fig. 12. Locality map showing the area between Lake Mweru and Lake Malawi.

An interesting example of these relics is the Siszya forest, which is situated at an altitude of about 1,500 metres near the Kalambo site. This forest can easily be found on the northern side of the road from Abercorn to Kalambo. It is not dependent on a watercourse and has a canopy of very tall deciduous trees, below which a closed understorey of evergreen trees occurs. A great number of the trees in this forest, such as *Celtis durandii*, *Blighia* sp., *Aningera altissima*, *Trema guineensis* and many other species, are common in the West African lowland forest, while some other types are also found in the montane forests. Examples of this last category are *Aningia adolfi-frederici* and *Cordia abyssinica*.

This forest shows, therefore, that two entirely different communities mix in this area and this forest type gives evidence of possible former plant migrations (Lawton, 1963). According to Lawton a number of Siszya species occur at present in deep gorges in the Abercorn District, and these may be an indication of the former greater area of this forest type.

Above the altitude of 2,000 metres the humid evergreen montane forest occurs on mountain slopes if the rainfall is more than 150 centimetres per year (Figure

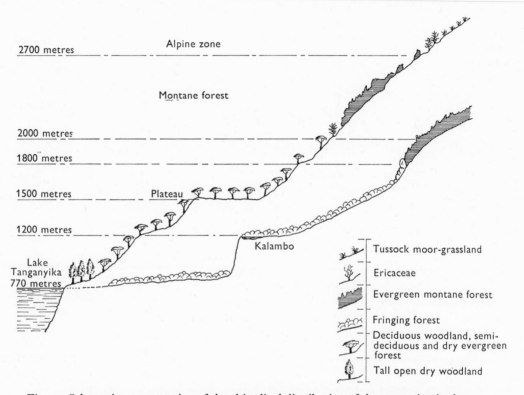

Fig. 13. Schematic representation of the altitudinal distribution of the vegetation in the area. The lower profile gives the fringing forest along the Kalambo River.

13). This closed humid forest, which is related to the montane forests of East and Southern Africa, contains species which are adapted to the cool climate of the higher regions, such as *Neoboutonia macrocalyx*, *Macaranga kilimandscharica*, *Chrysophyllum* sp., *Ficalhoa laurifolia*, *Podocarpus milanjianus*, *Entandrophragma stolzii*, *Ekebergia* sp., *Pygeum africanum*, *Ilex mitis*, etc. The humid evergreen montane forest is now very rare in the area under discussion. The Mbisi forest on the Ufipa plateau near Sumbawanga at an altitude of about 2,100 metres is an example of this type. Other relics can be found in the ravines of the Sunzu Hill near Abercorn at slightly lower altitude and on the Muchinga escarpment 20 miles (32 km) north of Mpika. These last-mentioned forests, which occur on the mountain slope above 1,700 metres altitude, can be seen from afar. They are surrounded by a swampy area and have apparently survived the fires because of a big supply of ground water. The Bwinginfumu forests have been described briefly by Lawton (1963). They are rich in *Podocarpus* and also contain *Ocotea*

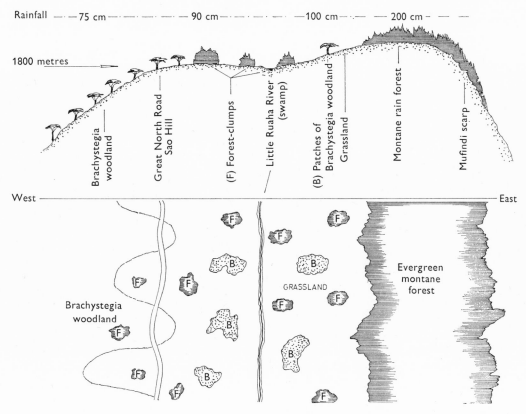

Fig. 14. The ecotone between montane forest and *Brachystegia* woodland near Sao Hill, Tanzania. (After J. Proctor.)

usambarensis, Ficalhoa laurifolia, Pygeum africanum and the Ericaceae: *Aguaria salicifolia* and *Philippia benguelensis* (altitude 1,750 metres).

A very interesting ecotone between the montane forest and the woodland can be seen on the plateau around Sao Hill at an altitude of 1,800 metres (southern Tanzania) (Figure 14). Patches of *Brachystegia* woodland and distinct montane forest-clumps occur here in the grassland which covers the plateau. The rainfall increases from the slope on the western side, which is covered with woodland and receives 75 centimetres annually, to 90 and 100 centimetres on the ecotone, to 200 centimetres on the Mufindi scarp on the east side of it. This ridge is covered with humid montane forest. Some of the trees which occur in these forest-clumps are: *Albizzia* sp. probably *gummifera*, *Bersama abyssinica*, *Dais cotinifolia*, *Parinari excelsa* ssp. *holstii*, *Podocarpus milanjianus* and *Pygeum africanum*. Some of the species which occur in these clumps have a wide range in the drier types of evergreen forest. (Information received from Mr J. Proctor, Mbeya.)

The highest types of vegetation occurring near the tree line and the alpine communities, which are so well known from the East African mountains, seldom occur in the region under discussion as very few mountains are high enough to harbour these vegetation types. A very good example of the dry conifer forest in which *Juniperus procera* dominates is the Ndumbi forest in the Kipen-

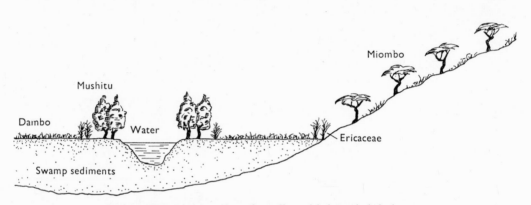

Fig. 15. Schematic section of a valley with impeded drainage.

gere Range (Gilchrist, 1952). Above the altitude of about 2,700 metres tussock moor-grassland occurs on the highest mountain tops.

Besides the plant communities which have been discussed briefly, some other types which depend on edaphic factors should be mentioned. Forests which are characteristic of areas with a high ground-water table occur along the shore of Lake Tanganyika at an altitude of 770 metres, but they are also found along the streams as riparian woodland. At lower altitudes they include such species as *Bridelia micrantha*, *Croton leuconeurus*, *Raphia*, *Allophylus abyssinicus* and some species of *Ficus*, *Parkia*, etc. Round the heads of streams at higher altitudes more species characteristic of evergreen montane forest are found in this riparian woodland.

This riparian woody forest community is closely related to the evergreen swamp forest or *mushitu*, which is found along the water margins in the depressions where the drainage is poor (Figure 15). The *mushitu* is usually surrounded by a grassy swamp vegetation or *dambo*, which borders on the woodland outside the swampy area. The typical *mushitu* is an interesting mixture of tropical swamp forest trees from West Africa and the Congo and of some species from the cool montane forest. We have seen that the dry evergreen forest shows the same two affinities. According to Lawton (1963) the first group of guinean elements is represented by *Mitragyna stipulosa*, *Syzygium owariense*, *Xylopia aethiopica*, *Uapaca guineensis*, and a great number of other species. Montane forest species of the swamp forest are: *Ocotea usambarensis*, *Podocarpus milanjianus*, *Ficalhoa laurifolia*, *Ilex mitis* and *Schrebera alata*.

The distribution of the Ericaceae is also of great importance for the explanation of the fossil pollen spectra. Shrubs and trees of this family are usually found in the area of the montane forest whenever they can compete with the trees. This is seldom the case unless the forest has been influenced by man. Under natural conditions the biggest concentration of Ericaceae is usually found in the zones just below and above the montane forest. In southern Tanzania and near the Mbisi forest, the Bwinginfumu forests, and similar localities Ericaceae grow in great profusion at altitudes between 1,500 and 3,000 metres. Some species, especially *Agauria salicifolia* and *Philippia benguelensis*, prefer the edges of the *mushitus* and *dambos* where it can be cold at night. In these circumstances Ericaceae can occur at lower altitudes of about 1,400–1,650 metres (Shiwa Ngandu, Kasama, Abercorn, etc.).

POLLEN ANALYSIS

The samples which have been received for pollen analysis usually contained sand and clay. They have first been boiled with 10 per cent KOH and then treated with cold fluoric acid prior to acetolysis. Unfortunately a great number of samples did not contain pollen in sufficient quantity for analysis and the results can therefore not be shown in a diagram. The isolated samples mostly give good evidence of the former vegetation and climate.

It is not possible to compare these results with those obtained in Europe as nearly all the trees of the forests and woodlands of Africa are insect-pollinated. The production of pollen is consequently much smaller than in European forests and the arboreal pollen is greatly under-represented in Africa as compared with the non-arboreal pollen. The fossil pollen spectra have therefore been judged more according to the ecological value of the plants which are represented than to their percentage value.

The plants which compose the pollen sum have been chosen according to the principle that this sum should include all the species which form an integral part of the regional vegetation. Only the pollen of plants which are of purely local importance has been excluded from the pollen sum. All the woody communities discussed above form part of the regional vegetation. The pollen of plants from the swamp and the water has, however, not been counted in the sum. These pollen types are: Cyperaceae, *Nymphaea*, *Typha*, *Potamogeton*, *Ottelia*, *Sphaerothylax* and *Tristicha*. Two species of Podostemaceae occur at present in great numbers on the rocks in the Sansia Falls, which are situated in the Kalambo River a few miles above the site of the excavation. These species could unfortunately not be collected in good condition as the area has only been visited during the dry winter season. The material could, therefore, not be identified. It is interesting that fossil pollen of the genera *Sphaerothylax* and *Tristicha* has been found in many horizons in great profusion. Spores of ferns, mosses and fungi have also not been included in the pollen sum. Grass pollen offers a problem in this connection as grasses certainly have been growing along the water margin of the former local basin at Kalambo but they can also occur among woody vegetation. The grass pollen produced by the swamp vegetation should not form part of the pollen sum, but pollen dispersed by grasses growing in the forest or woodlands is of great importance. The woody vegetation, especially at higher altitudes and on rocky slopes, is often open and this is reflected by the percentage of the Gramineae pollen. The grass pollen has therefore been included in the sum.

TRANSPORT OF POLLEN BY WATER

Before discussing the fossil pollen spectra we would like to deal with a possible source of error which can be of great importance. The Kalambo River, which comes from the Ufipa plateau where at present montane forest relics occur at an altitude of about 2,100 metres, could have transported pollen assemblages from the 'cooler' higher vegetation down to the site of the excavations. It is very difficult to investigate this matter with absolute certainty but a few points may be considered in this connection.

It is a very important point that the sites of the excavations are situated at the lowest end of the basin near the falls. Material brought down by the river will, in consequence, mostly have settled near the centre of the basin and not near the outlet. If the river has transported significant quantities of allochthonous pollen it will have done this especially during the periods with heavy rainfall and strong flow. These periods should then have pollen spectra which are contaminated with pollen from the cooler mountain vegetation. Periods of heavy flow will also have been favourable to the Podostemaceae growing in the river on the rocks above the Kalambo Falls. Excessively high percentage of Podostemaceae should be correlated with 'cooler' fossil pollen spectra if transport by the river really was of importance. The samples which have been investigated have been arranged according to the percentage of Podostemaceous pollen they contain (Table 1, p. 75). This arrangement shows very clearly that there does not exist a correlation between the number of Podostemaceous pollen and the montane pollen elements. This is very apparent for the last temperature minimum, samples 764, 765, 766, 2347. The pollen spectra of this period show that the temperature was then lower than during any of the former minima. The pollen spectra of the last minimum contain only 0–2·1 per cent Podostemaceous pollen. The reason for these low figures is presumably that during the winter the temperature of the water then was too low for the Podostemaceae to grow upstream from the Kalambo site. Pollen analysis of river deposits always has the disadvantage of possible contamination with allochthonous pollen but it can be accepted that transport of pollen by the river cannot in this case have had an appreciable influence on the results.

POLLEN SPECTRA

The pollen assemblages have been evaluated with the aid of ecological surveys of forest types made by Mr D. P. Bands. The pollen spectra can be divided into the following pollen zones, which are described in a sequence starting at the bottom of the profile:

Zone U

The oldest pollen samples both from Sites A and B are of more or less the same age and give an identical picture of former vegetation and climate. These samples include nos. 780, 781 and 2293 from Site B, and nos. 774, 2383, 2293, 3726, 3727, 3729 and 3731 from Site A. The four last-mentioned samples were collected by Professor J. D. Clark at the end of 1966 well below water level and they are the oldest of all the pollen samples so far studied in sub-Saharan Africa (see Figure 16).

The pollen spectra of this zone (Table 2) indicate that at the time of the deposition, the site was covered with water as is shown by the pollen of Podostemaceae (*Tristicha, Sphaerothylax* and *Inversodicrea*). A swamp vegetation with Cyperaceae, *Nymphaea, Polygonum* and an abundance of grasses was growing in the shallow water.

The riparian woodland was well represented as can be seen from the percen-

Kalambo site A excavation 1966

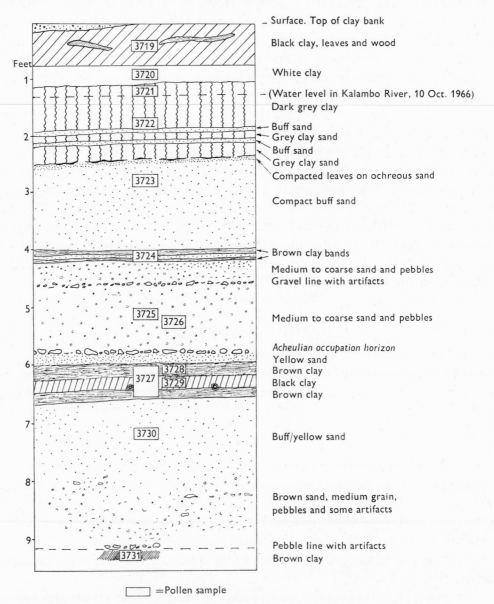

Surface. Top of clay bank

Black clay, leaves and wood

White clay

(Water level in Kalambo River, 10 Oct. 1966)
Dark grey clay

Buff sand
Grey clay sand
Buff sand
Grey clay sand
Compacted leaves on ochreous sand

Compact buff sand

Brown clay bands
Medium to coarse sand and pebbles
Gravel line with artifacts

Medium to coarse sand and pebbles

Acheulian occupation horizon
Yellow sand
Brown clay
Black clay
Brown clay

Buff/yellow sand

Brown sand, medium grain,
pebbles and some artifacts

Pebble line with artifacts
Brown clay

☐ =Pollen sample

Fig. 16. The position of the pollen samples collected in 1966, Site A, 1966 excavation.
The samples nos. 3720, 3723, 3724, 3725, 3728 and 3730 did not contain fossil pollen.

66

tages of *Syzygium, Myrica, Ekebergia* or *Khaya, Antidesma* cf. *vogelianum, Ilex,* and *Maytenus* cf. *acuminatus.* The pollen of the Meliaceae probably belongs to *Ekebergia meyeri,* a species which at present occurs in the fringing forest of Lake Bangweulu. This pollen was so much overrepresented in sample no. 774 (top) that it had to be counted outside the pollen sum. There are strong indications of the occurrence of a riparian forest of lower altitudes (about 900 metres) in which *Anthocleista, Allophylus, Parkia, Syzygium, Dissotis* and Meliaceae play an important part. *Antidesma* and *Maytenus,* which are usually indicative of higher-rainfall areas, can grow in a drier climate as long as the habitat is humid.

The woodland which occurred in the valley must have grown under fairly dry and hot conditions. The pollen of *Pterocarpus, Alchornea, Kirkia* cf. *acuminata, Allophylus, Erythrococca-Micrococca* and *Commiphora* indicate a higher temperature and a lower rainfall. The '*Croton*'-pollen could belong to *Ricinodendron* and would in that case strongly further support this climatic evidence. *Berlinia,* found in sample no. 2383, must have plenty of water available, if it is to grow at the site at present.

Indicators for cool conditions have not been found except for *Ilex* and *Olea* which occurred in very low percentages. These two species are found at present in the riverine forest in the Kalambo valley in which community, because of edaphic factors, montane elements can descend to lower altitudes. The *Podocarpus* pollen can have been blown in by the wind. The percentages of the Ericaceae are very low indeed and can have been produced by species growing along the *dambo* margin.

The general conclusion is that the groundwater level was high and that a swamp and riparian forest occurred along the water's edge. The surrounding vegetation could have been a semi-deciduous dry forest growing in a climate which was warmer and drier than that of today.

The following probable identifications of wood specimens have been done by Oxford from the level underneath no. 774 (from Floor 6): *Ziziphus, Ouratea, Cynometra* (possibly), Leguminous tree (possibly *Isoberlinia* or *Tamarindus*) (Appendix D).

Fruits have also been identified with more or less certainty from the same level at another site: viz. *Syzygium* (probably *S. owariense*), Annonaceae (perhaps *Xylopia*), *Diospyros* or *Chrysophyllum, Parinari* (either *P. curatellifolia* or *P. excelsa*) and two *Borassus* nuts (Appendix D).

From the nearby Site B, wood identified (Oxford) as probably *Burkea* and *Piptadenia* has been found (Appendix D).

The identifications fit very well with the pollen spectra. *Piptadenia, Ouratia* and *Cynometra* are trees from the tropical forests; *Xylopia* and *Syzygium* are

5-2

trees from the evergreen riparian forest; *Parinari* occurs in the evergreen dry forest and the *miombo* woodland, and *Tamarindus* indicates higher temperature.

Zone V

The following samples belong to a different biostratigraphic zone: nos. 768, 769, 2380, 2381, 2382, 3719, 3721, 3722 (from Site A) and nos. 2286, 2288, 2342 and 2343 (from Site B). The pollen spectra of these samples are given in Table 3.

The pollen assemblages of the above give the same picture for the water and swamp vegetation as the former zone because these vegetation types are not so much affected by climatic changes and are primarily determined by edaphic factors.

The riparian woodland was generally poorly developed and did not contain any strong indications for warmer conditions compared with the former zone.

The total assemblage points to cooler and wetter conditions than prevail at present at Kalambo. It may represent a difference in altitude of about 300 metres above the site, although in some samples (e.g. no. 2380) the difference from the present-day conditions on the site is not great. Spectra such as no. 2342 indicate present-day conditions at an altitude of up to 1,800 metres with a rainfall of about 150 centimetres (D. P. Bands).

A number of wood samples collected at the levels of samples nos. 768 and 769 at the nearby Site B have been identified by the Commonwealth Forestry Institute, at Oxford. The wood probably belongs to the following genera of trees: *Cassia*, *Acacia* (three species), *Parinari*, *Brachystegia* and *Albizzia*. These identifications are not absolutely certain. Some of them fit well with the conclusions drawn from the pollen spectra, but *Albizzia* and *Acacia* could also indicate present-day conditions (Appendix D).

Zone W

The pollen spectra 767, 2276, 2277, 2278, 2281 and 2378 represented in Table 4 originate from different levels, but, although they are not of the same age, they still give more or less identical pictures of the former vegetation and climate.

Sample no. 767 contains very little pollen and does not give a complete picture as only 94 grains could be counted. The spectrum represents today's conditions with a rainfall of 75–100 centimetres per annum.

The pollen assemblage of no. 2276 gives the same picture. The rainfall could have been slightly higher than in the previous sample, but a comparison is difficult because of the paucity of pollen in no. 767.

The woodland spectrum of no. 2277 indicates that the canopy could have been open and the occurrence of *Olea* may point to slightly cooler conditions. According to Mr D. P. Bands, however, *Olea* at present still occurs in some thickets near the Kalambo Falls site. Its fossil occurrence need not, therefore, indicate a change in temperature.

The spectra nos. 2278 and 2378 are more or less identical and both represent closed sclerophyll woodland. Sample no. 2378, however, indicates a higher temperature and higher rainfall (about 150 cm) as is shown by the high percentages of *Parkia*, *Allophylus*, the occurrence of *Acacia*, and the much lower percentage of *Olea* pollen. The rainfall indicated by sample 2278 is difficult to judge, but could be half of that of no. 2378.

The spectrum 2281 is difficult to explain as it contains a pollen grain of *Commiphora* which is an indication of a warm and dry climate. The rest of the spectrum could more or less represent present-day conditions. It should be pointed out that *Berlinia* must have plenty of water available to be able to grow at the altitude of the site, but the tree can have occurred in wet riverine forest.

The general picture of the samples of Zone W is more or less the same as that of the present-day conditions the only exception being that the rainfall was probably considerably higher at the level of no. 2378. The water will not have reached the site as Podostemaceae are generally very poorly represented.

Zone X

The composition of sample no. 2365 (Table 5) is entirely different. The fringing forest was apparently poorly developed and the *Brachystegia* woodland was very open. The influence of evergreen forest elements is demonstrated by the occurrence of *Opilia* and *Entandrophragma* in the riverine forest. The spectrum reflects a vegetation of a high altitude with a cooler and wetter climate than prevails at the site at present. Pollen of swamp or water plants was not found in this sample.

Zone Y

The samples no. 2349 and 2351 (Table 6) are very important from a chronological point of view as they are bracketed in between the C14 age figures of 27,000 and 30,000 years. These samples both represent a vegetation which is typical for present-day conditions on the site or of a slightly lower altitude, with probably a higher rainfall. The absence of species from higher altitudes and the presence of *Parkia*, *Alchornea* and *Combretum* strongly support the view that the samples belong to a warmer period. The fringing forest was very well developed and contained about as many species as the oldest samples of Zone U (nos. 780, 781,

2293, 774, 2383). The high figures for the Gramineae may have been caused by the *dambo* vegetation. The swamp plants were not represented in the former sample but Cyperaceae are now again present in these samples nos. 2349 and 2351, together with Podostemaceae.

Zone Z

The samples 764, 765, 766 and 2347 (Table 7) also belong to an important part of the sequence and again give a consistent picture of the former climate and vegetation. The spectra all belong to an open type of vegetation which is at present found at a high altitude of up to 2,000 metres. The fringing forest is very poorly developed and Podostemaceae hardly occur in the spectra. This may indicate that they could not grow well in the river because of the temperature minima occurring during the year.

Spectrum 764 could belong to a vegetation at a present-day altitude of at least 1,600 metres. The result of no. 765 is less convincing in this respect because of the occurrence of a pollen grain, which could belong to the Bombacaceae. This grain does, however, not belong to *Adansonia* or *Ceiba*, the only two genera of this family which occur in the region at present. The sample 766 is again typical for cool conditions such as prevail at present near the upper limit of the *Brachystegia* woodland at about 2,000 metres. The same conclusion can be drawn from spectrum 2347, which definitely comes from a cool site with moist atmospheric conditions. The high percentage of Ericaceous pollen in practically all these samples strongly supports this view. Ericaceae can also occur at lower altitudes, as has been discussed above, but the highest concentration is found near the edge of the montane forest. The cool habitat of the *dambo* is a typical biotope for *Agauria salicifolia* and *Philippia benguelensis*.

The samples of Zone Z are coeval with the last Würm maximum of Europe and they are very good proof of a downward shift of the vegetation during that period. This shift must have been about 800 metres during the coldest period.

CONCLUSIONS

The results of the pollen analysis show that during the Upper Pleistocene considerable changes in vegetation occurred at the Kalambo site, varying from more or less dry woodland from lower altitudes to open woodland growing at present at higher elevations under cool and misty conditions. The warmer periods can be compared with conditions prevailing at present at an altitude of about 1,000 metres, while the Kalambo site is situated at nearly 1,200 metres. The coldest minima represent the cool climate which is at present found at about 2,000

70

metres altitude near the lower limit of the humid montane evergreen forest. If a temperature gradient for this area of 0·51° C per 100 metres is accepted, the temperature maxima and minima can respectively be evaluated at +1° C and −4·1° C, compared with the present conditions. According to van der Hammen & Gonzalez (1960) the real decrease in temperature is bigger than can be calculated by using the temperature gradient for the evaluation of the downward shift of the upper forest limit. During the cool climatic periods the temperature cannot have been decreased by more than 4° C as otherwise the real montane forest would have reached the Kalambo site. It is very well possible that the sheltered position of the site in a valley exposed to the west counteracted the local decrease in temperature. On an exposed mountain slope this decrease may have been the same as has been calculated for the high East African mountains, viz. 5·1–8·8° C (Coetzee, 1967).

During the course of time the woodland round the site was more or less closed and consisted in the main of a number of elements of the evergreen and semi-deciduous woodlands. The pollen spectra of these woodland types give good evidence for climatic changes. The Kalambo site must at certain times have been surrounded by extensive *mushitu*. This swamp forest contained several species of the cool montane forest as is still the case at present in the Kalambo valley. The Cyperaceous pollen and also part of the grass pollen is explained as being derived from the *dambo* or grassy swamp vegetation which must have covered extensive areas at certain periods (van Zinderen Bakker, 1965, p. 227). The pollen produced by these swamp forests and *dambos* does not give proof for changes in climate but can be important for the understanding of the local conditions at the site.

The fossil pollen spectra give evidence for both rainfall and temperature, but it is obvious that the conclusions which can be drawn for the temperature variations are of a much more general importance than those for the rainfall. Vegetation types growing at various altitudes receive different rainfall. The amount of precipitation of a certain vegetation belt is a function of the temperature and wind conditions and is therefore of local importance for that specific habitat. Temperature is on the contrary a primary factor which is of more than local importance. From a vegetation indicating a higher rainfall in the Kalambo valley it can therefore not be inferred that pluvial conditions prevailed in this part of Central Africa. It should further be noticed that the presence of a high water table will have encouraged the growth of many species which can give the impression of a higher rainfall, as it is a well-known fact in plant ecology that ground water can replace rain to a certain extent. We therefore rely primarily on the results obtained in connection with temperature variations.

When the results are plotted and compared with the temperature curves known for Europe and America we see very striking similarities (Figure 17) which can be summarized as follows starting with the oldest pollen zone:

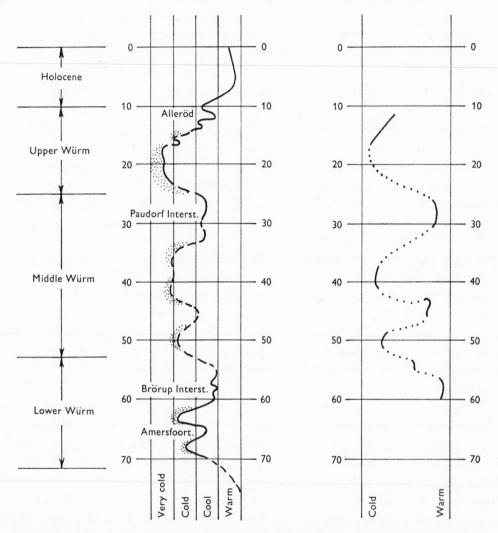

Fig. 17. Comparison of the temperature curve for the last 70,000 years in Europe (published by Wolstedt) with the results obtained at the Kalambo Falls (*Eiszeit und Gegenwart*, **13** (1963), 121).

Zone U

The fossil pollen of five samples together with the identification of many wood samples give good proof of warmer and drier conditions of Zone U. This result is very interesting as this warmer phase is preceded and followed by colder periods and is according to C14 age determination coeval with the Brörup Interstadial of Europe.

Zone V

Cooler conditions returned to the site and the pollen spectra in general indicate a drop in temperature of about 3·0° C compared with present-day conditions. The climate can, according to Mr D. P. Bands, be compared with that prevailing today at 1,800 metres with a considerable rainfall of 150 centimetres.

Zone W

The general picture offered by the pollen samples of this zone is that of climate, which was very similar to that of today, with a rainfall of 75–100 centimetres per annum.

Zone X

This zone is represented by only one sample and can therefore not be described with certainty. The only pollen spectrum indicates a cooler and wetter climate.

Zone Y

The two samples which have been analysed from this zone contained rich spectra of highly significant value indicating a warmer climate that can be compared with the present-day conditions on the site, although the rainfall seems to have been higher. These samples are of great importance as they are, according to the radiocarbon age determinations, bracketed between 27,000 and 30,000 B.P. The samples themselves are therefore coeval with part of the Paudorf Interstadial of the Würm chronology in Europe. Good proof for this same warm interstadial has recently been found in East Africa on Mount Kenya and the Cherangani Hills (van Zinderen Bakker, 1964). As the zone was in Africa first described (Clark & van Zinderen Bakker, 1964) from the Kalambo site it has been named the *Kalambo Interstadial* (Coetzee, 1967).

In Europe and on the high mountains of East Africa the temperature during this interstadial was slightly lower than at present. At Kalambo the temperature must, according to the evaluation by Mr D. P. Bands who is well acquainted with the forest ecology of the area, have been about the same as at present. This slightly more favourable climate may be the result of the setting of the site in a west-facing protected valley.

Zone Z

The pollen spectra give a clear picture of an open woodland vegetation such as is found today at an altitude of up to 2,000 metres. Conditions must have been cool, humid and misty as at present prevail near the montane forest limit and the temperature was about 4·1° C lower than now.

These samples are coeval with the cold stadial described as the *Mount Kenya Hypothermal* from the East African mountains (Coetzee, 1967). This cool stadial has also been described from pollen evidence from NE Angola (van Zinderen Bakker & Clark, 1962). The downward shift in vegetation at Kalambo during the coldest period must have been about 800 metres, which is less than in East Africa (Coetzee, 1964). It is possible, as has been explained, that the micro-climate of the site was responsible for a higher temperature.

TABLE I. *Comparison between river activity and pollen spectra*

Number of sample	Percentage pollen of Podostemaceae	Type of vegetation
2347	0·0	Cool
764	0·8	Cool
765	1·2	Cool
2277	1·4	Warm
768	1·5	Cool
766	2·1	Cool
2343	5·3	Cool
2349	7·7	Warm
769	11·5	Cool
2378	12·1	Warm
767	13·6	Warm
2288	14·4	Cool
2293	13·9	Warm
2380	21·6	Cool
2351	23·4	Warm
2342	28·8	Cool
2383	28·8	Warm
780 and 781	35·2	Warm
2382	63·1	Cool
774 top	72·0	Warm
2381	109·5	Cool
774 bottom	117·0	Warm

TABLE 2

Site	A	B	A	A	B	A	A	A	A
Number of sample	2383	2293	774 (top)	774 (bottom)	780–781	3731	3729	3727	3726
Number of grains counted ...	157	184	394	264	404	170	100	210	150
WATER AND SWAMP PLANTS									
Cyperaceae	5·4	13·1	1·8	16·2	28·8	8·8	18	12·9	5·3
Podostemaceae	28·8	13·9	72·0	117·0	34·8	4·1	4	10·9	12·6
Polygonum	—	—	—	—	0·4	0·6	—	1	—
Nymphaea	—	—	—	—	—	—	1	0·5	—
FRINGING FOREST									
Syzygium	28·5	4·3	12·5	6·2	8·2	4·7	11	8·6	19·3
Myrica	1·8	1·5	1·8	3·5	0·9	—	—	1·4	1·3
Memecylon-Dissotis	2·7	—	1·8	0·9	0·4	—	—	—	—
Ekebergia-Khaya	0·9	—	180·9	—	—	—	2	—	0·7
Other Meliaceae	—	—	3·6	7·0	—	—	—	—	—
Allophylus	1·8	—	—	—	—	—	—	—	—
Ilex	0·9	—	—	—	—	0·6	—	—	—
Parkia	—	0·7	0·9	—	—	—	—	—	—
Anthocleista	—	0·7	—	—	—	—	—	—	—
Antidesma cf. vogelianum	—	—	—	—	—	1·2	—	—	1·3
Maytenus cf. acuminatus	—	—	—	—	—	1·2	—	—	—
WOODLAND									
Gramineae	30·2	52·9	21·4	11·5	48·5	61·9	35	41·9	26·6
Compositae	3·6	5·1	5·3	3·5	6·0	1·2	3	1	3·3
Leguminosae	—	0·7	2·7	5·3	1·7	1·2	—	—	—
Protea-Allophylus	0·9	6·5	3·6	10·6	1·3	0·6	1	0·5	6·6
Commelina	1·8	—	—	—	—	—	—	—	—
Chenopodiaceae	1·8	0·7	—	—	—	0·6	—	1	—
Umbelliferae	—	—	0·9	0·9	0·4	—	—	—	—
Pedaliaceae	—	—	0·9	—	—	—	—	—	—
Sideroxylon-Chrysophyllum	1·8	—	—	—	—	—	—	—	—
Brachystegia	1·8	3·6	4·5	3·5	3·9	1·2	—	—	4
Bauhinia tomentosa	—	—	—	0·9	—	—	—	—	—
Bauhinia sp.	—	—	—	0·9	—	—	—	—	—
Berlinia	0·9	—	—	—	—	—	—	—	—
Isoberlinia	—	—	—	0·9	—	—	—	—	—
Uapaca	—	—	—	—	—	—	—	0·5	2·0
Croton type	3·6	0·7	—	0·9	0·4	1·2	—	0·5	0·7
Commiphora	—	—	—	—	—	—	—	0·5	—
Alchornea	1·8	0·7	—	0·9	1·7	2·9	3	1·4	0·7
Kirkia cf. acuminata	—	—	—	—	—	1·8	2	—	—
Olea	2·7	—	—	—	—	1·2	—	0·5	0·7
Micrococca-Erythrococca	0·9	—	—	—	—	—	—	—	—
Hymenodictyon	0·9	—	—	—	—	—	—	—	—
Rhus	0·9	—	—	—	—	—	—	0·5	—
Mimusops	0·9	—	—	—	—	—	—	—	—
Canthium	0·9	1·5	—	3·5	—	0·6	—	—	0·7
Justicia	—	—	—	—	—	—	—	—	1·3

76

TABLE 2 *(cont.)*

Site	A	B	A	A	B	A	A	A	A
Number of sample	2383	2293	774 (top)	774 (bottom)	780–781	3731	3729	3727	3726
Number of grains counted	157	184	394	264	404	170	100	210	150
WOODLAND *(cont.)*									
Other Acanthaceae	—	—	0·9	—	0·4	—	—	—	—
Commiphora	0·9	—	—	—	—	—	—	—	—
Podocarpus	—	5·1	2·7	3·5	1·3	—	1	1·4	4
Combretum	—	5·1	—	—	—	1·2	2	1	2·7
Celtis	—	—	—	—	—	—	1	—	—
Liliflorae	—	1·5	—	—	—	—	—	—	—
Malvaceae	—	—	—	—	0·4	—	—	—	0·7
Pseudolachnostylis	—	0·7	—	—	—	—	—	—	—
Acacia	—	0·7	—	—	—	—	—	—	—
Dichrostachys	—	—	0·9	—	0·9	—	—	—	—
Hippocrateaceae	—	—	3·6	—	—	—	—	—	—
Loranthaceae	—	—	0·9	—	0·4	—	—	0·5	0·7
Monocotyledons	—	—	—	—	0·9	—	—	—	0·7
Ericaceae	—	—	0·9	—	—	0·6	—	—	1·3
Varia	6·2	7·3	30·2	35·5	20·6	2·4	16	13·3	2·7
PORES									
Tetraploa (fungus)	0·9	—	—	—	1·3	0·6	1	1	0·7
Polypodiaceae	5·4	6·5	0·9	2·6	6·0	—	—	—	2
Other ferns	—	—	—	—	—	2·4	1	3·8	1·3

TABLE 3

Site	B	B	B	B	A	A	A	A	A	A	A	A
Number of sample	2343	2342	2286	2288	768	769	2380	2381	2382	3722	3721	3719
Number of grains counted	422	164	156	150	414	328	172	90	78	50	185	100
WATER AND SWAMP PLANTS												
Cyperaceae	38·0	5·8	2·1	17·1	33·0	42·0	19·8	26·0	4·3	6·0	8·7	14·0
Podostemaceae	5·3	28·8	—	14·4	1·5	11·5	21·6	109·5	63·1	18·0	26·7	24·0
Polygonum (Persicaria type)	—	—	3·4	0·9	—	0·5	—	—	—	—	0·5	—
Typha	9·6	—	—	—	—	—	—	—	—	—	0·5	—
Potamogeton	10·6	—	—	—	—	—	—	—	—	—	—	—
Eriocaulon	0·4	—	—	—	—	—	—	—	—	—	—	—
Nymphaea	—	—	—	—	0·5	0·5	—	—	—	—	—	—
Ottelia	—	—	—	—	—	—	0·9	—	—	—	0·5	—
Limnanthemum	—	—	—	—	—	—	—	—	—	—	—	—
FRINGING FOREST												
Syzygium	7·2	7·6	0·7	5·3	0·3	1·8	10·5	34·3	17·6	8·0	9·8	4·0
Myrica	2·4	5·8	4·7	18·4	4·4	4·1	5·3	—	2·2	2·0	1·1	6·0
Allophylus	—	—	—	—	—	—	3·5	2·6	2·2	—	—	—
Ilex	0·4	—	—	—	0·3	0·5	—	—	—	—	—	—
Cf. Eugenia jambos	—	—	—	—	—	—	—	—	—	6·0	—	—
WOODLAND												
Gramineae	59·8	10·9	76·5	45·6	60·9	60·7	37·5	31·6	26·4	28·0	15·1	26·0
Compositae	5·8	0·8	1·3	5·3	12·4	8·3	3·5	5·3	—	2·0	1·1	—
Leguminosae	0·4	—	—	—	—	—	1·8	—	—	—	—	—
Proteaceae	1·9	3·3	—	5·3	0·3	0·9	4·4	5·3	4·3	2·0	2·7	2·0
Commelina	—	—	—	—	0·3	—	0·9	—	—	—	—	—
Chenopodiaceae	—	0·7	—	—	1·0	0·5	0·9	—	2·2	—	1·0	1·0
Umbelliferae	0·9	—	—	0·9	0·5	0·5	—	—	—	—	—	—
Pedditea	0·9	—	—	1·8	—	—	—	—	—	—	—	—
Memecylon	—	—	—	—	—	—	3·5	—	—	—	0·5	—
Dichapetalum	—	—	—	—	—	—	—	—	—	4·0	—	—
Sideroxylon-Chrysophyllum	—	—	—	—	—	—	6·2	—	—	—	—	—
Brachystegia	2·4	0·8	2·0	0·9	1·4	2·3	3·5	2·6	2·2	2·0	3·8	1·0
Cf. Isoberlinia	—	—	—	—	—	—	—	2·6	2·2	—	0·5	—
Impatiens	—	—	—	—	0·5	0·5	0·9	—	—	—	—	—
Liliaceae	—	—	—	—	—	—	—	—	15·2	2·0	—	—
Olea	0·9	64·2	—	—	0·9	—	—	—	—	3·0	0·5	3·0

Taxon	1	2	3	4	5	6	7	8	9	10	11
Rhus	—	—	—	0·9	—	—	—	—	—	1·6	2·0
Podocarpus	0·4	0·8	—	4·4	—	—	—	—	—	4·3	4·0
Combretum	1·9	2·5	—	—	—	—	—	—	—	—	1·0
Dichrostachys	—	—	—	—	—	—	—	—	—	—	—
Myrsine	—	—	—	—	—	—	—	—	2·0	—	—
Loranthaceae	—	—	—	—	0·5	—	—	—	—	—	—
Cf. *Pandanus*	—	—	—	0·9	—	—	—	—	—	—	—
Cf. *Juniperus*	—	—	—	0·9	—	—	—	—	—	—	—
Caryophyllaceae	—	—	—	0·9	—	—	—	—	—	—	—
Crassulaceae	—	—	—	—	—	—	—	—	—	—	1·0
Rhopalopilia	—	—	1·3	—	—	—	—	—	—	0·5	—
Tribulus	—	—	—	0·9	—	—	—	—	—	—	—
Canthium	—	—	—	—	—	—	1·8	—	—	—	—
Justicia	—	—	—	—	1·0	—	—	—	—	—	—
Peltophorum	—	—	—	—	0·3	—	—	—	—	—	—
Sesamum	—	—	—	—	0·3	—	—	—	—	—	—
Moraceae	0·4	—	—	—	—	—	—	—	—	—	—
Polygalaceae	0·4	—	—	—	—	—	—	—	—	1·1	—
Bombacaceae	—	—	—	—	0·5	—	—	—	—	—	—
Rosaceae	—	—	—	—	0·5	—	—	—	—	—	—
Cassine–Mytroxylon	—	0·8	0·7	—	—	—	—	—	—	—	—
Cf. *Harpophyllum*	—	—	1·3	—	—	—	5·3	8·8	—	—	—
Cf. *Thespesia*	—	—	0·7	—	—	—	2·6	—	—	—	—
Antidesma	—	—	—	—	—	—	—	—	—	—	—
Cissampelos	—	—	—	—	—	2·6	—	—	—	—	—
Malvaceae	—	—	—	—	—	—	—	—	—	0·5	—
Adina	—	—	—	—	—	4·4	—	—	—	—	—
Celtis	—	—	—	—	—	0·9	—	—	—	0·5	—
Croton type	—	—	—	—	—	—	—	—	2·0	1·6	—
Uapaca	—	—	—	—	—	0·9	—	—	—	0·5	—
Craterispermum	—	—	—	—	—	—	—	4·3	—	—	—
Lindackeria	—	—	—	—	—	—	2·6	—	—	—	—
Cf. *Leonotes*	—	—	—	—	—	—	2·6	—	—	—	—
Monocotyledons	—	—	—	1·8	5·8	4·6	—	2·2	—	0·5	—
Ericaceae	—	—	—	5·3	9·6	8·3	—	2·2	—	0·5	—
Varia	3·9	2·5	6·8	5·3	—	3·5	—	4·3	14·0	16·2	9·0

SPORES

Taxon	1	2	3	4	5	6	7	8	9	10	11
Tetraploa (fungus)	—	—	—	—	1·0	0·5	—	—	—	—	3·0
Polypodiaceae	—	—	0·7	—	—	3·5	—	—	2·0	—	3·0
Other fern spores	46·1	0·8	0·7	1·8	5·4	7·0	2·0	2·2	2·0	7·0	3·0
Riccia	—	—	—	—	0·3	—	—	—	—	—	—

TABLE 4

Site	A	B	B	B	B	A
Number of sample	767	2276	2277	2278	2281	2378
Number of grains counted	94	148	158	150	156	135

WATER AND SWAMP PLANTS

Cyperaceae	31·0	7·7	8·4	7·1	19·2	15·8
Podostemaceae	13·6	—	0·7	—	—	3·5
Polygonaceae (*Persicaria* type)	—	—	0·7	—	—	10·5
Typha	—	—	—	—	—	1·6

FRINGING FOREST

Syzygium	8·6	13·4	5·8	14·1	3·2	6·2
Myrica	12·0	6·8	5·8	7·1	8·0	—
Ilex	—	—	1·4	—	—	—
Dissotis	—	0·7	—	—	1·6	—
Parkia	—	—	—	3·2	—	10·6
Allophylus	—	—	—	—	—	10·5

WOODLAND

Gramineae	34·6	26·8	51·5	16·5	44·2	22·7
Compositae	1·7	7·5	5·8	11·8	2·4	6·2
Leguminosae	—	2·2	—	—	—	—
Proteaceae	—	7·5	5·1	7·1	4·0	—
Commelina	—	—	—	—	—	0·9
Chenopodiaceae	—	—	—	0·8	—	—
Umbelliferae	—	—	1·4	0·8	—	—
cf. *Chrysophyllum*	—	0·7	—	—	—	0·9
Brachystegia	1·7	0·7	0·7	3·2	4·0	7·0
Memecylon	3·5	—	—	—	—	—
Berlinia	—	1·5	0·7	—	0·8	0·9
Croton type	—	—	—	—	—	0·9
Olea	—	—	6·6	11·8	1·6	0·9
Rhus	—	—	—	0·8	—	1·6
Mimusops	—	—	—	—	—	0·9
Commiphora	—	—	—	—	1·6	—
Podocarpus	3·5	3·0	4·4	0·8	2·4	1·6
Combretum	—	—	—	—	—	4·4
Pseudolachnostylis	—	—	—	—	—	0·9
Acacia cf. *albida*	—	—	—	—	—	0·9
Dichrostachys	—	—	—	0·8	—	—
cf. *Pandanus*	—	3·0	—	0·8	—	—
cf. *Justicia*	—	—	—	—	—	0·9
Peltophorum	—	—	—	3·2	—	—
Harpophyllum	—	—	—	—	—	3·5
Antidesma	—	—	—	—	—	0·9
Celtis	—	0·7	—	—	—	—
Trema-Celtis	—	—	1·4	—	—	—
cf. *Uapaca* (*U. nitida*)	—	13·4	2·2	4·0	1·6	—
Trichilia	—	—	—	—	—	4·4
Knowltonia	—	—	—	—	0·8	—
Sapotaceae	—	—	—	0·8	—	—

TABLE 4 (*cont.*)

Site	A	B	B	B	B	A
Number of sample	767	2276	2277	2278	2281	2378
Number of grains counted ...	94	148	158	150	156	135

WOODLAND (*cont.*)

Loranthaceae	1·7	—	—	—	—	—
Albizzia	1·7	—	—	—	—	—
Liliaceae	1·7	—	—	—	—	—
Morus	3·5	—	—	—	—	—
Pygeum	—	3·7	0·7	1·6	—	—
cf. *Borassus-Phoenix*	—	0·7	—	—	—	—
Fagara usambarensis	—	—	—	—	—	0·9
Monocotyledons	—	—	0·7	—	—	—
Ericaceae	—	1·5	0·7	—	3·2	—
Varia	25·8	6·8	4·4	11·0	22·2	12·3

SPORES

Polypodiaceae	—	1·5	2·2	—	3·2	4·4
Other fern spores	17·2	—	2·8	3·2	—	—

TABLE 5

Site	A
Number of sample	2365
Number of grains counted ...	150

RIPARIAN WOODLAND

Myrica	3·3
Allophylus	1·3
Opilia	1·3
Entandrophragma	1·3

WOODLAND

Gramineae	68·7
Compositae	6·7
Protea-Thesium	2·0
Brachystegia	2·0
Berlinia	1·3
Croton type	1·3
Olea	0·7
Podocarpus	4·7
Varia	1·3

TABLE 6

Site	A	A
Number of sample	2349	2351
Number of grains counted ...	150	148

WATER AND SWAMP PLANTS		
Cyperaceae	11·9	5·4
Tristicha	7·7	16·2
Sphaerothylax	—	7·2
FRINGING FOREST		
Syzygium	14·8	2·7
Myrica	2·2	5·4
Dissotis type	—	0·9
cf. *Allophylus*	6·7	—
Parkia	0·7	—
Cephaelis	0·7	—
WOODLAND		
Gramineae	49·9	65·8
Compositae	1·5	4·5
Proteaceae	—	1·8
Commelinaceae	—	0·9
Brachystegia	3·7	—
Memecylon	1·5	2·7
Olea	1·5	2·7
Canthium	0·7	—
Alchornea	0·7	—
Podocarpus	4·5	6·3
Combretum	—	0·9
Loranthaceae	—	0·9
Caryophyllaceae	0·7	—
Pseudolachnostylis	2·2	—
Trichilia	1·5	0·9
Chrysophyllum	—	0·9
Fagara	0·7	—
Croton-type	0·7	—
cf. *Urera*	0·7	—
cf. *Clitandra*	0·7	—
Justicia	—	0·9
Cruciferae	—	0·9
Varia	3·7	0·9
SPORES	4·5	4·5

TABLE 7

Site...	A	A	A	A
Number of sample	764	765	766	2347
Number of grains counted ...	133	213	109	167
WATER AND SWAMP PLANTS				
Cyperaceae	4·0	20·3	9·4	5·0
Podostemaceae	0·8	0·6	2·1	—
Polygonum	—	0·6	—	—
RIPARIAN WOODLAND				
Syzygium	—	0·6	1·0	2·5
Myrica	7·1	2·3	4·2	5·7
WOODLAND				
Gramineae	46·0	55·9	52·3	64·1
Compositae	12·7	9·3	6·2	4·4
Proteaceae	1·6	—	6·2	4·4
Umbelliferae	—	—	—	1·3
Brachystegia	0·8	—	2·1	1·9
cf. *Olea*	—	—	—	1·9
Podocarpus	1·6	4·6	3·1	0·6
Caryophyllaceae	0·8	—	—	—
Justicia	—	—	1·0	—
cf. Bombacaceae	—	0·6	—	—
Croton-type	1·6	—	—	—
Ericaceae	8·7	12·2	10·4	10·7
Varia	19·1	13·9	13·5	2·5
SPORES				
Fern spores	0·8	2·9	2·1	—
Riccia limbata	—	—	—	0·6

REFERENCES

Clark, J. D. & van Zinderen Bakker, E. M. (1964). Prehistoric culture and Pleistocene vegetation at the Kalambo Falls, Northern Rhodesia. *Nature, Lond.* **201** (4923), 971–5.

Coetzee, J. A. (1964). Evidence for a considerable depression of the vegetation belts during the Upper Pleistocene on the East African Mountains. *Nature, Lond.* **204** (4958), 564–6.

(1967). Pollen analytical studies in East and Southern Africa. In *Palaeoecology of Africa* (ed. E. M. van Zinderen Bakker), III, A. A. Balkema, Cape Town.

Fanshawe, D. B. (1961). Evergreen forest relics in Northern Rhodesia. *Kirkia*, **1**, 20–4.

Gilchrist, B. (1952). Vegetation types of Southern Tanganyika. In *Report on Central African Rail Link Development* Survey. Part D, 'Tanganyika', **2**, 58–67. U.K. Gov. Col. Office, London.

Lawton, R. M. (1963). Palaeoecological and ecological studies in the Northern Province of Northern Rhodesia. *Kirkia*, **3**, 46–77, 12 pl.

Rattray, J. M. & Wild, H. (1962). Vegetation map of the Federation of Rhodesia and Nyasaland. *Kirkia*, **2**, 94–104.

Streel, M. (1963). *La végétation tropophylle des plaines alluviales de la Lufira moyenne*, FULREAC, Université de Liège.

Trapnell, C. G. (1953). *The Soils, Vegetation and Agriculture of North-Eastern Rhodesia*. Report of the Ecological Survey, Gov. Printer, Lusaka.

van der Hammen, Th. & Gonzalez, E. (1960). Upper Pleistocene and Holocene climate and vegetation of the 'Sabana de Bogota' (Columbia, South America). *Leid. geol. Meded.* **25**, 261–315.

van Zinderen Bakker, E. M. (1962). A Late-Glacial and Post-Glacial climatic Correlation between East Africa and Europe. *Nature, Lond.* **194** (4824), 201–3.

(1964). A pollen diagram from Equatorial Africa, Cherangani, Kenya. *Geol. en Mijnbouw* **43**, no. 3. 123–8.

(1965). Über Moorvegetation und den Aufbau der Moore in Süd- und Ostafrika. *Bot. Jb.* **84**, 2, 215–31.

van Zinderen Bakker, E. M. & Clark, J. D. (1962). Pleistocene climates and cultures in North-Eastern Angola. *Nature, Lond.* **196** (4855), 639–42.

White, F. (1962). *Forest Flora of Northern Rhodesia*. Oxford Univ. Press, Oxford.

CHAPTER 4

THE EXCAVATIONS: SITE A

BY J. D. CLARK AND M. R. KLEINDIENST

INTRODUCTION

BY J. D. CLARK

During the three seasons 1956, 1959 and 1963, four main sites, named A, B, C and D (see Figure 2) were investigated. At Site A four separate excavations and two exploratory test pits, as well as work on the River Face Cliff itself, were undertaken: five areas were dug at Site B and one each at Sites C and D. The cultural material was found to occur usually on a series of surfaces of varying extent rather than dispersed throughout the deposits, which were largely sterile.

As the excavations progressed it became increasingly apparent that what, in 1953, had been interpreted as a fairly simple history of successive erosional and depositional phases was not simple at all and the more excavation that was carried out the more complicated was the succession seen to be. The amount of channelling and interlensing of sands and clays, rubble horizons and occupation surfaces that had taken place at almost all cultural periods rendered it difficult to correlate in detail the successions at excavations even as close together as those at Sites A and B. Where artifact-bearing horizons were concerned, however, the general correlation was, in most cases, quite clear, but it became increasingly difficult when endeavouring to distinguish between the various sandy channel fills, particularly in the Mbwilo Member and in the Ochreous Sands Bed of the Mkamba Member. These had much the same appearance in section and usually contained no artifacts. The complicated nature of this channelling and interlensing of deposits can be clearly seen from the section drawings and it has accordingly been necessary to number separately the succession of deposits at each excavation.

The rubble horizons and occupation surfaces were first completely uncovered and then lifted with small tools, a square at a time, and the artifacts cleaned, bagged and numbered. In 1956 the distribution patterns of artifacts on these rubble horizons were also plotted but this was not continued in later seasons as such plots, from natural accumulations of this kind, are without cultural significance. After initial checking with sieves of $\frac{1}{8}$ inch and $\frac{1}{4}$ inch mesh (3 mm and 6 mm) to ensure that no small finds were being missed, it was found that constant sieving was unnecessary except as a periodic check as, for example, in the case of some of the Acheulian floors. For the excavation of the microlithic and early Iron Age settlements at Site C, sieves of $\frac{1}{8}$ inch (3 mm) mesh were used.

The Acheulian occupation floors were found in deposits which lay at or immediately above the low water level in the river and, as the water content of these deposits was often considerable, it was necessary to allow the floors to drain before they could be properly cleaned and plotted. Site B, being open to the river at the west end, could be drained naturally until water level was reached. In the A 1 excavation at Site A, however, it was necessary to use a pump since the north wall adjacent to the river was not open. Attempts here to excavate below the water table were unsuccessful below a depth of 2 feet (61 cm) as the walls constantly collapsed, even where shuttering was used. The use of pollen-boring equipment was no more successful and even when casing was employed the coarse deposits and hard clays lying below water level effectively prevented the equipment from penetrating. In the 1966 excavation (A 6), situated at the north (river) end of the A 4 trench excavation, heavy, precast concrete casing was used. This was completely successful in enabling us to penetrate to a depth of 9 feet 2 inches (2·78 m) below low water level and to find evidence of three lower artifact-bearing horizons, but still without reaching bedrock. It is not as yet known, therefore, to what precise depth the occupation floors extend. It is probable that several more feet of living floors lie between the lowest level reached in 1966 and bedrock and a further attempt will be made at a future date to recover the complete sequence.

The artifact aggregates are usually found in two different kinds of contexts—in rubbles/gravels or as occupation 'floors' on temporary surfaces—separated by varying thicknesses of sterile, fine grained sediments. Rubbles/gravels are accumulations of debris and artifacts that mark former channels of the river or tributary gulleying, or they are surfaces of scree accumulation from the upper slopes. These are not 'living floors' in the sense the term is used here, but surfaces on which the cultural and other components may have collected naturally, though in some instances it is evident that man camped on the rubble when it was exposed as a land surface. The Lupemban is found in such rubble contexts.

On the other hand, the Acheulian and, in one or perhaps two instances, the Sangoan, occurs on surfaces which show no such natural accumulation of stone. During these periods the population made temporary camps on sand or fine gravel banks adjacent to the water's edge and all the larger pieces of stone lying on these surfaces can only have been carried there by man. The tools are quite fresh and must have been rapidly buried after the site was abandoned. This means that the patterns of distribution of artifacts on these floors are of the greatest importance since they can provide evidence of the behaviour and activities of their makers. The artifacts lay flat except in three instances where hand-axes were found standing on their side in a manner suggesting that they had been intentionally placed like this.

The quantity of wood and organic vegetable remains in the lower deposits of the Mkamba Member posed a problem as to excavation and preservation. The wood was completely waterlogged, presumably since the time of its burial, and was invariably soft so far as the exterior surface was concerned, so that it was very easily marked by metal excavating tools. In fact, where the wood had been lying next to a pebbly sand, the grains of sand had often been impressed into its surface by the weight of the overburden. When it rested in clay this stuck to the wood and was difficult to remove. The only sure way, therefore, to recover the wood undamaged was to excavate by means of water and the hands, supplemented by fine-haired brushes. By this means it was possible to be certain that, when a cut or other mark was visible on a piece of wood, this was contemporary and not the result of damage sustained in excavation.

Once removed from the excavation, the wood began to crack and split within a few hours, if not kept wet. All possible implements, bark and smaller finds were preserved in wet cotton wool in trays or on boards, the whole wrapped in plastic. For the longer pieces of wood metal tubes were used and all the material for treatment at the British Museum Laboratory was successfully transported to London in this way—usually by long-suffering friends and relations who happened to be flying over at convenient times and who were invariably faced with the difficult task of convincing sceptical customs officials at London airport that the curiously shaped parcels they were carrying contained, in fact, nothing more nor less than pieces of wet wood. Larger logs and wood fragments were kept damp in 44 gallon (207 litre) steel drums and sealed in plastic sheeting at the Museum at Livingstone to dry out slowly. This, incidentally, proved to be one of the most successful ways of drying the wood and after two to three years it could be handled without fear of damage. Samples of all the main logs and wood fragments were preserved and forwarded to the Commonwealth Forestry Institute for identification.

Peaty clay was worked by playing jets of water on to the deposit by means of a stirrup pump or, more effectively, with the motor-driven water pump. This separated the seeds, twigs and leaves from the surrounding clay matrix in a remarkably successful manner. Peaty clay was also kept wet and transported in metal boxes to Livingstone where the work of separation continued.

Each excavation was worked by having a 5 foot (1·52 m) grid laid out over it and the position of artifacts was recorded three dimensionally. Thus, the distribution patterns of all occupation floors and surfaces have been plotted to show the position of each individual specimen.

The deposits were excavated by layers in 6 inch (15 cm) spits and by the natural stratigraphy.

Geological samples were collected from each of the excavations and forwarded to Professor G. Bond at the University College in Salisbury, Rhodesia.

Pollen samples were collected from all deposits that might have been expected to preserve pollen, and complete runs of pollen samples were taken from A 4 and B 2 excavations and from the 'Tanganyika Cliff'. The location and stratigraphical position of the pollen-yielding samples used to reconstruct the Pleistocene temperature and vegetation pattern at the Kalambo Falls are set out in table form in Appendix I.

Radiocarbon samples were also collected wherever possible and submitted for C14 dating and the particulars of those that have so far been dated are given in Appendix J.

The provisional archaeological nomenclature used here will be defined and discussed in volume II but, for easy reference and better understanding of the artifact content of the various archaeological horizons as well as the location of these at the four main sites in the local basin, the nomenclature is set out here in table form in Appendix K.

A 1, A 2 AND A 3 EXCAVATIONS

BY J. D. CLARK

A 1 excavation, 1956 (Figures 18–23)

On 8 July a grid 30 × 25 feet (9·15 × 7·63 m) was laid out (see Figure 18) immediately adjacent to the river bank where the small river face sections had been exposed in 1953 and 1955, although all evidence of these previous excavations had been removed by the flooding of the intervening rainy seasons. The surface of this grid showed some slight disturbance due to mound cultivation but otherwise was fairly flat and sloped gradually up from northeast to southwest. It was situated on the edge of an area of fairly level ground bounded on the south and southwest by a low scarp formed by the eroded upper layers of the Mkamba

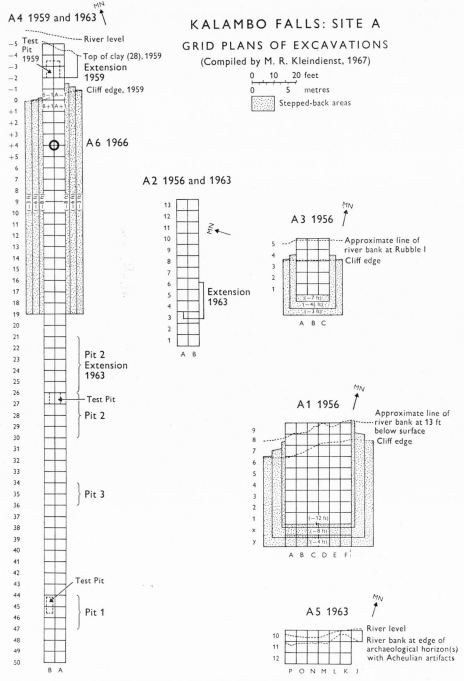

Fig. 18. Outlines of Site A excavations, showing grids.

Member and on the north and east by the river and tributary gulley. The sections exposed in these natural cuts showed that the upper half of the approximately 22 feet (6·7 m) high cliff was composed of red clay and the lower half of sands and sandy clays with several rubbles containing artifacts. Some potsherds lying on the river bank at and just above water level were believed to be derived from the upper part of the red clays.

The top-soil (1) (see Figure 20) was loose and brown to grey in colour to a depth of 4–6 inches (10·25–15·25 cm) with numerous charcoals—no doubt from the annual bush fires that sweep through the tall *Hyparrhenia* grass that covers the surface to a height of 7–8 feet (2·13–2·44 m). Several small, shallow patches of gritty, yellow soil (1a), 4 inches (10·25 cm) or so below the surface appeared to fill slight hollows in the top-soil and probably represent the depressions between the ridges or heaped soil in old mound gardens. Between 4 and 12 inches (10·25 and 30·50 cm) the top-soil was more compact and dark brown to grey in colour with some scattered charcoals, small pellets of burnt clay and one sherd of modern Lungu type pottery. At the 1 foot (30·50 cm) level there was little or no charcoal but in the grid squares adjacent to the eastern face one microlithic flake and some iron slag were recovered. Between 1 and 2 feet (30·50 and 61 cm) the soil became lighter, changing to buff at the west side and to red over the rest of the area (2). This red soil is a typical hillslope deposit and comprises interlensing layers of small pebbles and angular grit.

At 2 feet (61 cm) a layer of red, sandy clay (3) was encountered. This again is a typical hillslope deposit overlying a channel fill and, throughout its entire thickness, it consists of intercalated layers, sometimes more claylike and sometimes with a high gravel content. At a depth of 2 feet (61 cm) a layer of sandy red clay replaced the gritty and pebbly soil. When freshly excavated the clays are moist and easy to work but they become very hard on drying out.

At 2½ feet (76·25 cm) the red, sandy clay became more stony and yielded a tuyère fragment and a few pieces of slag and potsherds. Scattered charcoals were present between 2 feet (61 cm) and 2 feet 3 inches (68·7 cm).

The deposit at 3 feet (91·50 cm) was a lighter coloured, sandy and gritty clay or soil. It contained nothing except one piece of daga and a few charcoals from grid square A 1. There was a more stony lens of red soil between 3 and 3½ feet (91·50 and 106·75 cm) which intercalated with the red clay. Small spherical nests of ants or termites were found down to, but not below, 3½ feet (106·75 cm). The red, sandy clay and hillwash soil continued down to a depth of 4 feet (1·22 m) but contained only a few scattered charcoals, some daga fragments, one piece of iron slag, an abraded 'Middle Stone Age' flake of hard quartzite and two larger fragments of sandy quartzite.

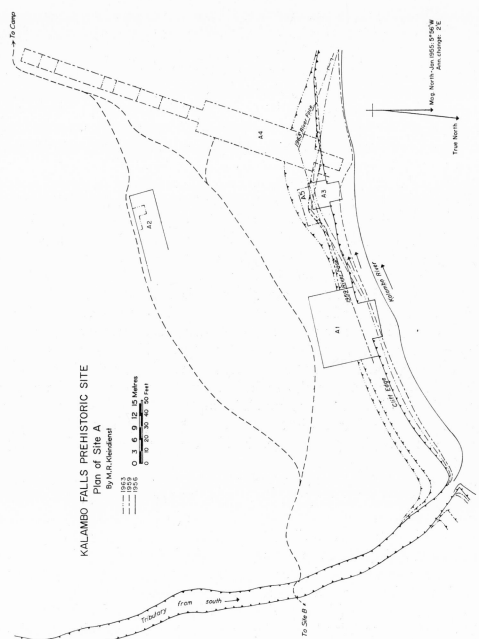

KALAMBO FALLS PREHISTORIC SITE
Plan of Site A
By M.R.Kleindienst

1963
1959
1956

0   3   6   9   12   15 Metres

0   10   20   30   40   50 Feet

To Camp

A4

1963 River Face

A5

A3

A2

1959 River Face

Kalambo River

A1

Cliff Edge

Tributary   from   south

To Site B

Mag. North - Jan 1955: 5°56'W
Ann. change: 2°E

True North

Fig. 19. Kalambo Falls Prehistoric Site: Plan of Site A, 1963.

At 4 feet (1·22 m) the sticky, red clay and sandy clay were found in the north-western two-thirds of the deposit while in the southeastern grid squares (B 1; C 2; D 3; and E and F 4) the deposit was a grey to red clay sand which yielded four potsherds with channelled decoration and two large pieces of slag. Charcoals now appeared in greater quantity than before.

Between 4½ and 5 feet (1·37 and 1·52 m) the red, sandy clay continued with intercalated patches of stony hillwash and lines of small pebbles. Increasingly large, sub-angular fragments of sandy quartzite were found and in grid squares C 1 and 2 and D 3 there were three groups of large stones which at first looked as if they might have been intentionally wedged into position with smaller stones. Daga, sherds, one derived 'Middle Stone Age' flake and a river pebble came from this level in the red clay, as also did a quantity of isolated charcoals.

In grid squares C–F 1–3, the deposit became a grey, clay sand (4). More stones began to appear in a line running diagonally from the northeast to the southwest. These were mostly small and lay at all angles in the clay and adjacent to the grey clay sand. At first it was thought that this irregular line of stones might be artificial but it appeared to have no beginning and no end and, as the excavation progressed, it became apparent that the stones lay close by the side of an erosion channel or gulley cut through the grey clay sand in the southeast corner of the excavation and that they thus represented a natural accumulation on the gulley bank. It was the grey clay sand that was found to contain the greater quantity of channel decorated pottery. The western side of this later gulley or channel can be seen in the River Face section (bed (3)) as exposed in 1959 (Figure 32). It was the eastern edge, therefore, that was exposed in the 1956 excavation.

The grey clay sand and buff, sandy clay (4) into which the eastern edge of the red, stony, clay-filled channel ('Younger Channel') had been cut, was itself later seen to have formed the fill of an earlier channel ('Older Channel') (also seen again in the River Face section). This is well shown in the section drawings of the east and south walls (Figures 20 and 21) where the 'Older Channel' can be seen to be either a meander of the river or a side channel running more nearly east and west and deepening from west to east and north to south.

Both these channel cuts (Events C7′ and C7″: Table 2, p. 149) dated to the earlier Iron Age and both contained only pre-Lungu pottery. Heavy mineral analysis showed that the grey, clay sands of the 'Older Channel' fill were derived from a source different from that of the red clay of the 'Younger Channel' cut, since they contain kyanite (iron 50 per cent, kyanite 48 per cent, zircon 2 per cent), while the red clay contains only iron and zircon (iron 98 per cent, zircon 2 per cent) (Appendix H). This may confirm the belief that the older deposit is river laid and the younger is the result of local gulleying. They are both overlain by 4½–5 feet (1·37–1·52 m) of hillslope soil with Lungu pottery in the top.

Between 5½ and 6 feet (1·67 and 1·83 m) there were fewer charcoals, but much more pottery began to appear in the grey clay sand (4b) of the 'Older Channel' fill (grid squares C–F 1 and the eastern half of 2) and the adjacent, gritty, red, clay sand. The sherds sometimes lay horizontally, parallel to the base of the channel but often at an angle or vertically in the clay sand. In the red, gritty, clay sand close to the line of stones, occurred a few sharp and derived flakes of chert and quartzite and it is possible that the former might belong with the pottery. In grid square D 3 was found a broken lower grindstone. A second lower grindstone was found in square F 4 at a depth of 6 feet 10 inches (2·08 m) and nearby was a flat upper grindstone of the 'bun rubber' type.

Between 6½ and 7 feet (1·98 and 2·13 m) the 'Older Channel' fill became more sandy and yellowish grey in colour (4c), still containing sherds. The red, sandy clay of the 'Younger Channel' fill was replaced over most of the rest of the excavation by a fine and coarse grained sand with some larger stones. The sand was red to yellow in colour. In squares D and E 2 occurred a lens of ochreous and ferruginous sand which represents the eroded top of the sterile, cross-bedded sands (8) that overlie Rubble I (Figures 20, 21 and 25) and into and through which both these Iron Age channels have been cut.

Between 7 and 7½ feet (2·13 and 2·28 m) the red, sandy clay of the 'Younger Channel' fill is replaced by fine and coarse-grained sand and some clay (3a), grey-brown in colour with occasional smoothed but angular rock fragments, a few derived flakes and one radially prepared core together with a few Kalambo Industry potsherds. There also occurred broken fragments of rubbers or upper grindstones and a flat whetstone of sandstone or sandy quartzite used for sharpening metal tools and bearing several cuts on one face made with such a tool. This will be illustrated in volume II.

The 'Older Channel' fill continued to produce sherds, slag and some charcoal and was easier to dig because of its less compact and sandy nature. Between 7½ and 8 feet (2·28 and 2·44 m), however, this grey clay sand (4d) in squares E and F 1 and 2 was replaced by a still blacker grey clay (5) which contained more sand on the northwest side. In square F 5 occurred a pocket of loosely cemented fine gravel with some larger stones and potsherds.

The deposit of the 'Younger Channel' fill is red, stony and sandy clay or clay sand with red clay and potsherds in squares E and F 6. These still contained charcoals which became increasingly scarce though occasionally a few larger pieces occurred. Samples of the black and red clays were taken to see if any pollen differences could be detected but no pollen was present.

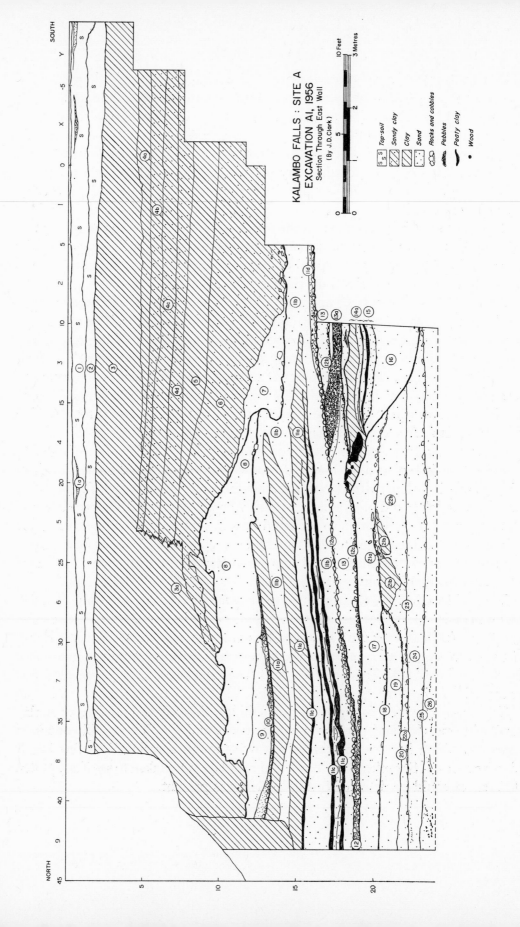

KALAMBO FALLS : SITE A
EXCAVATION AI, 1956
Section Through East Wall
(By J.D.Clark)

Fig. 20. Kalambo Falls Prehistoric Site A. Excavation A 1, 1956.
East Wall Section.

LITHOLOGY

Bed
no.

1 Grey-brown sandy loam with humus and lenses of yellow grit (1a); grading down into:

2 Light brown sandy loam; passing down into:

3 Red-brown clay (Younger Channel Fill) with channel decorated pottery, lenses and pockets of pebbles and grit, some larger stones including dolerite at the base and grey-brown sandy clay (3a) washed out from:

4 Stratified layers of buff sandy-clay (4a); grey sandy-clay (4b); light brown sandy clay (4c); grey sandy clay (4d). Contains early Iron Age channel decorated pottery.

5 Grey-brown clay with red streaks; a few Iron Age remains.

6 Grey sandy clay with quantity of channel decorated pottery and other Iron Age remains.

7 Grey sand and grit with pebbles. Sterile.

Beds 4–6 above fill this fill but might equate with a possible earlier phase represented by bed 7 in the A 4 Trench (Figure 28).

8 Ferruginous coarse sand and grit, loose and cross-bedded. Sterile.

9 Orange-coloured cross-bedded sands. Sterile.

10 Rubble Bed (Rubble Ib) with angular and sub-angular blocks, abraded Sangoan and Lupemban artifacts, set in a ferruginous sandy matrix and resting on grey clay. Cut out by erosion over the southern and western parts of the excavation.

11 Bedded, light brown and white sands and clay-sand alternating on the northeast with beds of grey and black clay; grey clay (11a); light brown fine sand (11b); black clay with pollen (11c); bedded buff sands and fine gravel (11d). Sterile.

12 Rubble Bed (Rubble Ic) with angular and sub-angular rock fragments and some well-rounded cobbles. Composite at the north end but divisible into three distinct rubble horizons (Ic(i), (ii) and (iii)) at the south end: (12a) Stoneline Ic(i) contains mostly large angular and sub-angular rock fragments and rounded cobbles; in (12b) and (12c) Stonelines Ic(ii) and Ic(iii) the number of large fragments decreases. The matrix is a medium grained sand, sometimes ferruginous, becoming finer at the north end where it contains also some clay. Many stone artifacts, mostly of Lupemban type, occur in the rubble together with some fresh Sangoan implements. These rubble horizons are separated by:

13 Coarse cross-bedded sand and grit (sterile), divisible into an upper and a lower part by a bed of fine gravel (13a) 6–9 inches thick which contained rare Lupemban artifacts.

14 Interstratified clay and sand with wood: black clay interbedded with fine white sand (14a). Sterile.

15 Coarse grey sand with intermittent pebble band and rare artifacts at base. Sterile.

16 Fine, bedded, light brown to white sand, sterile except for very rare, slightly abraded stone artifacts at the base.

Beds 14–16 are filling a channel cut in the underlying sandy deposits and thus lie disconformably upon them.

17 Fine white sand, compact and bedded. Sterile.

18 Pebble horizon having no thickness, with occasional large, angular rock fragments and cobbles and Acheulian artifacts in fresh condition (Occupation Surface IV).

19 Cross-bedded, coarse, white sand and grit. Sterile.

20 Pebble horizon with some large, angular rock debris and Acheulian artifacts in fresh condition (Occupation Surface V).

21 Clay pockets: black clay (21a); blue-green clay (21b). Sterile.

22 Cross-bedded, coarse sand and grit: coarse, bedded, light brown sand (22a). Sterile. Coarse sand and grit with some bedding (22b). Sterile.

23 Pebble horizon with some large angular and sub-angular rock fragments and Acheulian artifacts in fresh condition (Occupation Surface Vb).

24 Fine to medium, buff sand; disrupted brown clay layer at base in northwest corner. Sterile.

25 Pebble horizon with Acheulian artifacts and a few angular rocks (Occupation Surface VI).

26 Fine to medium sand with grit lenses, buff white in colour. Sterile.

95

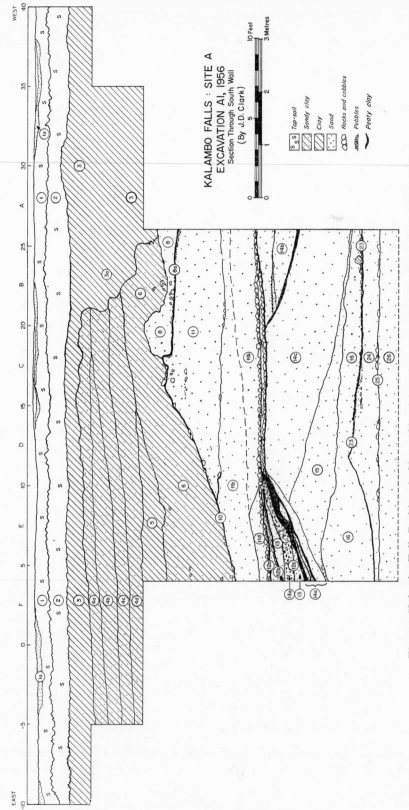

KALAMBO FALLS : SITE A
EXCAVATION AI, 1956
Section Through South Wall
(By J. D. Clark)

Fig. 21. Kalambo Falls Prehistoric Site at Site A: section at south wall of A I excavation, 1956.

LITHOLOGY

The descriptions of the East and West Walls (Figures 20 and 22) refer.

Between 8 feet (2·44 m) and 8½–9 feet (2·59–2·74 m) several large sherds were found together in the grey clay (6) and some of them joined to form a plain, undecorated bowl. Tuyère fragments, quartzite flakes and a chopper were also recovered and might be Iron Age tools. In the southwest corner of the excavation in grid squares B 1 and 2 at a depth of 9 feet (2·74 m) a group of larger stones was found which formed a ring round a hard, gritty, red clay 4 feet (1·35 m) in diameter. It was thought that this might be the daga floor of a structure of some kind, especially as at the north side of the circular area there appeared an oval patch of what looked like fire-hardened clay and might have been the base of a hearth. There also occurred one rubber, some daga and a few flakes and charcoals.

Today, gulleys in the local Kalambo basin are planted with bananas and oil palm, and garden huts and shelters are sometimes associated so that it would not be impossible for the area in squares B 1 and 2 to be the floor of a temporary shelter of this kind. The evidence, however, is inconclusive, especially since the clay patch rested on or immediately above the floor of the 'Older Channel' cut.

In grid square D 3, between 9 feet (2·74 m) and 9½ feet (2·90 m) one large stone was found standing on end.

Down to 11 feet (3·35 m) the grey, clayey sand (6) of the 'Older Channel' fill became progressively more claylike with some lenses of blacker clay and the line of the channel cut through the sands of beds (8), (9) and (11) (Figures 20 and 21). Potsherds, slag and tuyère fragments continued to occur in the 'Older Channel' fill.

The 'Younger Channel' fill became progressively coarser with depth from west to east and the channel in which it rests deepens from south to north, although the base was at a fairly constant depth of 12½–13 feet (3·81–3·96 m) in grid squares 4–8 at the west wall of the excavation. This is probably part of the channel fill of a tributary donga which divides into two gulleys at the southeast and southwest corners of the excavation and carried in sediments from the south slopes of the basin.

The walls of the excavation were carried down vertically for a depth of 11 feet (3·35 m) at which level, due to the weight of the Iron Age clays overlying the loosely compacted sands below, there occurred some substantial collapses, so that it became necessary to step back the sides. This task was generally un-rewarding but it was a necessary precaution carried out in most of the deeper excavations. The upper 7 feet (2·13 m) of the walls were stepped back 10 feet (3·05 m) in three steps. As the excavation progressed, further stepping back became necessary as can be seen in the section drawings.

Both the 'Older' and 'Younger' Iron Age Channels were cut down to

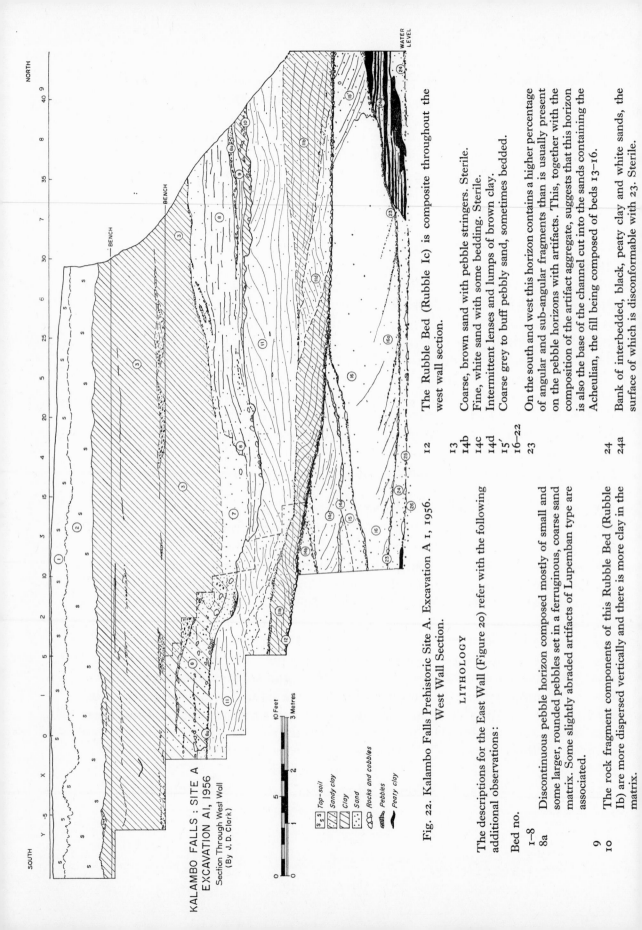

KALAMBO FALLS : SITE A
EXCAVATION A1, 1956
Section Through West Wall
(By J. D. Clark)

Legend:
- s s Top-soil
- Sandy clay
- Clay
- Sand
- Rocks and cobbles
- Pebbles
- Peaty clay

Fig. 22. Kalambo Falls Prehistoric Site A. Excavation A 1, 1956. Section Through West Wall Section.

LITHOLOGY

The descriptions for the East Wall (Figure 20) refer with the following additional observations:

Bed no.

1–8

8a   Discontinuous pebble horizon composed mostly of small and some larger, rounded pebbles set in a ferruginous, coarse sand matrix. Some slightly abraded artifacts of Lupemban type are associated.

9

10   The rock fragment components of this Rubble Bed (Rubble Ib) are more dispersed vertically and there is more clay in the matrix.

12   The Rubble Bed (Rubble Ic) is composite throughout the west wall section.

13   Coarse, brown sand with pebble stringers. Sterile.

14b   Fine, white sand with some bedding. Sterile.

14c   Intermittent lenses and lumps of brown clay.

14d

15'   Coarse grey to buff pebbly sand, sometimes bedded.

16–22

23   On the south and west this horizon contains a higher percentage of angular and sub-angular fragments than is usually present on the pebble horizons with artifacts. This, together with the composition of the artifact aggregate, suggests that this horizon is also the base of the channel cut into the sands containing the Acheulian, the fill being composed of beds 13–16.

24   Bank of interbedded, black, peaty clay and white sands, the surface of which is disconformable with 23. Sterile.

24a

approximately the same level—$12\frac{1}{2}$–13 feet (3·81–3·96 m) below the surface—and there is no appreciable difference in their archaeological content, which comprised channel decorated pottery, slag, daga and fresh and abraded stone artifacts, most of the latter being fragmentary. The makers of the Kalambo Industry occupied the valley during the whole of the time that the deposits of the 'Older Channel' cut were aggrading but there is reason to believe that the Channelled Ware sherds in the 'Younger Channel' deposits are derived. Pottery and larger stones with some gravel derived from the eroded Rubble Ib occurred in the lowest levels of the channel.

The sands and grits of the Mbwilo Member (8), through which these Iron Age channels and gulleys were cut, were sterile of artifacts, as also was the underlying deposit of sands (9) (Figure 20). These appear to belong with the underlying series of sands and clays which date to the closing stages of the Pleistocene and equate with bed (19) in the River Face section (Figure 32). Both these sands (8) and (9) were loosely compacted, cross-bedded in places and stained a dark brown or orange colour by iron. They had been largely cut out in the southern and eastern parts of the excavation but were well preserved at the northern end. They appear to belong to the period of increased rainfall termed Makalian in East Africa.

At the northwest side of the excavation the post-Pleistocene, ferruginous, bedded sands (8) rest on an erosion surface cut into an older sand, white to buff in colour (11) (Figure 22). Here at 9 inches (23 cm) above the base of the ferruginous sands (8), at a depth below the ground surface of approximately 11 feet (3·35 m), was a thin pebble line (8a) which contained some derived Lupemban together with fresh artifacts believed to be late 'Magosian' in age, but there was no pottery. At the southern end of the excavation this pebble line lies at the base of the sands (8) which, in turn, rest disconformably upon the feebly iron-stained sands (9) (Figures 20 and 22). The latter are cross-bedded, contain some lenses of coarse sand and small pebbles and are orange to buff and white in colour. This pebble line was again found to be present at Sites B and C, where the fresh, and so the latest, material is also ascribed to the 'Magosian'.

In the eastern half of the excavation (grid squares E–F 4–9) grey clays (11a), (11c), were interbedded with the white sands, and at a depth of $12\frac{1}{2}$–13 feet (3·81–3·96 m) a layer of grey clay (11a) approximately 1 foot (30·50 cm) thick had preserved portions of a pebble line that rested immediately upon it. This rubble (10) in Figure 20 and (22a) in Figure 32 is probably the same as Rubble Ib, the second of the three rubbles preserved at Site A ((20) in Figure 32). It contained the same mixed assemblage of typologically earlier and later Lupemban with some older artifacts that are found associated with the Rubble I accumulations at other sites in the valley. These tools mostly showed varying degrees of

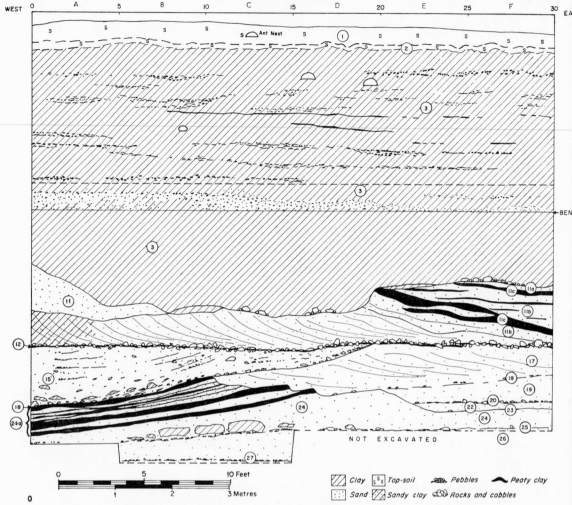

KALAMBO FALLS : SITE A
EXCAVATION A I, 1956
Section Through North Wall
(By J. D. Clark and L. E. Hodges)

Fig. 23. Kalambo Falls Prehistoric Site A. Excavation A 1, 1956. North Wall Section.

LITHOLOGY

This is a composite section: the upper half shows the north wall along the line 5–5′ before this was broken down and the excavation opened to the river; the lower half shows the section at approximately 18 feet to the north. That part of the section lying between the bench and the base of the Younger Channel cut was not recorded.

The descriptions for the East Wall (Figure 20) refer with the following observations:

Bed no.

1–3

11–11c

12   The Rubble Bed (Rubble Ic) is here composite with slightly abraded Lupemban and derived stone artifacts. The angular and sub-angular rock debris is greatest towards the eastern side of the section.

15′–17

18   Pebble horizon resting, on the west, on a bank of interbedded clays and sands and, in the centre and east, where this bank has been cut out by erosion, on the fine to medium sands (24). Two horizons may be represented here. The Acheulian artifacts are mostly found in the eastern half of the section.

19–26

27   Pebble horizon with rare flakes resting on sand and fine gravel (Occupation Surface VII).

abrasion and were lying associated with rounded but angular blocks of hard quartzite and sandstone that had probably made their way down the sides of the basin. Any dolerite present was appreciably weathered. The small tools were in chert and were mostly Lupemban artifacts. Notable were five core-axes and two hand-axes of lower Lupemban type. The tool count will be shown in a later volume.

The later channelling had not been able to cut below this clay layer but where it was absent over the eastern half of the excavation gulleying had cut approximately another 1 foot (30·50 cm) into the white/buff sands (11) (Figure 20). Here artifacts derived from Rubble Ib were mixed with the later material and pottery on the channel floor. Characteristic of the deposits of the Chiungu Member is the amount of unweathered but abraded dolerite blocks and cobbles present in the channel fill.

Below the floors of the later channels and under Rubble Ib the deposits were quite sterile of artifacts except for an isolated and abraded, short quadrilateral, chert flake of upper Lupemban type which was found at a depth of 14 feet (4·27 m) in grid square A 7. In the eastern half of the excavation the unbedded buff and white sands (11) and (11b) interstratified with the grey and black clays (11a) and (11c) had the appearance of a *dambo* deposit. Pollen samples (nos. 764, 765, 766, 2347—see Chapter 3) from these clays have produced clear evidence of cooler and wetter climatic conditions dating to the closing stage of the Pleistocene. A few scattered charcoals and organic remains were found in the middle layer of black clay (11c) and in the sand immediately overlying the Rubble Ic.

Over the western half of the dig, approximately to the west of grid squares C and D intersection, the clays were absent and the sands (11) were cross-bedded and mainly ferruginous in the upper half. The lower half of these sands had a fine, grey clay component (11b) which made them very hard to dig when they were dry and gave a buff to light grey colour to the deposit. These sands rested on a well-developed rubble—Rubble Ic(i) ((12a), Figures 20 and 21)—which was found to slope downwards, at first steeply and then more gently, from south to north. There was also a similar gentle gradient from west to east. At the southwestern corner the depth was approximately 14 feet (4·27 m) below the ground; at the southeastern corner this had increased to 15 feet 3 inches (4·64 m); and at the northeastern corner the depth was $17\frac{1}{2}$–18 feet (5·33–5·48 m) and this depth remained fairly constant along the north wall (Figure 23 and Plates 12 and 14).

This rubble (12) consists of a mass of angular stones with rounded and weathered edges—mostly hard and soft quartzites and sandstones with some rare and very weathered dolerite and hard quartzite pothole cobbles. The stones lie at all angles and are packed round with small gravel. They represent the floor and lower part of a channel bank believed to be a former channel of the river. At the northern end the debris was 9 inches (23 cm) thick and thinned to 4–5 inches (10·00–12·75 cm) at the southern, upslope, end.

Interspersed among the rocks were numerous artifacts belonging to several different industries. There were hand-axes, a few cleavers, core-axes, picks, numerous flake tools and evidence of the discoid and Levallois core techniques— artifacts from cultural stages ranging from the Acheulian up to the end of the Lupemban. A large proportion of these tools showed varying degrees of abrasion by the action of water with fine clay particles in suspension which has dulled the edges of the chert artifacts and imparted to them a soapy feel. Among the artifacts of Lupemban type were a number of anvils and fine examples of upper Lupemban core-axes, unifaced points and a trapeze as well as some good bifacially worked discoids and many other finely made tools, which all suggest an upper or final Lupemban rather than a 'Magosian' context for the latest artifacts in this rubble. The analysis of the artifacts from Rubble Ic(i) will be given in a subsequent volume.

The greater number of artifacts occurred in the northern half of the dig where the Rubble Ic had flattened out. It was mostly in the lowest, northwestern, part where the rubble was flattest that the largest stones were found, though a concentration of large rocks also occurred near the southwest corner where the rubble dips more steeply to the north.

The more gently sloping northern part of the rubble appears to be the floor of the channel. Upslope, south of the excavation, it would contain less water-rolled material and become a scree as was seen to be the case in A 4 excavation. The artifacts in these rubbles/gravels are naturally dispersed except in very rare instances and nothing, unfortunately, can be learned from the distribution pattern. The mixture of tools of different industrial stages indicates that some or all of them must have been derived. For example, the fresh appearance of the core-axes of Sangoan type suggests that they must have come directly from the lowest level to which the channel was cut for they have suffered no abrasion from the water. As is known from the 1959 and 1963 excavations in the A 4 trench, Lupemban artifacts could be and probably were derived from upslope also, but it is, nevertheless, possible that a proportion of them are contemporary with the channelling and found their way into Rubble Ic as a result of activities practised on the bank or in the stream bed itself during times of low water when the stones in the channel were exposed, as they are today in the present river during the dry season.

In this connection it is of interest to note the presence of three rough circles of stones which could have been artificially put into position (Plate 13). The first is a small oval, 2 feet (61 cm) in greatest diameter, composed of ten stones and is in grid square C 7. The stones lay in the centre of an iron-stained area which had the appearance of a hearth but, as there were no characteristic heat spalls or charcoals it is not possible to be certain. The second, in grid square F 6, is another small circle 1 foot (30·50 cm) in diameter. The third is a larger circle, less well defined, and with the greatest diameter of 5 feet (1·50 m) close to the west wall in grid squares A and B 8 and 9. Nearby, in B 9, was a large stone anvil which appeared to have been wedged into position for striking as the upper end showed numerous marks of battering (Plate 14). This suggests that stone-flaking was sometimes carried out close to the water and may be connected with the need to ensure that the stone being worked had the right moisture content to enable the best results to be obtained.

In grid squares C–E 5–6 was a narrow, elongate area without stones which had once held the upper end of a log of wood that had protruded into the rubble from the underlying deposit. The wood above the rubble had completely weathered away but was reasonably well preserved in the sand immediately beneath it. All that remained in the rubble itself were some very small flecks of carbonaceous material; this was a general indication that it was unlikely that wood would be found preserved in the deposits over Rubble Ic(i). In the lower part of the floor in square D 9 were found some further fragments of wood and another irregular area free from large stones, believed to show the form of a log no longer preserved.

At the southeast side approximately 9 inches (23 cm) to 1 foot (31·50 cm) below this rubble, in grid squares D–F 3 and separated from the Rubble Ic(i) by a coarse buff sand (13), was a thinner rubble—Ic(ii), (12b) (Figures 20 and 21). At the south end this rubble rested on a bank of fine gravel (13a) and at the southern and western sides it rose up to join the base of the main rubble—Ic(i). It was not represented in the rest of the excavation and must be closely contemporary with the formation of the main rubble above. There is no difference in the industrial content of the two, though that in the lower rubble is, perhaps, less abraded.

Over the eastern half of the excavation, in grid squares D–F 7–3, the main rubble was seen to be further divided into an upper and a lower separated by a coarse bedded sand with some small pebbles which reached its maximum thickness of approximately $1\frac{1}{2}$ feet (45·75 cm) at the east wall. At the southeast corner the gravel layer referred to above was intercalated. To the north and west the two rubbles/gravels joined to form a single horizon. The lower Rubble Ic(iii) had fewer large stones and was not so thick as Ic(i) but had the same cultural content, yielding some excellent examples of Lupemban tools.

In squares E and D 2 were found scattered charcoals lying in a thin, dark clay lens and white sand which appeared to intercalate with Ic(iii) and to lie immediately under the main and upper Rubble Ic(i). The charcoals from E 2 have been dated to between 29,750 and 27,500 years (Lamont, L-3991).

In the A 1 excavation Rubble Ic rested on an erosion surface cut into the Ochreous Sands and the upper part of the White Sands Beds of the Mkamba Member. Over the northeastern half of the excavation Rubble Ic rested on a fine buff to white sand (17) (Figures 20 and 23) compact, but with no evidence of cross-bedding. It was sterile of artifacts, was between $1\frac{1}{2}$ and 2 feet thick (45·75 and 61 cm) and covered the uppermost of the Acheulian occupation floors. Over the western half and at the south end of the excavation this sand and the occupation floors below it had been cut out by later channelling running in a southeast/northwest direction. The approximate northern edge of this channel, which contained only an occasional, abraded flake, is well seen in the plan of the uppermost Acheulian occupation floor (Floor IV). This channel post-dates the Acheulian horizons and thus dates to Sangoan times. In it were deposited coarse and fine sands, often cross-bedded, and some fine gravel lenses and clays which are the basal deposits of the Ochreous Sands here (beds (14)–(16)). At the southeast corner of the excavation some of the latest filling comprised interbedded black clays with organic material and white sands with some large sections of tree trunks and other wood fragments (14a) (Figures 20 and 21). At the southwest corner the sands immediately below Rubble Ic were coarser with some cross-bedding and lines of pebbles (14b). Both (14a) and (14b) overlay (14c) a fine, feebly bedded, white to buff sand which is distinguished from the top of bed (15) by an occasional pebble or flake fragment. In the west wall the base was marked by a thin, brown clay band with some derived lumps of a similar clay (14d).

Bed (15) was a coarse, grey sand with a more definite but discontinuous line of pebbles at the base, including a broken core-axe and a unifacially flaked cobble of Sangoan or Acheulian type. It was not continuous over the whole area excavated, being absent from most of the eastern part of the dig. At the southern end the uppermost levels were sometimes interstratified with fine, buff sand lenses as in the southwest corner. The same, or a similar, coarse, pebbly sand (15′) was present in the northwestern part of the excavation where it had cut down into the sands (16) and (17) overlying the uppermost Acheulian and to a zone of banded black clays and white sands (24a) preserved in the northwest corner. This deposit (15′) was sometimes bedded and was deepest at the northwestern corner. Here the base of the channel in which (15′) rested had been cut down to the upper black clay band on which was a little fresh Acheulian material. This is the same occupation surface (18) that is present at the base of the White Sands (17) immediately to the east and which is known as Occupation Floor IV.

The lowest of these channel deposits with Sangoan artifacts that cut out the White Sands and Acheulian horizons was a fine, bedded, light brown to white coloured sand (16) which became more extensive from east to west. In the upper levels it was very finely bedded but below cross-bedding was present and the sand was of medium grain. Over the western part of the excavation this sand rested on the disturbed occupation surface known as Vb. In the eastern part it rested against the White Sands (17) that preserved the Acheulian occupation floors.

This channel fill, represented in the A I excavation by the beds (14)–(16), forms a part of the Ochreous Sands aggradation that can be traced to beyond the A 4 trench downstream. The direction of the bedding is towards the west or northwest. Very little cultural material is contained in the intermittent pebble lines and this consists only of slightly abraded waste flakes of general Acheulian or Sangoan type.

Wood, as has been said, was present in the southeast channel fill and it was also preserved in grid squares C 8 and D 6 and 7, immediately underlying Rubble Ic (Plate 13). In D 6 was preserved the lower end of the log that had protruded up into Rubble Ic. In C 8 were found what appeared to be the *in situ* basal parts of the trunk or roots of a tree which gave the radiocarbon date of 43,000 ± 3,300 years (Lamont, L-399C) and thus determined the age of the channel fill of deposit (15) as Sangoan.

The uppermost of the Acheulian occupation floors within the White Sands Bed was a horizon of no thickness and was preserved only in the northern and northeastern part of the dig (18) (Figures 20 and 23). As with the lower horizons, this can have been an occupation of only very temporary duration—a season or two at the most—for all the evidence points to these floors' having been quickly covered by the overlying sterile and fluviatile sands before any humus could form or weathering of the surface take place. The only indication that this is a temporary surface is the presence of the artifacts and, sometimes, some small pebbles. Everything found here, except the small pebbles, must have been carried on to the surface by man; the distribution pattern shows no evidence of natural alignment and the tools themselves, on this and the other Acheulian floors, are absolutely fresh.

The northeastern part of Occupation Floor IV rests on a sterile white sand (19) but, as has been said, on the northwest side it rests on an eroded surface of the banded black clays and sands (24a). It was not possible to be certain whether this was precisely the same as or a slightly later phase than that of Occupation Floor IV on the eastern side since the grid squares C and D 8 and 9 contained practically no artifacts. The evidence suggests, however, that a single floor only is represented. Floor IV is generally fairly level though it slopes up on the east side in grid squares 6 and 7 where it rests on a partially eroded clay, grey to brown in colour on the exterior, though blue inside (21a and b).

A few small pieces of wood were found associated with the tools but none of them showed any evidence of having been shaped. Of particular interest are the two small concentrations of flakes in grid squares E and F 8 and 9 and in C and D 7, which are associated with anvils. There can be no doubt that this surface ((39) in the A 1 excavation (Figure 32)) represents a waterside camping place of very temporary occupation. This is believed to be the same occupation surface as that uncovered in the A 5 trench extension in 1963 ((37) in Figure 32) and may be the same as that in A 5 trench (43) (Figure 32).

Occupation Floor IV rested on a coarse, cross-bedded sand (22b) in the southeastern part of the dig. This was 1–1½ feet (30·50–45·75 cm) thick and lensed out towards the southern end of the excavation as also in grid squares C and D where it has been cut out by the later channelling. In squares D–F 6 where it runs up over the top of several pockets of the brown/blue clay Occupation Floor IV appears to merge with another surface with tools which lies immediately under the coarse sand (19) below Floor IV in the northeast grid squares; it is apparent that there can be little difference in age between the two. This is Occupation Floor V (20) (see Plate 15). The tools are associated with a number of large primary flakes in hard quartzite which were concentrated in a flaking area in squares D and E 4 and 5. Two of these flakes were found to join and they had been obtained by breaking up boulders of quartzite by anvil technique. On the floor, hand-axes and cleavers were found in small groups as if discarded where they had been used.

Floor V was seen to dip gently down towards the west and two small subsidiary patches of artifacts were found in grid squares C 5–7 and A–C 6. The eastern patch merged with the main horizon on the east side of the excavation and on the west side both patches lay in sand approximately 4 inches (10·20 cm) below Floor V. There was no difference in the artifacts on Floor V and in these subsidiary concentrations, known as Floor Va.

At the same level on the western side of the excavation the Floor V horizon was absent but 6 inches (15·25 cm) to 1 foot (30·50 cm) below, over the western half of the dig, was a further concentration of artifacts on a surface which appeared to run into Floor V though a little below it, along the junction of squares C D. On the northwest side it stopped short at, or merged into the occupation surface overlying the black clay. This area is known as Floor Vb (23). The general dispersal shown by the distribution pattern with some possible alignment by water, and the larger number of natural stones in this area, suggest that it is a part of the occupation surface naturally disturbed by water action and, as has been shown, the base of the channel containing the Ochreous Sands Bed lies at this level.

The continuation of this disturbed Vb surface, or a different occupation floor, was found at the same level in the eastern half of the excavation. This was separated from the upper Floor V by 6 inches (15·25 cm) to 2 feet (61 cm) of sterile, coarse, bedded sand with small pebbles (22a). The scatter of tools and waste on this eastern half of what is believed to be the undisturbed part of Floor Vb is sparse. It comprises several hand-axes and cleavers but very few flakes, showing that the large cutting tools had been carried in from elsewhere.

At the level of Occupation Floor V water began to stand in the excavation and it became necessary to try to drain this away. Accordingly grid squares B and C 8 and 9 were excavated for a further 3 feet (91·50 cm) below this horizon to form a sump which could be pumped out (see Plate 16). This proved fairly effective in so far as draining the remainder of the floor was concerned but it was difficult to keep the sand walls of the sump from collapsing.

Beneath the banded clays and white sand (24a) at the northwest corner was a compact, fine, white to buff sand with very little bedding (24) (Figures 20–23). At the base of this was a band of the brown to green clay with blue interior which was here preserved in the form of large, discontinuous lumps indicating that the layer had been partially broken down by erosion before it was buried. Patches of what may be the same disrupted clay layer protrude in places through the Occupation Floors IV and V in the central parts of the excavation. The clay was 9 inches to 1 foot (23–30·50 cm) thick in the sump section and immediately beneath it was found evidence of another temporary living floor—the line of the surface being marked in places by a thin line of small pebbles in addition to the artifacts ((25) in Figures 20–23).

This surface, Occupation Floor VI, lies approximately 1–1½ feet (30·50–45·75 cm) below Floor V which was at water level at the north end of the excavation. To the south it is separated from Floor V by a fine, compact, white to brown sand ((24) Figures 20–23) which is sterile. It is marked by a discontinuous pebble line—a few larger natural rocks and individual, or small groups of, cutting tools and a few flake tools but no great amount of waste. Again, it is the artifacts that distinguish this surface as a living floor. Unfortunately, this surface was reached only three days before the end of the 1956 season so that it was not possible to investigate it completely and plot the pattern of artifact distribution.

Typologically the tools are late upper Acheulian and in entirely fresh condition. They appeared to be concentrated towards the south end of the excavation in grid squares A–E 3 and 4. In squares A–E 5 there was a marked falling off in the number of artifacts though occasional examples were present in squares A–E 6 and 7. At the north side, however, they had practically disappeared and none was found under bed (24a) in the northwest corner of the excavation. In squares A 3, E 7, C 7 and C 8 were found several pieces of wood with smoothed surfaces but no definite evidence of having been worked by man. In square A 3 five pieces were lying next to and just beneath a cleaver and a hand-axe. The surface on which this occupation floor rested was composed of a fine to medium-grained sand with some coarser sand lenses and sloped slightly upwards at the south end, but otherwise was nearly flat ((26) in Figures 20–23). This floor appeared to represent the edge of a denser occupation area on a sand bank situated immediately south of the excavation. The fine white to buff sand (26) on which Floor VI rests was sterile of artifacts, but with some lenses of grit and small pebbles. Except in the small 'sump area' referred to above near the northwest corner of the dig, only the top 4 inches (10 cm) or so of this bed was exposed, but in the sump itself at a depth of between 1 foot and 1 foot 9 inches (30·50 and 52 cm) below the top was found a layer of small pebbles and an occasional waste flake which probably indicate the presence of yet another occupation horizon ('Floor VII').

The A 1 excavation was closed on 27 October 1956 (see Plate 15). It has provided a remarkably complete and rich assemblage of tools and other artifacts as the analyses show. When work was resumed at Kalambo Falls in 1959 the excavation was found to be much overgrown and collapsed and the north wall had been completely removed by the river.

The small, 1953 and 1955, excavations at the river bank were immediately north of the A 1 excavation and separated from the north wall by approximately 10 feet (3·05 m) of deposit. They were contiguous with each other, the earlier being at the upstream (east) end. Occupation Floor IV is here overlain by coarse, gritty sand and it yielded two divergent edged cleavers. The bedding of the sands underlying this floor was towards the west. The sands are here ochreous but are believed to represent a lateral facies of the white sands (17) in the A 1 excavation. At the western end of this 1953 excavation some wood fragments were found immediately above the level of Floor V.

Floor V showed the same scatter of finely made Acheulian tools as was preserved in the eastern half of the A 1 excavation, including the largest cleaver found at Kalambo. It was lying with two others close to a large, straight log of wood that protruded from a 1 foot (30·50 cm) thick layer of black clay at the base of which, and at water level, was another occupation horizon identified here with Floor VI in the A 1 excavation, resting, in turn, on a coarse sand with pebble lines.

Although the small area of this lowest floor which it was possible to excavate in 1953 yielded only two elongate ovate hand-axes, it produced several excellent examples of Acheulian scrapers made in chert.

The log dated to 60,300±750 years (Groningen GrN-2644) came from the 1955 excavation in this floor.

A 2 excavations, 1956 and 1963 (Figures 24 and 25)

This trench was dug between 29 July and 17 August 1956, under the direction of Mrs L. E. Hodges, in order to determine the nature of the deposits at the northern edge of the 60 feet (20 m) 'terrace' where it had been cut into by later erosion and, if possible to link up these deposits with those underlying the channel fills containing Iron Age remains in the adjacent A 1 excavation. The trench was 65 feet (19·50 m) long and 10 feet (3·05 m) wide.

The section through the north wall is seen in Figure 24 and the west end in Plate 17.

At the west end under the black to brown surface soil (1) and (1') was a buff to yellow sand or sandy soil (2) with some potsherds in the upper levels. In the southwest corner a wedge-shaped layer of stony rubble was present but did not continue across to the northwest corner. It is possible that this represents the broken-down northern limit of the Red Rubble to be seen in the A 4 trench, but it is more likely to be a resorted scree of more recent date.

The yellow sand passed gradually down into a clayey sand, mottled yellow to grey in colour and with iron pisolites in the lower levels (5). Six inches (15 cm) from the southeast corner and 6 inches (15 cm) above the base of the pisolitic zone was found in 1963 an isolated artifact. This was a broad, radially prepared flake with multifaceted striking platform, buff to white patina and quite fresh. Typologically, it is final Lupemban or 'Magosian' and suggests a connection between this deposit and (11) in the A 4 sections.

The clay sand (5) overlay, with no erosional break, fluviatile sands (6) with some cross-bedding and fine, thin, irregular bands of brown clay, probably connected, as on Site C, with the water table rather than belonging to the period of deposition of this bed. These yellow, clayey sands and the bedded sands had no artifacts associated.

At the west end was found a thin, sterile, grey clay (8) having a maximum thickness of 1 foot (30·50 cm). This was continuous in the northwest corner but

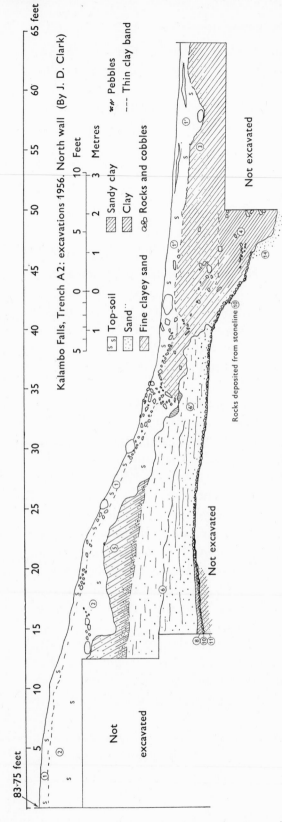

Kalambo Falls, Trench A2: excavations 1956. North wall (By J. D. Clark)

Figs. 24 and 25. Kalambo Falls Prehistoric Site A. Excavation A 2, 1956 and 1963. North Wall Section, 1956 and South and West Wall Sections, 1963.

LITHOLOGY

Bed no.

1 Brown sandy loam with angular rock debris derived from upslope. (1') Black sandy loam with occasional large boulders.

2 Brown sand loam with some boulders and angular rock fragments at the west end. Sterile. Probably correlates with (2) in A 4 Trench.

3 Red-brown, sandy clay of 'Younger Channel' fill with some angular and sub-angular rock fragments derived from upslope.

4 Brown-grey, mottled clay with some angular rock debris derived from rubble (10) below and Iron Age potsherds; probably correlates with the (4) in the A 1 Excavation.

5 Mottled yellow to grey sand with impersistent horizon of pisolitic iron nodules near the base. Probably correlates with bed (11) in A 4 Trench but could be the same as AA of the Pits Channel Member in A 4 Trench.

6 Buff to white sand, loose and cross-bedded, especially at the western end and thin intermittent lines of brown clay; the clay has been precipitated, probably as a result of groundwater action subsequent to the deposition of the bed. Sterile. Represents the infilling of a channel, the floor of which descends to the south or southwest. Probably correlates with the BB sands filling the Pits Channel in A 4 Trench Pits 2 and 3. Less likely is correlation with sands (12) in the A 4 Trench. A crack in the south wall of the 1963 excavation passing through beds (5) and (6) could be a potential slump line.

6' Buff sand (6) which has begun to break down and suffered some resorting following the erosion and channelling of Chiungu Formation times. Sterile.

7 Cross-bedded, fine white to light brown sand. Sterile.

8 Grey clay-sand and clay bed; partially broken down and cut out by subsequent channelling but preserved at the western end of the trench. A thin scatter of pebbles overlies the surface of this clay. Sterile. No equivalent in the A 4 Trench but possibly correlates with (16') where this is undisturbed in the northwest corner.

9 Fine gravel lens. Sterile. No equivalent in the A 4 Trench.

10 Rubble Bed of variable thickness with angular and sub-angular rock fragments, some more rounded stones and ?Lupemban and other stone artifacts, mostly slightly abraded, set in a ferruginous sand

Rocks deposited from stoneline (10)

Key
- S S | Top-soil
- | Sand
- (dotted) | Fine clayey sand
- (diagonal lines) | Sandy clay
- (diagonal hatching) | Clay
- Rocks and cobbles
- ⌁ Pebbles
- --- Thin clay band

Metres
Feet

83·75 feet

65 feet

Not excavated

Not excavated

110

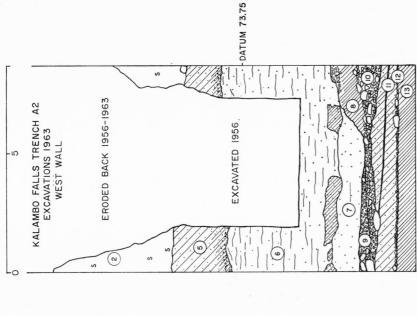

KALAMBO FALLS TRENCH A2
EXCAVATIONS 1963
WEST WALL

ERODED BACK 1956–1963

EXCAVATED 1956.

DATUM 73.75

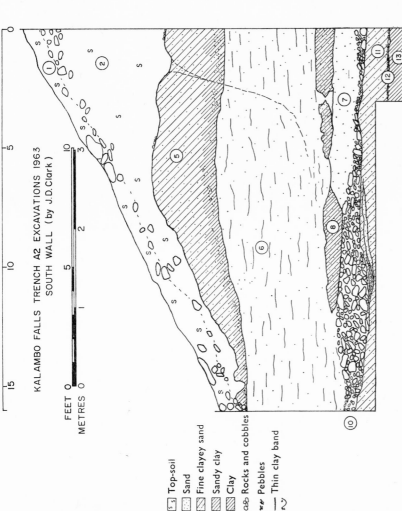

KALAMBO FALLS TRENCH A2 EXCAVATIONS 1963
SOUTH WALL (by J.D.Clark)

FEET 0
METRES 0

	Top-soil
s s	Sand
	Fine clayey sand
	Sandy clay
	Clay
	Rocks and cobbles
	Pebbles
	Thin clay band

III

matrix. At the east end of the trench, between the 30′ and 40′ lines, the stone artifacts that lie on this rubble bed are of 'Mago-sian' type and in fresh condition. Rubble bed (10) probably correlates with the rubble line at the base of the Pits Channel Fill of the Mkamba Member in the A 4 Trench, while the eastern end was exposed also during the time of the formation of Rubble I.

11 Grey clay-sand with ferruginous orange mottling together with some lenses of fine gravel, sand and a thin band of darker clay. Sterile. Correlated with (17) in the A 4 Trench sections.

12 Thin rubble line of small, mostly rounded pebbles, sub-angular stones and an occasional larger sub-angular rock. Yielded a sparse collection of stone artifacts with no particular diagnostic characteristics but probably of general 'Middle Stone Age' affinities. Provisionally correlated with Rubble II in the A 4 Trench.

13 Dark grey clay which becomes very hard after drying out. Sterile. Correlated with (19) in the A 4 Trench sections.

14 Feebly ferruginous, mottled yellow and white bedded sand. Sterile. Provisionally correlated with bed (20) in the A 4 Trench.

appeared to have been broken down at the south side by the channelling that deposited the overlying bedded sands. It rested here on a fine, white, bedded sand (7).

Below this sand and clay was a rubble (10) which was believed at first to be the same as the main mixed Rubble I (either Ib or Ic) in the A 1 excavation. It varied in thickness, with an average of 5 inches (12·75 cm), and rested on a fine, yellow, bedded sand or clay sand (11). It was composed of the usual unsorted angular rocks with not many artifacts. At the western end it was dipping in a westerly or southwesterly direction and also at the eastern end of the trench it dipped more gradually towards the northeast up to the point where it was truncated by the later channelling.

The western edge of the channelling containing the Iron Age remains was exposed at the eastern end of the trench and, adjacent to the rubble, it was found to be marked by redeposited and slumped rubble and rocks. The filling consisted of sandy clays as in the A 1 excavation. In the lower levels there was a mottled clay (4) grey to brown in colour, which may represent the 'Older Channel' fill, while in the upper levels the red clay (3) can be identified with the clays and clay sand of the 'Younger Channel' fill. Both yielded Iron Age potsherds, slag and daga.

At this end of the trench also the rubble was in places divided into two parts, the upper being a single line of stones associated with a thin, brown clay or soil separated from the main rubble by 2 or 3 inches (5 or 8 cm) of sand and clayey sand. A fresh or only very slightly rolled group of artifacts is typologically final Lupemban or 'Magosian' and came from the eastern end of the trench. This part of the rubble was, therefore, exposed at the time of the erosion and initial stages of aggradation of the 30 feet (9 m) 'terrace' deposits. The sands (6') that overlie the rubble at this end of the trench, while they post-date the 'Magosian' have also been resorted at a later date. In the remainder of the rubble unmodified artifacts in chert are present with older implements but in no great abundance; characteristic retouched tools are absent.

In 1956 it was assumed that this rubble/gravel (10) equated with one or other of the divisions of Rubble I. However, the 1963 excavations in the A 4 trench suggest that the A 2 stoneline represents, in fact, the floor of a channel that is intermediate in age between Rubbles I and II (see p. 131).

In 1963 a further small excavation was carried out at the western end of this site to compare the stoneline and its contents with Rubble II and the overlying deposits with the stratigraphy in Pits 2 and 3 in the A 4 trench (see Figure 25). The western end of this dig was situated approximately 12 feet (3·6 m) east of the west end of the 1956 trench and the excavation was cut back approximately

2 feet (61 cm) to the south and west of the sections exposed in that year. The archaeological content of this rubble indicates that it must post-date Rubble II but it seems possible, because of the elevation, that it represents the base of the channelling found in Pits 2 and 3 of A 4 during 1963 and not the main erosion surface of Rubble I. Thus the overlying sands would equate with the sands (BB) of the Pits Channel Fill (see Figures 28 and 29).

The 1963 excavation in A 2 was taken a short way below the rubble (10), and 1 foot (30·50 cm) below this a second thin stoneline (12) was found. The cultural material from this stoneline was very sparse and quite indeterminate but it seems likely that it represents Rubble II since it also rests on grey clay (13) like that exposed in A 4. The association of the A 2 rubble/gravel (10) is further discussed below in the general correlation of the Site A excavations.

A 3 excavation, 1956 (Figure 26)

Since at least one rubble with artifacts of Lupemban type was present in the river bank section immediately downstream from the A 1 excavation at heights above that which had mostly been cut out by the pre-Chiungu Member channelling, it was decided to open a section here. Accordingly A 3, an area 24 × 15 feet (7·3 × 4·5 m) was excavated, 65 feet (19·5 m) west of the A 1 excavation (Figure 19). The overburden above the rubble was removed under the direction of Mrs L. E. Hodges between 29 August and 16 September. In spite of stepping back the lower levels, the loose sands of the lower part of the section would not support the weight and some collapse occurred at the east wall on 15 September. Figure 26 and Plate 18 show the sections exposed in the south and west walls.

At the surface was some 9 inches to 1 foot (23–30·50 cm) of black to dark grey humic soil (1) beneath which was a layer of light brown soil (2) 1 foot (30·50 cm) thick at the north end of the excavation but lensing out to only some 3 inches (7·75 cm) at the south end. Beneath this were between 3 and 4 feet (91·5 cm and 1·22 m) of dark brown (3) and red brown (3') clays and clay sands, deepening from south to north. These contain earlier Iron Age remains and probably represent the 'Older Channel' fill. Pottery, slag, daga and charcoals occurred in the excavation from 9 inches (23 cm) below the surface down to a depth of 4 feet (1·22 m), that is to say to near the gravelly base of the clays. Below this the deposits were sterile of artifacts until Rubble Ia was reached.

The red/brown clays rested in a channel that had been cut into an orange to buff-coloured sand (4), fairly fine grained and with no clearly defined bedding. This passed, with no apparent break, down into a buff-coloured, cross-bedded sand (5) with thin, contorted bands of brown clay which, as Site C shows, are

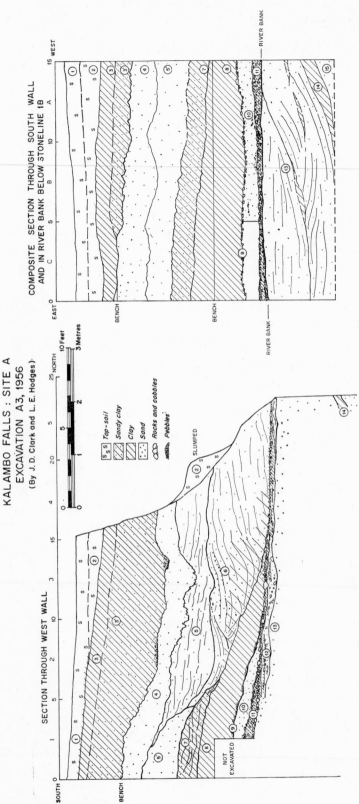

KALAMBO FALLS : SITE A
EXCAVATION A3, 1956
(By J. D. Clark and L. E. Hodges)

SECTION THROUGH WEST WALL

COMPOSITE SECTION THROUGH SOUTH WALL
AND IN RIVER BANK BELOW STONELINE 1B

Fig. 26. Kalambo Falls Prehistoric Site A. Excavation A3, 1956.
West and South Wall Sections.

LITHOLOGY

Bed
no.

1   Dark grey humic soil or loam. Sterile. Grading into:

2   Light brown sandy loam.

3   Dark brown sandy clay passing into red-brown mottled clays and
    clay-sand with some fine gravel lenses at the base (3'). Contains
    Iron Age remains. Correlated with (3) in the A 4 Trench.

4   Fine orange to light brown sand with feeble bedding. Sterile and
    grading into:

5   Light brown cross-bedded sands, loosely compacted with thin, dis-
    continuous and contorted lines of brown clay believed to have
    been formed *in situ* by fluctuation in groundwater level. To the
    south the sands are darker brown in colour and only feebly bedded
    (5'). Sterile.

6   Bedded, coarse and fine white to light brown sands, loosely com-

7   At the south end (6) is replaced by grey-brown clay-sand with
    interbedded lines of thin, brown clay similar to those in (5) above.
    Sterile and grading down into:

8   Grey clay lensing out or cut out from south to north by the sands
    (6) above. Sterile.

9   Pebble line with small pebbles and angular and sub-angular rock
    fragments and rare Lupemban and 'Magosian' stone artifacts,
    slightly abraded (Rubble Ia). Correlated with (15) in the A 4
    Trench.

10 White, unbedded sand with small pebbles of quartzite. Sterile.

11 Rubble Bed (Rubble Ia and Ib) with many large and small angular
    and sub-angular rock fragments and some cobbles set in a brown
    clay matrix. Sometimes composite, the bed sometimes forms two
    rubble lines separated by brown, ferruginous clay-sand. Contains
    Lupemban and 'Magosian' stone artifacts. Correlated with (15)
    in the A 4 Trench.

12 Coarse sand and sandy clay with rock rubble without artifacts.

13 Fine grained, bedded, ochreous to white sands. Sterile. Correlated
    with (20) in the A 4 Trench.

14 Grey clay lens. Sterile. Correlated with (21) in A 4 Trench.

post-depositional in origin. At the south end these sands are darker brown in colour and only feebly bedded (5′).

At the north end of the excavation the sands became alternately coarser and finer and white to buff in colour—very loosely compacted and with much cross-bedding (6). The lower part had a percentage of clay mixed with the sand which gave it a grey appearance. At the south end of the dig the clay content of this sand increased considerably and the deposit became a grey brown, clayey sand interbedded with layers of brown clay (7). These sands overlay a bank of grey clay (8) rising fairly sharply at the southern end and lensing out some 12 feet (3·6 m) to the north of the south wall. These deposits represent the filling of a channel which, it would seem, was flowing approximately east–west. From the cultural content and a radiocarbon date on charcoals from the underlying Rubble I it is apparent that this filling took place in Recent times and is the same as the sands (12) that fill this channel in the A 4 trench (Figures 28 and 29).

At the base of the grey clay at the south end the deposit was sandier and below this there occurred a thin, undulating stoneline, Rubble Ia (9). This was composed of small pebbles and irregular lumps of quartzite and sandstone in a matrix of brown clay and was separated from a much more massive stoneline (11) (Rubbles Ib and Ic combined) 1 foot to 8 inches below (30·50–20·50 cm) by a layer of fine-grained, sterile, white sand (10). The upper rubble dips down from south to north and merges with the lower one in a line running obliquely from grid square A 2 at the west wall to C 3 at the east wall. It contained very few artifacts almost all of which were concentrated in grid squares C 2 and C 3 and consequently they may be considered to have been derived from the main rubble an inch or two below. Here, against the east wall and at the junction of the C 2–3 grid lines, was found a very fine, but desilicified example of a Lupemban lance-head. Rubble Ia covers grid squares A–C 1, C 2 and two-thirds of C 3; the assemblage of artifacts is given in a later volume and, besides a core-axe, a chopper and a small scraper, consists mostly of waste. Twenty-five artifacts were in fresh condition.

In grid squares C 2 and C 3, where Rubble Ia merges with Rubbles Ib and Ic composite, at a depth of 12 feet 4 inches to 13 feet 3 inches (3·7–3·97 m) from the surface, were found a few small, scattered charcoals which have given a radiocarbon date of 9550±210 years B.P. (Lamont L-395D). Besides dating the contemporary later 'Magosian' artifacts this shows that the channelling and overlying cross-bedded sands, which are the same as those of the 30 foot (9 m) terrace at Sites C and D, were aggraded about ±7,500 B.C.

The underlying Rubble Ib and Ic, which rests on the main erosion surface, was composite and some 9 inches (23 cm) thick at the north end, while at the southeast end of the excavation it was just beginning to separate into two. As in the A 1 excavation, it is here composed of sub-angular blocks and lumps of quartzite and sandstone with an occasional spheroidal lump of completely weathered dolerite. These components are wedged at all angles in a sandy clay matrix, grey-brown in colour. As exposed in A 3 this rubble forms part of the south side of a river channel and the artifacts mostly show abrasion from washing in fine clay sand. A very few scattered charcoals were present in the sandy clay matrix of the rubble at a depth of 13 feet 3 inches (3·97 m) from the surface, but were insufficient to give a radiocarbon date. Besides two hand-axes and three cleavers the assemblage contained seven core-axes, a pick and several other heavy-duty tools. The light-duty tools are predominantly Lupemban in form and made of chert. One hundred and ninety-one artifacts are fresh, amongst which are a microlith and four small scrapers, typologically 'Magosian'. The use of the chalcedony which is present in a small percentage, also indicates a 'Magosian' context.

Below the rubble was a thin layer of coarse sand with clay and larger stones but without artifacts (12). This rested disconformably, at the north end of the excavation, on a fine white to orange, ferruginized, cross-bedded sand ((13) and (15)) with some lenses of clay interbedded and a grey clay band (14) dipping from west to east in the lowest point to which the excavation was taken, at the north-west corner at the river bank. Both these deposits were sterile. They are the same as the sands and clays (20) and (21) of the Ochreous Sands Bed of the Mkamba Member in the A 4 trench.

The A 3 excavation thus indicated that the main channelling which marks the base of the Chiungu Member was in the vicinity of A 1 and further east, though the 1959 excavations showed that additional channelling of this time was present also immediately west of A 3. Although it was not recognized in 1956, the rubbles/gravels in A 3 represent all three subdivisions of Rubble I which come together here and in A 4. It might be expected that in those excavations where the rubbles are composite, many more artifacts would be found than when they are separate, but this is not necessarily the case. The greatest number of artifacts occurred in A 1 and B sites but this is believed to be because the focus of occupation was more towards the centre than at the western edge of the basin. The relationship of the A 1, 3 and 4 excavations is seen in the River Face sections (Figure 32).

A 6 EXCAVATION: 16–24 OCTOBER 1966 (Figure 27)[1]

BY J. D. CLARK

This excavation was undertaken to try to recover details of the stratigraphy in those parts of the Mkamba Member that lie below the low water level in the Kalambo River; to collect additional pollen samples and to determine, if possible, the depth at which bed rock occurs, immediately upstream from the Spillway Gorge.

The technique adopted was to excavate within and under the wall of heavy, precast concrete pipes which, by virtue of their weight, then sank into the deposit in pace with the progress of the excavation. Pipes 4 feet (1·22 m) in diameter, 4 feet (1·22 m) high and 3 inches (7 cm) thick were chosen and two of these were successfully transported from Abercorn and set up at the site. This work took the greater part of two days since the pipes weighed half a ton (500 kg) each and a special ramp, pathway and cutting had to be built so that they could be lowered to the foot of the river without breaking.

The excavation was sited on the centre line of the A 4 trench on the immediate edge of the river which now coincides approximately with gridline +4, where the black clay bank (bed (28), Figure 28) that forms part of the White Sands Bed of the Mkamba Member was exposed. The rubble and talus that had fallen from the River Face Cliff since the 1963 season were removed and an area some 15 × 15 feet (4·5 × 4·5 m) of the clay bank was exposed. It was here overlain by a coarse, pebbly sand containing some large and water-abraded wood fragments. This sand was buff in colour or grey where the clay content was greater.

At the start of work the top of the clay bank (28) was 1 foot 3 inches (37 cm) above the level of the water in the river but groundwater was seeping from the cliff face and the cleared area at the junction of the buff sand and the grey clay and, by the close of work on 24 October, rain falling in the catchment had raised the level of the water in the river by 1 foot (30·50 cm) to 3 inches (7 cm) below the top of the clay bank. The place selected for the excavation made it possible to fix its position exactly in relation to earlier work at Site A.

Excavation was carried out by setting the first tube on end on the cleared space of the clay bank and beginning to dig out the deposit that lay within the cylinder. Generally the weight of the concrete was sufficient to keep the pipe moving down with the progress of the excavation but the surface tension of the clay on the wall

[1] The help received from Dr Glen H. Cole, from Mr D. W. Phillipson the Secretary/Inspector of the Zambia National Monuments Commission, from Mr John and Mr Colin Carlin and from the Abercorn Town Council, which materially contributed to the success of this operation, is most gratefully acknowledged here.

of the cylinder sometimes prevented this. After an hour or two, however, percolating water was enough to lubricate the clay and release the pipe. On only one occasion was it necessary to free the pipe by partly digging away the clay from the outside wall.

Down to a depth of 4 feet (1·22 m) below the surface of the Black Clay (28) it was possible to remove the water by bailing but, below this point, pumping (1½ h.p. Alcon pump) became necessary. Down to 7 feet (2·13 m) the excavation could be cleared of water and some 8–10 minutes were available for examination of the deposits before pumping again became necessary. Below this point, however, the water entered more rapidly through the base of the excavation and more frequent pumping became necessary. When the first tube had been lowered to the level of the top of the Black Clay (28) the second was placed on top of it. In this way both tubes were lowered and a depth of 8 feet (2·4 m) below the surface of the Black Clay was reached. By pumping and digging it was possible, in the inside of the cylinder, to penetrate to a total depth of 9 feet 2 inches (2·78 m) and, if a third cylinder had been available and time had permitted, it should have been possible to have carried the excavation still deeper.

The main disadvantage of this type of excavation is that, as the work progresses, the stratigraphic section is hidden by the concrete wall of the cylinder so that it is doubly necessary to ensure that all information is carefully recorded as the excavation is deepened. Also, when the deposit is loose and water-charged, as are the coarse to medium-grained sands that underlie the clay banks, sand from the outside of the cylinder will be washed under the base and into the excavation. If pebbles and artifacts occur in the sands, these will, similarly, be washed into the excavation and may even be let down from higher in the same bed. The recorded levels of finds in these sands must, therefore, be considered as approximate only. Where pebble lines or artifact horizons are present the same problem does not arise though some artifacts may still enter the excavation under the base of the wall.

The profile of the sediments which, in the A 6 excavation are nearly horizontally bedded, is shown at Figure 27. The black clay bank under the coarse sand with wood fragments comprises three parts: (28a) a sticky, black clay, 7½ inches (19 cm) thick, with a black, peaty layer containing compressed leaves, reed stems and fragments of tree branches up to 2 inches (5 cm) in diameter with the bark still in place, none of which, however, show any sign of artificial working; (28b) a white, structureless clay, 3½–4 inches (8–10 cm) thick, with very occasional impressions of small, pinnate leaves; (28c) a dark grey to black clay 1 to 1 foot 2 inches (30·50–35 cm) thick, with two 1 inch (2 cm) layers of fine, compact, buff-coloured sand separated by 2 inches (5 cm) of black/grey clay. At

KALAMBO FALLS: SITE A

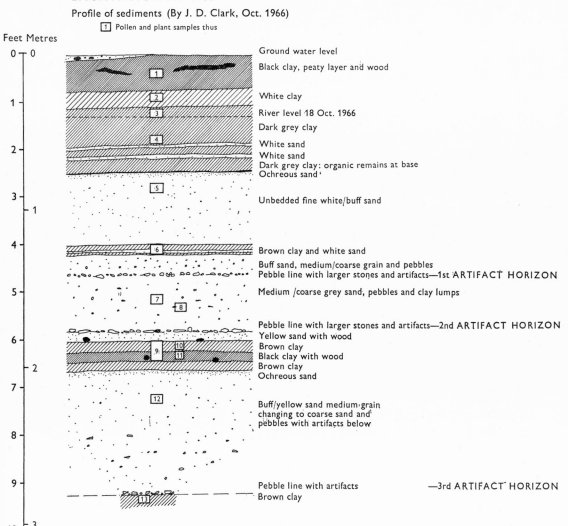

EXCAVATION A6 1966·

Profile of sediments (By J. D. Clark, Oct. 1966)

1 Pollen and plant samples thus

Feet Metres

Ground water level
Black clay, peaty layer and wood

White clay
River level 18 Oct. 1966
Dark grey clay

White sand
White sand
Dark grey clay: organic remains at base
Ochreous sand

Unbedded fine white/buff sand

Brown clay and white sand
Buff sand, medium/coarse grain and pebbles
Pebble line with larger stones and artifacts—1st ARTIFACT HORIZON

Medium /coarse grey sand, pebbles and clay lumps

Pebble line with larger stones and artifacts—2nd ARTIFACT HORIZON
Yellow sand with wood
Brown clay
Black clay with wood
Brown clay
Ochreous sand

Buff/yellow sand medium·grain
changing to coarse sand and
pebbles with artifacts below

Pebble line with artifacts   —3rd ARTIFACT HORIZON
Brown clay

Fig. 27. Kalambo Falls Prehistoric Site, Site A: section of A 6 excavation, 1966.

the base of this clay is a further peaty layer with organic matter, compressed leaves and small fragments of fibrous stemmed plants and rootlets; this layer was between $\frac{1}{4}$ and $\frac{1}{2}$ inch thick (5–10 mm). This profile through the black clay bank, here 2 feet $\frac{4}{5}$ inch (61·16 cm) thick, is closely comparable with that from the A 4 trench (see pp. 137–8) and of approximately the same thickness.

The clay bank rests on compact, unbedded, fine white to buff sands which can be identified with bed (29) (White Sands Bed) of the A 4 trench. These sands are 1 foot $\frac{5}{6}$ inch (32·67 cm) thick and are quite sterile. At the junction of the sand and the overlying clay the topmost inch (2·5 cm) of the sand is more compact and stained an ochreous colour by the concentration of iron.

At a depth of 4 feet (1·22 m) a narrow band of brown clay was encountered which was separated from a second and similar band by a thin layer of white, medium-grained, clay sand. This overlay a medium to coarse-grained sand with small pebbles (= (29)) in which, at a depth of 4 feet 6 inches (1·37 m), occurred a pebble line containing a number of artifacts of Acheulian type. Together with the tools were angular and sub-angular rock fragments and cobbles. The artifacts comprised fifteen unmodified flakes including two hand-axe trimming flakes and thirteen flake fragments and chunks, one utilized piece, one small tool and one bevel-based core scraper. They are mostly fresh or slightly abraded. A white clay or clay sand adheres to some of the specimens on this horizon which probably represents the floor of a channel into which the artifacts were washed from a nearby bank. This horizon is referred to as the first artifact horizon and is believed to be part of the same horizon as that uncovered at the base of the A 4 trench in 1959 and about 4 feet (1·22 m) below river level in that year.

Below this first artifact horizon was a further 1 foot (30·50 cm) of the medium to coarse-grained sand with pebbles of up to half an inch (1 cm) long axis and small lumps of grey clay (probably derived and redeposited from a nearby clay bank) and some small fragments of wood. This lower part of the sand is looser, probably bedded, and greyer in colour on account of the increasing amount of fine clay mixture. It rests directly on a second artifact horizon at a depth of 5 feet 8 inches (1·75 m) below the top of the black clay bank (28). This horizon has no thickness and is marked by an accumulation of artifacts and natural stones resting on a 2 inch (5 cm) thick compact, yellow to white, sterile sand. The natural stone component is analysed below and it is immediately noticeable that there are more than three times as many natural stones in this as there are in the underlying, or third, artifact horizon (and the same is true also for the first artifact horizon). The artifacts are, by contrast, also much more numerous, are mostly fresh or very slightly abraded and are, therefore, believed to form part of an actual occupation floor. They comprise three hand-axes and two broken fragments of hand-axes, two cleavers and one cleaver flake, one pick, one chopper, one discoid, five core scrapers, ten small, retouched tools, nineteen utilized pieces, 176 flakes, 219 flake fragments and sixty-six chunks. Not all these are derived from the surface area of the floor within the cylinder, some having been washed into the excavation from outside the wall. Wood fragments also occurred in association with this horizon and the yellow sand, though none showed signs of having been worked by man. The nature of the horizon, as noted above, and the richness of its archaeological content indicate that it represents an Acheulian occupation floor.

The base of the sterile, yellow sand was ochreous in colour and, at a depth of 6 feet (1·83 m) below the surface, rested on a dark brown clay. This was found to be 5 inches (14 cm) thick and consisted of an upper 2 inches (5 cm) thick brown clay, a middle layer of black clay and a lower brown clay also 2 inches (5 cm) thick. Wood fragments were associated with the black clay and one of these has been partly reduced to charcoal from having been burnt in a fire. This deposit probably represents a clay bank that had been dried out and oxidized at some time in the past. Beneath this again was a further deposit of unbedded and sterile, fine white to buff sand, stained to an ochre colour at the contact with the brown clay. This deposit continued for a further 1 foot 4 inches (40 cm) to a depth of 8 feet (2·44 m) when the sand became looser, buff in colour and of medium grain with some small pebbles and artifacts. This rested on yet another brown clay bank on the surface of which was a horizon with larger pebbles, some cobbles and artifacts. This pebble line and the sand immediately above is the third and lowest artifact-bearing horizon encountered in the excavation. It yielded two small scrapers, one of them a finely worked, semi-circular scraper in chert, seven utilized pieces, forty-seven flakes, fifty-seven flake fragments and eighteen chunks. Again the material is fresh or very slightly abraded and this also most probably represents an occupation surface. The excavation was not continued below this line.

The upper part of this profile, down to and including the first artifact horizon, can be correlated with that found in the base of the A 4 trench in 1959. The sediments and two artifact horizons below this are now known for the first time. Since they are lower in the basin, practically horizontal and in primary archaeological context, they presumably represent older horizons than those previously described from Site A, unless it can be shown that the Acheulian occupation horizons at the A 1 end of the river face cliff dip to the west between the A 1 and A 6 excavations to reappear in the latter some 6½ feet (2 m) lower down. Only further excavation of this kind between the two localities can determine this point. The aggregates from the three archaeological horizons are typical of the Acheulian tradition at the Kalambo Falls.

Thirteen more samples for pollen analysis and determination of the macroplant remains were obtained (see Chapter 3) as well as valuable information for future use on the potential of this method of excavation.

COUNT OF NATURAL STONES ON ARTIFACT HORIZONS:
A 6 EXCAVATION

Artifact horizon 2

mm	Qte. block	Qte. cobble	F/Q	Sdst.	D.	Ch.	Qz.	
< 50	4	2	—	4	—	2	—	12
50–100	16	5	4	17	2	7	1	52
100–200	18	—	1	6	1	1	—	27
200–300	—	—	—	—	—	—	—	—
Totals	38	7	5	27	3	10	1	91

Artifact horizon 3

mm	Qte. block	Qte. cobble	F/Q	Sdst.	D.	Ch.	Qz.	
< 50	—	1	—	—	—	—	1	2
50–100	7	2	2	4	—	3	—	18
100–200	8	—	—	—	—	—	—	8
200–300	1	—	—	—	—	—	—	1
Totals	16	3	2	4	—	3	1	29

Qte. Hard quartzite.   D. Dolerite.
F/Q. Feldspathic quartzite.   Ch. Chert.
Sdst. Sandstone.   Qz. Quartz.

THE A 4 TRENCH AND THE SITE A RIVER FACE CLIFF, 1959 AND 1963

BY MAXINE R. KLEINDIENST

Excavation A 4 (Figures 28 and 29)

The A 4 trench was laid out on 4 June 1959, as a cut primarily for stratigraphic purposes. Ten feet wide (3·05 m) and extending 250 feet (76·2 m) back from the edge of the River Face Cliff at Site A, it is located about 20 feet (6·1 m) downstream from the 1956 A 3 trench which had been almost eroded away in 1959 (Figure 19). Areas are designated by a 5 × 5 foot (1·52 × 1·52 m) grid: A and B refer to the east and west halves of the trench; grid lines are 0 to +50, with 0 at the cliff edge; as depth increased it was necessary to add grid lines −1 through −5 on the river end. When reference is made to grid squares, those with a plus number will have the number of the boundary grid line to the south; those with a minus number that of the boundary grid line to the north (Figure 18).

Excavations commenced on 5 June, over the entire length of the trench, using 6-inch 'spits' (15·2 cm)[1] and following the contours of the present surface. At a

[1] The top of the red soil below the humus line was excavated in two 3-inch 'spits' (7·6 cm): from −6 to −9 inches (−15·2 to −22·9 cm) and −9 inches to −1 foot (−22·9 to −30·5 cm). Six-inch 'spits' recommenced below 1 foot.

depth of about 5 feet (1·52 m), on 30 July, the area of excavation was reduced to that of two deep pits upslope—Pit 1 (grid lines 47 to 44) and Pit 2 (grid lines 30 to 26)—and the area downslope of grid line 21 (Plate 19). A north wall was maintained on the o line until 8 August, when it was removed to facilitate the disposal of backdirt into the river downstream. It was also necessary in the course of the downslope digging to step back the heavy clays which contain Iron Age remains and which overlie unconsolidated sands, from 22 August to 10 September.

Until 14 August, Mr Mario Bick and Miss Barbara Anthony were in charge of excavations under the direction of Professor Clark or Mrs Lilian Hodges. From 14 August to 27 September, supervision was undertaken by Mrs Florence Anderson and Mrs Peggy Tindall. I arrived on 21 September, and commenced supervision with Miss Anthony on 28 September. At that time Archaeological Horizon Rubble I-composite (Sections, Figures 28 and 29, bed no. 15) was cleared and ready for removal (Plate 20). Archaeological Horizon Rubble II (bed no. 18) was discovered in the course of investigating what happened to Rubble I near the 21 line. The very thin sloping scatter of Rubble I debris and artifacts had been removed in the course of excavation before the heavier concentration was found downslope at a depth of about 14 feet (4·27 m). The stratigraphically lower Rubble II was preserved in the area between grid lines 16 and 21.

As soon as Rubble I could be lifted, excavations recommenced in the underlying sterile sands and clays (on 7 October). For convenience, an arbitrary datum 'X' was established, which was surveyed-in later as being 66·3 feet in elevation, relative to the trench datum taken as 100·0 feet (20·2 m relative to 30·48 m). I attempted to lessen the danger of slumping by slightly battering the walls below the level of Rubble I (Plate 22). However, the rains began on 5 October, and as depth increased several large falls occurred, fortunately always during the lunch hour. Excavations were consequently moved out to the 12 line on 20 October. The increasing rains limited the final complete clearance of the stratigraphic section to the extreme river end of the trench, where however, a small eastern Extension was made to clear a larger area of the lower pebble line containing Sangoan artifacts (bed no. 24), and of the wood and associated artifacts lying just above the lower black clay bank (bed no. 28). Excavations terminated on 10 November, in a final attempt at least to reach the Acheulian horizons below the clay, and below river level, which was supervised by Mr Neville Chittick, then Director of the Antiquities Division of the Tanganyika Government.

In 1963, from 10 July to 20 August, further work on the upslope half of the

A 4 trench was aimed at more clearly defining the cultural content of Rubble II, and at classifying the sequence below the Red Rubble Bed of the Mbwilo Member (bed no. 14) in Pit 1. This resulted in: the deepening of Pits 1 and 2; the removal of the section between Pit 2 and grid line 21 (the face at line 21 had been eroded back somewhat); and the excavation of Pit 3 (grid lines 36 to 34). Under the direction of Professor Clark and myself, Mr Charles Keller was in constant supervision of Pit 1; Miss Sue Bucklin and Mr David Phillipson of Pit 2 and its northern Extension; and Miss Barbara Anthony of Pit 3. Digging proceeded according to natural horizons in Pit 2 and Extension, by 6-inch 'spits' (15·2 cm) in Pit 1, and by 1-foot 'spits' (30·5 cm) in Pit 3. The deepening of Pit 1 at length required a system of hoists and buckets; Mr John Clark assisted in the construction and maintenance of this device, and also in the deep augering into the bottom of Pit 1.

Stratigraphy and cultural content

The sections of the A 4 trench are shown in Figures 28 and 29. In these sections, the beds have been numbered, so far as is possible, in stratigraphic order from top to bottom and references are made accordingly.

The red and grey clays or sandy clays of the Chiungu Member rest unconformably on the unconsolidated current-bedded sands of the Mbwilo Member. At the base of the latter, the Rubble Bed (I-composite or Ic) of the alluvial facies rests on the 'main erosion surface', and is traceable upslope into the Red Rubble Bed of the colluvial facies. Hence, the Mbwilo Member rests unconformably on various of the deposits of the underlying Mkamba Member. Beds nos. (3) and (5) to (7) are included in the Chiungu Member; beds nos. (9)–(15) in the Mbwilo Member; and beds nos. (16)–(29) in the Mkamba Member. Beds nos. (1), (2) and (4) are parts of the soil profile and have not been classified in any named geological unit, nor has bed no. (8).

The section is capped throughout by red (upslope) to red-brown (downslope) sandy loam (2) with a dark grey to black layer at the surface containing humus and ash (1). Soil-filled pits at top (2a) are connected with Lungu occupation and cultivation in the area prior to excavation. A sample of charcoal found in the top of (2), 13 inches (33 cm) below ground surface, during the stepping-back of the old east face of Pit 1 in 1963, yielded a date of 2,470±40 years B.P. (GrN-4226). The date is older than expected, since it falls within the range of a date from above the microlithic horizon at Site C, rather than being in the range of the Iron Age or post-Iron Age. Hence, the charcoals probably do not date the horizon in which they were found (Appendix J).

Upslope, there is little apparent change in the texture of the soil with increasing depth, although it becomes slightly more gritty and compact, and contains an impersistent horizon of pisolitic iron nodules and pebble horizons near the base (4). Sherds were found to a depth of about 18 inches (45·7 cm); artifacts of 'Magosian' type in mint condition began to be found in (4). These pebble horizons may be traces of short-lived land surfaces, but may equally well be 'stonelines' in the sense of soil science in which both artifacts and debris have been concentrated, presumably due to the activities of soil fauna (Anderson, 1957, p. 6). The soil at Pit 1 rests directly on the Red Rubble Bed (14) without any clear erosional break between although the matrix of the Red Rubble is coarser and more consolidated. At Pits 3 and 2 the soil is in clear contrast with the buff sandy clay (11) that overlies the Red Rubble Bed. The cultural content, if the 'Magosian' is in archaeological context, indicates that the base of the soil profile upslope is older than the red soil downslope.

The top-soil shows indistinct wavy irregular bedding, caused by the grading-out of coarser particles, suggesting an accumulation through colluvial action from the red weathering products on the hills to the south. This banding, or bedding, is more distinct where the sandy loam grades imperceptibly downward into red-brown and brown sandy clays and clays (3) and (5) that contain Iron Age remains.[1] Where these clays are deepest (grid lines o to +6), sherds, daga and slag, and some stone artifacts were found to a depth of 7 feet (2·13 m); below this the deposits seem to have been largely sterile, according to the field notes. Bed (3) is also irregularly bedded at the river end of the trench, due to the sorting-out of grit, fine gravel and pisolitic iron nodules; there is a band of pea-sized gravel and nodules near the base in places where it overlies the more clayey (5) or (6). On the west wall, cutting-back exposed in section a depression filled by dark brown sandy clay (2b) containing sherds, slag and daga, which may have been man-made.

Underlying the brown clays is grey clay (6) which grades down into light grey sandy clay or clayey sand (7). The colour break is clear, but there does not appear to be any discordance between the grey and the overlying brown deposits. The lower contact of (7) with sand (12) is an abrupt change in sedimentation, and appears to be an erosion surface, although (7) might merely have been deposited on the top of (12).

Unfortunately, in these horizons the excavated 'spits' cut across the various natural bedding planes; however it seems clear from the field notes that sherds did not occur in the grey deposits (6) and (7). Only one piece of burnt clay is recorded as coming from a 'grey clay', which must be (7), in grid square A +5 at a depth of 10 feet to 10 feet 6 inches (3·05–3·20 m) below the ground surface.

[1] The sediments described for convenience as 'clays' are actually silts, or clayey silts in grade.

These deposits, or at least (7), did contain a number of stone artifacts in various stages of abrasion, including a few of 'Magosian' aspect in fresh condition which may or may not be in archaeological context. (The point to be shown in volume II from grid square A 20 or 21 in the 'spit' from −5 feet 6 inches to −6 feet (−1·52 to −1·67 m) below the ground surface, is probably from (7).) Some artifacts may have come from the contact with or the top of sand (12), and one small accumulation including a small 'point' (also illustrated in volume II) came from the lens of fine sand with grit (9) between grid lines 0 and +2. This material is of small size, but most shows evidence of transport. For the purpose of a counted sample, all these artifacts have been grouped as those found above Rubble I in Trench A 4.

Sand (9) and a lens of grey to dark grey clay (9') appear to be intermediate between (7) and (12). In 1959 it seemed certain that (7) was distinct from buff sandy clay (11) in the Pit 2 area, being separated from it by a patch of buff sand (10). In 1963, (11) was found to contain mint or fresh artifacts of 'Magosian' type in the Pit 2 Extension. These seemed to be in archaeological context, although they were scattered through some 6 inches (15·2 cm) of the deposit, at a level about 5–6 feet (1·5–1·8 m) below the present ground surface. This cultural evidence suggests the slim possibility that (7) and (11) might be the same deposit, and that (10) may only be an area of disturbance caused perhaps by water seepage, a falling tree, or man. If, however, (7) is the basal deposit in a later channel as seems most probable, then artifacts of 'Magosian' type could easily have been supplied from (11), which was also encountered in the Trench A 2 section (bed no. (5), Figure 24).

Bed (11) is considered as belonging to the Mbwilo Member. In fact, the sections suggest that (11) could interfinger with the Red Rubble Bed between Pits 1 and 3. However, bed (11) is distinct from the matrix of the Red Rubble in Pit 3, and in Pit 2 is different from the matrix below the upper few inches in the Red Rubble; bed (11) overlies the thinned-out and probably resorted Red Rubble in the Pit 2 Extension, but it is not much different from the matrix of the gravel there. Consequently, it is taken as later than the accumulation of the Red Rubble Bed upslope.

Bed (12) is unconsolidated, current-bedded and cross-bedded sand, stained orange by ferruginization, particularly along the bedding planes. The general dip on the cross-bedding is to the north-northwest. The brown colouration at base overlying Rubble I-composite (12a) appears to be a post-depositional feature, although the sand is slightly clayey here and contained a few flecks of charcoal above the rubble line. These resemble fragments of grass blades such as are blown about during and after bushfires. At the river end of the trench (12) grades into and in part overlies (13), a coarse gritty brown sand, somewhat consolidated and containing a few angular fragments of dolerite completely weathered to yellow clay, together with fine gravel.

Only a few artifacts were found just above the level of the main erosion surface and Rubble I-composite (15) at the base of (12). The erosion surface cut through the earlier sterile sands (20) and clay (19), Rubble II (18), and its overlying deposits (16) (17); on it the contents of the Red Rubble Bed and Rubble II have been combined and redistributed. Rubble I probably includes the contents of other, older artifact-bearing horizons as well, since the bulk of medium-sized prepared flakes and cobble anvils at least do not seem to be attributable to either of the two local sources. Alternatively, these may have been added during the time of formation of Rubble I. Some fresh material might be 'Magosian', but diagnostic pieces are lacking.

Elongate cobbles and artifacts in Rubble I showed directional orientation (Figure 10, Chapter 2). Taken in conjunction with the facts that the rocks rest on clean, sorted sand in the bottom of a channel-cut, and are overlain by current-bedded, clean, sorted sand, the orientation probably results from current action. A similar orientation can be measured on cobbles found in the bed of the Kalambo River today (Figure 9, Chapter 2).[1]

The accumulation varies from one stone (3 inches, 7·6 cm) to as much as 18 inches (45·7 cm) in thickness, with the larger artifacts tending to occur with the larger cobbles, again indicating water sorting. Artifacts in all stages of abrasion occur, and there are no really clear-cut groupings according to physical condition. The bulk of the material is slightly abraded to abraded, with the arêtes just rounded-off. Most flakes in this category also have irregular nibbling and chipping of the edges, which can be attributed to the early stages of transport (Kuenen, 1956, p. 352). The fresher large material is probably from Rubble II, and the fresher small material from the Red Rubble Bed—one being older, and the other presumably younger than most of the slightly abraded to abraded cultural material. In the area of grid lines +6 to +8, where the matrix was harder with more fine gravel, the thicker accumulation could in places be divided into two parts with lenses of up to 6 inches (15·2 cm) of coarse sand and fine gravel

[1] It has been suggested by G. Bond (personal communication) that the orientation measured in both Rubble I and II results from slow mass movement (creep), since it is most probable that slopewash and creep transported the material from the slopes surrounding the local basin. However, in the archaeological excavations, the rubbles rest in channels or at least on eroded surfaces; they are generally in a matrix of sorted sand, and in places the overlying deposits are current-bedded. The possibility that the orientation is inherited from transport by mass movement, and unaffected by the later current action indicated by the bedding in the sands, seems unlikely. Because river action is the last process of transport which affected the rubbles seen in excavations, they are here regarded as 'gravels', although most of their components are not well rounded.

between. These might represent Archaeological Horizons Rubbles Ia and Ib in the Mbwilo Member as found in the A 3 trench; because this is uncertain, the entire A 4 artifact content from horizon (15) has been considered to be combined Rubble I-composite. Since these are channel deposits, and moreover contain mainly redistributed artifacts, no great differences could be expected in comparing such small local units, nor were any observed when they were counted separately.

The heavier concentrations of artifacts and rubble were found between the 8 and 12 lines, and north of the +6 line. On the north, or river end of the trench (grid squares A and B +1, +2, −1) where the deposit was 12–14 inches thick (30·5–35·6 cm), the matrix was hard, dark brown sand with fine gravel to 1 inch in size (2·5 cm). Flakes here seemed more weathered. Some large angular chunks 14–18 inches (35·6–45·7 cm) in greatest dimension were encountered here, but these did not show any evidence of use as anvils. The majority of the shaped tools were found north of the 10 line, and these include nearly all which might be considered to be characteristic of the middle to upper parts of the Lupemban range on typological grounds. Most of the shaped tools found south of the 10 line are types which could have come from Rubble II.

The non-artifactual debris was counted in grid square B +1. Nearly all the debris was between 2 and 10 cm in size (0·8–3·9 inches—pieces less than 2 cm or 0·8 inches were not counted). Only fourteen stones ranged between 11 and 16 cm in size (4·3–6·3 inches); only one stone was 25 cm (9·8 inches) in greatest dimension, and one was 30 cm (11·8 inches). The composition of the debris is shown in Table 1. Dolerite was rare in Rubble I, and presumably the fairly abundant weathered dolerite pieces in the Red Rubble Bed, and those from Rubble II, were destroyed by the resorting. The debris did not appear to be much more rounded than that of the Red Rubble however, although the number of angular pieces seems to be somewhat less. Rubble I, from the evidence above, in the A 4 trench was probably first a channel deposit left on the erosion surface, then a lag deposit developed on an exposed slope (when material may have been added by slopewash and creep, as well as by man), and then again at least briefly a channel deposit when sand (12) was being laid-in.

The (? last) channel was obviously cutting against the upper clay bank (19) and the slump-block feature at grid line 16 may be contemporary, since angular fragments of grey clay were included in Rubble I at the foot of the block; also the various thicker accumulations of debris on the erosion surface could be former slumps from which the fine sediments have been removed. The slumping could also have taken place at any later time, perhaps caused by the weight of overburden and seepage along the clay/sand contact. The smaller channel at grid line 22, exposed in the 1963 Pit 2 Extension, may be a high water overflow channel relating to the larger cut downslope. In that case, the area of slumping and contact between the Rubble Bed (I) of the Mbwilo Member and the Rubble Bed (II) of the Mkamba Member is probably more disturbed than it appeared to be in the field in 1959. The small channel could also be an entirely separate, and local feature of drainage into the basin.

The Red Rubble Bed (14) is made up mainly of angular to subrounded fragments of dolerite, quartzite, feldspathic quartzite or quartzitic sandstone, and 'chert' (Table 1, p. 148), in a matrix of more-or-less ferruginized coarse sand and grit. Thus, it seems to be a scree or creep accumulation on an existing land surface, such as can be seen exposed by gullying on the slopes and at the foot of Polungu Hill to the south, although the interbedded lenses of sand suggest that water action—possibly only slopewash—also played a role in its formation. The deposit thins rapidly downslope from Pit 1 to Pit 2 and also, apparently, eastward but seems to be fairly continuous westward and downslope. (It was always encountered in any pitting in the area of the camp.) If the trench is cutting only the northeastern edge of the deposit, it suggests that it is a fan of coarse material that spread out over the area near the mouth of the Spillway Gorge at about the level of the confining ridge of the local basin. Soundings indicate that it is continuous upslope, where it undoubtedly interfingers with the present-day accumulation of hillslope rubble. In the Pit 2 Extension, where the rubble has thinned to become a single unit and a channel deposit, it has probably been resorted.

Components of the Red Rubble Bed range as large as 2 feet (61 cm) in longest dimension in Pit 1, averaging about 4–6 inches (10·2–15·2 cm) in size however; the size range is much more restricted in Pit 2, where debris 2–4 inches (5·1–10·2 cm) in length is most common. Table 1 gives the composition of a sample from the Pit 2 Extension. Unfortunately, no samples were taken from the upslope Pits; the dolerite content in the counted sample is undoubtedly lower than that seen in Pits 1 and 3.

Artifacts typologically assignable to all the Kalambo Falls cultural stratigraphic units might be expected; however, Acheulian and Sangoan types are rare, and the included cultural material seems to be, on typological grounds, late in the range of industries exhibiting prepared-core methods (? Lupemban). The latter observation is based particularly on the small size of some prepared cores. The artifacts cluster in the upper and lower stone concentrations in the pits, and are relatively scarce in the intervening sand lenses, indicating that they have naturally accumulated with the rubble. The cultural content of the Red Rubble Bed in the pits has therefore been grouped into that from the upper, and that from the lower portions. Most of the artifacts are at least slightly abraded, with nibbling and chipping on edges and arêtes either from water transport or from inclusion in scree deposits, which makes utilization from human agency difficult to determine. Most have patination with brown ferruginous staining, and in some cases the chipping and subsequent wear of the chipped edge post-dates the ferruginization. Some material in fresh condition occurs in both top and base, however.

The time relationship between the beginning of the accumulation of the Red Rubble and the initiation of the phase of downcutting of the main erosion surface cannot be determined. Rubble I is traceable upslope into the Red Rubble, but it is not possible to say to what extent the period of formation of the colluvial deposit in the A 4 area equals that of the formation of Rubble I.

The base of the Red Rubble does not clearly rest on an eroded surface. Although the underlying clays of the Mkamba Member (A) (AA) may be swamp or *dambo* deposits and therefore cover some range of time, no evidence of a dry land surface of any duration—marked by a soil for instance—was noted below the base of the Red Rubble Bed. Consequently, its formation may have begun fairly soon after the upper clays of the Mkamba Member ceased being deposited.

It is, in fact, only possible to say that the Red Rubble formed after the top deposits of the Mkamba Member and prior to the channel action and sand deposition of the aggrading river which laid-in sand (12). Thus, the resorting of the Red Rubble into Rubble I could have begun at any point in the existence of the latter deposit. If the C14 date from Rubble Ic in the A 1 trench (*c.* 30,000 years B.P.) actually marks the time at which the downcutting of the main erosion surface had reached nearly to the present river level (see p. 104), then the occurrence of typologically evolved prepared core methods in both the Red Rubble and various areas of Rubble I-composite suggests that the latter may have been exposed as a land surface for a comparatively long period of time—something in the order of 10,000–15,000 years. (Some very small prepared cores were also found in Rubble Ic.) The archaeological evidence fits better with an age of approximately 30,000 years B.P. for Rubble II (pp. 133–5), rather than for Rubble Ic.

The 1963 excavations both clarified and complicated the stratigraphy, as might be expected in dealing with riverine deposits. The Pit 2 Extension uncovered the steep north bank of a hitherto unsuspected phase of channelling, which had just been missed by the edge of Pit 2 in 1959. This Pits Channel Fill is the uppermost deposit of the Mkamba Member which has been found. In Pits 2 and 3, the fill is capped by cream/white (dry colour) sandy clay, clay, and clayey sand (AA) grading down into fine white ferruginous-mottled sand with crumpled thin bedding planes and clay bands (BB) that are possibly post-depositional in origin. The crumpling is most likely to be a slump or compaction phenomenon (slumping of the hillslope can be seen to have taken place in the A 2 trench area). The fine sand continues down to the black clay (16′) overlying Rubble II; the top of the clay is considerably disturbed by the erosion, and chunks were caught-up into the base of the overlying sand. A few artifacts were found in the disturbed zone at the bottom of the Pits Channel, although no rubble is associated. Most could have come from the underlying Rubble II complex. The collection also includes an unmistakable prepared flake (Levallois method) with a faceted platform off a radially prepared core quite unlike any found *in situ* in Rubble II, and seven prepared flakes with parallel dorsal trimming. The incidence of eight prepared flakes out of a total of twenty-six is very high compared with Rubble II. On this slim evidence, the Pits Channel Fill can perhaps be regarded as being within the range of the Lupemban proper.

The south bank of the Pits Channel could be within the still unexcavated area between Pits 3 and 1. However, it appears likely on stratigraphic grounds that the 'rainbow clay' (A) underlying the Red Rubble Bed in Pit 1 grades laterally into clay (AA) (grey-green coloured when wet) which occupies the same position in Pits 3 and 2. There is a distinct break in sedimentation, and probably an erosional break, at the base of the 'rainbow clay' in Pit 1. The correlation is supported by the pollen content: the two samples no. 2349 ('rainbow clay' (A), Pit 1) and no. 2351 (clay (AA), Pit 2) taken in 1959 are regarded as similar (Clark & van Zinderen Bakker, 1964, p. 3; see also Chapter 3, pp. 69–70, and Appendix I). The pollen is interpreted as indicating a woodland of present site altitude or lower, with probably a higher rainfall. These are the only samples at this height above the present river (*c.* +40 feet, 12·2 m) which have yielded pollen counts at present. The clay can be regarded as swamp or overbank deposits at about the upper limit of basin filling allowed by the +31 foot (9·4 m) notch in the Spillway Gorge (see Figure 8, Chapter 2), if the river was graded to that level.

In 1963 a small area of the old A 2 trench was cleared to locate the level of Rubble II there; a 'mixed' rubble with some prepared flakes was found to overlie it. This was taken as Rubble I-composite, as it had been in 1956. However, the characteristics of the overlying sands suggest that they may in fact be the fill of the Pits Channel as in Pits 2 and 3 in the A 4 trench, and therefore that this rubble in A 2 is older than Rubble I (see pp. 112–13).

Immediately below (A) in Pit 1, or separated from it by a few inches of orange-mottled fine sand, is a thin rubble (B) with small components (2–6 inches, 5·1–15·2 cm in size). This rubble included a few artifacts, but no evidence of prepared core methods or diagnostic evolved shaped tools. It might belong, from its position, to the fill of the Pits Channel with (A), or might be an upper member of the Rubble II complex. The latter is considered the more likely possibility.

Below (B) is cross-bedded sand (C), with a general dip on the bedding planes 10° to 20° southwest. It is finer at top and coarser at base overlying a pebble line (D) with pebbles measuring to 1·75 inches (4·6 cm), and lumps of brown clay to 6 inches (15·2 cm) in size. This contained some artifacts, again without prepared core methods, that are considered as part of the Rubble IIa series. Of this material, one small triangular core-axe and one end scraper will be illustrated in volume III.

Coarse, bedded pebbly sand (E), with a dip on the bedding of 6° to 8° southwest, overlies rubble/gravel (F), correlated with Rubble IIa. This in places is separated from rubble/gravel (H), correlated with IIb, by fine and coarse ferruginized sand (G). Below (H) is current-bedded medium and coarse pebbly sand resting on an eroded surface; this surface is correlated with the top of clay (19) downtrench. Below this surface the deposits were explored in a test pit and deep auger holes (see west wall section, Figure 28).

In the test pit, fine clayey sand (I) with clay bands grades down into (K), a bank of black to brown clay and sandy clay which contained two flakes. Both of these are unprepared: one is an end struck, secondary flake of sandstone, fresh but disintegrating, with a plain platform, $70 \times 50 \times 30$ mm in size; the other is a primary, side struck flake of quartzite, fresh, with a cortex platform, $90 \times 95 \times 30$ mm in size.

A small sample of charcoal from (K), obtained 8 feet 9 inches to 10 feet (2·67–3·05 m) below the datum in grid squares B 44 and 45, gave a date of $> 43,850$ years B.P. (GrN-4261). This is comparable to dates on samples from below clay (19), taken in 1959 (below).

Below the dark clay, the auger holes indicated a series of alternating variously coloured sandy clays, clayey sands, and fine sands (beds (L) through (S)), until the auger was stopped at a depth of about 19 feet 6 inches (5·94 m) below the Pit 1 1963 datum of 78·8 feet (24·01 m) by disintegrated pebbles of quartzite and dolerite (T). The black/brown clay (K) appears to be the equivalent of grey-banded clay (19) downtrench, or may be slightly lower stratigraphically. The augered series compares with the sterile sands and clays (20) to (23), and the pebbles (T) with the pebble lines containing Sangoan artifacts (24) (24′).

In the Pit 2 Extension, the uppermost deposit which predates the Pits Channel is a buff clay (CC′) on the east wall, underlain by grey sandy clay (CC), grading into fine grey clayey sand (DD) and laterally into fine white sand on the west wall; then comes a weathered grey clay (EE) grading down into a less weathered, darker grey clay (FF), with banded clay and fine clayey sand at the base. Clays

(EE) and (FF) seem to be part of a soil profile. The basal clay and clayey sand can be seen on the west wall to grade laterally into a bank of unconsolidated fine white sand with ferruginous mottling (16) that becomes coarse sand at the 21 line, and against which the overlying fine sediments are banked. These sediments, together with the underlying black clay (16') which contains pebble stringers and artifacts above Rubble IIa proper, appear to be bank and/or overbank deposits of a laterally migrating stream that was depositing the Rubble II complex (18) and its coarse grey sand with silt or clay matrix (17) in the channel. This channel would also appear to have been graded to the +31 foot (9·4 m) notch in the Spillway Gorge, with infilling here proceeding from north to south as does the filling by the Kalambo River today in the Site A area.

In Pit 2, and presumably also in Pit 3 although here only IIa was excavated, Rubble II (bed 18) is overlain by or in part contained within a matrix of black to grey-brown clay (16') and in coarse sand with silt or clay matrix (17) which rests on the surface of a massive grey-and-white banded clay bank (19). The top of this clay seems to be equivalent to the erosion surface between beds (L) and (J) in Pit 1. The colour banding, which can also be seen in places in the lower clays (21–22) (21'–22'), is actually a kind of varving due to the sorting of coarser from finer particles in thin layers.

Charcoals found in the dark clay (16') in grid squares A and B 23 and 30 gave a date of 31,660 ± 600 years (GrN-4648). Although from slightly above Rubble II proper, this seems a reasonable date for Rubble II, and its included cultural content.

Archaeological Horizon Rubble II is divisible into two parts, Horizons IIa and IIb, in most of Pit 1, and downtrench as far as the 21 grid line, beyond which it is in places a composite accumulation. Single stones, artifacts, and pebble stringers were also found in Pit 2 above the main IIa, but below the zone of Pits Channel disturbance, and these have been considered part of IIa as was pebble line (D) in Pit 1. With the small sample obtained, the artifact content of Rubble II in Pit 1 can only be regarded as the same as that found in the other pits, based particularly on the occurrence of parallel-sided core-axes, supporting the correlation of (D) (F) (H) with (18). (The artifact aggregate from Rubble II undoubtedly covers some time span: the gravels are laterally time-transgressive, and the collection from any one area includes some transported artifacts which might pre-date the gravels.)

Most artifacts from Rubble II are fresh, or only very slightly abraded, and differences between groups separated on the basis of physical condition can be better explained by the processes of natural sorting than by typological development. The artifact aggregate can be regarded as early in the range of industries

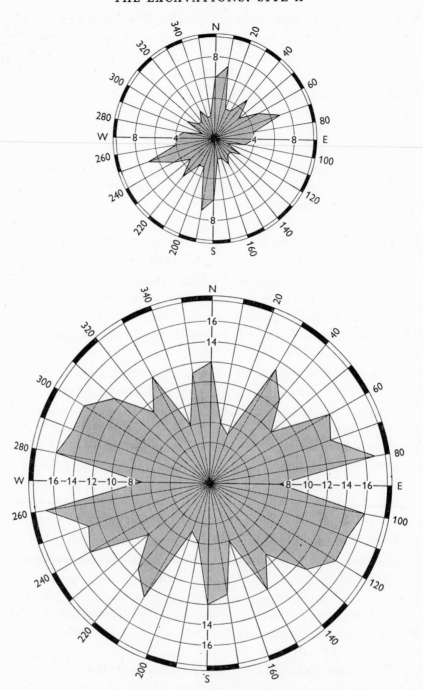

Fig. 30 Diagrams showing frequency and orientation of long axes of boulders in Rubbles IIa and IIb at A 4 excavation, 1963.

with prepared core methods (? lower Lupemban), although the incidence of these methods is low. Parallel-sided core-axes make their appearance here. The sample from the trench A 4 Rubble II may not be entirely representative. Some types of artifacts, such as the large blades found elsewhere in Rubble I—particularly in the A 1 and River Face trenches at Site A—for which no original context is yet known, would appear to fit typologically with the Rubble II material. Their absence is as likely to be caused by the processes of natural sorting as by human activities—or rather the lack of them—in the A 4 area since no flakes of the large size range were found in the A 4 Rubble II sample.

The possibility that during the phase in which Rubble II gravels were deposited channelling actually cut well down into the local basin cannot be entirely discounted, because the remaining areas of exposure are restricted. This adds another unblocking and blocking of the Spillway Gorge, however, and the remaining areas of Rubble II show only a low dip toward the axis of the local basin.

The source of the coarse material in Rubble II then is a problem. If the river could not remove the sediments filling the basin, it can hardly be assumed to have been actively transporting gravels even at flood stage. A steeper tributary or scree from the south may have supplied the coarse material, since the dolerite content amounts to 3 or 4 per cent (sight estimate) (Table 1). An older, as yet undiscovered, rubble/gravel at this altitude is also a possibility.

Orientation diagrams are given in Figure 30, for measurements taken in Pit 2 and the Pit 2 Extension. In IIa only sixty-five elongated cobbles could be measured, but these show a strong orientation north-south, and east-northeast to west–southwest. In IIb, on a more adequate sample of 203 elongated cobbles, the orientation is not as marked, but seems to be east-northeast to west-southwest and west-northwest to east-southeast. These, together with the direction of dip on the cross-bedding in the sands in Pit 1 suggest the downstream current direction was southwesterly at this point.

The bulk of the deposits below the banded grey clay bank (19) belong to a single continuous period of deposition, and to the Ochreous Sands and Grey Clay Beds of the Mkamba Member. They are uniformly sterile,[1] structureless fine sand (20) (20′) with ferruginous staining, grading down into intercalcated lenses of grey brown sandy clay (21) (21′) that in turn grade down into brown clay (22) (22′). Charcoal flecks and pieces were found in the upper part of the sand. One sample (GrN-3196) from just north of the 15 line, in the west wall,

[1] The only finds in bed (20) were two quartzite cobbles found about 1 foot (30·5 cm) below Rubble I, one in grid squares 16 and the other in grid squares 10, and one trimming flake thought to have fallen from above.

and 6 inches (15·2 cm) below Rubble I-composite gave a date of 40,600±1,300 years; another small sample of charcoal from about 6 inches (15·2 cm) lower and underneath clay (19) in grid square 16 near the west wall (GrN-3226) gave 46,000+3,500−2,400 years, considered less exact than the first. Charcoal flecks also occurred in the brown clay (22'), but on the small sample obtained only a determination of > 32,000 years could be given (GrN-3608).

The date of > 43,850 years from (K) in Pit 1, approximately correlated with clay (19), may be interpreted as in general agreement with these dates from slightly below (19). If these dates are correct for the top of the Ochreous Sands, the approximately 31,000 years date for the top of Rubble II complex suggests that clay (19) covers some appreciable time span and/or that the erosion preceding Rubble II was more marked than it appears in the restricted exposures in Trench A 4. The C14 dates from the Ochreous Sands do not all agree with the stratigraphic positions of the samples, however (below).

A pollen sample from (22') at the 16 line, about 6 feet (1·83 m) below the C14 samples in bed (20), suggests open vegetation with cooler and wetter conditions than the present (no. 2365, Chapter 3). Professor van Zinderen Bakker noted that many grains were contracted in this sample, and all samples from above this level have proved to be barren except for those from the clay at the top of the Pits Channel Fill. This must indicate either that conditions for the preservation of pollen were poor at the time of deposition of the various sediments, or that at some later time the water table had fallen sufficiently in the basin to allow these sediments to dry out completely so that contained pollen was destroyed. Today, however, all the sediments are moist when excavated during the dry season, and water seepage through Rubble II hindered the digging. The pollen in the top of the Pits Channel Fill may have been preserved by constant surficial moisture below the Red Rubble Bed.

A sudden change in sediment grade takes place at (24) where the fine sand gives way to current-bedded, discontinuous stringers of fine gravel with pebbles to 2 inches (5·1 cm) in size—most being under 1 inch (2·5 cm)—in a matrix of coarse ferruginized sand (25), interstratified laterally with fine sand and clay lenses. This deposit varies considerably in thickness (from a few inches to several feet), and can be roughly separated in the excavated portion into two levels: an upper portion, exposed from the +6 to the −1 line where it petered out; and a lower portion, exposed from the +1 to the −5 line. The pebble stringers contained a few larger cobbles of sandstone, quartzite, dolerite and chert up to 9 inches (22·9 cm) in greatest dimension, together with Sangoan artifacts. These last are mainly primary and secondary trimming flakes in mint or very slightly abraded condition, with only a few small flake tools, cores, picks, and core-axes.

Their condition indicates little or no transport, and their size is not in equilibrium with the grade of fine gravel which the stream was then moving. However, it is possible that the artifacts and few cobbles were the only material of larger size available to the stream. There is no visible erosion surface, and the artifacts were found at various levels in the deposit (24). The pebble stringers are separated by 3–18 inches (7·6–45·7 cm) of fine sand (26) from the top of the lower black clay bank (28), except in the Extension and in A 4 grid square −5 where there is a single band of pebbles resting on or almost on the clay.

Resting on or just above clay (28) in sand (26) are tree-trunks and branches, some patches of matted vegetal matter (27), and flat lumps of clay to 10 inches (25·4 cm) in diameter which contain organic matter, together with a few artifacts, and angular and rounded cobbles to 9 inches (22·9 cm) in diameter—dolerite being weathered to clay. The top of the black clay was taken as the base of the Ochreous Sands and Grey Clay Beds in 1959; however, the 1963 excavations on the River Face (A 5 trench) indicated that sand (26) is likely to be a remnant of, or resorted, upper White Sands and Dark Clay Beds. This is supported by the C14 date on one of the logs of > 49,000 years (GrN-3211), which exceeds any of the dates on material from the Ochreous Sands at either Site A or B. It is not absolutely clear where the boundary should be drawn in the A 4 trench since there is no distinct eroded surface. The channel action at the base of the Ochreous Sands can be traced across the River Face Cliff from the A 1 to the A 5 trench at a level about 6 feet 6 inches (1·98 m) above 1959 low water level (see Figure 32), and the pebble stringers with Sangoan artifacts continue downstream at approximately the same level from A 4. In consequence, sand (26) is provisionally included in the White Sands Beds of the Mkamba Member.[1]

A pollen sample taken from just above the wood at the −1 line, west wall, in sand (26) (no. 2378, Appendix I) gave evidence of closed woodland, with higher temperature and precipitation than the present day.

The top of clay (28) dips southwest (13° to 211°); the tree-trunks are all resting with their crowns in the direction of the dip suggesting first that this was the downstream direction, and second that the area may have been, or been near, a channel bank at the time of their deposition. The location of an Acheulian occupation area (A 5 trench) a short distance away tends to confirm the last interpretation. (As noted, the logs might have been disturbed or even deposited by later channel action however.)

The black clay bank consists of a black peaty layer made up of organic matter

[1] Sands (26) may be White Sands or basal Ochreous Sands; in either case, the wood may belong to the uppermost White Sands time range. It could also belong to the time range of the Ochreous Sands, though this seems less likely. The pollen sample should also be evaluated with these uncertainties in mind.

(flat-lying leaves, twigs, and seeds) in a silty-clay matrix (28a) that included a few artifacts assigned to the latest Kalambo Falls Acheulian on the basis of evidence in the A 5 trench (below); a blue-white structureless layer in the centre (28b); a second black layer with organic matter (28c); and in places a thin band of brown colour at the base (28d). The origin of the white layer is puzzling. Spectrographic analysis (Appendix B) indicated only that it is composed of finely divided silica.

Below the clay bank are the unbedded, fine white sands (29) that characterize the Acheulian horizons in the A 1 trench and at Site B. The attempt to verify this in 1959 uncovered only a thin pebble band about 4 feet (1·2 m) below the river level of that date. This horizon included only one hammerstone, one small scraper, thirty-nine small flakes, most of which were slightly abraded or abraded, and eight chips and chunks.

Two samples, taken from the −3 grid line on the east wall of the A 4 extension, at depths of 1 foot 6 inches (45·7 cm, no. 2387) and 2 feet 3 inches (68·6 cm, no. 2388) below the base of the black clay both contained a little pollen. The vegetation might be interpreted as that characteristic of a stream bank today (van Zinderen Bakker, personal communication). The next higher sample, from 1 foot (30·5 cm) above the base of the black clay (28c) at the −3½ grid line on the west wall (no. 2383, Appendix I) provided good evidence of a fringing forest along an active river, and of vegetation characteristic of warmer and drier conditions than the present. Although no depositional break is observable, samples taken from 5 inches (12·7 cm) higher in (28c) (no. 2382), from (28b) (no. 2381), and from (28a) (no. 2380) all indicate conditions cooler and wetter than the present, with the surroundings covered by open woodland. Thus the black clay accumulation covers some appreciable time period of real climatic change, even if some shift in the pollen spectrum can be taken as due to the migration of the river channel. (Redeposition of older pollens is always possible, but no evidence was observed to suggest that such is the case here.) The Acheulian people first occupied the site during a period similar to the present, and occupation continued during a cooler and wetter time.

River Face Cliff, 1959 and 1963, and the A 5 trench (Figures 31 and 32)

When it became apparent that the stratigraphy in the 1959 A 4 trench differed from that found in the 1956 A 1 trench, I decided to clear to some extent the entire cliff facing the Kalambo River in order to connect the two trenches directly. Time allowed only Rubble I and its subdivisions to be traced across the cliff face, with two test pits into the underlying sediments (Plate 23). A few work-

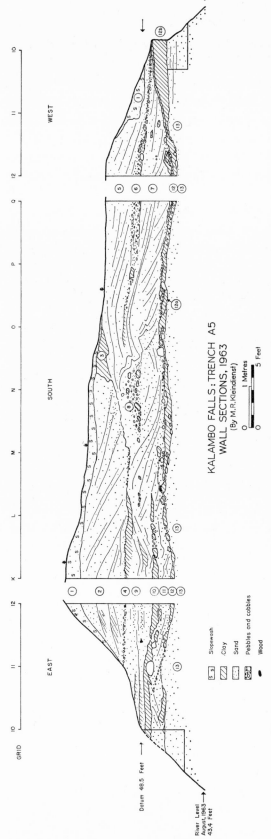

KALAMBO FALLS: TRENCH A5
WALL SECTIONS, 1963
(By M.R.Kleindienst)

Fig. 31. Kalambo Falls, Site A, River Face (1963) Excavation A 5.

LITHOLOGY

Bed
no.

1 Surface wash, redeposited sand.

2 Bedded fine and medium sand, with some sorting out of coarse
   sand at base of foreset bedding; ferruginized on bedding planes.

3 Grey clay.

4 Pebble stringer, clayey in part, containing flakes.

5 Fine sand, cross-bedded, and ferruginized on the bedding planes.

6 Pebble band composed of coarse sand, pebbles to 1 cm size,
   lumps of buff clay to 5 cm size or occasionally larger, and Sangoan
   flakes and core-axes; clayey in places.

7 Cross-bedded fine sand, with a few flakes in south wall, changing
   to medium sand in west wall where it includes pebbles to 1·5 cm
   and clay lumps to 2 cm size.

8 Patch of pebbles and coarse sand containing lumps of clay to
   15 cm size—some rolled, some angular—and flakes.

9 Alternating layers of fine and coarse sand, with some clay lenses;
   contained charcoal flecks and pieces in southeast corner of trench,
   and 1 piece of wood at base.

10 Band of grey clay, containing cobbles and some flakes in the
   southeast corner of the trench.

11 Bedded coarse sand, containing numerous flakes at base, together
   with pebbles to 5 cm size, and a few pieces of wood; changes to
   medium sand at the 'N' line.

12 Horizon(s) containing Final Acheulian artefacts, pebbles, cobbles,
   and lumps and patches/lenses of brown or grey clay. In the south
   wall are undisturbed areas of brown clay, with white lenses (12a);
   here, artefacts were found on, in, and under the clay which is continuous with the top of the black clay bank in the west wall (12b).

13 Fine white to buff sand, with some patchy ferruginization; sterile
   to river level.

men carried out the clearance, from 22 October to 10 November, supervised by Miss Anthony and myself.

I briefly visited the site on 5 September 1961 in company with Dr E. G. Haldemann. The high river, during the heavy rains of 1959 and 1960, had cutback and cleaned the section, showing that an *in situ* Acheulian horizon was present on what seemed to be a sandbank situation between Trenches A 4 and A 1. The black clay (28) was then seen to rise and grade laterally into white silt upstream of A 4, to thin-out over the top of a bank of fine sand, and to recommence as a dark clay bank containing logs of wood on the A 1 side. It was not clear, however, which, if any, of the A 1 Acheulian horizons was involved. Consequently, excavations were planned for this area in 1963. Further cutting by the river in the intervening two rainy seasons had again changed the observable section, and undoubtedly removed a valuable sector of the A 5 trench Acheulian occupation area, much of which today can be found on the adjacent bed of the Kalambo River.

The 1963 River Face Trench (A 5) and an Extension eastward to the area of the old A 1 trench at a level just above the water line were excavated from 12 August to 23 August. Miss Anthony and Miss Bucklin aided in directing the excavations. A portion of an Acheulian occupation area was uncovered, over an area of 10 × 30 feet (3·05 × 9·14 m), in part disturbed by stream action which marks the base of the Ochreous Sands Beds; this could be placed as approximately contemporary with or older than Floor IV in the A 1 trench.

Stratigraphy and cultural content

On the detailed section of Trench A 5 (Figure 31), bed no. (1) is surface wash, beds (2) to (10) belong to the basal Ochreous Sands and Grey Clay Beds, and bed (11) is considered to be a remnant of the White Sands and Dark Clay Beds of the Mkamba Member. Bed (12) was brown clay on the east, tracing into black clay (12b) on the west which is the same as at least the upper portion of clay (28) in Trench A 4. Acheulian artifacts were found in bed (12), which was doubled in the northwestern part of the trench; the central portion had been the base of later channelling, but on the eastern end of the A 5 trench the artifacts appeared to be in primary archaeological context, and in the southwestern corner were found, undisturbed, in and under clay (12), and also resting on top of the clay in less certain context. Bed (13) is fine white sands, which continue below river level.

The Composite Section (Figure 32) and its description are a compilation of 1956, 1959, and 1963 excavations, with some additional information from the 1961 observations. Because of the erosion of the Kalambo River in this area between 1956 and 1963 (Figure 19), the section does not represent a single vertical plane. It must therefore be taken as somewhat generalized, but with correct elevations. Reference should be made to the detailed discussions of the stratigraphy of the various trenches. The following bed numbers apply only to the Composite Section.

At the top of the River Face Cliff, the red sandy loam (2) with its upper greyblack horizon (1) is continuous across the face, grading down into three (possibly only two) separate channel fills. The 'Younger Channel' fill, containing Iron Age remains where excavated in the A 1 trench, is made up of red clay and sand with charcoal lenses, and a grit and fine gravel horizon at base (3). It was seen to cut the 'Older Channel' fill just downstream of A 1, and in the west wall of that excavation. The channel fill in the A 4 trench is made up of the red to brown clayey horizons containing Iron age artifacts at the top, and grey deposits at the base (4). Only the upper portion with red-brown clays can be traced to the A3 trench, and then, apparently, to the 'Older Channel' fill near A 1, or even to the top of the 'Younger Channel' fill. The upper part of the River Face Cliff could not be cleared in 1959, although (4) seemed to be traceable to (5) (Plate 23). In 1963, only (1) and (2) could be seen overlying the sands of the Mbwilo Member between A 4 and the 'Older Channel' fill.

In the 'Older Channel' fill, the top-soil (2) grades down into red-brown clays (5), and then into yellowish clay (6), which is underlain by red sandy clay and clay (7), and by grey-brown clay (8) and grey clay (9). In the A 1 trench, black silts and brown sand (10) overlie gritty orange sand (11). Bed (11) was traced to a coarse gravel deposit at the base of the 'Older Channel' in the River Face, made up mostly of sub-angular blocks including large fragments of fresh dolerite to 2 feet (61 cm) in largest dimension, which suggests that they were supplied directly from the source of dolerite to the south. The small area of clearance in 1959 produced only a few abraded flakes, and some potsherds. In the top of bed (9) the greater portion of a restorable Channelled Ware pot was found, associated with a fragment of broken grinding stone. The 1963 excavations at Site C indicate that this is likely to have been related to a burial; no evidence of an artificial fill was noted in 1959.

Although in the A 4 trench deposits (4) might conceivably follow almost directly on the deposition of the underlying sands, in the River Face Cliff the 'Older Channel' clearly cuts across the fill and minor rubbles overlying Rubble Ic. The base of the channel in A 4 is about 10 feet (3·05 m) above the bottom of the channels in the River Face. The fill of the A 4 channel may be the same as that of the 'Older Channel', this is by no means certain, since these channels may relate to a southern tributary of the Kalambo, very likely the same as enters upstream of the A 1 trench today: the tributary appears to have been shifting its channel eastward as the Kalambo cut down (but see pp. 92–3). Although all these channels and fills belong to the same general phase of river activity, the cutting and filling at different spots are unlikely to be strictly contemporary, and probably overlap in a complex fashion. Abandonment of a channel presumably led to its silting-up, a process which is likely to have been facilitated by man. The Lungu are today impeding the active tributary by growing bananas in its lower course. Obstructed or abandoned channels would be areas of overbank deposition by flooding from the main river, and of deposition of sediments brought in from the valley slopes.

The sediments overlying Rubble I-composite in A 4 at the cliff face (16') (16) (17) were not directly traceable to A 3, although a grey clay which is probably (16) was exposed in the southwestern corner of that trench (bed 8, Figure 26). In A 3, variously coloured sands (12) (13) (14) (15) overlie the main erosion surface; in the River Face clearing of 1959, sand (14) was coarse to medium, and somewhat ferruginized, and (15) was fine sand. On tracing Rubble I-composite upstream from the A 4 trench, it was found to bifurcate just beyond the area of the A 3 trench—as it did locally in A 4, and in the southern part of the A 3 excavation—into Rubbles Ia (18) and Ib (20) with bedded, fine ferruginized sand between (19). It almost immediately again split to become Ib and Ic (25). The deposits between include a lens of light grey clay (21) in the River Face Cliff which is probably more-or-less the same as the sequence in the eastern half of Trench A 1, where orange-red sand overlies a pebble band (22a) that contained a mixture of Lupemban artifacts. This band may correlate with (20) or it may be a different pebble horizon altogether. It is underlain by a series of interbedded grey clays and fine buff sands (22), followed by cross-bedded medium sand, gritty at base (23), and coarse brown sand (24) which contained pebbles and flakes scattered through the more gritty central portion. The artifacts seem to be the usual mixture of types probably belonging to various industries within the range of prepared core methods (Lupemban). All show some degree of abrasion. Pollen samples from the (22) series all indicate open woodland with a cooler climate than the present (nos. 764, 765, 766, 2347, Appendix I).

Rubbles Ia and Ib seem to be minor breaks in the refilling of the basin when coarse material from the exposed lag/gravel deposits upslope was redistributed downward, with some addition of (?) contemporary artifacts of 'Magosian' type, and charcoals. In the face clearance no artifacts were found in Ia, and only a few in Rubble Ib. All of these showed some degree of abrasion, and practically all are small (< 60 mm); the only shaped tools are three small side scrapers.

Rubble I-composite/Ic represents an erosional break, and contains an increasing concentration of artifacts as it cuts through earlier implementiferous beds. It is thought that a gravel bar exposed by the present river just east of the confluence of the southern tributary, and the A 1 trench, may also be Rubble Ic (Plate 26); this then would be the lowest exposed level of that horizon. In A 1, although not in the plane of the River Face section, Rubble Ic is also in part subdivided by sand lenses into three parts (Ic(i), Ic(ii), and Ic(iii)). In the River Face, just adjacent to A 1, it had doubled in one area. Because this is probably not contemporary with the more important subdivision in A 1, the River Face collection has all been considered to be Rubble Ic. Rubble Ic can be seen to truncate the underlying Ochreous Sands deposits containing Sangoan artifacts (especially 32) and even those with Acheulian (37). Therefore in the A 1 trench area it can be expected to contain, and does include, some Acheulian artifacts, and more tools of Sangoan type than it does upslope in A 4 where most of the heavy-duty tools must come from Rubble II.

In the A 4 trench, interbedded sterile fine sands and clays (26) (27) have a coarser horizon at, or near, the base which contains mint to very slightly abraded artifacts (29). This horizon is traceable for some distance downstream of A 4 (29e); upstream it traces to patches of coarser material containing Sangoan artifacts in the A 5 trench (29a) (29b) (29c),[1] which are 1 foot 6 inches to 3 feet (46–91 cm) above the horizons with Acheulian tools. Other, basal lenses of pebbles contain artifacts, as at (31) and (32) where the southwesterly dipping fine sands with ferruginous mottling (26a) rest in a cut through the upper horizons of the White Sands with Acheulian artifacts. It is difficult to say in these cases how much of the artifact content is Sangoan; the few large tools seem to be of Acheulian type although there are no firm grounds for restricting them to that techno-typological tradition.

A fragment of wood found in the east wall of Trench A 5 in fine sand (26a), above clay (31) and stratigraphically slightly below the patches with Sangoan artifacts dated 37,450±600 years B.P. (GrN-4259). (This is the wood shown in bed no. (9) on the A 5 section, Figure 31.) Charcoal flecks scattered through the sand for about 1 foot (30·5 cm) above the wood fragment dated >38,850 years (GrN-4260).

The radiocarbon dates from the Ochreous Sands are not consistent with their stratigraphic positions (Appendix J). Those from near the top in the A 4 trench are 'older' than those from near the base in the A 5 trench, and roughly of the same order as that from near the base in the A 1 trench (L-399C). In addition to

---

[1] A C14 date (GrN-4227) on a wood fragment from the clay at (29a) gave an unexpected, completely modern date. The physical appearance of the wood was the same as that of pieces giving dates in the 40,000 year range in A 4, and as that of sample GrN-4259.

the usual sources of error, the discrepancy may in some cases be due to the fact that dated wood fragments are actually root fragments whose age does not reflect that of the horizon in which they are found (?L-399C, GrN-4259). Using two standard deviations of error, the base may be as old as 50,000 years B.P. (L-399C); the top as young as 38,000 years B.P. (GrN-3226). Sample GrN-3228 from the B 2 trench suggests a still lower date for the upper Ochreous Sands.

The erosional break between the Ochreous Sands Beds and the White Sands Beds of the Mkamba Member could be seen in the southern part of the A 1 trench. It is not as clearly marked in the River Face Cliff, and, as noted above, the division in A 4 is provisional. Sands (33a) (34) (35) and (35a) all appear to be part of the Ochreous Sands; sands (33) (33b) (36) and (38) of the White Sands, which in places may be disturbed or resorted remnants. These contain flakes in areas of coarser sand deposition, many of which were probably caught up from disturbed Acheulian horizons as was seen to be the case in the 1963 A 5 excavation; here, a floor originally associated with a thin clay layer (= top of 43a) was subsequently torn up, but the larger tools and cobbles at least were not removed.

The uppermost Acheulian horizons at Kalambo Falls are themselves discontinuous pebbly layers (37) (39) (41) and (43) separated by fine sands (38) (40) (42), which in the A 1 trench bank against the eroded clay bed (43c). This clay in 1963 was traced in the A 5 Extension to the cut-out by (31), and seems at least in part contemporary with the clay (43) and the black clay bank (43a) associated with Acheulian artifacts. The pollens included in (43c) and the upper part of (43a) are similar in pertaining to a cooler, wetter period (sample nos. 768, 769, and 2380, 2381, 2382, Appendix I). A C14 date (GrN-4228) on a piece of wood from horizon (37) where it overlies (38b) and (43b) in the A 5 Extension has given a count of $> 52,000$ years, which roughly parallels the date of $> 49,000$ years on wood from (33) in A 4 (GrN-3211). An enriched sample of this wood (GrN-4896) gave a finite date of $61,200 \pm 1,280$ years, approximately the same as the date of $60,300 \pm 750$ years (GrN-2644) from lower in the White Sands at Trench A 1 (1955).

The deposits underlying the dark clays (43) (43a) (43b) and (43c) are the same wherever they have been exposed. These are fine white sands (44) (48) and (50) containing wood, pebble horizons (45) and (46), and Acheulian occupation areas (47) and (49). The A 5 Extension uncovered a few artifacts at (45) in 1963: one large scraper;[1] twelve small flakes, all between 31 and 60 mm in size, with only

---

[1] The end and side scraper is of particular interest in that there is a use facet on the undersurface at the end, at an angle of 148° with the flat ventral surface. This appears to result from bruising and rubbing motions, and has a 'pecked' rather than a polished surface. The angle of steep, resolved

two slightly abraded and one abraded; and two chips and chunks. The depth to which these sands continue below river level—where logs of ancient wood can be seen outcropping—has not been ascertained (see Trench A 6).

Conclusions

The evidence is summarized in Table 2. At Site A, deposits bearing Acheulian artifacts reached an elevation of about 3 feet (0·9 m) above the approximate present-day low water level of the Kalambo River. These deposits are separated by some time interval from the stratigraphically higher horizons containing Acheulian artifacts, represented by the deposition of most of a 4 foot (1·2 m) thick clay bank in the A 4 trench, and by deposition and erosion of a more-or-less contemporary clay bank in A 1. The uppermost Acheulian artifact-bearing horizons in places have been disturbed by river action, but do not appear to have been completely formed by that action. Rather they seem to have been associated with an area of temporary sandbank deposition and removal, resulting in frequent minor discordances and many stratigraphic puzzles during excavation. The lower part of the White Sands Beds seems to have accumulated during somewhat more stable conditions of deposition, and without question the Acheulian artifacts are found in these as occupation areas in primary archaeological context. The difference may be due to varying proximity to the river channel at different times, although pollen analyses show that a climatic change to cooler, wetter conditions was also involved. The topmost Acheulian horizons are found to a level of about +6 feet (1·8 m) today, and some may have been removed by the later erosion. Deposits to about this elevation may well have been formed by a river flowing at approximately the same level as today, since it can be observed that the Kalambo River is laying-in—from the gravel-covered channel bottom to the top of the presently forming sandbank—some 10–12 feet (3·05–3·7 m) of sediments on the point bar opposite the mouth of the A 4 trench.

As shown on the plan of Site A (Figure 19), the Kalambo River today is cutting against the south bank, and in the course of seven years has shifted its bank from 15 to 30 feet (4·57–9·14 m) southward in this area. Deposits are forming concurrently on the north bank: the sandbank mentioned opposite Trench A 4 was much enlarged between 1959 and 1963. The lateral infilling from the north must encroach on whatever sediments lie on the river bed (an erosion surface). Observations made when swimming in the river indicate that the larger cobbles

trimming is 78° to 95°, and the facet suggests that the trimmed edge was held approximately vertical to the plane of work. The scraper is of hard feldspathic quartzite in fresh condition, made on a chunk, and measures 110 × 90 × 50 mm.

and artifacts obtained in some abundance from the eroding south bank at Site A can be found on the river bed in the adjacent area; flakes also appear not to have been removed although the quantity of these is harder to estimate under water. A certain amount of wood—both ancient and modern—can also be found.

The river regimen has undoubtedly been somewhat upset by the supply of backdirt from the excavations, and further by a large slump in 1962 near Site D, on the right bank of the Kalambo, south of the mouth of the Kaposwa River. There the Kalambo was compelled to shift to the back channel while re-excavating its normal channel; the coarse debris, consisting of angular fragments from the hillslope colluvium and some large subrounded boulders to 2 feet (61 cm) in size which appear to derive from the base of the colluvium, was left behind even though when it broke through the barrier one can assume the river had more than its normal competence for transport.

Most coarse material is deposited by the Kalambo before it reaches the excavation areas in the older riverine sediments (see Chapter 2 and Appendix A). It is probable that if some of the coarse debris obtained from the erosion of these sediments is shifted downstream, much or most of it is not moved out of the local basin as even medium-grade sands are being left on the sandbars. Therefore, under present-day conditions, the Kalambo River accumulates coarse debris in the Site A area while removing the fine sediments, and as it migrates laterally southward it forms contemporary sand deposits overlying the gravel deposits in the channel bottom. Some finer materials are deposited in the back channels as overbank deposits, and these at times include coarser pebble horizons with small stone artifacts and sherds (see Figure 6, Chapter 2).

At Site A, the channelling which separates the Ochreous Sands, with Sangoan artifacts, from the White Sands, with Acheulian artifacts, does not appear as a major erosion episode or as a major time break, and it seems the White Sands deposits may have nearly their original thickness. (At Site B the channel at the base of the Ochreous Sands cuts deeply below present river level, but into the lower part of the White Sands.) However, if the C14 dates from the A 1 and A 5 trenches actually pertain to the lower part of the Ochreous Sands, then the dates from the upper part of the White Sands in the A 5 Extension and A 4 suggest that a longer time interval is involved than is apparent geologically. There is little convergence between the Acheulian and the Sangoan at Kalambo Falls, aside from a few artifacts with specific Sangoan attributes found in the uppermost Acheulian horizons. If a cultural continuum is assumed, this might also be taken as evidence of a time break.

The accumulation of the Ochreous Sands and grey clay deposits, favoured by Lungu ladies for making pottery today, probably initially coincided with a swing to warmer conditions but spanned at least one later cooler phase, and presumably requires a blockage of the Spillway Gorge. Sedimentation continued until channelling with Rubble II as its basal deposits, at about $+30$ feet ($9 \cdot 1$ m). This did not remove the blockage, and filling continued to about $+40$ feet ($12 \cdot 2$ m) in A 4. This fill may be just about contemporary with the channel gravels as indicated above. Yet another channel, the Pits Channel, cut to about $+32$ feet ($9 \cdot 8$ m) and filled again to about $+40$ feet ($12 \cdot 2$ m). This was followed by the accumulation of the Red Rubble Bed of the Mbwilo Member to about $+50$ feet ($15 \cdot 2$ m). The last deposit followed conditions known to approximate the present day, but the time of initiation of its deposition relative to the immediately underlying deposits, or to the cutting of the main erosion surface, is not definitely known.

The river suddenly was able to begin excavating the older deposits of the Mkamba Member, forming Rubble I-composite/Ic at the base of its channel. It is not clear that climate exercised any simple control on either cutting or filling in the local basin. The deposition of the Ochreous Sands and Grey Clay Beds, which presupposes a blockage of the present outlet, appears to belong mainly to a period with conditions approximating the present day, while deposition of the sands and clays of the Mbwilo Member overlying Rubble Ic, also presupposing a blockage of the present outlet, belongs to a period with cooler, probably 'wetter' conditions. Two breaks in the deposition of sands are marked by Rubbles Ib at about $+12$ feet ($3 \cdot 7$ m) and Ia at about $+15$ feet ($4 \cdot 6$ m); sand accumulation reached an elevation of at least $+27$ feet ($8 \cdot 2$ m). The top of the buff sandy clay taken as the upper bed of the Mbwilo Member reaches $+45$ feet ($13 \cdot 7$ m).

It would appear that the grey clays and red sediments containing Iron Age remains in A 4 may not be the same as the fill of the 'Older Channel' in the River Face; they may belong to a slightly older channel, and fill which reaches an altitude of about $+38$ feet ($11 \cdot 6$ m). On the River Face and in A 1 a 'Younger Channel' fill and an 'Older Channel' fill are seen, both reaching an elevation of about $+20$ feet ($6 \cdot 1$ m). It is possible that the various deposits of the Chiungu Member containing Iron Age remains result from combined colluvial action and overbank deposition from the main river as it cut down to its present level and northward, and that no further blockage of the Spillway Gorge need be envisaged. Human interference in the ecological-hydrological setting may have been the deciding factor (bush fires, tree cutting and clearance, cultivation resulting in an oversupply of fine sediments from disturbed soils).

Even though these Site A excavations are minute compared to the whole area of the local basin, they are in the crucial outlet area and therefore show a larger part of the depositional history than might otherwise be expected. There are gaps in the story, however, only some of which can be filled by evidence from

10-2

other sites in the basin. Whether the Sangoan mainly derives from or is unrelated to the latest Acheulian at Kalambo Falls cannot be clearly demonstrated. The evidence for the association of the large blades, and large prepared cores, with the ?lower Lupemban has not been found. No unmixed or undisturbed context for the Lupemban proper is yet known, and that for the typologically most developed Lupemban is not satisfactory. Evidence from pollen concerning the vegetation and climate in the area is lacking for much of the section. Evidence for dating the various geological and climatic events as yet consists of a limited number of C14 dates. The clarification of these problems awaits further excavations.

TABLE I. *Composition of debris in some horizons of Trenches A 4 and A 5, Kalambo Falls Prehistoric Site*

		Rock types					
Year and location of sample		Feldspathic quartzites	Quartzite	Silicious mudstone ('Chert')	Dolerite	Other	Totals[a]
1959	A 4, Rubble I-composite, ½ of grid square B +1						
	Number	39	183	14	3	1[b]	240
	Percentage	16·3	76·3	5·8	1·2	0·4	100·0
1963	A 4, Rubble I-composite, ½ of grid square A 25, = resorted Red Rubble						
	Number	79	285	69	80	—	513
	Percentage	15·4	55·6	13·4	15·6	—	100·0
1963	A 4, Rubble IIa, north ½ of grid square B 29						
	Number	35	321	29	3[c]	—	388
	Percentage	9·0	82·7	7·5	0·8	—	100·0
1963	A 4, Rubble IIb,[d] north ½ of grid square B 29						
	Number	97	307	11	11	—	426
	Percentage	22·8	72·0	2·6	2·6	—	100·0
1963	A 5, Horizons with Acheulian artifacts, total area						
	Number[e]	80	280	7	22	—	389
	Percentage	20·6	72·0	1·8	5·6	—	100·0

a Debris over 2 cm (0·8 inch) in greatest dimension counted.
b Angular fragment of feldspar.
c Other squares were observed to contain more dolerite, sight-estimated to be 3–4 per cent.
d Counted by Miss Sue Bucklin.
e Counted from floor plan.

TABLE 2. *Summary of evidence: Geological events at Site A, based on Trench A 4, and the River Face clearance to Trench A 1*

Phases of downcutting (C), and filling (F)	Elevation above the present approximate low water level of Kalambo River	Remarks (C14 dates in counted elapsed years)	Named geological units[a]	Pollen evidence
{ Soil	Top c. +32 feet on River Face Cliff	Slopewash from south. Soil formation/deposition presumably began considerably earlier. Base of soil upslope in A 4 contains artifacts of 'Magosian' type. C14 date near top of soil in A 4, Pit 1, 2,470 ± 40 years		Nil
Chiungu Member				
F 7″ Red sandy or silty fill[b] of 'Younger Channel'	Top c. +20 feet Base c. +10 feet	Iron Age remains. ?C14 date 970 ± 150 years in A 1	Nil	
C 7″ 'Younger Channel'	Base c. +10 feet	A 1, and River Face Cliff	[Erosion]	
F 7′ Predominantly grey silty-clays, with gravel at base containing dolerite from south	Top c. +20 feet Base c. +10 feet	Iron Age remains. C14 dates 1,080 ± 180, 1,400 ± 150 years in A 1; date of 970 ± 150 years may refer	Nil	
C 7′ 'Older Channel'	Base c. +10 feet	A 1, and River Face Cliff	[Erosion]	
F 7 Red-brown to brown clays, A 4, A 3	Top, highest c. +38 feet Base, lowest c. +20 feet	Iron Age remains. Possibly related to F 7′, or F 7″, in time of deposition	Nil	
Grey sandy clay and clay at base of brown deposits, A 4	Top, highest c. +36 feet Base, lowest c. +20 feet	Possibly the same as in F 7′, but no pottery found and a few included stone artifacts of 'Magosian' type	Nil	
C 7 Channelling, river begins downcutting	Base c. +20 feet	A 4, ?earlier phase of C 7′	[Erosion]	
Mbwilo Member				
{ Buff sandy clay overlying Red Rubble, A 4	Top, highest c. +45 feet Base, lowest c. +36 feet	Possibly same deposit as at base of F 7, but more likely earlier. Included artifacts are of 'Magosian' type; A 4 Pits, A 2		Nil

149

TABLE 2 (*cont.*)

Phases of downcutting (C) and filling (F)	Elevation above the present approximate low water level of Kalambo River	Remarks (C14 dates in counted elapsed years)	Named geological units[a]	Pollen evidence
F 6 Current-bedded sands	Top, highest c. +27 feet	Sterile. A 4, A 3, and River Face Cliff		Nil
[Break in deposition of fine sediments]				
Rubble/gravel	c. +15 feet	Mixed cultural material, A 3 and River Face Cliff; latest is 'Magosian'. C14 date of 9,550 ± 210 years in A 3	Rubble Bed (Ia)	Nil
Sands		Sterile. A 3, and River Face Cliff		Nil
[Break in deposition of fine sediments]				
Rubble/gravel	c. +12 feet	Mixed cultural material, A 3 and River Face Cliff, ?A 1	Rubble Bed (Ib)	Nil
Sands and clays		Sterile. River Face Cliff and A 1		Cooler, wetter
[Possibly a long break in the deposition of fine sediments]				
F 6 Gravels and rubble-lag deposit	From c. +22 feet to 0 or −0 feet	Mixed cultural material; much of Lupemban type, and latest possibly late in the Lupemban range, or 'Magosian' upslope. Rubble I-composite in A 4 and A 3; Ic in River Face Cliff and A 1, where subdivisible in places. C14 date of 30,500 ± 2,000 years (on treated residue) at c. +8 feet in A 1	Rubble Bed (I-composite, or Ic)	Nil
Beginning of deposition of red rubble upslope prior to or during C 6, or later during F 6?	Top c. +50 feet, Base c. +40 feet	Mixed cultural material; latest is probably late in the Lupemban range. A 4 Pits	Red Rubble Bed, colluvial facies	Nil
C 6 Downcutting by river	Top of sediments removed, at least +40 feet. Base of visible channelling, c. +22 feet to 0 or −0 feet	'Main erosion surface' from A 4 to A 1	[Erosion]	
Mkamba Member				
F 5 Clay, sandy clay and fine sand	Top c. +40 feet	Mainly sterile. Some of scarce cultural material at base may be Lupemban	Pits Channel Fill	Warmer, ?wetter at top Nil

Unit	Deposit	Elevation	Remarks	(Bed name)	Climate
C 5	Channel cut	Base c. +32 feet	Pits 1, 2, 3 in A 4, ?A 2	[Erosion]	Nil
F 4	Sands and clays	Top c. +40 feet Base c. +31 feet	Sterile	Rubble Bed (II-composite or IIb)	Nil
	Gravels, coarse sand, dark clay at top	Base c. +30 feet	Included cultural material possibly early in Lupemban range. C14 date, A 4, Pit 2, 31,600 ± 600 years for top of complex		Nil
C 4	Channelling, possibly little downcutting	Base c. +30 feet	Pits 1, 2, 3 in A 4, ?A 2	[Erosion]	Nil
F 3	Ochreous sands of varying grade, coarser at base, and grey clays	Top c. +30 feet Base c. +2 feet	In A 4 base marked by a change to coarser sediments. Sangoan artifacts included in A 4, A 5, and River Face Cliff. C14 dates: near top, A 4, 40,600 ± 1,300 years, 46,100 + 3,500 − 2,400 years, > 43,850 years; middle, A 4, > 32,000 years; near base, A 1, 43,000 ± 3,300 years, A 5, 37,450 ± 600 years and > 38,850 years	Ochreous Sands and Grey Clay Beds	Cooler, wetter Present day
C 3	Channelling in places	Base c. +2 feet	Cut into older deposits, or disturbed their presently preserved uppermost horizons. A 1 to A 4	[Erosion]	
F 2	White sands and black clays with impersistent pebbly horizons	Top c. +6 feet Base at −0 feet	Truncated in places. Acheulian occupation areas. C14 dates: > 49,000 years,[c] A 4; > 52,000 and 61,200 ± 1,280 years, A 5 Extension	White Sands and	Present day, wetter[d] Cooler, wetter
C 2	Minor channelling	Base at −0 feet	Cut into older deposits, A 1	[Some erosion]	Nil
F 1	White, structureless fine sands with dark clays, and pebbly horizons	Top c. +3 feet	Acheulian occupation floors. C14 date 60,300 ± 750 years, in A 1	Dark Clay Beds	Cooler, wetter
C 1	Cut to bedrock?	?	?	[Erosion?]	Warmer, ?drier
					?

[a] Terms in parentheses are used in the archaeological nomenclature.
[b] The three channel fills at Site A probably overlap in time of deposition.
[c] This sample may be in sediments of the basal Ochreous Sands.
[d] This sample may pre-date the erosion (C 3), indicate conditions during the channelling, or even post-date it.

REFERENCES

Anderson, B. (1957). *A Survey of Soils in the Kongwa and Nachingwea Districts of Tanganyika*. University of Reading and Tanganyika Agricultural Corporation.

Clark, J. D. & van Zinderen Bakker, E. M. (1964). Prehistoric culture and Pleistocene vegetation at the Kalambo Falls, Northern Rhodesia. *Nature, Lond.* **201** (4923), 971–5.

Kuenen, Ph. H. (1956). Experimental abrasion of pebbles. 2: Rolling by current. *J. Geol.* **64**, 336–63.

CHAPTER 5

THE EXCAVATIONS: SITES B, C AND D

BY J. D. CLARK AND G. H. COLE

B 1 EXCAVATION, 1956 (Figure 35)

BY J. D. CLARK

Approximately 350 feet (106 m) upstream from Site A, where the river bends round in a right angle, changing its direction of flow from northeast to south-west, on the north side of the tributary donga an Acheulian floor was found in 1953, exposed at river level with Rubble I some 8–10 feet (2·4–3 m) above it. Several very fresh hand-axes and cleavers were collected as well as a pointed piece of wood and the tip of another which may have been utilized (Clark, 1954). Since the thickness of overlying deposits here was not as great as at Site A, it was hoped that it might be possible to uncover a larger area of this floor (Figure 33).

For the Pan-African Prehistory Congress excursion in 1955 a small section of the floor was exposed on the river bank at water level immediately upstream from the B 1 trench to be excavated the following year. Some 3½–4 feet (1·06–1·22 m) of laminated black and grey clays with intercalated sandy layers overlay the occupation floor and contained much organic material in the form of leaves, twigs and other compressed vegetable matter. Later, at the time that this floor was lifted, a small excavation was also made in the culturally mixed horizon, Rubble I.

On 7 July 1956 a grid 20 × 25 feet (6·1 × 7·6 m) was laid out next to the river bank; when the excavation was taken to water level, the length of the north and south walls was extended from 20 to 38 feet (6·1 to 11·5 m). Mrs L. E. Hodges supervised the excavation of this area (Figure 34).

Ground level sloped gently from west to east. At the surface was a fine, sandy, black to grey soil (1) with minute flecks and some larger pieces of charcoal and also potsherds and slag. At approximately 1 foot (30·50 cm) below, the grey sand was replaced by buff-coloured sands (2) of rather coarser texture. These were found to be 2 feet (61 cm) thick at the river bank (west) end but continued to a depth of nearly 4 feet (1·22 m) over the rest of the area and it was apparent that this deposit was dipping eastwards. At the east end, at a depth of 2 feet 3 inches (68 cm) was a thin, discontinuous lens of yellow clay (3). Lenses of this kind were also found in the 1959 excavation and it is possible that they represent consolidated ash from burned vegetation. Concentrations of ash are present on

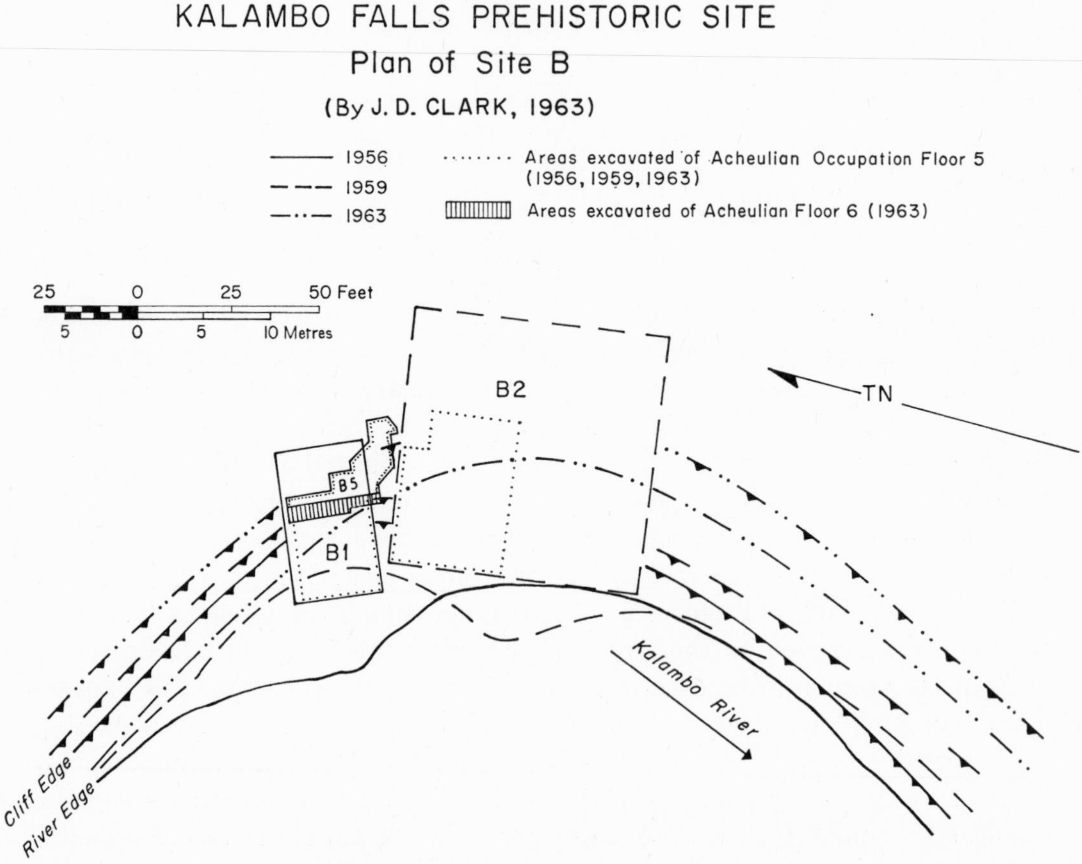
KALAMBO FALLS PREHISTORIC SITE
Plan of Site B
(By J. D. CLARK, 1963)
1956
1959
1963
Areas excavated of Acheulian Occupation Floor 5 (1956, 1959, 1963)
Areas excavated of Acheulian Floor 6 (1963)
25 0 25 50 Feet
5 0 5 10 Metres
B2
B5
B1
TN
Kalambo River
Cliff Edge
River Edge

Fig. 33. Kalambo Falls Prehistoric Site: Plan of Site B, 1963.

the surface of the modern swamp after the annual burning of the *Phragmites* and other dambo vegetation. Below this lens and similarly intercalated with the buff, sandy soil (2) was a band of grey coloured sand (4) which is believed to be an immature soil and so a temporary occupation surface. At the base of the buff sand (2), which was now seen to be dipping fairly steeply towards the northeast, was a light brown to yellow, sterile, medium textured sand (6) and this passed downslope into, and was overlain by, a mottled, brown/grey clay (5), 6–7 feet (1·83–2·13 m) from the surface.

These deposits (1)–(4) contained thick, red and grey Kalambo Industry pottery, slag and daga with charcoals, rubbers and grindstones and an occasional flake and hollow scraper in quartzite and chert, heat spalls of quartzite—mostly

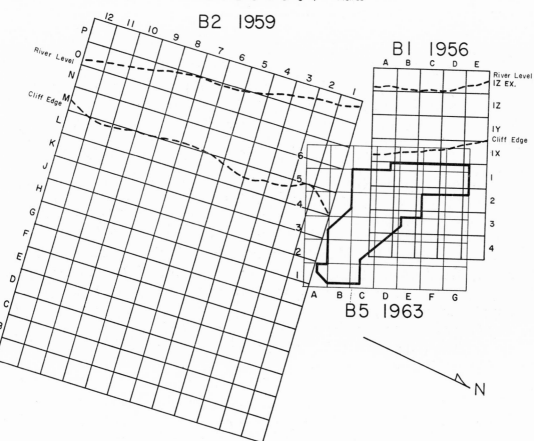

Fig. 34. Site B excavations, showing grids.

from the western side of the excavation—in fact, a typical sparse midden refuse from an occupation site nearby, on the surface of the bench between Sites B and C. Volume II will give the list of finds from these Iron Age deposits.

The mottled, brown/grey clay, which became greyer in colour with depth, yielded the same assemblage and continued for a depth of 12 feet (3·66 m) at the eastern end of the dig. This deposit had every appearance of being a swamp clay, the brown mottling being due to oxides of iron. It contained small flecks of charcoal and some larger pieces as well as small pellets of red and yellow clay-like material. The upper levels of the clay, present only over the eastern half of the dig, contained only broken stone but pottery, slag and rubbers appeared again in the next 1 foot (30·50 cm) down and continued, becoming scarcer, to the base. Between 5 and 6 feet (1·52 and 1·82 m) in square A 4 an abraded hand-axe was found. Its top had been struck and reused, probably by the 'Later Stone Age' or Iron Age inhabitants. At 6 feet (1·82 m) several scattered sherds were found on the same level suggesting that they had been deposited on a temporary surface.

At this point it was decided to take down only the grid squares A and B 3 and 4 to the base of the clay. Squares C–E 3 and 4 were left as a means of access to the rest of the dig. At 8½ feet (2·58 m) the clay became moist and the broken half of a flat bored-stone of schist was found, together with a number of sherds. Between 9 and 10 feet (2·74 and 3·04 m) below, potsherds decreased in numbers but were still present as was also the usual scatter of microlithic flakes and a very few abraded stone artifacts. As discussed elsewhere, it was thought at the time that this association of Iron Age and microlithic finds might point to a symbiotic existence of both agricultural and hunting groups in the locality, but the 1963 excavations at Site C showed this not to have been the case there.

Over the western half of the excavation a loose, buff to white, cross-bedded sand sterile of artifacts (7) forms the upper part of the bank into which the grey clay (5) has cut. It contained horizontally bedded, thin, contorted bands of brown clay and dipped down towards the east; from the Site C excavations these clay lines can be shown to be post-depositional in origin. It was quite clear that the B 1 excavation has been cut through the lower part of the old bank of the 30 feet (9 m) terrace, as this existed during the period of the early Iron Age occupation and probably during that of the 'Later Stone Age' also. The cultural content of the swamp clays here represents midden refuse that had spilled down this bank from a settlement area lying above and to the west of Site B that has since been destroyed by the eastward erosion of the river but must have been identical with that found at Site C further to the north in 1963. Thus it was anticipated that the pre-Chiungu Member channelling had not cut down to and removed the Acheulian later Pleistocene surfaces and work was, therefore, concentrated on the western half of the dig.

There were 7 feet (2·13 m) of the sterile, current-bedded sands (7) at the western end, at which level a thin, discontinuous and irregular line of small pebbles (8) occurred. This also contained a small scatter of artifacts. It was interstratified with a lens of grey, clayey sand, sterile except for some half-dozen artifacts lying on the surface. The plan of this horizon and line of the Iron Age erosion will be shown in volume II.

A few scattered charcoals and minute pieces of what may be wood were associated with this horizon as were also two small pieces of white clay. The pebble line is a water-laid deposit and the artifacts are, therefore, redeposited. As with the same pebble line in the A I excavation, the latest and fresh material is 'Magosian' and certainly post-Lupemban.

This pebble horizon rested on a 2–8 inch (5·1–20·50 cm) layer of loose, white sand (7') similar to the overlying sands which, in turn, rested on approximately 1 foot (30·50 cm) of coarse, ferruginized and bedded sand, the bedding planes having an eastward dip. This is also sterile and the top of this layer is stained black by iron and manganese. All these sands, which overlie Rubble I-composite at trench B I, belong to the Mbwilo Member with Rubble I at its base.

In the 1955 excavation immediately to the west and north this Rubble I-composite was found to dip northwards and to bifurcate, the two stonelines being separated by some 6 inches (15·25 cm) of coarse, ferruginous sand. In the B 2 excavation to the south it was later found to be similarly divided. Over the area of B I Rubble I is generally horizontal, though it dipped gently from north to south in the southeastern corner, indicating that the higher ground was towards the west or southwest. On an average it was 3 inches (7·75 cm) thick but some deeper pockets 4–5 inches (10·25–12·75 cm) thick were found. The lithology is the same as at Site A. At the bank where it was cut out by the later channelling, slumping was observed which has let down the rubble and overlying coarse sand nearly 1 foot (30·50 cm).

The distribution of artifacts on this rubble and the position of the larger stones are shown elsewhere. As on Site A the artifacts showed varying degrees of abrasion and several different cultural stages are represented. There can be little doubt that this is a channel deposit and that water was the primary agent responsible for redistributing the artifacts, though the abundance of tools and the slight degree of abrasion exhibited by many of them indicate that they were made in the immediate vicinity, probably on the surface of the rubble when this was exposed. No charcoals were preserved with the rubble/gravel but, in square D I, were several stones showing heat spalling that may have been associated with a hearth and there is a suggestion that the clay-sand which forms the matrix may have been reddened and baked. In grid square D I x was found an anvil stone which appeared to have been wedged into position and had marks of battering on the upper face; near by were two specimens of the split cobble type of anvil. Although this rubble cannot be considered as an occupation surface in the way that the Acheulian surfaces can, yet there are indications, as shown above, that it represents an area which was available at times of low water for temporary settlement.

Below Rubble I-composite were a series of cross-bedded, mostly ferruginized sands and clay of the Ochreous Sands Bed of the Mkamba Member, into which the main erosion surface had cut. On the northeast side of the excavation were coarse, ferruginized, bedded sands (11) dipping to the north or northeast. These rested on a fine, bedded sand (12), white to ochreous in colour where it had been stained by iron. The top of this sand at the east was heavily ferruginized and on both east and north was marked by a thin pebble band without artifacts. This deposit is again sterile and appears to be a channel fill, the bedding planes dipping towards the northeast. At the northeast corner it abutted against deposits of grey (13), black (14) and buff-coloured clay (15) which occupy the bottom of the channel. These clays were similarly sterile and the brown clay could be seen on the north side to be forming a lens which was interbedded with the sands (12). Although no stratigraphic break was apparent it is possible that the lower part of this deposit (12) under the level of the brown clay (15) is a slightly older sand than that lying above.

Under the brown clay band was a layer of ferruginous, cross-bedded, orange sand of fine to medium grain (16) which changed to a clayey sand (16'), grey in colour, resting on the grey clay (17) at the northeast corner. At the base of deposits (16) and (17) at the north side of the dig and at the base of the sands (12) on the east side was a thin pebble band (18) which may represent a temporary surface. It yielded one chopper and one primary flake in hard quartzite, both slightly rolled. At the south and west sides of the dig this pebble stringer was absent, but the surface, if such it be, may be represented by the facies change from ferruginized, coarse sands to white, ochreous, bedded sands.

The pebble line is a minor disconformity resting on a fine, buff-coloured, unbedded sand (19) with some layers of coarse sand and fine gravel. This covered most of the area excavated. At the north and east sides the sands (11) were underlain by and in part interbedded with sands of coarser texture (20), grey to yellow in colour and it is apparent that they fill a channel running in a northeast–southwest direction. Another pebble horizon (21) with some larger stones—and, in square A 1 y, a piece of wood—was present in the lower levels of these sands and, at the north side, appeared more likely to represent an occupation horizon that had suffered disturbance by channelling. The same surface was found during the B 2 excavation in 1959. A small but important collection of artifacts, including two elongate core-axes, clearly belonging to the Sangoan and all quite fresh was found and this horizon is referred to as Occupation Surface IV (it should not be confused with Floor IV at Site A 1). The distribution of the specimens and the analysis of the material will be given in volume III.

On 9 and 11 October, when the excavation had reached this level there occurred two collapses of the south wall. In order, therefore, to prevent a similar collapse of the north wall a $2\frac{1}{2}$ feet (76·25 cm) bench was left unexcavated along the whole length of this wall.

Below the disconformity of Sangoan Occupation Surface IV over the western half of the dig were laminated black and grey clays (22) with wood and bark preserved in the lower layers. These clays overlay fine, greeny white to pale grey, unbedded, compact sands (23), on which the Sangoan occupation area rested over the eastern half of the dig and through which channelling at the base of the Ochreous Sands had cut at the east end down to the underlying Occupation Floor V with the Acheulian: these are the White Sands Bed of the Mkamba Member.

This floor was continuous over the whole area excavated and is preserved also under the unexcavated sections below the Iron Age clay, as was learned in 1963.

There was now much water seeping through the east wall of the excavation below the deposits of the Chiungu Formation and it was necessary to try to drain this away so that the floor might dry out sufficiently to be properly excavated. Since this floor sloped very gradually towards the east it was, regrettably, necessary to excavate the central section of grid squares C 1–1 z without plotting the distribution of the artifacts, to a foot below the main floor. This was effective in draining the remaining parts of the occupation surface and the two areas on either side provided evidence of a magnificent Acheulian floor with quantities of tools but comparatively little waste. Again, the tools were in a perfectly fresh condition and it was certain that this was part of a camping floor which had suffered little or no disturbance.

The tools lay in the greatest profusion (109 hand-axes and 93 cleavers) in an area $21 \times 24\frac{1}{2}$ feet (6·4 × 7·4 m) in the southeast part of the floor, together with a comparatively small number of larger cobbles and stones set in a 2 inch (5·1 cm) thick matrix of coarse to medium grained sand with small pebbles. This surface was overlying sand of fine to medium texture (25) representing a sandbank that had been exposed by the side of the water and on which Acheulian man had made his temporary camp. The stream that had laid down this sandbank would not have been capable of transporting any stone larger than 30 mm diameter so that anything larger can only have been carried in by the inhabitants. There is no evidence of natural sorting or alignment of the material nor does it show evidence of weathering. The underlying sands show no soil structure so that the occupation floor must have been covered rapidly by the fine white sand (23) after its abandonment and a rise in water level in the basin. Only two pieces of wood were found in direct association with the tools on this floor. One of these shows signs of intentional shaping and may have been a knife; it was found next to an area of grey clay in grid square A 1 z. The C section grid squares which had to be lifted without plotting have produced four core-axes that had been let down to this level by the channelling exposed in the east wall which reached to, but not below, the Acheulian floor level at this end of the dig. The plot of this floor and analysis of the finds will be found in volume III and discussed in the chapter on the Acheulian in that volume.

Since water continued to seep through the east wall and the deposits at the northeast corner, causing slumping of the saturated sands, it was decided to reduce still further the area of the excavation, which was therefore restricted to grid squares B, C and D with 1 foot (30·50 cm) of A and of E giving an area of 17 × 20 feet (5·18 × 6·10 m).

Acheulian Occupation Floor V rested on a medium to fine white to buff-coloured sand (25) with no artifacts and changing laterally into a coarse, pebbly sand. At a depth of 1 foot (30·50 cm) below the occupation floor a number of large logs and other pieces of wood, some of which had been partly uncovered when the drain was first dug, were encountered. There was no regular pattern in their distribution and they lay partly in the base of the sand and partly resting on and in a black clay (27) full of compressed vegetable matter. There were no tools associated with the wood in the sand at this level but in grid squares D and E 1 y at a slightly lower level was an oval area of brown clay sand 3½ feet (1·06 m) in diameter which had been reddened as if by fire. A sample of this was submitted to the British Museum (Natural History) through the courtesy of Dr K. P. Oakley and it was confirmed that this was burnt clay. The distribution of the wood at this level will be shown in volume III. The main logs had a diameter of 1 foot (30·50 cm) or more and one was 19 feet (5·79 m) long. At the northwest corner a large tree-trunk some 18 inches (45·75 cm) in diameter protruded from the bank into the river and appears to have been charred, though this might be due to cracking on drying owing to its having been partly exposed over a period by the river.

Due to its antiquity the wood in this and lower horizons has been partially carbonized by natural ageing processes. The ends of a log will sometimes have had the heartwood and part of the exterior removed thus forming a concavity, while in other cases the process is reversed and the end will exhibit a blunt point. Both these phenomena are frequently, but not exclusively, met with in instances where African hardwoods have been charred and burned in a fire. Unfortunately, at the Kalambo Falls Site, water washing sand over the logs at the time of their burial has effectively smoothed and abraded the exterior of the wood so that direct evidence of charring or charcoal, if once present, has been removed. Moreover, on drying, the exterior of this partially carbonized Kalambo wood cracks and often exhibits a surface simulating the charring seen on logs from a camp or bush fire, so that it is difficult to distinguish between this and contemporary charring. While, therefore, the direct evidence of charcoal and charred wood is lacking from the logs at this particular level adjacent to the burnt clay, its unequivocal presence at a lower level with artifacts lends support to the view that this restricted burnt clay area may represent a hearth.

In grid square B I x was a log 77 inches (1·96 m) long, 9 inches (23 cm) wide across the short axis, narrowing and rounded at both ends, and $5\frac{1}{2}$ inches (14·25 cm) thick at the centre. It has roughly parallel sides and a plano-convex section but there is no clear evidence of tool marks or intentional shaping. Approximately across the centre of the log on the convex face is a broad, shallow groove, the surface of which is rubbed smooth by the action of water as is also the rest of the log. The groove runs the full width of the log and does not look natural, though it might have resulted from the wind's rubbing two boughs together. This is commoner than might be expected with African savannah trees and several examples of such rubbing and grooving were collected for comparison. The curvature of the exterior of this particular log shows that it must have formed part of the trunk of a tree or of a very thick limb, whereas the present-day examples of natural grooving found are all associated with branches of 3 inches (7·62 cm) or less. The wood surface in this groove is without the irregularities that result from the use of a chopping tool. If it was, indeed, humanly produced then it is more likely, as experiment shows, to have been formed by charring with fire and scraping. None of the other logs or wood fragments at this level showed any possible evidence of human activity and some of the logs are substantial and heavy and would have needed several men to move them. In view of their position—immediately underlying the Acheulian V living floor—the possibility cannot be entirely ruled out that they formed part of a platform on the edge of the water where man may have camped for reasons of protection and, conceivably, because below it, and pressed into the black 'peaty' clay on which it rests, artifacts began to appear again. Some of the material might have formed part of a structure, such as a windbreak.

With the first appearance of the wood the problem arose as to how it should be cleaned as, being heavily waterlogged and partially carbonized, it was easily marked with the metal trowels used for excavation. Accordingly, as has been said, all wood was cleaned with water, the hands and fine hair brushes.

Beneath this upper wood layer the black 'peaty' clay (27) filled the greater part of the excavation but did not extend to the north and south walls, though it may have done so below the level to which we were able to excavate. The clay formed, therefore, a rather restricted area some 15 × 12 feet (4·5 × 3·6 m) in the centre of the dig. There were two main layers of 'peaty' clay—an upper (27) and a lower (29)—separated by from 6 to 12 inches (15·25–30·50 cm) of coarse, grey clay sand and subsidiary clay layers (28). On the surface of each of these clays (26) and (28) was a pebbly gravel and coarse sand with artifacts.

Since the clay was full of delicate organic remains it was impossible to use any metal tools in its excavation. A stirrup pump was, therefore, used and the more powerful motor-driven pump also to play a jet of water on to a particular area. This most successfully removed the vegetable remains from the clay and facilitated the recovery of a quantity of seeds, leaves and other delicate specimens of this kind which would otherwise have been damaged in excavation. In addition, seventeen pieces of wood of various lengths were found showing evidence of modification and utilization. Side branches and bark had sometimes been removed and controlled charring in a fire had also been employed further to shape the tool. One partially burned log from the lower 'peaty' clay had the whole of one face reduced to charcoal. For the reports on these remains see Appendices C and D and volume III.

The technique employed to excavate the 'peaty' clay made it impossible to obtain a plot of the distribution of the artifacts or to separate adequately those from the two horizons. The number of tools was small compared with the quantity from the floor above and those that did occur were predominantly side scrapers and utilized flakes. Whether the pebbly sands in which this assemblage was found represent an occupation area or areas seems doubtful, though they could more justifiably be described as an occupation surface. In 1963, when the area immediately to the east of where the 1956 dig had stopped was excavated, this surface was found represented by a single horizon and was quite clearly a living floor. It is, therefore, known as Occupation Floor VI (subdivided in 1956 into VIa and VIb).

The B 1 excavation closed on 27 October at river level, without, however, having penetrated to the base of the lower 'peaty' clay (29). This deposit had produced some most important organic remains including several utilized pieces of wood, logs that had clearly been charred and some charcoals.

B2 EXCAVATION, 1959 (Figures 36–39)

BY J. D. CLARK

In 1959 it was found that, since 1956, some 5 feet (1·52 m) of river bank had been eroded. The south and east walls of the 1956 excavation had suffered collapse and gullies had been cut into them, while from the base of the old dig there issued a clear spring of water which was used for drinking water by Dominico's (Chiungu) village nearby.

A gridded area (B 2) 70 × 50 feet (21·3 × 15·2 m), having the long sides running approximately north and south, was laid out immediately adjacent to the south end of the B 1, 1956, excavation. The east–west axis was later prolonged down to river level giving a total area of 70 × 70 feet (21·3 × 21·3 m). It was hoped to be able to determine the extent of the Acheulian occupation floor on the south and east sides and the excavation was intended to uncover as large an area of this floor as possible. The top of the river bank was 50 feet (15·2 m) west of the northeast corner of the excavation and some 16 feet (4·88 m) of deposit overlay Floor V (Figures 33 and 34).

On the west or river bank side, the surface soil was grey and sandy (1) but eastwards this changed rapidly (grid squares A–D 1–12) to a red-brown soil or loam (1b). In the easternmost grid squares the surface of this loamy soil had recently been disturbed by mounding for cassava gardens and the incorporation of this area in the excavations was only accomplished after prolonged negotiations with the owners of the garden.

The top of the bank was located in sections J–M; it sloped very gradually towards the east. Excavation was begun by taking down grid squares A–K 1–12. Iron Age midden debris with channel decorated ware and a few Lungu sherds occurred even in the surface soil where also were found a few recent bones.

Over the western half of the dig (grid squares E–K) the deposit below the top 6 inches (15·25 cm) was a grey clay sand (6) changing to a true clay (7) in grid squares G–K. This contained a considerable number of potsherds (fifty-three from J and eighty from H) but the majority came from the sandier parts of the deposit in grid squares E–G. The cultural material from these clays and sands included, besides the potsherds, slag, daga and some worked iron.

At a depth of 1½ feet (45 cm) the grey clay in sections G–K 6–8 was underlain by a sterile, white river sand (10) but the remainder of the area continued to yield pottery. The number of sherds fell off considerably in the red clay soil (5) of squares A and B 1–12. For example, at depths of 1–1½ feet (30·50–45·75 cm) there were no sherds in the A squares, three in B, six in C, three in D, twelve in

E, twenty-three in F, twenty-three in G, forty in H, thirty-six in J and thirty in K. The easternmost sections continued to produce very little or no cultural material and the majority of finds came from sections E–G down to a depth of 3 feet (91 cm). The white sand extended over the central grid squares in sections G–K and contained no artifacts.

At 3 feet 3 inches (98·75 cm) the red clay soil in squares A–C was replaced by a mottled grey clay or clay sand (7) with some redder patches (7′). Westwards this changed into a grey clay sand which was replaced in the central grid squares of the G–J section by the sterile white sand. In the grid squares at the north and south sides of the excavation where the grey clay persisted, it contained numerous sherds.

The L section of grid squares which formed the bank was taken down when the rest of the excavation had reached a depth of 4 feet (1·22 m). Potsherds (101) occurred down to a depth of 1 foot (30·50 cm) in the hard grey clay (7b). Sixty-four of these sherds came from grid square L 12. This 'concentration' of pottery contained rim sherds from five different pots and it is possible that it may represent a collection of grave pottery that had slumped down the bank of the old Iron Age channel in the same way as the bank had slumped at Site C and so prompted in 1963 the examination of what proved to be the settlement area. Below 1 foot (30·50 cm) this section was composed of hard grey clay and white sand and was sterile.

The mottled red-grey clay and clay sand (7) of the eastern section gave place westwards to grey clay sand and continued down to a depth of 4 feet 9 inches (1·43 m), still containing the same channel decorated sherds, clay and daga, but the wedge-shaped area of sand in the central grid squares steadily increased with depth. It was present in grid squares D 6–8 at the 4 feet (1·22 m) level and between 4½ feet and 4 feet 9 inches (1·36 and 1·43 m); it appeared also in the central grid squares of C section. Most of the Iron Age finds continued to come from the areas of grey clay sand and clay at the north and south sides of the excavation.

At 4 feet 9 inches (1·43 m) on the west side there appeared in the sterile, white sand a band of small pebbles with artifacts and a few larger stones (Rubble Ia) (11).

It is apparent that the triangular area represents a spur of older deposits of the Mbwilo and Mkamba Members that protruded into the swamp during deposition of the Chiungu Member. The Iron Age cultural material was found next to the old bank on either side of the spur and over the western half of the dig, thus indicating that it was debris from occupation that had spilled down the slope from the settlement area to the west.

The deposits of the Chiungu Member which contained Iron Age remains are probably divisible into two stages. The upper and later stage is deepest at the eastern end of the dig where it attained a thickness of 3½ feet (1·06 m) or more. The clays and clay sands (3) and (5) are predominantly red in colour with some gritty and pebbly lenses and thin discontinuous patches of yellow 'loam' (4) which, it has been suggested, may represent consolidated ash from burnt vegetation. In the northeast corner down to a depth of 5 feet (1·52 m) or more and, again, in the middle of the east wall, there is also some disturbance (1c) which is probably due to Borassus palms that once grew there. The red clay sands contained few sherds and all of them, except for three from the surface, are of channelled ware type. If they are not derived from the earlier Iron Age deposit they would indicate that the Kalambo Industry population was still present in the basin but that the centre of settlement had already shifted from the B and C site terrace.

It is now considered probable that these red clay sands are the equivalent of the 'Younger Channel' fill at Site A, though no stratigraphic break separating them from the grey clays and clay sands on which they rest could be satisfactorily demonstrated at Site B and it is possible that deposition was more or less continuous nearer the centre of the swamp. Lithologically, they are similar and they have the same sparse archaeological content as the 'Younger Channel' fill at Site A. If this correlation is valid then the rare Kalambo Industry sherds that are found in them are more probably derived than contemporary.

A radiocarbon sample from a depth of 2–3 feet (61–91 cm), consisting of charcoal from the section stepping back the south wall and coming from this upper red clay/sand portion of the Chiungu Member has been dated to A.D. 1580 (GrN-3189:370±50). Due, however, to known variations in the C14 content of the atmosphere at this time, an age of about A.D. 1350 is also possible. If the Channelled Ware sherds contained in these clay sands are derived, this would indicate that, by the end of the sixteenth century A.D., perhaps by the middle of the fourteenth century, the makers of the Kalambo Industry had disappeared from the local Kalambo basin. As has been said, these later channel fill deposits at Site A may also be connected with the formation of the low ±6 feet (1·8 m) terrace on the Tanzania side of the river and, if this were the case, this result would give a possible date for the time of the formation of this terrace.

The lower and earlier deposits of the Chiungu Member—the grey clay and grey clay sand (7) containing the bulk of the channel decorated pottery—would be the equivalent of the 'Older Channel' fill on Site A. It contains pottery and other cultural debris down to the lowest sections excavated (13 feet 8 inches (4·16 m)) mixed with some derived artifacts of microlithic and Lupemban type.

A radiocarbon charcoal sample from these clays in grid square D 7 at a depth of 7 feet (2·13 m) gave an age of A.D. 1020 (GrN-3580: 930±40 years), which agrees well with the dates (L-395B and C) obtained for the upper to middle levels for the A 1 excavation. These deposits are banked against the spur of the 30 feet (9 m) terrace and dip fairly steeply down towards the east cutting through Rubbles Ia (11) and Ib (13) and resting on an erosion surface cut into the Ochreous Sands (14) of the Mkamba Member that underlie these rubble/gravels. The A–C sections below the 7 feet (2·13 m) level were left unexcavated.

The remnant of rubble preserved in the projecting spur of older sediments with the apex in grid square D 8 seemed to dip downwards towards the east and south (Figures 37 and 38) and was highest at the northwestern corner. It contained only Lupemban and 'Magosian' artifacts. There were few large natural stones and also comparatively few of the large heavy-duty implements. This is the uppermost rubble/gravel at Site B and is known as Rubble Ia. It merges with the composite Rubble I (Ia and Ib) in the 1956 B 1 excavation. It dips 2 feet 8 inches (81 cm) between grid squares K 1 and K 2 at the western end and an estimated 2½–3 feet (76–91 cm) at the southwest corner and at D 8 where it occurred at 7 feet (2·13 m) below the surface. In grid squares J–K 5–6 and J–K 8 it was found to be discontinuous, having probably been cut out by subsequent erosion. From J–K 9–12 the southward dip was more pronounced.

In E and F sections Rubble Ia lay immediately above Rubble Ib and the deposit here was stained dark brown to black and cemented by iron. Proceeding westwards the two rubbles were separated by an increasing thickness of river sands (12) which reach a depth of 4½ feet (1·36 m) on the line K–L at the river bank. The sand (10) overlying Rubble Ia was of medium to fine grain and white to buff in colour but that of the stone line itself was coarse with a scattering of small pebbles stained occasionally red to black by iron.

The cultural assemblage from this rubble will be analysed in volume III. The surface still preserved was approximately 1,590 square feet (180 sq.m), and yielded 3,721 artifacts. Very occasionally a few flakes derived from the rubble were found in the adjacent clays.

This rubble (11) probably represents the base of a stream channel that was seasonally dry, for the 'Magosian' tools in the assemblage are fresh or only very little worn. Of particular interest is the discovery at the base of the rubble in grid square M 12 of half a bored stone. This shows the typical ferruginous staining exhibited by many of the artifacts from this surface and it lay in quite undisturbed deposit so that there is no doubt of its contemporaneity with the rubble. As the assemblage is quite lacking in 'Later Stone Age' cultural material this bored stone must belong with the 'Magosian' artifacts and is confirmation for the evidence from other sites in Zambia and Rhodesia that the bored stone was known to the makers of the 'Magosian'. Among typical 'Magosian' implements from this rubble are unifaced and bifaced points, backed blades, burins and small scrapers.

Immediately underlying Rubble Ia at the northwestern end was a coarse, buff sand with small pebble stringers containing artifacts (12). This in turn rested on finer grained sands and some clay (12a) and (12d) which overlay buff to ochreous sands (12f), fine grained in the northern half and coarse and bedded, with pebble stringers with artifacts (12b) over the southern half of the dig. These rested on Rubble Ib (13).

These sands separating the two erosion surfaces contain an assemblage of 'Magosian' and earlier and later Lupemban implements similar to that from Rubble Ia. The total number of artifacts was 4,667 of which 2,865 came from between 4 feet 9 inches and 7 feet (1·43 and 2·13 m) over the northern half of the excavation. Only 1,802 specimens came from the deeper southern levels between 7 and 11 feet (2·13 and 3·35 m). Notable are two finely made 'Magosian' bifaced points, *outils écaillés*, a dimple-scarred rubber and anvil stone, small scrapers and a small, bifaced, pointed pick which, from its very fresh appearance, is also included as 'Magosian'. The tip end of an abraded, long Lupemban lancehead also came from these sands. Physically it is identical with the butt end of a similar lancehead from the underlying Rubble Ib and these are likely to have been two parts of the same tool. If this is so, it lends support to the belief that most of the artifacts from Rubble Ia and the underlying sands are re-deposited largely from Rubble Ib. There is also a small percentage of thermally fractured fragments of quartzite.

The second and lower erosion surface, Rubble Ib, was found to dip southwards from the northwest corner, as did Rubble Ia but, unlike Ia, it did not also dip appreciably eastwards. In fact, towards the southeast it appeared to rise slightly. At the northwest corner this rubble/gravel lay approximately 6½–7 feet (1·98–2·13 m) below the surface and 2½ feet (76 cm) below Rubble Ia, although, as the B 1 excavation showed, the two had merged some 10 feet (3·05 m) or so to the north.

At the southwest end the rubble/gravel is 11–12 feet (3·35–3·66 m) below the surface, separated only by 1 foot (30·50 cm) of sand from Rubble Ia above and it is clear that the two run together a few feet south of the excavation. They actually do so, or are separated by a few inches of sand only, east of the H grid square section, as can be seen from the section drawing (Figure 37). Between K 1 and K 7 the southward dip is very gradual but in grid squares 8 and 9 it dips more steeply and is represented by only a thin pebble line for a short distance in grid square 9. Over the rest of the excavation the rubble (13) has the characteristic appearance of those on Site A and in trench B 1, 1956, consisting of numbers of sub-angular rocks with some rounded cobbles set in a pebbly sand and with numerous Lupemban and other artifacts in varying stages of abrasion. The sand matrix is coarse with ferruginous staining and mottling.

On the north side of grid section 9 the rubble is some 4–5 inches (10–13 cm) thick with many artifacts and pieces of natural debris. South of this line, however, it is thinner and contains fewer artifacts, and those mostly of later Lupemban type. There is a sterile or nearly sterile eroded area running east–west along the length of the stone line, which may indicate that the southern half was buried more quickly than the northern half or that some later redeposition of the southern half may have taken place.

The surface area of Rubble Ib (approximately 1,615 square feet (190 sq.m)) produced the greatest accumulation of artifacts from any of the mixed rubbles at Site B—a total of 11,157 artifacts most of which can be assigned to the lower and upper Lupemban and show varying degrees of abrasion. There is, however, also a smaller and unabraded 'Magosian' assemblage. Artifacts from the following grid squares constitute what has later been referred to as the 'measured sample' and total 4,067 specimens: E 6–8, F 6–11, G 4–12, H 3–12, J 2–12 and K 1–2.

The distribution of the artifacts on this rubble/gravel suggests that natural sorting has taken place, since heavier and lighter artifacts have in some cases been concentrated separately. Whether this rubble, when exposed, formed a suitable site for human settlement is uncertain. In grid square K 6 were twelve rounded cobbles and other groupings were found in squares J 8 and K 8. Though none of them bore evidence of use these groupings are suggestive, especially as the surface also contained split cobbles and nine thermal spalls of hard quartzite and a full range of Lupemban tools including split cobble anvils. If this was ever an occupied surface no precise evidence of a living floor now remains and the artifacts have been later redistributed by water.

The total assemblage is described in detail elsewhere but it may be noted here that it contains an excellent series of heavy duty and other tools assigned to the ? lower Lupemban—in particular core-axes, picks and some fine lanceolates. As was mentioned above, the butt end of an early lanceolate came from M 12 and is believed to belong to the same tool as the point found in Rubble Ia. The upper Lupemban was equally well represented and there was again a comparatively large number of 'fabricating tools'—hammerstones, grindstones, split cobble and block anvils—thus suggesting that the occupation area cannot have been far away.

From the stratification seen in the river bank sections in 1956 and 1959 it was apparent that Rubbles Ia and Ib continued to dip towards the south beyond the limits of the excavation, where they presumably merged and reached low water level at a point where a line of stones outcropped in the bed of the river, half-way between Sites A and B. At this point the channel containing clays of the Chiungu Member had cut down to the level of this rubble and the overlying sands of the Mbwilo Member were missing. At Site C also the Rubble I composite was, at its lowest point, only just above present-day low water level so that, while the river was flowing at this level, the upper surfaces of the rubble would have been exposed and available as camping places.

At a depth of 8–9 feet (2·44–2·74 m) the Chiungu Member clays (7e) were very moist and water began to stand in the grid squares causing a collapse of the south wall and making it necessary to step this back. The stepping back was carried out down to the level of Rubble Ib.

Rubble Ib rested disconformably on a medium textured, bedded, buff sand with differential ferruginous staining (14). This represents the filling of a channel and, from the evidence of the bedding, was deposited by a stream flowing from northwest to southeast. The uppermost levels of this deposit contained no artifacts but at 13½ feet (4·11 m) in grid squares H 2 and 3 were found a rather poorly made hand-axe, one bifacially trimmed chunk, one primary flake of quartzite and two chunks of weathered chert. They lay at approximately the same level in the sand associated with a scattering of small pebbles, but there was no evidence of any disconformity. They are clearly water deposited, but very little abraded and are of Sangoan type. This 'horizon' might be the equivalent of the disconformity, observable in the stratigraphy in the B 1 excavation at approximately the same depth below Rubble I-composite.

These bedded sands are characterized by the presence of discontinuous bands of small pebbles, some of them containing artifacts, and have yielded the greater part of the Sangoan tools from Site B. There was, however, evidence of minor channelling or ponding in the central grid squares 8–5 and again in 3–1 in the M–F sections, the lower parts of which were filled with black clay containing plant remains, some being the stems of water plants (14c). These organic clays also contained pollen but no artifacts though the pebble line marking the base of the channel in grid squares 5 and 6 contained flakes and some utilized pieces. The line of this channel or channels can be seen from the section drawings in Figures 38 and 39.

Over the southern half of the excavation the sands (14) became coarser and there was much cross-bedding with pebble stringers, flakes and an occasional piece of wood at a depth of 14–14½ feet (4·26–4·41 m) below the surface or *c.* 1½–2½ feet (45–76 cm) below Rubble Ib at the south wall. One of the wood fragments from coarse sand over a pebble line (15) in M 10 has given the radiocarbon date of 35,950 B.C. (GrN-3228: 37,900±1,500/1,200). There may be a minor disconformity between the upper sands and clays (14) and the lower sands (15)–(20) since the carbon date would indicate that the upper sands at Site B are somewhat younger than the Ochreous Sands with Sangoan artifacts at Site A. If a disconformity exists, the break lies at the base of the clay-filled channel (14c) in the central and northern half of the excavation and the pebble lines and thin clay band to be seen in the south wall of the dig (15) and (15a). The cultural content of this upper sand series might then be described as later Sangoan and that from the lower sands as earlier Sangoan. In any case there can have been no great time difference and they both form an integral part of the Sangoan series.

At the north side below beds (14)–(14c) was a coarse, cross-bedded sand, grey in colour from its clay content (15b) and (15c). Within this were several lenses and two more persistent bands of small pebbles and gritty gravel (15′) and (15″) with many flakes and some small tools all showing varying degrees of abrasion. These are mostly in quartzite and lay horizontally to the bedding and there can be little doubt that they were deposited by water. One large, proto-biconical core in friable feldspathic quartzite was found in square L 2 at a depth of 13½ feet (4·11 m), but could not be preserved. Another fine gravel stringer (17′), underlying and separated from (15″), dipped westwards and southwards towards the river. These two lenses produced a quantity of factory waste and some tools which are important for comparison with the Acheulian and Lupemban.

At the southern side of the excavation the sands were of coarse to medium grain and grey in colour and, when wet, they had the appearance of sago pudding (16). Few artifacts occurred in them and then only in the rare pebble stringers. One such fine pebble band with flakes was found to dip steeply to the east (17) and the sand eastward of this was of finer texture, sterile and buff to grey in colour, showing little bedding (16). Figure 38, depicting the west wall, shows the typical facies change from finer to coarser sand from north to south.

Over the southern half of the excavated area coarser and finer sands were interstratified with fine gravel and pebble bands down to the base of the excavation at river level (18). The cultural content of these deposits was clearly contemporary Sangoan that had been caught up and redeposited in the course of the filling of the basin. In this respect the succession in the lower levels of the excavation was quite different from that at the northern side of the dig. The base of the Ochreous Sands Bed, of which these beds (16)–(20) form a part lies below water level at the south side of B 2 excavation.

At a depth of 7½ feet (2·28 m) under Rubble Ib in grid square M 12 (i.e. 20 feet (6·10 m) below the surface) several small wood fragments were found isolated in an otherwise sterile and coarse grey sand (18b). These have been dated by the C14 method and give an age of 40,050 B.C. (GrN-3237: 42,000 ± 2,000 years).

At the northern side of the dig under a coarse sand and gravel (18c) lenses of pebbles and fine gravel containing artifacts (19) were interbedded with medium to fine grained, buff-coloured sands. At the extreme northwestern corner these gave place to fine gravels (19a) dipping westward and immediately overlying dark brown to black clays (20c) which had been partly broken down by erosion and redeposited as lumps in the overlying gravel. Eastward of these gravels was a pebble line (19b) extending over grid squares J–L 1–2 and containing Sangoan artifacts. Below this again was more sterile, buff sand of medium to fine grain (20) at the base of which was another pebble horizon with Sangoan tools (20b). In grid square L 1 this pebble horizon bifurcated and the lower band dipped eastward and developed into a fine gravel layer with tools (20b'). The two are separated by a fine grey sand (20d).

Discontinuous with these pebble layers there also occurred, in grid squares M–G 2–6, another pebble horizon, this time dipping to the south. This was the most definite and continuous horizon that had been encountered below the mixed rubbles and it is believed to represent a temporary surface that had later suffered some natural disturbance when the overlying sands were deposited but which was occupied for a short time by the makers of the Sangoan. The number of tools was not large but they are quite characteristic—core-axes, picks and other heavy- and light-duty tools as well as some small flake tools. They are fresh or very slightly abraded. This surface lenses out to the east and north and its probable continuation can be seen in the pebble line in the southern half of the dig. Both are equated with the pebble lenses (20b) and (20b') in the north wall section and are believed to form part of the similar patchy distribution represented by surface IV in B 1 excavation at approximately the same level.

This occupation surface IV in grid sections 4–6 is on approximately the same level as the Acheulian occupation floor but, in the sections 1–3 it is somewhat higher, as has been seen, and its place is taken by several discontinuous pebble lines with artifacts. Under the lowest of these (20b'), however, a totally different deposit is found—a fine grey to light brown, unstratified sand (21), sterile of artifacts. This is identical with the White Sands that overlie the Acheulian floors in the B 1 and Site A excavations. The cross-bedded sands and fine grained lenses with the Sangoan rest disconformably on this sand and have also eroded it from the grid square sections south of 1–3. Some 2 feet (61 cm) of this sand remained overlying the main Acheulian occupation floor and running through it was a thin but continuous band of brown clay (21') which may represent a temporary soil horizon. At the base of this sand Acheulian Occupation Floor V was located.

This horizon was the southward continuation of the main Acheulian floor excavated in 1956 at B 1 and lithologically it is the same. It had no thickness and the tools lay horizontally thickly scattered in 'clusters' on the flat surface of a fine, white river sand. Several areas of sand from which artifacts and natural stones were absent have significance, as well as a rough semicircle of larger stones at the southeast end of the floor. The number of natural stones on this horizon was not large and all of them had been carried into the site by man since the load capacity of the stream was quite inadequate for them to have been deposited by the river. The aggregate of artifacts and manuports on this horizon represents the accumulation of occupation debris that followed the temporary habitation of this riverside sandbank.

In two places only was a narrow band of sand some 3–5 inches (7·75–12·75 cm) thick seen to separate an upper from a lower layer of artifacts that might represent a single season's deposition (grid squares O–P 1 and G–H 1). The tools themselves were in mint condition and showed no evidence of having been disturbed.

This part of Acheulian Floor V extended over grid squares G–P 1–2 and in the more eastern part into grid sections 4 and 5. To the south of these squares, however, the floor was quite absent and it was apparent that it has been cut out by the later channelling. This proved a considerable disappointment as we had expected to find and plot the southern limits of the artifact distribution. However, the approximately 600 square feet (55·5 sq.m) still remaining yielded an abundant and full range of tools associated with wood and other carbonized vegetation. As in the 1956 excavations this floor had to be drained but this was achieved by removing the near sterile Ochreous Sands in the erosion channel to the south.

The east and west sections in Figures 38 and 39 show the manner in which the floor has been cut out by the later channelling. Some of the artifacts have spilled down the channel bank but it appears that the velocity of the stream was inadequate to displace them other than downwards. While the tools on the floor are lying horizontally, the derived artifacts conform to the contour of the channel bank. In square N 4 on the channel bank 12 inches (30·50 cm) below the level of the floor a wooden club was found. Next to the club in square N 3 was another short but finely pointed implement of wood. These, with two further utilized pieces of wood were lying with hand-axes, cleavers and smaller flake tools that had started to spill down the bank of the channel from the Acheulian floor. Below Acheulian Floor V a large log protruded into the channel bank and associated with it were several other pieces of wood and carbonized vegetable material—grasses and woody plants—the significance of which is discussed later.

In marked contrast to the Acheulian artifacts were the occasional Sangoan hand-axes and core-axes found in the Ochreous Sands (16)–(18) of the channel. In square L 6 was found a log of wood, hollow on one face, that had been charred in a fire. In G–K 5 and 6 the channel filling contained a number of fine roots and stems of water plants set vertically in the sand and clearly contemporary. Most of the larger artifacts found in the channel fill were lying horizontally with no particular orientation of the long axis whereas the lighter and smaller natural stones were inclined, the upper end to the west and orientated east and west.

Under the main Floor V the white, medium- to fine-grained sand (23) was sterile, except for an occasional flake in M and N 2, down to 9 inches to 1 foot (23–30·50 cm) below the floor. This sand continued to the base of the excavation on the north side at a depth of $3\frac{1}{2}$–4 feet (1·06–1·22 m) below Floor V. In the western grid squares N and O 1–2, however, two lower temporary occupation floors, termed VI and VII respectively (23′), and (23″) were found where tools and wood were preserved in association with a thin scatter of pebbles. How far these floors extended southwards is not known as they had been cut out by the later channelling. They probably correlate with the VI and VIb horizons in the B 1 excavation immediately to the north and, similarly, are distinguished from the main Acheulian Floor V by their limited extent and the relative scarcity of artifacts.

Floor VI (23′) is that associated with the large log and patches of carbonized vegetation. The stone artifacts comprise some large cutting tools and a number of flakes, again all in quite fresh condition and there are seven pieces of wood that appear to have been utilized. Floor VII (23″) is of considerable interest as, although again limited in extent, it shows a small group of large cutting tools in association with several pieces of wood. All the logs of wood lie at right angles to the line of the later channel. In square M 3 a large piece of bark was found that might have formed part of a carrying tray. This has been identified as Leguminosae bark (see Appendix E). One of the hand-axes was found standing vertically in the sand, on one long edge, as if it had been placed there artificially. All this material lay in the white sand (23) as the 'peaty' black clays of this level present in the B 1 excavation had already been replaced laterally by this sand near the south wall of the excavation.

Below Floor VII grey-black clay (23a) appeared at the north side of the excavation together with another tree-trunk and a number of wood fragments two of which are believed to have been utilized. Beneath the large log were found a hand-axe and a cleaver which were associated with a pebble line dipping east-wards and extending south over grid squares 3 and 4, forming a minor erosion feature (23′″). Because water was now standing in the excavation at river level it was difficult to clear this horizon and the precise artifact distribution could not be plotted. It is known as Surface VIII and appears to have been an occupation floor similar to VI and VII; it produced some fine examples of both large and small tools, mostly fresh and unabraded. The general standard of stone working is inferior to that on Floor V. Besides stone tools this horizon produced one piece of worked wood and other possibly utilized pieces.

As the excavation had now reached river level it was impossible to continue it further though it was clear that the White Sands containing Acheulian horizons, where not cut out by later channelling, extended below water level. At the close of the day on 29 October rain had caused the collapse of the north wall, though fortunately not before all the plotting had been completed and the tools lifted from the Floor VIII area. It had been hoped to clear the small area between the 1956 and 1959 excavations but early rains and the need to return to Livingstone prevented this. Sufficient was obtained, however, to show the wide extent of the main Acheulian Floor V and the contrastingly more limited areas of the occupation surfaces below this, besides providing a large collection of stone tools and waste and several more wooden implements. A large number of wood samples was collected from the Acheulian horizons and examples for identification were forwarded to the Commonwealth Forestry Institute at Oxford (see Appendix D).

As might be expected, the stratigraphy in the B 2 excavation is similar to that in B 1. The succession at Site B can be generally correlated with that at Site A though it naturally differs in detail. The swamp clays of the Chiungu Member, containing Iron Age remains, can be divided into older, predominantly grey clays and younger, predominantly red clays. These are found filling a cut through the bedded sands and rubble horizons of the Mbwilo Member, which rests on the main erosion surface with Rubble I-composite or Ib at its base. The succession of the Mkamba Member is more complete at Site A, for at Site B the Ochreous Sands containing Sangoan implements and possible occupation areas, are the uppermost preserved deposits of that formation. In the B 2 excavation the channel in which the Ochreous Sands were deposited was cut below the present river level, through the White Sands and the Acheulian occupation floors. The White Sands continue to an unknown depth below river level.

B3 EXCAVATION, 1959 (Figure 39)

BY J. D. CLARK

A small pit 10 × 5 feet (3·05 × 1·52 m) was excavated in the swamp approximately 100 yards (91 m) to the north-northeast of B 2 within the reed bed area. This work was carried out between 22 and 31 July by J. H. Chaplin. The excavation was made to try to determine the extent of the swamp clays with Iron Age remains east of the main excavation and the relationship of these to the Boulder sub-facies of the Chiungu Member. The stratigraphy of the pit is shown in Figure 39.

The upper 1 foot (30·50 cm) consisted of fine grey sand with some narrow lenses of darker material, probably ash from natural fires since this area is burnt annually. Below this was 6 inches (15 cm) of well-rounded cobbles, mostly of fist size. At a depth of 2 feet (61 cm) the layer of cobbles was replaced by a 6 inch (15 cm) layer of smaller material with a few well-abraded flakes. Below this again the coarse gravel was encountered and it continued down to water level at 6½ feet (1·98 m) when the excavation had to be abandoned. The well-rounded quartzite and sandstone boulders and cobbles were set in a matrix of coarse pebbly sand. Between 5 feet (1·51 m) and 5½ feet (1·67 m) was a layer of smaller gravel with, below that again, more boulders. The deposit was now damp and some thin lenses of organic clay were present.

This pit yielded only a few cultural finds all of which were well abraded.

0–1 foot (0–30·50 cm) one small rubber and a prepared flake with some retouch; also a very abraded core-axe.

1–2 feet (30·50–61 cm) four possible rubbers and two flakes.

2–2½ feet (61–76 cm) seven waste flakes, an angle core and three possible rubbers.

2½–3 feet (76–91 cm) twelve waste flakes (three with retouch), one hammerstone and one piece of slag with impression of the tuyère wall.

3–3½ feet (91 cm–1·06 m) seven flakes, two cores, one rim sherd of channel decorated pottery.

3½–4 feet (1·06–1·22 m) two flakes.

4–4½ feet (1·22–1·36 m) sixteen flakes and two pieces of iron slag.

4½–5 feet (1·36–1·52 m) ten flakes.

5–5½ feet (1·52–1·67 m) nine flakes and one piece of slag.

5½–6 feet (1·67–1·83 m) sterile.

6–6½ feet (1·83–1·98 m) three cores and one flake.

B 4 EXCAVATION, 1959 (Figure 39)

BY J. D. CLARK

A second pit was dug a further 25 yards (22·8 m) north of B 3 on the edge of the swamp area in order to see if the Boulder sub-facies was present at the same level. This pit was similarly 10 × 5 feet (3·05 × 1·52 m) and was excavated by J. H. Chaplin.

At the surface were approximately 1½ feet (45 cm) of dark grey sandy soil which became lighter with depth, changing to a light brown colour between 1½ feet (45 cm) and 2 feet (61 cm). Here was found a thin layer, 5–7 inches (12·75–17·75 cm) of yellow, loamy, clay-like material similar to that found in the upper levels of the red clays of the younger series of the Chiungu Member in trenches B 1 and B 2. This may represent consolidated ash from the burning of reeds or it might be a leached zone. Beneath this was a medium to coarse brown sand, in part ferruginous. At 3½–4 feet (1·06–1·22 m) was an irregular layer of dark brown moist clay sand and below this, between 4 and 5½ feet (1·22 and 1·67 m), was a grey mottled swamp clay. At 5½ feet (1·67 m) boulders and cobbles began to appear and continued to a depth of 6 feet (1·83 m) where excavation was stopped by water which now filled the trench. No archaeological finds were made in this pit but two small pieces of charcoal were found between 2½ and 3 feet (76 and 91 cm) and between 3 feet 2 inches and 4 feet (96·5 cm and 1·22 m). The boulders occurred at the same level in both pits.

It would seem that the topmost levels of the clays with Iron Age remains in excavations B 1 and B 2 may, if the loamy, yellow clay layers formed at approximately the same time, be contemporary with the fine-grained sediments overlying the Boulder sub-facies in pit B 4. The abraded state of the Iron Age sherd and the slag in the B 3 pit indicates that these were most certainly derived, as were those from the pit excavated in the low level terrace at ± 6 feet (1·83 m) on the Tanzania side of the river. It is possible, therefore, that the formation of the Boulder sub-facies of the Chiungu Member in the central part of the basin was contemporary with that of the low terrace nearer the Spillway Gorge. As has been seen, this event may have taken place as late as the sixteenth century.

B 5 EXCAVATION, 1963

BY J. D. CLARK

It had not originally been the intention to do any work at Site B in 1963 but the high floods of the 1961–2 season and the following year had eroded the whole of the remaining narrow portion of the sandy sediments of the 30 feet (9 m) terrace in the stretch downstream between B 2 and Site A (Figure 33). The bank of the river was now some 25–30 feet (7·6–9·1 m) east of where it had been in 1959 and showed Chiungu Member clays lying directly upon a rubble only a few feet above the water level in August 1963. The whole of the western half of the B 2 excavation had also been cut out back to the line J–H.

Up-river from B 2 erosion had not been so extensive due to the fact that it was just upstream from the bend. Here several tree-trunks and logs could be seen sticking into the river from the bank at and just below water level. Since these were associated with black clay that did not seem to have been disturbed it was thought that the concentration of wood might represent an artificial platform and it was decided to excavate it and, if possible, to establish its relationship to B 1 and B 2. The work was carried out by Sue Bucklin, J. W. D. Clark, C. M. Keller and myself between 10 and 24 August.

The bank was cut back to clear an area in which to work and in doing so hand-axes and cleavers began to appear in the area downstream and east from the wood. It was apparent that here was preserved part of the area of Acheulian Floor V which had remained unexcavated in 1959 between B 1 and B 2.

As work progressed it became clear that the tree-trunks that had led to the excavation were in part those that had already been uncovered in the B 1 excavation immediately below the level of Floor V and, indeed, a trowel from the 1956 excavation was found lying beside one of the logs. The line of the north wall of B 1 was also picked up; the south wall had already collapsed at the end of the 1956 season.

It also proved possible to pick up the eastern edge of the area of Acheulian Floor V excavated in 1956 and to extend the excavation of the undisturbed part of this floor further to the east and southeast. Unfortunately the post-1959 erosion had cut out the westward part of the unexcavated portion of the floor between B 1 and B 2. However, the eastward portion was preserved and produced some excellent examples of large cutting tools and a full range of waste and small tools. The plot of this floor, which measured approximately 23 × 10 feet (7·01 × 3·05 m) and the analysis lists will be given in volume III. This excavation provides important additional evidence for estimating the extent of the occupation site which can now be seen to have been more than 2,000 square feet (215 sq.m) in area. It was found to rise very slightly from north to south, it has no thickness and, again, all the artifacts and natural stones have been carried in.

Re-excavation of the tree-trunks and wood fragments in the river bank showed that several of them were, indeed, the same as those uncovered in 1956 while others had since been exposed by the river erosion. As previously described, it is possible, though no conclusive proof was forthcoming, that these logs had formed an artificial platform. At the river bank itself, immediately upstream from the tree-trunks in B 1 excavation, erosion had exposed clean sections and a pointed piece of wood was found here sticking from the river bank and lying in black 'peaty' clay. This was excavated without using metal tools and the specimen was found to be a flat stick 3 feet (91 cm) long with a flattened, oval section curved at one end and pointed at the other. The extreme tip end had been broken off and carried away by the river. The specimen is a stout, straight branch from a shrub or bushy tree with part of the root preserved, gently curved, probably from the weight of the overburden, and has the appearance of having been used. It was situated at the same level as, or immediately below, the Acheulian Floor V which here was just above water level and yielded a fine elongate ovate hand-axe in hard quartzite.

When the remaining area of the old B 1 trench had been re-excavated it was possible to identify the eastern limit of the area over which Floor VI had been excavated in 1956. A further part of this floor—16 × 6 feet (4·88 × 1·83 m)— lying to the east of the 1956 dig was now excavated and the distribution of arti- facts plotted. This work was carried out by C. M. Keller and Sue Bucklin. The plot shows a concentration of considerable interest for comparison with that from the B 2 excavation. The detailed analysis of the collection from the 1963 area of this floor still remains to be undertaken.

The stratigraphic and cultural evidence from Site B is summarized in Table 1.

TABLE I. *Summary of evidence: geological events at Site B*

Phases of downcutting (C) and filling (F)[a]	Elevation above the present approximate low water level of the Kalambo River	Remarks (C14 dates in counted elapsed years)	Named geological units[b]	Pollen evidence
Soil	Top c. 20 feet on River Face Cliff	Thin soil formed on fluviatile sands containing Iron Age remains		Nil
			Chiungu Member	
F 7" Predominantly red sandy clays with grit lenses	Top c. 18 feet Base c. 14 feet	Iron Age remains C14 date 370 ± 50 years in B 2		Nil Nil
C 7" Break in deposition of red sands and clays	Base c. 14 feet	B 1 and B 2	[Erosion?]	Nil
F 7' Predominantly grey silty clays and clay with gravel at base including some dolerite	Top c. 18 feet Base c. 6 feet	Iron Age remains C14 date 930 ± 30 years in B 2		Nil
C 7' Channel cut	Base c. 6 feet	B 1 and B 2 cut down from c. 18 feet to 6 feet	[Erosion]	
			Mbwilo Member	
F 6 Current-bedded sands	Top highest 19 feet Base lowest c. 12 feet	Sterile B 1 and B 2		Nil
[Break in deposition of fine sediments]	From 12 feet to 11 feet B 1			
Pebble horizon		Artifacts of 'Magosian' type B 1		Nil
F 6 Current-bedded sands	Top highest c. 12 feet Base lowest c. 10 feet	Sterile B 1		Nil
[Break in deposition of fine sediments]				
Rubble/gravel	From + 15 feet to ± 10 feet	Mixed aggregate of Lupemban and earlier artifacts: latest is 'Magosian', B 1 and B 2	Rubble Bed (Ia)	Nil
F 6 Coarse bedded sands, grits and impersistent pebble horizons: some clay and fine sand	Top highest c. 15 feet Base lowest c. − 8 feet	Mixed cultural material of Lupemban and 'Magosian' type B 2		Nil
[Break in deposition of fine sediments]				
Rubble/gravel	From c. 13 feet to ± 8 feet	Mixed aggregate of Lupemban and earlier artifacts: latest is 'Magosian', B 2	Rubble Bed (I-composite or Ib)	Nil
C 6 Down cutting by river	Channelling c. + 15 feet to ± 10 feet and 0 or − 0 feet south of B 2	'Main erosion surface' B 1 and B 2	[Erosion]	

TABLE I (*cont.*)

Phases of downcutting (C) and filling (F)[a]	Elevation above the present approximate low water level of the Kalambo River	Remarks (C14 dates in counted elapsed years)	Named geological units[b]	Pollen evidence
			Mkamba Member	
F 3 Ochreous fine and coarse sands, some bedded, impersistent pebble lines and fine gravel; grey 'peaty' clays in upper part	Top +12 feet Base − 0 feet	Sangoan artifacts in gravel stringers and on temporary pebble horizons in B 1 and B 2. C14 dates 37,900 ± 1,500/1,200 years from upper part 42,000 ± 2,000 years from lower part	Ochreous Sands and Grey Clay Beds	Warmer and wetter Nil ?Warmer Present day
C 3 Channelling and some down cutting	Base at − 0 feet	B 1 and B 2	[Erosion?]	
F 2 White, structureless, fine sands and black clays with impersistent pebble horizons	Top c. 6 feet Base c. 2 feet	Top truncated Acheulian occupation floor V at base	White Sands and	Cooler, wetter
(C 2) [Minor break in deposition of fine sediments]				
F 1 White, bedded, fine to coarse sands and black clays with impersistent pebble horizons	Top highest c. 3 feet Base at − 0 feet	Acheulian occupation floors VI–VIII	[?Erosion] Dark Clay Beds	Warmer ?Drier
C 1 Cutting to bedrock?	?	?	[Erosion]	?

[a] C 5 and C 7, F 5 and F 7 are not represented at Site B.
[b] Terms in parentheses are used in the archaeological nomenclature.

SITE C EXCAVATIONS, 1959 AND 1963

BY J. D. CLARK

As the cliff section is described in the chapter on the geology (see also Plate 31 and Figure 11) and the microlithic and Iron Age settlements will be discussed in volume II, it is necessary here to refer only to the cultural content of the rubble at the base of the fluviatile, bedded sands. This rests here on an erosion surface cut into cross-bedded, buff to ochreous sands which are probably the same as those under the clays near the base of the Site D sections (see below). If so, it would indicate that these clays had been cut out from the central part of the valley by the channelling that preceded the deposition of the Mbwilo Member before the rubble bed was deposited.

No archaeological excavation was done at this site (C) in 1959 but material was collected from the rubble that showed the usual assortment of upper Lupemban artifacts with older material indicating that it was probably Rubble I composite. In 1963, however, several slightly abraded earlier Lupemban type core-axes were found and these suggested the possibility that Rubble II might also be represented here. Accordingly, it was decided to excavate a small exploratory section and this was done by C. M. Keller between 16 and 21 August. An area was selected at the foot of the cliff immediately downstream from the south wall of the settlement excavation and a trench 20 × 5 feet (6·1 × 1·52 m) was excavated. The rubble/gravel dipped gently towards the north and consisted of the usual angular rocks and tools. It was only one stone thick (4–5 inches (10–13 cm)) and rested disconformably on the Ochreous Sands.

The excavation proved beyond any doubt that this surface was, in fact, Rubble I-composite resting on the main erosion surface.

Only 350 artifacts were recovered, including eighteen shaped tools, and the incidence of the prepared core method is low. The blades and blade cores and dorsally prepared flakes with faceted striking platforms (seven in all, since two of the utilized flakes have prepared platforms) and flat, discoid, prepared cores are of upper Lupemban form but, as at Site D, the parallel-sided and double-ended core-axes and those with a core scraper edge worked on the butt, as well as the number of plain platformed flakes, show that a high proportion of the contents of the rubble belongs to the lower Lupemban or to the Sangoan.

Some 9 inches to 2 feet (23–61 cm) above this rubble in the base of the overlying, loose, cross-bedded sands was a thin pebble band in places as at B 1 excavation. This yielded a small collection of sixty-two artifacts, including only four shaped tools, four blade fragments and a blade core; all are to some extent abraded and are, therefore, presumably derived.

SITE C EXCAVATIONS, 1966 (Figure 40)

BY G. H. COLE

Introduction

During a brief stay at Kalambo Falls from 16 to 28 October 1966, the writer was invited by Dr Clark to excavate at Site C, where it appeared from surface material that a Sangoan occurrence might have been present. A relatively flat area which is part of the high water stream channel contained quite a few large artifacts of Sangoan type. Excavations failed to locate a Sangoan occurrence, however, and it became evident that the artifacts had derived from some of the higher lying deposits at this site. The Kalambo River in flood, evidently, is not competent to move the larger stone artifacts but readily sorts out the smaller tools and flakes which are by far the most important constituents of the occurrences encountered in excavation.

This note will describe the stratigraphic situation at Site C. It has not been possible, at the time of preparing this statement, to study the artifacts which were recovered during the excavations.

The excavations (Plate 31)

Excavation number 1 was a 20 feet long trench which extended from near the edge of the dry season stream into the bank of the high-water channel. This trench covered a vertical distance from the water table to 8·5 feet (2·6 m) above, where it overlapped with a section cleared in excavation number 4. The latter was simply made to clear a section upwards from that exposed at the headward end of trench number 1 and to clear a portion of the single rubble line present at this part of the site. No artifacts were collected from either of these excavations.

Excavations 2 and 3 were put in to expose sections and to recover artifacts from a portion of the site where superimposed rubble lines could be seen to occur. In addition, a 32 foot section of the steep wet season stream bank was cleared to facilitate tracing and correlating the rubble lines present at the two extremes of the excavated area (Figure 40).

The sediments

About 27 feet of fluvial deposits with occasional rubble lines occur above low water level at Site C.

The sediments are mainly in the size range of sands and fine gravels. Coarser

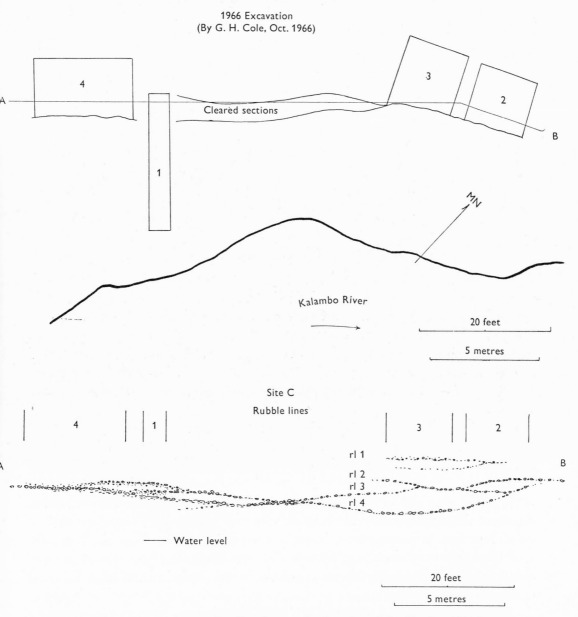

KALAMBO FALLS: SITE C

1966 Excavation
(By G. H. Cole, Oct. 1966)

4

A

Cleared sections

3

2

B

1

MN

Kalambo River

20 feet

5 metres

Site C

Rubble lines

4

1

3

2

A

rl 1

rl 2

rl 3

rl 4

B

Water level

20 feet

5 metres

Fig. 40. Plan of excavations at Site C and generalized section of the Site C rubble lines as
seen in excavations and cleared sections.

183

pebbles are occasionally found and clayey sands and silts also occur. Clay lumps are common in some of the beds and clay seams or lenses sometimes occur. The few of these encountered in excavation appeared rather to be the result of fusing of an aggregate of clay lumps than a product of slack water deposition. Interfaces are sometimes simply non-depositional surfaces between two minor depositional units while others are erosional surfaces. The latter usually are marked by angular fragments, or sometimes pebbles, with artifacts.

The entire sequence at Site C would appear to be comprised of channel deposits, except for the few feet at the top which contain 'Iron Age' artifacts and which have been investigated at this site by Clark and van Noten in 1963.

The lowermost deposits at the southwest end of the excavated area as exposed in excavation number 1 are coarse cross-bedded ferruginous sands. These sands are truncated by a 3 foot thick lens or wedge, which pinches out away from the river, made up largely of clay lumps with an intercalated sand lens. Another sand layer, varying from 6 inches to 2 feet thick separates this deposit from a rubble zone (= Rubble I-composite (J.D.C.)) including clay lumps, chunks of sandstone, and ferruginous sandstone slabs, all derived from the Kalambo Falls Formation. Quartzite and other rock fragments from the surrounding hills as well as artifacts are also found in this rubble. A thin lens of sand separates this rubble from a fine gravel with artifacts but the sand pinches out quickly and is not present in excavation 4 where the gravel lies directly on the rubble line. Three feet of cross-bedded sands lie over the rubble. These have been truncated in this section and are now covered by a dark loam containing potsherds which has slumped from the deposits containing Iron Age remains at the top of the terrace.

At the downstream end of the site excavations were not taken to water level but in excavation number 3, an 18 foot section was cleared upwards from the lowermost rubble line (= Rubble I-composite (J.D.C.)) (about 4 feet above river level) that could be seen exposed in the river bank. In this section, four distinct rubble lines were distinguished although minor non-persistent pebble or rubble stringers with a few artifacts were also encountered (Figure 40). These are marked 1 to 4 from top to bottom since it was not possible to relate them more exactly with any of the subdivisions of Rubble-I at Sites A and B. Due to the unconsolidated nature of the sediments, this excavation was made in three steps to avoid slumping. At the front of the excavation the two lowermost rubble lines (3 and 4) are separated by about 3 feet of sand. These rubble lines merge in excavation 2 and this merged rubble in turn joins rubble line 2 a few feet further to the northeast to appear as a single rubble line in the river bank. Rubble lines 2 and 3 are separated by more than 2 feet of sand at the front of excavation 3 but merge towards the back and at its downstream end to separate again in the adjacent excavation. Several feet of sand including many clay lumps and a weakly developed unconformity with a few artifacts lie between rubble lines 1 and 2 at the back of the excavation. Cross-bedded sands and gravels lie over rubble line 1 to a depth of 8 feet in the cleared section and appear, in exposed portions of the terrace riser, to extend at least to the dark coloured deposits with Iron Age remains. No artifacts were seen *in situ* in these sediments but a small straight-backed blade was found on the surface of some material slumped from the upper part of the terrace, apparently having washed out of it.

Rubble line 1 lies at about $12\frac{1}{2}$ feet (3·8 m) above the river and contains not very abundant artifacts in a gravel band lying on an irregular eroded surface which contains many clay lumps. This rubble line, not as strongly marked as the other three, passes beneath slumped material between excavations 3 and 4 and did not reappear as a recognizable feature in the latter. Similarly, rubble line 2 seems to have disappeared in the same area. The two lower rubble lines, however, were followed by means of clearing the steep river bank between excavations 1 and 3. These two rubbles merge about half-way between and then separate only to come together again in excavation 4. In the vicinity of excavation 1, the lowermost rubble line is marked more by the presence of a layer of clay lumps than by artifacts or rubble.

The artifacts

Artifacts found in the rubble lines are generally unworn and apparently pertain to industries of the sort which at other of the Kalambo Falls sites have been referred to as the Lupemban and 'Magosian'.

More large Sangoan-type artifacts and large rock fragments were found in the lower rubble lines than the upper. This is not necessarily because more of these artifacts were manufactured at the time of formation of these rubbles, for these large pieces could well have settled as lag material much as similar artifacts and rubble characterize the present seasonally exposed channel floor.

Although there is no particular reason why there should be an appreciable time span involved in the deposits spanning the rubble lines 1 to 4 part of the sequence, it did seem on preliminary examination of artifacts during excavation and labelling that material which would seem to have been typologically in advance of that of rubble lines 3 and 4 was to be found in the uppermost rubble lines.

Small bits of charcoal were found in excavation 3 in a thin sand layer occurring between rubble lines 2 and 3. It is thought that enough of this substance was found to permit C14 dating.

Conclusions

It can be suggested that the environment of Site C was one of a somewhat sluggish, shifting stream, much like that of the Kalambo River in this area today. The sediments all appear to be channel deposits. Remnants of overbank deposits are probably represented by the abundant clay lumps. The more pronounced rubble lines doubtless represent old channels which were, in part at least, seasonally exposed. Thus, as is true at the Site C today, streamside living areas were available. As most of the artifacts are unabraded and would seem to have suffered little or no transport, it is likely that most of them are in archaeological context although some lag accumulation and transported material is also present. Evidence in other of the Kalambo Falls excavations indicated that the Kalambo River had erosional and aggradational phases but there is no reason to think that the deposits at Site C, excepting the few feet of sediments at the top of the sequence which contain 'Iron Age' material, represent any more than a single aggradational phase with such minor erosional activity as is associated with lateral shifting and seasonal variation in flow.

SITE D EXCAVATION, 1956 (Figure 41)

BY J. D. CLARK

This site lies to the west of Site C, near the quartzite ridge that bounds the basin on the western side. A well-defined rubble/gravel was present half-way down the cliff section exposed by the river and it was hoped to be able to correlate the stratigraphy here with that at Site B and the 'Tanganyika Cliff'.

A grid 20 × 15 feet (6·1 × 4·5 m) was laid out on 26 July and excavated down to the rubble during August. When uncovered, the additional slope of the river bank at the level of the stoneline gave a surface area of 25 × 20 feet (7·6 × 6·1 m). By 1963 the river had cut back at Site D so that the top of the bank was then within 5 feet (1·52 m) of the south wall of the 1956 excavation.

Below the black-grey surface soil (1) was a thin layer of lighter coloured, buff soil (2) and below this to a depth of 3 feet (91·5 cm) from the surface was a grey, fairly sandy deposit (3) which is the Iron Age occupation midden that appears to cover the greater part of the top of the 30 feet (9 m) terrace between Sites B, C and D. The surface soil produced a nineteenth-century annular bead of blue glass and a number of the Kalambo Industry sherds. Some slag and daga were also found in the midden soil down to a depth of 3½ feet (1·06 m). This material is of little interest except for the finding of a complete, undecorated, globular pot with an incised glyph, engraved after firing, on one side of the body of the pot. Following the evidence of the 1963 excavation on Site C, it would seem likely that this pot may have been associated with a grave and the engraving could have been a representation of the burial.

As on Site C the grey sand of the midden gave place to a light buff sand (4) which extended down for a further 7–9 feet (2·1–2·7 m) and rested on the rubble/gravel. This sand (4) was loosely compacted and cross-bedded with thin, contorted bands or lenses of dark brown clay which are also, presumably, like those on Site C, post-depositional in age. At the south end brown clay is diffused more extensively in some of the sand layers. This sand is clearly the same as those that overlay Rubble I-composite at Sites A, B and C and forms the upper member of the 30 feet (9 m) terrace. The sand contained no artifacts and the discontinuous pebble line immediately above the base at Sites B and A 1 is absent at D.

The rubble (5) is composed of the usual sub-angular rocks and smaller stones, unsorted and lying wedged together at different angles in a brown to grey clay matrix which becomes sandier at the northeast side of the excavation. This surface is some 4 inches (10 cm) thick and, as elsewhere, yielded a number of artifacts which appear to belong to the earlier 'Middle Stone Age' or lower Lupemban, though older and younger material is also associated.

Since this is a rubble/gravel no significance can be attached to the distribution pattern of artifacts and there is, moreover, a tendency for the large tools to be aligned with the long axis in a north–south direction suggesting redistribution by water. The rubble rises gently towards the south and is between 14 and 15 feet (3·27 and 3·57 m) above low water level. It is not possible to be certain which subdivision of Rubble I is represented here and, from the height above the river, it is likely to be composite as in the A 4 and B 1 excavations and to have been exposed for the greater part of the time covered by the three subdivisions. The large-sized blocks of quartzite must have reached their position by colluvial action down the slopes of the adjacent quartzite ridge and must then have been redistributed by an early phase of the channelling which preceded and/or deposited the overlying sands of the Mbwilo Member. The majority of the artifacts are abraded but not severely, suggesting that they cannot have travelled very far and the large tool element, in particular the parallel-sided and elongate core-axes, is of lower Lupemban rather than of Sangoan form. The prepared core element is present though no very evolved forms of core, radially prepared flake or blade occur.

During 'Magosian' times this rubble was an exposed slope since the few (10) fresh artifacts are in absolutely mint condition and include one very typical

'Magosian' backed blade. As at the other sites the tools of this type must have been covered rapidly by the aggradation phase that deposited the sands of the Mbwilo Member.

The composite Rubble I at Site D rested on an erosion surface cut in a white or greyish white clay (5), possibly weathered bedrock from the hill to the west. In some places this deposit approached kaolin in consistency while in others it was more of a sandy clay. It was at least 10 feet (3 m) thick, contained no artifacts or pebbles and must have been laid down in still, open water.

Investigation of the deposits below Rubble I-composite at this site was confined to the river bank section and the excavation was stopped here at water level.

The base of the grey clay (5), where exposed, was seen to dip fairly steeply to the south and was separated by a minor disconformity from a buff-coloured clay (7) that passed down into grey and black clay (7′), all of which were seen to be filling a channel that appeared to have a southeasterly direction. In the black clay near the base of this channel fill were found several pieces of wood, much decomposed. A sample of this was dated to > 40,000 years (Lamont, L-399A) which places it in the range of samples from the Ochreous Sands at Sites A and B, or, perhaps, on the evidence mentioned below, slightly earlier.

The bank or side of the channel on which the clays rest is an ochreous brown clay (8) and lying on the sloping surface of this clay in the lower part of the excavation, almost at water level, were found two artifacts in hard quartzite. The first of these is a very slightly rolled, elongate hand-axe (20·5 × 9·5 cm) with convergent sides and a rounded, linguate end. It is bifacially worked and was probably made on a flake. The butt is square rather than U-shaped and similarly shows bifacial retouch. This is characteristic of a form found on the uppermost Acheulian floors at Site A. The second specimen is a large, utilized flake (8 × 6 cm), irregular in plan form with one, convex, unifacially trimmed edge. This specimen is fresh. These two tools might be contemporary with the channel surface on which the clays rest or they might be derived from the immediately underlying deposit. This latter is a fine bedded sand (9), buff to orange in colour from ferruginous staining. At a height of 6–9 inches (15·25–23 cm) above the base of the excavation at water level, were found in this sand two quite fresh, irregular, primary flakes of hard quartzite. They lay just below the brown clay (8) and almost at the same level as the wood in the black clay of the channel fill. This ochreous sand passed upwards at the west side into an unstratified, fine, white sand and downwards into an unstratified, medium- to coarse-grained sand with a fairly high grey clay content which was sterile and passed below water level.

The fill of the channel appears to belong to the Ochreous Sands as in the B 2 excavation and the older eroded deposits to the White Sands of the Mkamba Member. The fine-grained deposits that were found below Rubble I-composite at Site D are typical of those in the north and northwest of the local basin, grading into more sandy beds somewhere between Sites B and D. These beds extend towards the southwest adjacent to the Spillway Gorge.

REFERENCE

Clark, J. D. (1954). An early Upper Pleistocene site at the Kalambo Falls on the Northern Rhodesia Tanganyika Border. *S. Afr. Arch. Bull.* **9**, no. 34, pp. 51–6.

CHAPTER 6

CORRELATION OF ARCHAEOLOGICAL SITES IN THE LOCAL BASIN AT THE KALAMBO FALLS

BY J. D. CLARK

The foregoing chapters have shown something of the complexity of cutting and filling that is observable in the later Quaternary sedimentary sequence, as well as of the rapidity of facies changes in the sediments in the local basin at the Kalambo Falls. The lateral swing of the main stream course together with the local cutting and aggrading of secondary channels and the deposition of fine overbank sediments in back channels, makes it impossible exactly to correlate the succession at each of the four main sites investigated. However, the coincidence of the main Beds and deposits of the three Members is never in doubt, not only on lithological grounds, but also on account of their archaeological and pollen content and the chronology established by the radiocarbon method.

The Mkamba Member is the earliest of which record exists and is preserved in the north and south sides of the basin to a height of ±50 feet (15·2 m) above low water level in the river. It is best known from the excavations at Site A. All except the lower beds of this Member have been removed from the central parts of the basin by subsequent erosion which, following the unblocking or cutting of the Spillway Gorge, lowered the water level to that of the present-day stream, at the same time entirely removing the upper part of the Member. The base of the Mkamba Member lies at an unknown depth (though in excess of 9 feet (2·75 m)) below low water level. The Member consists of bedded, coarse and fine sands and clay layers with organic remains, together with pebble lines and primary archaeological horizons that occur up to a height of 6 feet (1·83 m) above the river and contain Acheulian artifacts. The aggregates are mostly quite undisturbed by natural agencies and lie on very temporary surfaces on which there had been inadequate time for soil to form or vegetation to become established.

The Acheulian is contemporary with a period of uninterrupted and probably fairly rapid aggradation. At the top, the latest Acheulian horizons in the White

190

Sands Bed are dated at Site A to > 61,700 years B.P. (GrN-4228) (Vogel & Waterbolk, 1964). An older horizon, 3 feet (91 cm) lower at the same site dates to 60,300±750 years (GrN-2644).[1] The lower Acheulian 'floors' at Site B, which are stratigraphically older again, are contemporary with a warmer and probably drier climate. However, by the end of Acheulian times at the Kalambo Falls, the pollen spectra at both Sites A and B show that cooler and wetter conditions permitted the growth of higher altitude vegetation in the immediate vicinity of the basin.

A black clay bank occurs near, or at, the top of the White Sands Bed at both sites and has in each case been truncated by later erosion which cut a channel into the sands to an as yet undetermined depth below present river level. There is no indication that this channelling represents a major phase of erosion, nor that any great length of time elapsed between the end of the Acheulian contained in the White Sands Bed and the first appearance of the Sangoan found in the overlying Ochreous Sands Bed that fills this channel. However, if the radiocarbon age of 43,000±3,300 (L-399C) (Olson & Broecker, 1959) for wood from the top of the truncated channel fill with Sangoan tools beneath Rubble Ic at the A 1 excavation can be accepted as dating the sands in which the wood was found, this would indicate that at least 18,000 years separate the latest Acheulian from the Sangoan present in the lower foot of the Ochreous Sands at Site A or an even longer period of time at Site B. The geological evidence gives little indication that the erosion period separating these two beds of the Mkamba Member was so great but, since the compositions of the Acheulian and Sangoan artifact aggregates at the Kalambo Falls (Clark, 1965) are sufficiently divergent to show that they are at least not derived the one from the other, sufficient time must have elapsed for the differentiation of the Sangoan to have taken place.

At Sites A, B, C and D the Ochreous Sands pass below the level of the present river so it is possible that the earlier 'transitional' stages, that appear to be missing at the Kalambo Falls, lie within the lower part of these sands in the base of the erosion channel. That part of the Ochreous Sands that is exposed above water level and reaches a height of 30 feet (9·15 m) above the river accumulated comparatively rapidly in some 3,000–5,000 years or less, on the basis of the radiocarbon dates for the top and lower part of the Ochreous Sands Member at Site A. The finite dates from Sites A and B on wood and charcoals in these sediments lie between 37,900±1,500/1,200 years (GrN-3228) at Site B 2 and 46,100±3,500/2,400 years (GrN-3226) at A 4. As, however, the latter date is derived from a charcoal sample coming from near the top of the Ochreous Sands at A 4 and is greater than both those from the lower part of these sands at A 1 (43,000±3,300 years (L-399C)) and at B 2 (42,000±2,000 years (GrN-3237)), it

[1] Suggesting the replacement of Acheulian by Sangoan took place at least 60,000 years ago.

is probable that some contamination exists, either due to leaching in the upper levels, or more probably to absorption of younger carbon from groundwater in the lower part of the deposit which is always moist and where there is much seepage from the present swamp, especially at Site B.

These dates for the Sangoan from Kalambo are in general agreement with those from northeast Angola (Mufo) (Clark, 1963) and from Rhodesia (Pomongwe Cave) (Cooke, 1963), so that no major discrepancy exists. They indicate also, as does the lithology, that the Ochreous Sands accumulated fairly rapidly and that the Sangoan aggregates contained within them belong with a later rather than with an earlier stage of that industrial complex. This confirms the archaeological data that there is no direct continuum between the Acheulian and the Sangoan at the Kalambo Falls though it is possible, as previously stated, that the missing stages lie in the lower part of the channel below river level.

The sterile pale grey sands and clays, well represented at Site D up to a height of 14 feet (4·27 m) above river level and again in the lower part of the 'Tanganyika Cliff' section, show that, while coarser sediments were accumulating in the main channel, some open, still water probably existed at the northwest side of the local basin. Such fine sediments could have been laid down in abandoned meanders as overbank deposits following seasonal flooding from the main stream. The pollen spectra of this time indicate somewhat warmer and wetter climatic conditions, but with a cooler phase towards the end. The aggradation of the Ochreous Sands and grey clays only became possible through the blocking of the Spillway Gorge and the continued building up of this blockage which permitted the aggradation of a further 20 feet (6·1 m) or more of sands, clays and fine gravels to a height of ±50 feet (15·2 m) above the river. A temporary halt in sedimentation or the northward swing of the main channel is represented by the accumulation of Rubble II at Site A which contains what has been tentatively described as lower Lupemban. This event is dated to 31,660±600 years B.P. at A 4 (see Appendix J). The artifact aggregate from this horizon is characterized by elongate core-axes and picks, retouched blades and the first appearance of the Levallois technique. Further channelling and aggradation followed (Pits Channel Fill Bed) at Site A and is probably also represented in the 'Tanganyika Cliff' section on the north side of the river by an interface at +28 feet (8·5 m) though no artifacts are present here. Two pollen samples from the upper part of the Pits Channel Fill give warmer and wetter values and a correlation has been suggested with the Paudorf interstadial of Europe. Rare artifacts found in the base of the Pits Channel in A 4 and at A 2 are probably Lupemban.

The top of the fine sediments filling the Pits Channel represents the top of the Mkamba Member and, after building up to a height of between 40 feet (12·2 m) and 50 feet (15·2 m) above the river the base level in the local basin was rapidly lowered to the present level by the breaking and removal of the blockage in the Spillway Gorge. Whether or not this event and the stratigraphic break that separates the Mkamba from the succeeding Mbwilo Member were the direct result of climatic change cannot be determined, though it is possible that this was a contributory cause. As has been stated, the pollen evidence shows that the climate in the closing stages of the aggradation of the Mkamba Member was warmer changing to cooler and perhaps wetter than the present day, but no pollen evidence is yet available from the base of the Mbwilo Member. A radiocarbon date of 30,500±2,000 years (L-3991) (Broecker & Olson, 1961) from charcoals at a height of 8 feet (2·44 m) above river level, thought at one time to date the Rubble/Gravel Ic is, in view of the date of Rubble II, now less likely to reflect the true age of this Ic rubble and channel gravel which is expected to be younger. The length of time represented by this discontinuity in the aggradation of fine-grained sediments in the local basin is unknown. If the time interval between the formation of Rubble Ic and the deposition of the overlying fine sediments was short, then the pollen spectra from the black clays overlying Rubble Ic at A 1, which clearly indicate a cooler and wetter climate, provide evidence that climatic change could have played a major role in the unblocking of the Spillway Gorge. On the other hand, if the break was a long one, these pollens give no indication of the climate at the beginning of Mbwilo Member times. Once the aggradation of fine sediments recommenced approximately 30 feet (9·15 m) of sands and clays were deposited with two further rubble/gravels in the lower part. Probably contemporary with the initial down cutting and continuing through most of the time represented by the Mbwilo Member, was the accumulation of the Red Rubble Bed on the southern slopes of the basin at Site A. These later rubble/gravels are well represented at Sites B, C and D but the rubble becomes increasingly less the further away from the source on the southern and western hill slopes. At Sites C and D there is appreciably less rubble than at Sites A and B. These rubble/gravel horizons that line the bottoms of the stream channels must have been covered fairly rapidly, but those on the slopes were exposed for a longer time and would have provided a suitable surface for occupation and sources of raw material for the human population.

The archaeological content of these Rubble Beds of the Mbwilo Member is mixed and so far it has not proved possible to locate occupation horizons of the Lupemban and 'Magosian' that are in primary archaeological context though the remarkable quantity of tools and artifacts, which often show minimal evidence of wear or abrasion, indicates that living sites must have been in the immediate vicinity of the Site A excavations. In addition to the derived artifacts of Acheulian and/or Sangoan type, at least two stages of the Lupemban are represented in these horizons. The latest artifacts are of 'Magosian' type lying on Rubble I-composite at A 3 dated to 9,550±2,110 years (L-395D) and sealed by current-bedded sands; 'Magosian' tools are, similarly, the latest at Sites B, C and D. The top of the sterile sands that seal these horizons in the western part of the basin and represent the latest deposit of the Mbwilo Member constitutes a terrace approximately 30 feet (9·15 m) above the present river. The aggradation of these sands was coincident with the reblocking of the Spillway Gorge up to at least the height and the deposition of the Older Boulder Beds at the eastern end of the basin. The evolved 'Magosian' artifacts from the upslope sandy clays over the Red Rubble at Site A are probably in part contemporary with the accumulation of current-bedded sands in the central part of the basin. Unfortunately, no pollen data are available for the later events in the local Kalambo basin and, again, it is not possible to know whether the subsequent unblocking of the Spillway Gorge in post-Mbwilo Member times and the re-excavation of the river channel to its present level were climatically controlled. Pollen spectra from east Africa and northeastern Angola indicate a warmer temperature in early post-Pleistocene times (van Zinderen Bakker, 1967) and probably increased rainfall and it may be inferred that the same was true at the Kalambo Falls. If the erosion that preceded the aggradation of both the Mbwilo and the Chiungu Members was contemporaneous with a warmer and probably wetter climate, as we have now seen that there is reason to believe was the case and, since there is no evidence of tectonic movement at those times, then climate and coincident vegetation changes may have played a significant part in controlling the blocking and unblocking of the Spillway Gorge.

By approximately 2000 B.C. (3,920±40 and 3,850±40 years) erosion had proceeded sufficiently far to have exposed the top of the 30 foot (9 m) terrace, which formed an attractive camping area for 'Later Stone Age' groups at Site C. The archaeological aggregate is now fully microlithic but with the addition of edge ground axes/adzes, bored stones and other large tools. The area was subsequently occupied in early Iron Age times contemporaneously with two or more stages of channelling, which lowered the river to its present level. In these channels at the western end of the basin there accumulated grey, silty clays, followed by red clays in which collected a scatter of occupation debris from the settlement areas; upstream to the east the fine grained sediments gave place to coarse gravels—the 'Younger Boulder Bed' (Chiungu Member). The early Iron Age food-producing population was present by the middle of the fourth century A.D. (1,605±40 years, B.P.) (GrN-4646) and continued to occupy the local basin until the close of the tenth century and probably later. A later plain ware pottery tradition which is presumed to have superseded the Channel Decorated Wares in the basin by the sixteenth century A.D. is known from the hill slopes above Site A and may have been ancestral to the wares made by the Mambwe and Lungu peoples who occupy the Kalambo Falls locality today.

Although the sedimentary succession in the local basin at the Kalambo Falls and its contents provides a unique record of events and changing human technology from early in the Upper Pleistocene to the present day, there are, as this record shows, still gaps to be filled, chronological events to be confirmed and problems, both geological and archaeological, to be solved. Indeed, although the deficiencies in this record are all too apparent, nevertheless, it is the most complete that we have for this time in sub-Saharan Africa and it is sufficiently demonstrated that it can be used to provide a basic framework within which the cultural content of the archaeological horizons that are analysed and discussed in subsequent volumes of this work can be studied, cultural units can be established and an attempt can be made to understand the relationship of these to the ecosystems of which they formed an integral part.

REFERENCES

Broecker, W. S. & Olson, E. A. (1961). Lamont radiocarbon measurements VII. *Radiocarbon*, **3**, 172.

Clark, J. D. (1963). Prehistoric cultures of northeast Angola and their significance in tropical Africa. *Diamang. Lisbon. Publicações Culturais*, no. 62, p. 18a.

(1965). The influence of environment in inducing culture change at the Kalambo Falls Prehistoric Site. *S. Afr. Arch. Bull.* **20**, no. 75, pp. 93–101.

Cooke, C. K. (1963). Report on excavations at Pomongwe and Tshangula Caves, Matopos Hills, Southern Rhodesia. *S. Afr. Arch. Bull.* **18**, no. 71, pp. 146–51.

Olson, E. A. & Broecker, W. S. (1959). Lamont natural radiocarbon measurements V. *Radiocarbon*, **1**, 23–5.

van Zinderen Bakker, E. M. (1967). Upper Pleistocene and Holocene stratigraphy and ecology on the basis of vegetation changes in sub-Saharan Africa. In *Background to Evolution in Africa*, ed. by W. W. Bishop and J. D. Clark. Chicago University Press. Pp. 125–47.

Vogel, J. C. & Waterbolk, H. T. (1964). Groningen radiocarbon dates V. *Radiocarbon*, **6**, 350–2.

13-2

APPENDIX A

THE GEOLOGY OF THE KALAMBO FALLS PREHISTORIC SITE

By Geoffrey Bond[1]

1. INTRODUCTION[2]

The Kalambo River flows into the eastern shore of Lake Tanganyika near the southern end of the lake. For some miles eastward of this point the river forms the territorial boundary between Tanzania and Zambia. About 4 miles (6·4 km) upstream from the lake the river plunges 720 feet (220 m), in one pitch, over the Kalambo Falls, which have become a well-known tourist attraction. In consequence the area is more accessible than it would otherwise be. It can be reached quite easily by car from Abercorn about 21 miles (33·5 km) to the south.

In 1928 Mrs E. Gordon-Gallien organized an expedition to the Kalambo Falls and took with her a surveyor, Lieut. J. W. Cornwall, R.A., and a geologist, Colin Rose. Their purpose was to fix the position of the falls, measure their height and map the area topographically and geologically. An account of their work appeared as three papers in the *Geographical Journal* for 1929. This expedition produced what was probably the first reliable map of the area and the coordinates, shown on the geological map (Figure 5), were taken from it.

Rose (1929) published two geological maps, one on a scale of $\frac{1}{2}$ inch = 1 mile on which the outlines of the alluvium (Quaternary) are shown, and another on a scale of 1 inch = 1,500 feet on the detailed geology in the immediate vicinity of the falls. His views on the origin of the falls will be discussed in a later section of this paper.

The Quaternary Geology of the area was briefly described by Dr J. D. Clark in the first paper published on the archaeology of this site (Clark, 1954). His description was based on the sections disclosed by his first excavations, before any detailed geological mapping had been done.

During October 1956 I spent ten days at Kalambo at the invitation of Dr Clark. By that time a good topographic map had been prepared by Mr Clayphan on a scale of 1 inch = 500 feet and air photographs were also available. At the time of my visit Dr Clark's major excavation had reached an advanced stage and provided large clean sections. The time was spent making a detailed geological map of the Quaternary deposits of as much of the Kalambo basin as possible and in examining the sections exposed by excavation.

[1] I would like to express my thanks to Dr J. D. Clark for the privilege of taking part in so important an investigation; for making all the arrangements for my visit, and for his hospitality at Kalambo. We discussed the geology in great detail during my visit and we have done so since, but the conclusions reached in this account are entirely my own responsibility.

I also wish to record my indebtedness to the Wenner-Gren Foundation of America, since my travelling expenses were paid out of the grant they had made for the 1956 excavations at Kalambo.

[2] The manuscript was submitted in 1957. The author, who is now Professor of Geology at the University College of Rhodesia and Nyasaland, Salisbury, Rhodesia, was unfortunately unable to revise the text for the present volume.

The geological map (Figure 5) was based on Mr Clayphan's topography. It covers an area about 1½ miles long and 1 mile wide, but traverses were made well beyond these limits, which are roughly those of the Quaternary deposits in the basin. Observations were also made on geomorphology in an attempt to explain the development of the Kalambo Falls and the basin in which Quaternary sediments were able to accumulate so near its lip.

The resulting picture of the Quaternary geology is more complex than Clark's brief description, and that of the development of the drainage pattern, including the origin of the Falls themselves, differs from Rose's.

2. THE GEOLOGICAL SETTING

Solid geology and raw materials of artifacts

There was no time to attempt to map the solid geology. Reference should be made to Rose's map (1929, p. 43), on which the distribution of the various rock types is shown.

The rocks consist of cherts and quartzites of various kinds belonging to the 'Plateau Series'. They are only gently folded and in the vicinity of the falls they dip gently eastwards. There is some faulting, with the formation of well-cemented breccias, and there are a few quartz veins. There is also an intrusion of post-Plateau Series dolerite on the west flank of the basin. Although its area is small and it was impossible owing to poor exposures to decide whether it is a dyke or sill, its outcrop is shown roughly on the map, as it had some bearing locally on the nature of the Quaternary deposits. Rose (1929) mentions quartz dolerite in the area, but did not show it on his map.

The quartzite and chert outcrops on the western flank of the basin provided prehistoric man with abundant good raw materials. Most of the rock types among the implements are easily matched in outcrops close to the site and, apart from some beautifully smooth egg-shaped pebbles up to 4 inches in longest diameter, there is no reason to suppose that the early inhabitants needed to import raw materials of any kind.

The purer quartzites are very resistant to weathering. They are cream and buff-coloured rocks, and fine to medium in grain. The feldspathic quartzites weather more easily, and implements in this material from the lower floors were generally fragile. The feldspars appear as tiny white dots of clay decomposition products.

Some of the finest implements were made from extremely fine-grained pale grey cherty rock, with a very good fracture. This outcrops on the western flank of the basin just north of the Spillway Gorge leading to the lip of the Kalambo Falls. It is shown on Rose's map (1929, p. 43) and indicated on mine (see Figure 5).

Dolerite pebbles and boulders are uncommon in the lower beds in the excavations. Most of these seen were rotten right through. They were represented by concentric shells of soft clay, sometimes with a hard core in the larger pieces. In general, however, dolerite pebbles were seen only as pale green circles on the walls of the pits, often sliced right through by the diggers.

Soils on the quartzite flanks of the valley are pale pink and loose textured. They are shallow on the steeper slopes, but surprisingly thick on the more gentle ones. On the east there is difficulty in drawing the boundary between soils and the Quaternary deposits, as the slope is gentle and soil creep has obscured the junction. There is difficulty also round the northern end of the basin. Where uncontaminated by quartzite soils from the valley sides, the Lake Beds[1] give loose grey soils, but their northern limit is hard to see. Rose (1929) included more ground to the north in his alluvium than has been shown on the present map. Around the rest of the basin the lines agree.

Geomorphology

The Kalambo River flows in a general westerly direction for a number of miles before joining Lake Tanganyika. On entering the Quaternary basin it turns northwards for about 4 miles (6·4 km) before making an abrupt turn to the west again. It then passes through a short narrow gorge, the Spillway Gorge, before reaching the lip of the Kalambo Falls.

This short northerly section is part of a long valley feature which continues north for some miles, until it gradually swings west to the lake. At Kalambo it is about 600 feet (183 m) deep and 2 miles (3·2 km) wide and the river leaves it by a lateral exit, although the easiest course would seem to be northwards. The valley follows the strike of the quartzites and there may well be some measure of structural control.

North of Kalambo Falls this valley contains only an insignificant stream, the Kawa, which rises on a low divide within the valley and flows northwards. On the south side of this divide a small stream, the Kaposwa, flows south into the Kalambo just north of the entrance to the Spillway Gorge. The Kawa and Kaposwa, rising on a divide within a valley feature, are obvious misfits and help to suggest the sequence of events which produced the present drainage pattern.

Seen from the higher points on the quartzite hills, the skyline of the country to the east is remarkably even. It is part of an old surface into which the present drainage is cut. King (1951, map) shows it as the Gondwana surface at an altitude of about 5,000 feet (1,525 m).

Before the formation of the present rift scarps the Kalambo probably followed a general westerly course across this surface, now represented by the level crests of the interfluves. The formation of rifts usually results in some backtilting of the surfaces near the faults. In the case of the Kalambo this would break its westerly course and divert it northwards. It could eventually have reached Lake Tanganyika some distance to the north, as the Kawa does now. It is suggested that this valley was eroded along the strike of the quartzites by the Kalambo and the long N–S valley was the result. Alternatively it might be argued that this was a pre-rifting valley into which the Kalambo was diverted by the faulting, but considered in conjunction with certain features of the Kalambo Gorge this suggestion loses some of its appeal.

The newly formed scarp of the eastern wall of the Tanganyika rift would initiate a series of steep consequent streams. One of these, favourably placed to collect drainage, cut back actively into the scarp and in time broke through the quartzite ridge bounding the N–S part of the Kalambo valley on the west. It thus captured the Kalambo and formed the falls. The consequent on the rift scarp which made the capture must have had some initial advantage over its neighbours. It seems quite possible that it originated in the truncated part of the original Kalambo valley. There is a strong suggestion of a wide upper valley into which the deep notch of the gorge is cut. The wide upper part of this double feature might be part of the old Kalambo valley, in which case the capture has merely restored the pre-rifting direction of the river.

---

[1] For reference to Lake Beds here and subsequently see footnote 1, p. 203.

Rose (1929, p. 41) summarized his views as follows: '...first a general uplift of the whole region, probably a direct cause of the anticline in the gorge (which was thus subjected to strain) and the flooding of the old Kalambo system, the overflow from the temporary lake thus formed being by way of the gorge, so that the river began to carve itself a new course; secondly, further uplift or uplifts which increased the gradients of all the streams, including the Kalambo, draining into the gorge area, with the effect that every stream has been re-juvenated, and they are beginning to cut new valleys in the bottoms of their old ones.'

His explanation links the formation of the falls and the Kalambo Lake directly with the uplifts. The archaeology of the Lake Beds gives them a rough date, which is so late that it is impossible to believe that 4 miles (6·4 km) of the Kalambo Gorge have been cut since their formation. My own view is that only a small amount of erosion in the gorge has been possible since the Lake Beds began to form. The existence of a lake in the Kalambo basin was a Quaternary event which has had no direct influence upon the erosional history of the gorge. This must have existed in much its present form at the time the Acheulian lake beds began to form.

An outline of the suggested history of the Kalambo is, therefore, as follows:

(1) Westerly course of Kalambo river on Gondwana surface.
(2) Formation of Tanganyika rift in its present form.
(3) Diversion of Kalambo northwards.
(4) Cutting of N–S valley along strike of quartzites.
(5) Vigorous erosion by favourably placed stream on scarp.
(6) Capture of Kalambo by this stream.
Later
(7) Periodic formation of temporary lakes in the Quaternary.

This seems a logical sequence of events leading to the present drainage pattern. It provides an explanation of the basin in which Quaternary deposits formed. It accounts for the misfit nature of the opposed Kawa and Kaposwa rivers rising on a divide within the valley, for the lateral outlet of the Kalambo river and for the existence of a fall at this point.

3. THE QUATERNARY BASIN

The Kalambo valley

The Quaternary basin lies between quartzite ridges about 600 feet (183 m) high. It narrows at its southern end, but the northern end is broad and indefinite, and it is impossible to define the limits of the deposits. They merge imperceptibly into the low soil covered divide on which the Kawa River rises to flow northwards along the continuation of the main valley.

Where the Kalambo River enters the basin it is a fast-flowing stream with coarse torrent gravels in its bed. It maintains this character on a straight northwesterly course until the first major bend is reached. At this point there is a sudden change of gradient and beyond it the nature of the stream changes abruptly. It becomes deep and sluggish and can only be crossed by canoe. It meanders, extending to a point about ¼ mile (402·6 m) north of the Spillway Gorge. Then it turns back and flows south, shallowing somewhat. At the entrance to the gorge it turns west and after passing through a short gorge, the floor of which is covered in large boulders, it plunges over the falls. At the abrupt change from a fast to a slow-running stream a small delta is forming, with well-rounded boulders of quartzite more than a foot in diameter. Between these points deposits must be fine grained, as the stream has already dumped its coarse load. Beyond the limit of the present delta there is a swamp area, covered in *Phragmites* reed beds. Even at the end of the dry season this swamp is still wet. Slow accumulation must be taking place here, but the coarse deposits of the active delta are building up much faster. The present swamp seems to be a relic of a larger area which is being steadily covered as the delta advances and is crescent shaped in consequence.

Since the Spillway Gorge is separated from the fast-flowing part of the Kalambo by the meander section, the massive subangular to subrounded boulders covering its floor cannot have been transported by the Kalambo itself.

The present pattern of sedimentation by the Kalambo River is, therefore, one of strongly contrasted coarse and fine facies. The recent behaviour of the river has an important bearing on the interpretation of the older deposits. Just as facies variation of an extreme kind can be seen in the deposits forming now, so it can be seen in earlier stages of the Quaternary history. Unless the present pattern is appreciated, it is impossible to understand the earlier sediments. Even so it is difficult to correlate the various facies of the earlier deposits.

The Spillway Gorge

About 100 yards (91·5 m) above the falls the river emerges from a short gorge about 500 feet (152·5 m) long cut in hard quartzite. The north wall is vertical and about 30 feet (9 m) high. On the south it is vertical for about 15 feet (4·5 m) and this is followed by a steep slope. The dip of the quartzites is gently upstream and the gorge follows a strong joint direction.

The top of the walls of this gorge is about level with the flat bench-like feature formed by the top of the oldest Quaternary deposits. The flat top of beds containing Iron Age remains is not much below this level. The local base level of the basin is the floor at the entrance to the Spillway Gorge, and Clark (1954, p. 52) suggested that the overflow from the Kalambo Lake had lowered this base level since the height of the Gamblian Pluvial.

Although the level of sedimentation and erosion within the basin has been controlled by this outlet, it seems unlikely that a gorge 30 feet (9 m) deep and 500 feet (152·5 m) long has been cut in hard quartzite by the outflow from the basin in the time implied by this interpretation. Furthermore, the Quaternary history is not one of continuous sedimentation. There were periods of erosion, to lower levels, and later deposits were then built up unconformably on earlier ones. The base level must have fluctuated, and if the control was simply the bedrock level in the Spillway Gorge sedimentation and erosion could not have taken place in this way. Progressive erosion by the river, even allowing for fluctuations in rate due to climatic changes, could only produce a falling base level. Yet even as late as Iron Age times, sediments were deposited up to a level near the top of the gorge, while at earlier periods, erosion within the basin cut down very nearly to the level of the present outlet. It seems more likely, therefore, that this gorge was cut before the sediments containing the earliest artifacts were laid down. The answer may lie in periodic damming of the gorge by sediments, perhaps stabilized by vegetation. Such sediment is more likely to have been brought in by the tributary stream flowing into the basin near the A pits from the southwest than by the Kalambo itself. This tributary, at present of no great size, drains a large embayment in the hills on the west. In times of heavy rainfall this stream, with its steep gradient, would sweep boulder gravels down into the valley and might form an outwash far across the Spillway Gorge faster than the Kalambo, with its low gradient in this section, could scour it out. In this way ponding could take place.

Bedrock is not exposed in the floor of the gorge at present. The river flows over sub-angular torrent boulders which the main Kalambo stream would have difficulty in moving, even in time of flood. These boulders are less rounded and generally larger than those in the delta forming at present further upstream. The Kalambo could not transport such large rocks over its sluggish section and they may be the remnants of the last dam formed in the entrance to the Spillway Gorge.

The Kawa–Kaposwa Divide

As stated earlier, the Kawa River running north, rises on a low divide within a continuous N–S valley. On the south side of this watershed a short tributary, the Kaposwa, only ¼ mile (402·6 m) long, flows south into the Kalambo. At the divide the transverse profile of the valley is almost a smooth curve, with a very short flat central portion. The Kawa is entrenched into this surface, but does not seem to expose solid rock anywhere near its source. If this was the old valley of the Kalambo the bedrock surface must fall northwards. After capture, however, this section of the valley would be left without longitudinal drainage, and lateral wash from the flanks would creep across it, until the beheaded stream could begin headward erosion into it. The result would be to leave a barrier of hill wash across this part of the valley, behind which the Kalambo would be able, at times when the Spillway Gorge was blocked, to form a lake or swamp. Presumably the headward erosion of the Kawa will eventually cut back through this barrier and the lake beds behind it. The Kalambo could then be recaptured, unless the lip of the falls can be lowered fast enough to maintain the present pattern.

The formation of the Quaternary basin in this part of the Kalambo valley was, therefore, only one event in the long erosional history of the area. The nature of the earliest sediments remains unknown, as they are nowhere exposed by natural erosion, and cannot be reached in excavations since they are below the water table. When sedimentation began has not been determined. Neither has the date of the capture been fixed, but it seems to have occurred well before the Quaternary.

The suggestions made above about the behaviour of the Spillway Gorge are rather complicated. If it could be believed that the Kalambo had cut this gorge since the deposits of the early Iron Age were formed, it might be thought unnecessarily so, but the difficulty of a fluctuating base level would still remain.

4. THE QUATERNARY DEPOSITS

The Lake Beds (Plate 11)[1]

The oldest Quaternary deposits so far known are those shown as Lake Beds on the geological map (Figure 5). They cover an extensive area and are moderately well exposed in natural sections. The lower parts were well displayed in the excavations at the time of my visit.

The scarp feature shown on the map running round the northern and eastern parts of the basin is cut in these deposits. It forms a terrace with a level surface, breached in places by small gulleys. It is so continuous, however, that there can be no doubt that it is cut into deposits of the same age throughout. The height of the terrace shows that in these early times, sedimentation reached a slightly higher level than at any subsequent period.

In the excavations (A 2, A 3, B and D) only the lower parts are preserved. Details of the lithology were carefully recorded by Dr Clark during excavation, and are described by him. The beds vary considerably both laterally and vertically even over short distances. Except for black peaty lenses, these beds as exposed in excavations were predominantly pale cream sands of fairly fine grain. They were not pebbly except where occupation debris was present, and this was all sharp and unworn.

Facies variation is considerable in these beds and they appear to be full of minor non-sequences. The sands and black clays are both sub-aqueous deposits, though indicating different conditions. The sands are often current-bedded, but the peaty clays must have accumulated in quiet water. Truncation of the peat lenses by sands shows that conditions changed rapidly locally from calm to current action.

The prehistoric floors can only have been formed at times when the underlying surface was exposed as dry land. This could only happen when the area of open water was temporarily reduced and prehistoric man could encroach on the lake floor, around the margin at least.

The best natural exposures of these beds are in the cliffs on the Tanganyika bank of the Kalambo River near the ferry crossing, leading to Mkamba village. The base is not exposed, but the middle and upper parts of the succession are well seen in this cliff, whereas in the area of the excavations a later erosion cycle has cut deeply into the beds, and later deposits rest on a low horizon in them.

The Lake Beds in the excavations can be traced by natural exposures into the cliffs on the Tanganyika bank, but there is some additional evidence of their equivalence. Since there are considerable facies changes this evidence should be taken into account. Although floors with abundant implements have only been exposed near the western margin of the basin, a few implements and waste flakes have been found in the Lake Beds at the northern and eastern sides. These are of a type consistent with the age of those recovered from floors found in the main excavations.

The cliff at the ferry is over 30 feet (9 m) high and is composed throughout of fine-grained white- and cream-coloured sediments. Stratification is not obvious until the beds are closely

---

[1] Professor Bond subsequently agreed with Clark and Kleindienst that the deposits were fluviatile. In the general nomenclature now recognized this rock stratigraphic unit is the Mkamba Member, Kalambo Falls Formation.

examined, when bedding can be made out. The deposits are mainly sandy clays, with a few clay bands up to 2 feet (61 cm) thick. Pebbles up to $\frac{1}{2}$ inch (1 cm) across occur in thin bands, but, on the whole, the grain size of the sediments is finer than the sands of the main excavations.

As the cliff feature cut in these beds by the Kalambo River is followed round the eastern side, the colour and grain size change. The colour changes to yellow and the sediment is sandier. Clay lenses disappear. Traced southwards towards the Vundwe River, the colour continues to darken until it becomes dark red. In the gulley cut by the Vundwe, cellular lateritic ironstone more than 20 feet (6·1 m) thick (base not seen) is exposed. This ironstone cements coarse and even pebbly sands. At a point 250 yards (228·7 m) south of the Vundwe this has passed into coarse boulder gravels firmly cemented by iron oxide.

The feature formed by these beds can be traced all the way along and there seems no doubt that they are all the same age. Just as the present river is forming coarse torrent gravels and fine swamp beds simultaneously, so, at the time of the formation of the Lake Beds, contrasted facies of sediments were also deposited.

Since deposition there has been a period of ferruginization, resulting in the formation of the coarse sandy laterite of the Vundwe section, and the cemented gravels further upstream. Even the clays and fine sands at the ferry show incipient ferruginization, but they were apparently so deficient in iron originally that little redistribution was possible. Nevertheless, iron cemented nodules, about as big as marbles, are scattered through the top 10 feet (3 m) or so, and these beds are noticeably more consolidated than those below.

The Lake Beds must have filled the basin to the outlet level at the time. Open water was probably restricted and variable in extent, which would account for their rapid variations in lithology.

Older Boulder Beds [1]

After the formation of the Lake Beds there was a period of lowered base level during which active erosion took place, and much of the basin was re-excavated. The next deposits rest against the erosion feature formed at this time, but do not reach to the top of it. They are torrent gravels with well-rounded quartzite boulders up to 2 feet in diameter. They are widely distributed in the southern part of the area of the map, and have a level soil-covered top. Their age in relation to the cultural succession is unknown, since no implements have been found in them. This is not surprising, as their very coarse nature indicates conditions which would have rolled any tools beyond recognition in a short time.

In the main excavations the eroded Lake Beds are followed unconformably by a coarse boulder floor, only 6 inches (15 cm) thick, but this is regarded as a land surface deposit, and cannot be equated with the Older Boulder Beds. It contains implements up to later 'Middle Stone Age'. It is succeeded by sands which show strong current bedding and were obviously deposited by water. These sands may be the fine facies deposited at the same time as the Older Boulder Beds. The only certain fact is that these sands are unconformable on the Lake Beds, and that the Older Boulder Beds have a similar relation to beds of that age.

The Older Boulder Beds form fresh-looking scarps, particularly well seen on the Tanzania side of the valley due east of the Spillway Gorge (Plate 4).

[1] Now the Chitambala Gravel Beds; coarse alluvial facies of the Mbwilo Member, Kalambo Falls Formation.

The deposits formed at this time must have extended over the whole of the re-excavated part of the basin. Their formation was followed by another period of erosion, in which about half their area was removed, again forming a basin in which later deposits could form when conditions leading to sedimentation returned.

The Younger Boulder Beds [1]

The Younger Boulder Beds rest unconformably against the erosion scarps cut into the Older Boulder Beds. Their level soil-covered top is not far above the highest flood level of the present Kalambo River, which is however, entrenched into them.

Lithologically they are similar to the Older Boulder Beds, and to the boulder delta which at the present stage is still forming. The vegetation in the vicinity of the delta is so dense that it is impossible to be certain whether the present delta is, in fact, part of the Younger Boulder Beds, or whether there has been a minor erosion period in which some of the basin was re-excavated.

Since in the area away from the delta the top of the Younger Boulder Beds is distinctly above flood level, it seems likely that there has been a break, during which the small basin containing the present swamp was cleared out.

No archaeological material has been found in the Younger Boulder Beds and their age remains in doubt. They are separated from the Older Boulder Beds by a period of deep erosion, in much the same way as the Older Boulder Beds are separated from the Lake Beds. During this period of lowered base level it is probable that the upper mixed floors (1 and 2) of the excavations formed as land surface deposits, and the Younger Boulder Beds probably post-date this period.

Swamp deposits and Red Talus

The crescent-shaped area of the present swamp is being encroached on by the boulder beds now being formed by the Kalambo River. Even in October (end of dry season) much of it is waterlogged and it is heavily overgrown by beds of *Phragmites* reeds. Paths through it give glimpses of the deposits, which are fine sand and silt. They are dark coloured when wet, but dry out to a pale grey.

The level topped stretch of ground between the B and D excavations stands up above the lowest sand-covered terrace, and is capped by grey structureless deposits of fine sand and silty clays. These beds contain Iron Age slag and pottery. They appear to have been formed under conditions similar to the present swamp.

Iron Age deposits of the A excavations must be of approximately the same age as those of B and D but they are red stony earths. They conform in level with the grey beds, but seem to have been formed mainly by soil creep from the dolerite area on the west flank of the basin. They contain some sub-angular rock waste derived in this manner from the slope. This red talus material can be followed some distance southwards along the west flank of the basin, when it has crept down over the earlier deposits. Further still to the south, beyond the limits of the dolerite, it loses its identity, merging into the much paler sandy soils derived from the Plateau series quartzites.

[1] Now the Chisiya Gravel Beds; coarse alluvial facies of the Chiungu Member, Kalambo Falls Formation.

There is an area of grey soils, very like the Iron Age beds of sites B and D around the village of headman Dominico. The level of this ground is slightly below the Iron Age swamp beds, but above that of the recent swamp. It has been shown on the map as Swamp Beds of an intermediate age on these grounds alone. There is no direct evidence of age, as no excavation has been done and its true age and nature remain in doubt.

pH profile

One of the most interesting features of the Kalambo Site is the amount of wood preserved in the 'Older Stone Age' deposits, but not a single fragment of bone or tooth has been found, in spite of the most careful methods of excavation. Conditions leading to the preservation of bone may be very different from those under which wood will survive. Bone is soluble in acid conditions of soil and ground water. Where the reaction of the sediment is alkaline bone may survive. This is expressed as the pH value of the soil or ground water.

Robinson (1949) has discussed the problems of measurement of pH in soils and its significance. He concluded (p. 164) that to some extent the pH of a soil at any given moment must be a conventional figure, and that no single figure can adequately represent the pH pattern within an actual soil. The same arguments apply to sedimentary deposits such as these at Kalambo, but the influence of acidity or alkalinity of the moisture within the sediments determines whether bone will survive or not. The pH, as measured now, may not be related to conditions which existed at the time of formation, but in the lower parts of the sediments, which have probably been waterlogged since their formation, variations of pH have probably been less than in the upper parts which have been subjected to seasonal fluctuations of water table.

Measurements of pH at Kalambo were limited to a single profile in the A 1 excavation. They were made with a simple B.D.H. portable pH outfit, which can, under favourable conditions, give readings to ± 0.25 of a pH unit. A number of determinations were also made on surface soils in the area, and these gave consistent values of 5.5. The Iron Age red earths at the top of the section in A 1 also gave values of 5.5. Down the profile this increased somewhat to a depth of 11 feet, where a mixed floor, of talus origin, indicates a land surface and a pause in sedimentation. The value a little above this horizon is 7.5.

In the false-bedded sands below the value falls to 4.5, and maintains this figure almost unchanged down through the lower mixed floor and into the late Acheulian sands at the bottom of the section.

Above the upper mixed floor the material is a transported stony soil, whereas below it the deposit is a water-laid sandy sediment. The two are not directly comparable. However, the acidity of the lower levels is such that it is not surprising that bones and teeth are absent. The preservation of wood is probably favoured by acid conditions, but even more by continuous waterlogging and the exclusion of atmospheric oxygen.

The full profile gave the following figures:

0 ft 3 in. (7.5 cm)	Grey humus	pH	5.5
2 ft 2 in. (66 cm)	Red clay		5.5
4 ft 0 in. (1.22 m)	Red sandy clay		7.0
6 ft 0 in. (1.83 m)	Pale red gritty clay		6.5
7 ft 6 in. (2.28 m)	Grey brown sandy clay		7.5

9 ft 0 in. (2·74 m)	Coarse grit current bedded	No reaction
10 ft 0 in. (3 m)	Coarse grit current bedded	No reaction
11 ft 0 in. (3·3 m)	Coarse grit current bedded	No reaction

Upper Mixed Floor[1]

12 ft 0 in. (3·6 m)	Grey clay	?6·0
12 ft 6 in. (3·8 m)	Grey silty sand	5·5
12 ft 11 in. (3·88 m)	Fine buff sand	4·5
13 ft 6 in. (4·11 m)	Grey sandy clay	4·5
14 ft 0 in. (4·22 m)	Grey clay lens	4·5
14 ft 6 in. (4·37 m)	Fine grey sand	4·5
15 ft 0 in. (4·52 m)	Dark grey clay lens	No reading possible
15 ft 3 in. (4·59 m)	Sand lens between clays	5·0
15 ft 6 in. (4·67 m)	Buff sand	No reaction
16 ft 0 in. (4·83 m)	Buff sand	No reaction
16 ft 9 in. (5·05 m)	*Lower Mixed Floor*[2]	No reaction
18 ft 0 in. (5·49 m)	Fine pale sands (with tree-trunks)	4·5
	(Base not seen).	

5. FLOORS EXPOSED BY EXCAVATION

Chelles-Acheul (Floors 5–7)

These floors form a group which are similar in occurrence and were all deposited in the same manner. They lie on slightly uneven surfaces within the clean sands of the Lake Beds. There is no obvious break in the sediments at their horizons. The sands which enclose them are similar to those now forming on the shores of Lake Chila near Abercorn, and it is probable that they were either the sands on the shore of the Kalambo Lake, or near the normal shore line. The floors are only one stone thick, and every stone is either an artifact, flake, or anvil. The enclosing sediments are non-pebbly and on the floors themselves there are no pebbles which were transported by natural means; they were all left in their present positions by pre-historic man. They are sharp and unworn, nor were they apparently moved significantly from their original positions by the action of water. They were factory floors in the best sense of the term.

Although the floors exposed in the excavations were near the sloping margin of the basin, they were probably within the normal limits of the water. The sand on which they rest was either exposed by exceptional shrinking of the lake during drought years, or during short cycles of reduced rainfall. There is evidence that many implements of this period were made further up the sides of the basin and found their way into the mixed floors lying higher in the succession at a later date. Those found on these floors within the Lake Beds must, however, have been made and left by Acheulian man in the positions in which they are now found.

Such floors do not represent long periods of occupation. Each was probably the work of a

[1] Archaeological Horizon Rubble Ib; see Figure 20, bed 10.
[2] Archaeological Horizon Rubble Ic; see Figure 20, bed 12.

small group, or even a single individual, who occupied the site as a purely temporary camp, at a time when the level of the lake was abnormally low. At other times, when the level was higher, the makers of these tools must have camped and worked further up the slope.

These factory floors are, therefore, an extraordinarily interesting feature of the site, and one which could only have been studied in such large and carefully controlled excavations. Since there are probably many of them, each covering a limited area, and all dating from the same general period, it is not to be expected that sections in different pits would give exactly the same number of floors at exactly the same horizons. Even the same group of people, returning to the area in successive years, would hardly be likely to occupy exactly the same site.

If the floors represented normal seasonal retreat of the lake margin it is unlikely that sufficient sediment would have accumulated during the next seasonal rise of the water, to prevent the disturbance of the floors in the next dry season. As they appear completely un-disturbed, with anvil stones still wedged in position in the sand, it seems more likely that they were only formed in exceptionally dry years, then covered by water and sediment when the level returned to normal, and so sealed permanently in position.

The only stones on the Acheulian floors which were shaped by natural abrasion are perfectly rounded or egg-shaped quartzite pebbles, generally about 4 inches (10 cm) in long diameter. They are the kind of pebble which is formed by the swirling action of water in pot holes in solid rocks, and they are completely foreign to the sedimentary environment of the basin, or of the Kalambo River in the part of the valley above the falls. Although their shape is natural, they must have been brought to the camp sites by Acheulian man, but for what purpose is not clear. They show no signs of fire cracking, but some of them appear to have been rubbed on one or more sides, as though they had been used for grinding.

The Acheulian floors seem to be confined to the western margin of the basin. Only a few scattered flakes and tools have been found in the equivalent beds nearer the centre, which seems to indicate that the lake did not dry out completely during this period, though abnormal regressions did take place. Rare artifacts have been found on the eastern side, but the western side was probably more favoured since it was so much nearer good outcrops of raw materials for tool making.

The lower mixed floor (Floor 3 and 3a)[1]

This floor is a striking feature in all three excavations of the A group; it is poorly developed in B, but again well developed in D. Lithologically it is a great contrast to the beds above and below it. Its thickness varies, but on the average it is perhaps 6 inches (15 cm) thick. Unlike the Acheulian floors, it contains many naturally shaped boulders, and only a small percent-age of the stones are tools. In appearance and derivation it is different from the floors below, and its archaeological content is also quite different. Tools from late Acheulian to late 'Middle Stone Age' are found indiscriminately mixed throughout. So coarse a deposit, in which the natural boulders reach a maximum size of about a foot, and one so thin compared with the size of its components, can hardly be expected to show stratification. The boulders are unsorted for size and shape, and neither they nor the implements among them show a

---

[1] In the archaeological nomenclature, Archaeological Horizons Rubble Ic(i) and Ic(iii) (the Rubble Bed of the Mbwilo Member, Kalambo Falls Formation).

high degree of rolling. The natural stones are mainly sub-angular to sub-rounded. Judged by the mixed typology of the contained artifacts this small thickness of deposit could represent a considerable time. It will be shown later that some of the older types must be regarded as derived, so that its duration is not so great as the total assemblage of artifacts would indicate.

The floor rests unconformably on the sands and clays of the underlying Lake Beds, although the unconformity is not very obvious in the excavations. There is no sign of it in the high cliff of Lake Beds near the ferry, and it seems certain that a considerable thickness of these beds was removed by erosion in the area of the A, B and D excavations before the mixed floor began to accumulate. The unconformity must, therefore, mark a considerable time interval.

The condition of the artifacts, boulders and smaller stones which make up Floor 3 (and 3a) does not suggest deposition by running water or wave action on a lake shore, and some other mode of transport must be looked for. The surface on which the floor rests is not flat. In sites A 1 and A 3 which are close together, it has a gentle northerly slope. Its base is somewhat irregular and in places the floor itself divides into two parts with a few inches of coarse gravel between.

In excavation A 2 the floor was clean but uplifted at the time of my visit. This pit is on the flank of the basin, whereas A 1 and A 3 are on slightly lower ground. Floor 3 was well exposed in A 2 and the surface had a pronounced slope parallel with the flank of the basin at this point. The surface of the floor was broken by several wrinkles as though the whole sheet had slumped slightly down the slope.

The B site is further away from the edge of the basin than the A group and in this excavation Floor 3 was very poorly developed, though its horizon could be traced at the base of the succeeding sands. In D site which is again closer to the confining rim of the basin, Floor 3 was again well developed.

The development of Floor 3 is, therefore, related to the slopes surrounding the basin; it is well developed near the edges and dies out away from them. Its distribution and the absence of signs of rolling by water shown by the components suggest an origin by soil and talus creep down the valley side into the floor of the basin. No doubt a considerable quantity of fine detritus crept down the slope during the same period, only to be continually washed out of the deposit and removed from the basin by the Kalambo River.

An origin of this kind is suggested by the internal evidence of the deposit itself, and supported by the nature of the deposits now forming on and near the steep slopes on the west of the Kalambo River, north and south of the entrance to the Spillway Gorge.

The feature formed by the top of the Lake Beds abuts against the solid quartzites along this part of the edge of the basin, but the angle between solid and alluvium is obscured by soil and talus creep down the slope. This deposit is exposed in new gulleys and where strong rainwash has removed the finer particles on the open slopes. It consists of a thin layer of unsorted rock fragments, which are sub-angular to sub-rounded in shape, and the general similarity to Floor 3 is striking. It dies out rapidly on reaching level ground.

The slope above, from which the talus is derived, must have been the source of raw material for Stone Age man, and no doubt he made and abandoned implements on it. These implements were then ready to join the general downhill movement of the loose surface material. A very mixed archaeological assemblage is found in the talus now forming. 'Older Stone Age' hand-axes and cleavers are rare, but are present. They are in a very poor state of preservation, the material having decayed under the weather except in the case of the very pure quartzites. No doubt they are rare because only those which originated far up the slope remain to creep down in the recent talus. Those which were left lower down have crept down into earlier talus deposits, such as Floor 3 of the excavations.

In the recent talus 'Middle Stone Age' flakes are more abundant, and they are generally in much better condition, although the angles between flake scars are blunted by abrasion (as distinct from rolling by stream action). There are also lumps of iron slag and potsherds and, more recent still, rusty bully beef tins which were probably left by the German troops who occupied the area in the First World War. The talus now forming thus contains an even more mixed assemblage of artifacts than Floor 3, ranging from 'Older Stone Age' to Iron Age in its broadest sense.

Reverting now to the archaeological content of Floor 3, the youngest material is typo-logically late 'Middle Stone Age', and the earliest is Acheulian. 'Older Stone Age' tools make up a considerable fraction of the total, which is to be expected since at the time during which this floor accumulated, less of the scatter left on the valley side by 'Older Stone Age' people had been removed from the slope which was feeding the deposit.

The physical condition of the 'Older Stone Age' tools from Floor 3 is interesting. Those made of pure quartzite appear to be fresh and are certainly unrolled in the sense that they have not been carried along by an active stream, but they are no longer sharp. The crests between flake scars and the edges themselves, are blunted by abrasion in much the same way as seen in the 'Middle Stone Age' flakes found in the recent talus. A comparison between hand-axes and cleavers from the Acheulian floors and those from Floor 3 brings out this con-dition very well. The difference between them can be seen and felt with the fingers. Those from the undisturbed Acheulian floors are in absolutely mint condition. Those from Floor 3 are by comparison blunt.

The 'Middle Stone Age' tools from Floor 3 are generally sharper, but some of them are distinctly blunted. The distance which a flake had to travel down the slope to reach its rest-ing place determined the degree of wear. Some, no doubt, were made at the base of the slope, almost where they are now found, and these should be in fresh condition. Examination of tools from this floor discloses just such a state in the 'Middle Stone Age' collection. Some are abraded, some are fresh. A few of the smaller ones are even slightly rolled. The land surface deposit is covered by coarse current-bedded sands, which were deposited by moving water after a return to a condition of raised base level. The smaller flakes were slightly rolled in the resorting which took place at this time, but current action was not strong enough to disturb the larger tools and boulders.

The conditions indicated by Floor 3 are, therefore, very different from those under which the Acheulian floors were formed. The mixed floor was a land surface deposit of some dura-tion, during which time the basin was more or less completely drained. The total assemblage of contained artifacts cannot be used to date the start of this period, since the 'Older Stone Age' material is derived. But it cannot have begun before the erosion phase which came after Acheulian and part of Sangoan times. The end of the period is dated by the latest contained culture which is later 'Middle Stone Age'.

The upper mixed floor (Floors 1 and 2)[1]

The lower mixed floor (Floor 3) is covered by a few feet of coarse gritty sands. There are some peaty clays and the deposits are slightly ferruginous, generally having a chestnut colour. They are current bedded and indicate a return to sedimentation controlled by a higher base level.

The Upper Mixed Floor rests, probably with a non-sequence, on these deposits. It resembles Floor 3 but contains more fines. The archaeological content is mixed, and the latest culture is typologically 'Magosian'. It seems to have accumulated in much the same way as Floor 3, and to represent a period of lowered base level during which the basin was more or less drained again, and talus crept down over the earlier deposits.

The Iron Age beds

The upper mixed floor is succeeded in the A sites by a red, earthy deposit containing Iron Age slag and potsherds. This is really a transported soil derived from the dolerite area. In B site however, the Iron Age deposits are grey swamp deposits. These two differing lithologies must have been more or less contemporaneous, and the conditions under which this could have occurred were discussed earlier in this account.

It is possible that after its formation Floor 3 was also covered by a similar deposit of transported soil. The next period of erosion may have washed out the fines and left any artifacts which it had contained on the surface of Floor 3. The very latest cultural content of that floor may, therefore, postdate its main period of formation. Until further evidence for this is forthcoming the latest date which can be assigned to Floor 3 cannot be more precisely stated.

6. CORRELATION AND CLIMATIC INTERPRETATION[2]

The Kalambo Site is an isolated one, and correlation with better known areas must, in the absence of fossils, be based on the use of stone tools as zone fossils, and on climatic evidence. Both these approaches have their limitations. The use of artifacts entails the assumption that similar cultures were practised simultaneously over large parts of Africa, and Clark (1954) has already suggested that the Acheulian people may have lingered on later at Kalambo than elsewhere. This is treating Kalambo as a special case, and the evidence should be re-examined to see if this is really necessary.

Climatic correlation involves the interpretation of the observed geological succession in terms of climate, which is never easy, and then comparison with some standard succession of climatic events. The most generally accepted standard is that of East Africa, based largely on lake levels, but again depending on the climatic interpretation of geological events. The various African Quaternary correlation tables which have been produced over the years show how difficult the problem is, and there are even those who deny that there have been significant climatic changes.

[1] In the archaeological nomenclature Archaeological Horizon Rubble Ib. Excavation A 1.

[2] To be read in relation to the evidence, nomenclature and opinions current in 1957 when the report was written.

Correlations based on artifacts as zone fossils and on sequences of climatic changes are independent lines of argument. If both lead to similar conclusions there is some hope that they are well founded. It is possible to apply both to the Kalambo basin.

The current-bedded gritty sands, which occur at several horizons in the succession, were deposited by water. The stony mixed floors were land surface deposits. Thus it would be logical to interpret the sands as products of a wetter climate and stony floors as those of a drier climate. There are non-sequences at the horizons of the stony floors, and they were formed at or immediately after periods of erosion. Hence at Kalambo periods of erosion were times of drier climate.

On theoretical grounds it can be argued that during a dry phase the products of rock decay would remain on the slopes surrounding the basin, because there was insufficient transporting power to remove them. At the onset of wetter conditions this material would be rapidly removed from the slopes, and deposited on the floor of the basin. Under such conditions, the tributary which now enters the Kalambo near the A excavations might block the gorge with its outwash fan, and lead to a period of filling of the basin with swamp and lake deposits. These conditions would persist until the onset of a drier phase, when the Kalambo, draining a considerable area of country, would be likely, in times of flood, to be able to break through the barrier and drain the basin. After the break through, erosion of the deposits would follow, and partial re-excavation of the basin would ensue. Such considerations would again lead to the interpretation of the mixed floors as products of drier phases of climate.

Column 1 of the correlation table sets out the generalized stratigraphy as shown by the excavations. Accepting the East African succession of climatic events as a standard, and correlating on drier phases indicated by erosion surfaces, leads to the conclusions in column 4.

The sequence is reasonable, but doubt must remain about the sands containing the final Acheulian floors. The erosion period which followed was the most important in the whole succession. Many feet of the Lake Beds were removed at this time, and it could be held that it should be equated with the Kanjeran-Gamblian interval. The sands containing the Acheulian floors would then be Kanjeran.

Turning now to the artifacts as zone fossils, it is most convenient to begin in the middle of the succession, at Floor 3, and to work up and down from this horizon. The correlation of this floor is difficult, since part of the cultural content must be regarded as derived. In such a mixed assemblage the only material which is reasonably reliable for dating purposes is the latest.

The large collection made in the 1956 excavations contained material which is typologically later than was found in the earlier digs. It is late 'Middle Stone Age', and on these grounds this land surface must be put in the late Gamblian. The floor is covered by sterile water-laid sands which must, therefore, be referred to the last (?3rd) peak of the Gamblian.

The upper mixed floor (Floors 1 and 2) contains an even later industry, which Clark refers to the 'Magosian'. These deposits, therefore, belong to the drier phase between the Gamblian and Makalian, and the sands above them to the wetter part of the Makalian. Completing the column upwards, the oldest Iron Age material occurs in swamp beds which could be regarded as Nakuran. An erosion period follows which logically belongs to the post-Nakuran to Recent time during which the climate has been drier.

Working down the succession from the drier period represented by Floor 3 and the non-sequence on which it rests, there is an impersistent gritty sand, cross-bedded and sometimes slightly ferruginized, between Floors 3 and 4. This should belong to the wetter period before Floor 3. Probably most of it has been lost by erosion in the area excavated and this seems to be all that remains of sediment laid down by the 2nd Gamblian maximum.

Floor 4 contains a Sangoan industry and rests on a non-sequence, which is perhaps the drier phase between 1st and 2nd Gamblian maxima. The major break referred to above lies below Floor 3, and again a possible alternative dating would be to regard the final Acheulian floors as late Kanjeran, the major break being the expression of the Kanjeran-Gamblian interval. This alternation, also suggested by the climatic approach, avoids the need to regard Kalambo as a retreat area in which the Acheulian people lingered on later than elsewhere.

Column 3 of the correlation table gives the results derived purely from the cultural succession which are in reasonable agreement with those based on the geological-climatic approach.

The tentative correlation put forward by Clark (1954) was based on the preliminary excavations which followed his discovery of the site. In the light of the much more extensive excavations of the 1956 season, slight modifications of these views were necessary, and these have been adopted above, and in the correlation table.

The only other account so far published is by Mortelmans (1956, pp. 86–8) who visited the site on the Zambian excursion of the Third Pan-African Congress of 1955.

In addition to quoting Clark's views as expressed in his published account (1954), and giving a typical stratigraphical succession from the area of the A sites, he has briefly discussed dating and the origin of one particular horizon, which seems to have given rise to a certain amount of debate among the delegates.

The beds in question were the impersistent sands and grits between the horizons called III and IV by Mortelmans (1956, p. 87). These floors are now numbered 4 and 3. The conclusion of the Congress delegates seems to have been that these thin beds represented the arid period between the end of the Kanjeran and the onset of the Gamblian. Since Floor 4 contains Sangoan and Floor 3 ended in the later 'Middle Stone Age' this conclusion seems less well founded than Clark's original interpretation. Furthermore, if the sedimentation of the basin followed the pattern described above, periods of erosion should be equated with drier phases, and water-laid false-bedded sands and grits of this type with the wetter periods.

Generally speaking, therefore, satisfactory correlations of the Kalambo succession can be obtained by both geological and cultural methods. Pollen analyses and C_{14} tests are to be carried out on materials from some of the horizons and may well be expected to shed further light on the problems posed by this important site.

Correlation table

(1) Stratigraphy	(2) Inferred climate	(3) Culture	(4) Geological Age
Erosion	Drier	Iron Age	Recent
Red talus and grey swamp beds	Wetter	Iron Age	Nakuran
Erosion	Drier	—	—
Sterile grits and sands	Wetter	—	Makalian
Land surface gravels (Floors 1, 2) on erosion surface	Drier	Magosian (mixed with older cultures)	—
Sterile false-bedded sands, etc.	Wetter	—	Gamblian (? 3rd max.)
Land surface gravels (Floors 3 and 3a)	Drier	Late MSA (mixed with older cultures)	—
On erosion surface	—	—	—
Thin sands and grits, sometimes cut out by erosion	—	—	—
Gravel of Floor 4	—	—	Gamblian (? 2nd max.)
Erosion	Drier	Sangoan	—
Sands with factory Floor 5 Sands with factory Floor 6 Sands with factory Floor 7	Wetter	Final Acheul	Gamblian (? 1st max.) or late Kanjeran
Base not seen	—	—	—

REFERENCES

Clark, J. D. (1954). An early Upper Pleistocene site at the Kalambo Falls on the Northern Rhodesia Tanganyika Border. *S. Afr. Arch. Bull.* **9**, no. 34, pp. 51–6.

Cornwall, J. W. (1929). The survey of the Kalambo Gorge. *Geogrl J.* **74**, no. 1, 33–8.

King, L. C. (1951). *South African Scenery* (2nd ed.). Oliver and Boyd, London and Edinburgh.

Mortelmans, G. (1956). Le troisième Congrès pan-africain de préhistoire. *Acad. Roy. Sci. Col.* Memoir in 8vo New Series. **4**, pt 3, pp. 1–128.

Robinson, G. W. (1949). *Soils, an Introduction to Pedology*. Murby, London, no. 1.

Rose, C. (1929). The geology of the Kalambo Gorge. *Geogrl J.* **74**, no. 1, 38–46.

APPENDIX B

DESCRIPTION OF WHITE CLAY BAND, LOWER CLAY BANK, TRENCH A 4, SITE A, KALAMBO FALLS PREHISTORIC SITE

Tanganyika Ministry of Commerce and Industry
Geological Survey Division Laboratory Services

Ref. No. X/7677/2

Dodoma
5 October 1961

LABORATORY REPORT

Sample: One clay for identification.

Submitted by: Dr M. R. Kleindienst, Coryndon Museum, Box 658, Nairobi.

Locality: Kalambo Falls, D.S. 68 SE.

The specimen is largely composed of quartz (X-ray photograph no. 1612), probably with a small percentage of clay mineral giving the rock its clay-like feel and appearance. It is not diatomite since the silica is crystalline quartz (against opaline silica in diatomite), and the rock has too high a density (S.G. = 2·37: diatomite is less than 2·35) and is not sufficiently porous.

D. R. C. KEMP
Geologist

APPENDIX C

IDENTIFICATION OF FRUITS AND SEEDS FROM SITE B, KALAMBO FALLS

By F. White

The specimens illustrated (by Mrs Janet Dyer) at Figure 42 and coming from the Black Clay layer (White Sands Beds of the Mkamba Member) associated with the artifact horizon 'Acheulian Floor VI' in Excavation B 1, 1956 at Site B, are provisionally identified as follows:

A. ?*Aidia micrantha* (K. Schum.) Bullock ex F. White. Characteristic of evergreen thicket. This identification is uncertain and it might be one of a number of other Rubiaceae (Figure 42 A).

B. Seed of a member of the Annonaceae. The deeply ruminate endosperm is distinctive. This could easily be *Xylopia rubescens* Oliv. a swamp forest species, but confirmatory evidence would be needed (Figure 42 B).

C. Not yet identified but sufficiently distinctive for illustration (Figure 42 C).

D. *Harrisonia abyssinica* Oliv. The identification is reasonably certain. It is a species of semi-evergreen and evergreen thicket and of the edges of evergreen forest—montane and sub-montane (Figure 42 D).

E. ?*Chrysophyllum.* ?*C. boivinianum* (Pierre) J. H. Hemsley. A montane forest species. The fruits are edible. Unknown today in the Abercorn district but occurring not far away in the Mafinga Mountains (Figure 42 E).

F. Either *Parinari excelsa* Sabine, a forest species, or *P. curatellifolia* Planch. ex Benth., a savanna woodland species. Without the leaves it is impossible to be certain (Figure 42 F).

In addition to those illustrated at Figure 42, the following further identifications have been made.

G. Parts of pods of *Isoberlinia* (savanna woodland trees) or *Berlinia* (forest, riparian trees); it is impossible to be more specific.

H. Immature fruit of the palm, *Borassus aethiopum* Mart.

A number of leaf specimens submitted were also examined but could not be identified with any confidence.

All these specimens, except E, have been recorded from or are likely to occur in the Abercorn district today.

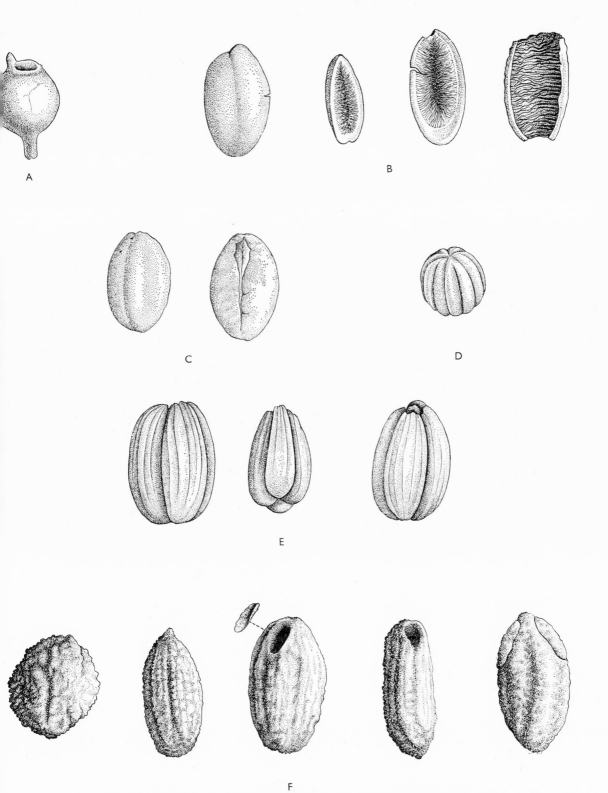

Fig. 42. Drawings of seeds from Acheulian horizon VI at Site B, 1956, Kalambo Falls
Prehistoric Site. (A, B and D: 3 × life size; C, E and F: 1½ × life size.)

APPENDIX D

PROVISIONAL IDENTIFICATIONS OF CHARCOALS AND WOOD SAMPLES FROM THE KALAMBO FALLS PREHISTORIC SITE

By L. Chalk assisted by A. C. Hoyle and J. F. Hughes, Commonwealth Forestry Institute, Oxford; and J. D. Brazier and E. W. J. Phillips, Forest Products Research Laboratory, Princes Risborough

From the numerous samples submitted by the excavators between 1956 and 1964, the following provisional identifications have been made:

1 CHARCOALS

Charcoals from Site A, Excavation A 1, 1956. Depositional phases F 8 ('Older Channel' fill) and F 9 ('Younger Channel' fill) associated with Iron Age remains.

Identifications by L. Chalk (11 June 1958).

Catalogue number	Depth		Identification
14	4 ft 6 in.–5 ft 0 in.	F 9	Hardwood
15	4 ft 6 in.–5 ft 3 in.	F 8	Hardwood, possibly *Uapaca* sp.
16	5 ft 0 in.–5 ft 6 in.	F 9	Hardwood, possibly *Piliostigma thonningii*
17	5 ft 0 in.–5 ft 3 in.	F 9	Hardwood, possibly the same as 19 below
19	5 ft 0 in.–5 ft 6 in.	F 8	Hardwood
20	5 ft 6 in.–6 ft 0 in.	F 8 and F 9	Hardwood, possibly Flacourtiaceae or Rubiaceae
23	6 ft 0 in.–6 ft 6 in.	F 8 and F 9	Possibly *Cynometra* sp.
24	6 ft 6 in.–7 ft 0 in.	F 8	Possibly *Brachystegia*
26	7 ft 0 in.–7 ft 6 in.	F 9	Hardwood
27	7 ft 6 in.–8 ft 0 in.	F 9	Hardwood, possibly same as 26 above

2 WOOD

(*a*) Site A. Depositional Phase F 3. Ochreous Sands Beds, Mkamba Member. Excavation A 4 and River Face, 1959. Associated with Sangoan artifacts.

218

APPENDIX D

Provisional identifications by J. F. Hughes (3 February 1964).

Catalogue number	Identification
36, 37, 49	*Guibourtia* sp. (3 specimens)

(*b*) Site A. Depositional Phase F 2. White Sands Beds, Mkamba Member. Associated with latest Acheulian artifacts (Occupation Floor IV). Excavation A 4, Extension and River Face, 1959.

Provisional identification by J. F. Hughes (3 February 1964).

Catalogue number	Identification
14	*Guibourtia* sp.
18	*Manilkara* sp. or *Mimusops* sp.

Excavation A 1, 1956

Provisional identification by L. Chalk (5 May 1959).

Catalogue number	Identification
16 (A 1/56/IV/e and f 4)	*Colophospermum* sp. or *Tamarindus indica*

(*c*) Site A. Depositional Phase F 2. White Sands Beds, Mkamba Member. Associated with Upper Acheulian artifacts (Occupation Floor VI) Excavation A 1, 1955 and 1956.

Provisional identifications by L. Chalk and A. C. Hoyle.

Catalogue number	Identification
II/55	*Zyziphus* sp.
—	*Ouratea* sp.
12 (A 1/VI/63)	*Cynometra* sp. J. D. Brazier has suggested the following alternative identifications for 12, either *Afrormosia, Dalbergia* or *Swartzia*

(*d*) Site B. Depositional Phase F 2. White Sands Beds, Mkamba Member. Associated with Upper Acheulian artifacts on Occupation Surface V. Excavation B 1, 1956.

Provisional identification by L. Chalk.

Catalogue number	Identification
B/V/6	?*Coleospermum mopane* or *Monopetalanthus richardii*

(*e*) Site B. Depositional Phase F 2. White Sands Beds, Mkamba Member Associated with Upper Acheulian artifacts. (Occupation Layer VI). Excavation B 1, 1956.

Provisional identifications by L. Chalk, A. C. Hoyle and J. D. Brazier, made 31 May 1956, 10 December 1956, 5 May 1959, 31 October 1959, 3 February 1964.

Catalogue number	Identification
1	Sapindaceae, possibly '*Blighia* type'
2	*Cynometra*, possibly *C. alexandri*
3	Leguminosae, possibly *Burkea* sp.
4	?*Coleospermum mopane*, or *Monopetalanthus richardii*
7 and 14	*Isoberlinia* sp. or *Tamarindus* sp.
9	*Piptadenia* sp.
11	Leguminosae, possibly '*Newtonia* type'
18	?*Coleospermum mopane* or *Monopetalanthus richardii*
C/A 6	Mimosaceae, ?*Albizzia* sp.
C/A 6	*Brachystegia* sp. ('*longifolia* type')
C/A 6	*Parinari* sp.
C/A 6	*Acacia campylacantha*
C/A 6	*A. chariensis* (-'*stenocarpa*' Oliv.)
C/A 6	*A. sieberiana*
C/A 6	*Cassia singueana*
A/17, 33, 72	*Guibourtia* sp.
A/25, 30	Similar to *Guibourtia* but with tangential rows of vertical resin canals not shown in A/17, 33 and 72

Three further collections of wood samples, made in 1959, have recently been examined and identified by the Forest Products Research Laboratory at Princes Risborough. We are much indebted to Dr E. W. J. Phillips, Head of the Wood Structure Section, who organized these identifications.

Woods from White Sands associated with Acheulian horizons VI–VIII from Site B, B 2, 1959 Excavation.
From Grid Squares G–N 1–4.
(63 samples: nos. 1–35, 54, 62–88).

All these are identified as Leguminosae (but excluding *Cynometra*, *Ouratea*, *Brachystegia*, *Afzelia* and *Amblygonocarpus*). They comprise eight different timbers, six of which (nos. 3, 6, 14, 27, 29 and 30) cannot be further identified.

Sixteen samples are provisionally identified as ?*Tessmannia* or *Guibourtia* (nos. 5, 7, 24, 32, 54, 62, 63, 70–3, 81, 82, 86 and 88).

Twenty-seven samples are probably a species of *Tamarindus* (nos. 1, 2, 4, 8–13, 15–19, 21–3, 25, 26, 28, 31, 33–5, 65, 67 and 77).

The remaining samples were not suitable for critical examination.

Woods from Ochreous Sands over black clay bank associated with Sangoan artifacts from Site A, A 4 and A 5 Excavations.
From Grid Squares A 4 and River Face Pits.
(26 samples: nos. 36, 38–61 and 217).

With the exception of eight samples (A 5, nos. 52, 61 and 217; A 4, 56, 6/54, 7/46, 11/53 and 59) all these woods are identified tentatively as *Tessmannia* or *Guibourtia*.

APPENDIX E

REPORT ON BARK AND OTHER SPECIMENS FROM SITE B, KALAMBO FALLS, DEPOSITIONAL PHASE F2, WHITE SANDS BEDS, MKAMBA MEMBER

Associated with Upper Acheulian artifacts on Occupation Surfaces V and VI, Excavations B 1 and B 2, 1959

By T. C. Whitmore

The specimens listed below were packed in five groups which are here described together. One well-preserved fragment of bark ($12 \times 5 \times \frac{1}{2}$ inches) from Occupation Surface VI may, it is thought, have served as a carrying tray or dish similar to those still made as a temporary expedient by many African peoples; it bears no unquestionable signs of shaping by man, however.

(1) The enclosed detailed inventory of the five parcels shows that many of the 'bark' fragments are, in fact, fragments of wood.

(2) Some of the wood fragments and all the bark fragments, except one, have decomposed so that, though they retain their shape, they are soft and brittle and the tissues are now soft, homogeneous and blackish-brown—?carbonized. No trace of structure remains visible at magnifications of up to ×20 in these samples and it is unlikely that they can be identified. Some of the bark fragments retain surface pattern but identification from this alone is impossible.

(3) The remaining wood fragments retain structure visible especially on tangential and radial surfaces. These might be identifiable at one of the institutes with a reference collection of wood slides.

(4) One bark fragment, the 'tray' in parcel 4, is in an excellent state of preservation. A separate report is enclosed which concludes it is probably bark of a tree in Leguminosae.

Packet number	Accompanying description	Note on sample	Comment
1	B 1, 1956, Upper Acheulian Occupation Surface V. Collected 1959	(a) Wood fragment (b) Wood fragment (c) Wood fragment	See note (1). Very friable, mostly gravel; thrown away
2	B 2, 1959, Upper Acheulian Occupation Surface V	Flattened wood $12 \times 3 \times 1\frac{1}{2}$ inches with grid-cracked surface skin $\frac{1}{8}$ inch thick (charred)	See note (1)

221

Packet number	Accompanying description	Note on sample	Comment
	B 2, 1959, Upper Acheulian Occupation Surface V	(a) Many small fragments; most wood, some bark	Perhaps shattered in transit. See note (2)
		(b) Several small packets of bark and one of twig wood	See note (2)
4	B 2, 1959, Upper Acheulian Occupation Surface VI. Possible bark 'tray' from grid square M 3	A well-preserved bark 'tray' $12 \times 5 \times \frac{1}{2}$ inches trough shaped; and several slightly smaller 'trays'	Identified as Leguminosae bark (see separate report). For others see note (2)
5	B 2, 1959, Upper Acheulian Occupation Surface V	(a) Two flat wood fragments $12 \times 4 \times 6$ inches	See note (1)
		(b) Sapwood fragment with bark attached, 12 inches long	See note (1)
		(c) Several small wood fragments	See note (1)
		(d) Three bark fragments 8 inches square	Tissues structureless; thrown away

NOTE (1) This wood retains some structure and could, perhaps, be identified.

NOTE (2) Tissues soft, homogeneous, blackish brown (?carbonized), no trace of structure remaining visible, probably cannot be identified.

Identity of Fossil Bark 'Tray' (sample 'B 2/52 Bark Tray/M 3 Acheul 6') from Kalambo Falls

I. *Characters of the cross-section possibly of taxonomic value*

1. Cortex-like layer in outer part of inner bark (pseudo-cortex of Whitmore, 1962a).
2. Rhytidome present of one (two) layers; outer bark 4 mm thick.
3. Phelloderm (secondary cortex) consisting of several close lying sheets of stone cells.
4. Phellem multilayered; narrow black inner and broad fawn outer layers; the outer layer in places with mid-brown tangential streaks.
5. Conspicuous, pale, isodiametric, stone cells scattered throughout bark, except close to cambium.
6. Fibre blocks very small.
7. Sample has exuded resin.

II. *Comment on these characters*

1. Barks with pseudo-cortex are slow growing (Whitmore, 1962*b*). This means that they slough slowly too. Correlated with this, many barks with pseudo-cortex have no rhytidome and merely slough as powder (e.g. English beech). The presence in one bark of pseudo-cortex and rhytidome is unusual. It may be connected with a fire-swept habitat.

2. Thorenaar (1926) made a comprehensive study of Indonesian trees in search of reliable diagnostic characters. He discovered that, of the characters of this fossil 'tray', the following are useful:

(*a*) presence of phelloderm;
(*b*) phelloderm made of stone cells (sclerotic);
(*c*) layered phellem;
(*d*) colour of phellem layers.

III. *Comparison of fossil with present-day barks from the Kalambo Falls Area* (*see Appendix F*)

1. Of the 80 present-day bark samples, 18 have pseudo-cortex.

2. Of the 18 samples with pseudo-cortex, five are from boles of small girth. Whitmore (1962*b*) shows that all small girth members have bark with pseudo-cortex. The fossil bark does not come from such a member.

3. Of the 13 large girth samples with pseudo-cortex, a group of five has:

(*a*) phelloderm with several close-lying stone cell sheets (none of the other eight samples has this);
(*b*) a rhytidome of one (two) layers, (only three of the other eight samples have this).

All 13 samples have conspicuous, pale, isodiametric stone cells. None of the samples has multi-layered phellem, nor is there conspicuous resin exudation. Several have very small fibre blocks. The group of five samples is all Leguminosae.

4. Thirteen of the 67 present-day bark samples without pseudo-cortex are Leguminosae. Of these eight have a multi-layered sclerotic phelloderm as described above; it is many layered in five, few layered (or present only in part) in three samples. The degree of development of the layering varies between trees of a species (*Afrormosia angolensis* samples 20 and 27).

5. Some Leguminosae have resin.

IV. *Conclusion*

I conclude from the above that the bark of the fossil 'tray' is of a tree in the Leguminosae. The presence together of multi-layered sclerotic phelloderm is diagnostic of the family and there is a certain amount of corroborative evidence.

I am unable to assign this fossil bark to a genus but will state that it is unlikely to be *Brachystegia*. Only one (no. 57) of four (57, 12, 77 and 78) samples of present-day *Brachystegia* bark has a pseudo-cortex and this differs substantially in its other features from the other samples.

V. *Comment*

Nowadays, the forests in the Kalambo Falls area contain more Leguminosae than any other family of tree, if the present-day samples are representative. There are 13 species of Leguminosae out of a total of 70 species in the collection. *Ficus* with five species is the second most abundant.

If the flora was the same when the 'tray' was made the use of Leguminosae would not be surprising. However, the 'tray' is not made of *Brachystegia* although this is the codominant genus of much of present day Central African savanna woodland.

REFERENCES

Thorenaar, A. (1926). Onderzoek naar bruikbar kermerken ter identificatie van boomen naar hun bast. *Meded. v.h. Proefst. v.h. Boschwezen 16: Wageningen.* English translation: *Investigations on useful characters for the identification of trees from their bark* (of part only), in Botany School, University of Cambridge.

Whitmore, T. C. (1962*a*). Studies in systematic bark morphology, II: General features of bark construction. Bark studies outside Dipterocarpaceae. *New Phytol.* (1962).

Whitmore, T. C. (1962*b*). Studies in systematic bark morphology, III: Bark taxonomy in Dipterocarpaceae. *Gdns' Bull.* (1962).

APPENDIX F

CHECK LIST OF EIGHTY-TWO BOTANICAL SPECIMENS
OF TREES AND SHRUBS COLLECTED IN THE VICINITY OF
THE KALAMBO FALLS LOCAL BASIN
BY MRS MARY RICHARDS IN 1959[1]

Identified by Mary Richards and D. B. Fanshawe

1. *Isoberlinia angolensis* (Welw. ex Benth.) Hoyle & Brenan (Leguminosae).
2. *Afzelia quanzensis* Welw. (Leguminosae).
3. *Julbernardia globiflora* (Benth) Troupin (Leguminosae).
4. *Marquesia macroura* Gilg. (Flacourtiaceae).
5. *Craterosiphon quarrei* Staner (Thymelaceae).
6. *Lannea discolor* Engl. (Anacardiaceae).
7. *Albizzia antunesiana* Harms. (Leguminosae).
8. *Cassine buchananii* Loes (Celastraceae).
9. *Strychnos innocua* Delile (Loganiaceae).
10. *Papea capensis* Eckl. & Zeyh. (Sapindaceae).
11. *Dichaetanthera erici-rosenii* (no reference).
12. *Brachystegia longifolia* Benth. (Leguminosae).
13. *Combretum ghasalense* Engl. & Diels. (Combretaceae).
14. *Uvariastrum hexaloboides* (R. E. Fries) Stockh. (Anonaceae).
15. *Uapaca nitida* Muell. Arg. (Euphorbiaceae).
16. *Monotes* sp. (Dipterocarpeae).
17. *Boscia salicifolia* Oliver (Capparideae).
18. *Strychnos innocua* Delile (Loganiaceae).
19. *Parinari curatellifolia* Planch. ex Benth. (Rosaceae).
20. *Afrormosia angolensis* Harms. (Leguminosae).
21. *Uvariastrum hexaloboides* (R. E. Fries) Stockh. (Anonaceae).
22. *Viridivia suberosa* (no reference).
23. *Memecylon flavovirens* Baker. (Melastomaceae).
24. *Uapaca pilosa* Hutchinson (Euphorbiaceae).
25. *Memecylon flavovirens* Baker. (Melastomaceae).
26. *Syzygium guineense* (Willd.) DC var. *macrocarpum* Engl. (Myrtaceae).
27. *Afrormosia angolensis* Harms. (Leguminosae).
28. *Anisophyllea pomifera* Engl. & Brehmer (Rhizophoraceae).
29. *Isoberlinia angolensis* (Welw. ex Benth.) Hoyle & Brenan (Leguminosae).
30. *Bauhinia petersiana* C. Bolle (Leguminosae).

[1] This collection is now housed in the Department of Botany, University of Cambridge, England.

31. *Diplorhynchus condylocarpon* Welw. ex Ficalho & Hiern (Apocynaceae).
32. —
33. *Syzygium guineense* (Willd.) DC. var. *afromontanum* (Myrtaceae).
34. *Voacanga schweinfurthii* Stapf. (Apocynaceae).
35. *Syzygium guineense* (Willd.) DC. var. *afromontanum* (Myrtaceae).
36. *Ziziphus mucronata* Willd. (Rhamnaceae).
37. *Ficus sycomorus* Linn. (Moraceae).
38. *Parkia filicoidea* Welw. (Leguminosae).
39. *Trichilia roka* (Forsk.) Chiov. (Meliaceae).
40. *Kigelia pinnata* DC. (Bignoniaceae).
41. *Acacia albida* Delile (Leguminosae).
42. *Combretum zeyheri* Sond. (Combretaceae).
43. *Ficus wakefieldii* Hutchinson (Moraceae).
44. *Combretum zeyheri* Sond. (Combretaceae).
45. *Piliostigma thonningii* (Schum.) Milne-Redhead (Leguminosae).
46. *Trichilia prieureana* A. Juss. (Meliaceae).
47. *Ficus thonningii* Blume = ?*Ficus microcarpa*, Linn. (Moraceae).
48. *Pterolobium stellatum* (Forsk.), Brenan (Leguminosae).
    Acacia sieberiana DC. (Leguminosae).
    Acacia pentagona (Schumach.) Hook (Leguminosae).
49. *Celtis durandii* Engl. (Ulmaceae).
50. ?*Grewia* Linn. (Tiliaceae).
51. *Minusops zeyheri* Sond. (Sapotaceae).
52. *Trichilia prieureana* A. Juss. (Meliaceae).
53. *Teclea nobilis* Delile. (Rutaceae).
54. *Grewia flavescens* Juss. (Tiliaceae).
55. *Ficus dekdekena* A. Rich. (Moraceae).
    Ficus cyathistipula Warb. (Moraceae).
56. *Bridelia micrantha* Baill. (Euphorbiaceae).
57. *Brachystegia* sp. (Leguminosae).
58. *Vitex buchanani* Baker, ex Guerke. (Verbenaceae).
59. *Diplorhynchus cordylocarpon* Welw. ex Ficalho & Hiern (Apocynaceae).
60. *Erythrophloeum guineense* G. Don. (Leguminosae).
61. *Syzygium cordatum* Hochst. (Myrtaceae).
62. *Pterocarpus angolensis* DC. (Leguminosae).
63. *Ficus congensis* Engl. (Moraceae).
64. *Pseudolachnostylis maprouneifolia* Pax (Euphorbiaceae).
65. *Dichaetanthera erici-rosenii* (no reference).
66. *Vitex doniana* Sweet (Verbenaceae).
67. *Afzelia quanzensis* Welw. (Leguminosae).
68. *Hymenocardia acida* Tul. (Euphorbiaceae).
69. *Pterocarpus angolensis* DC. (Leguminosae).
70. *Sclerocarya caffra* Sond. (Anacardiaceae).
71. —
72. *Anthocleista schweinfurthii* Gilg. (Loganiaceae).

73. *Syzygium guineense* (Willd.) DC. var. *afromontanum* (Myrtaceae).
74. *Entandrophragma delevoyi* De Wild. (Meliaceae).
75. *Terminalia sericea* Burch. ex DC. (Combretaceae).
76. *Dracaena reflexa* Lam. (Liliaceae).
77. *Brachystegia spicaeformis* Benth. (Leguminosae).
78. *Brachystegia spicaeformis* Benth. (Leguminosae).
79. —
80. *Steganotaenia araliacea* Hochst. (Umbelliferae).
81. *Erythrophloeum guineense* G. Don. (Leguminosae).
82. *Maytenus senegalensis* (Lam.) Exell. (Celastraceae).

APPENDIX G

LIST OF USEFUL PLANTS, TREES AND SHRUBS COLLECTED IN THE IMMEDIATE VICINITY OF THE KALAMBO FALLS LOCAL BASIN IN 1956

Collected by L. E. Hodges and J. D. Clark

Details of the way in which these plants are prepared for use by the Lungu population were obtained but are omitted here.

Of the specimens collected, the following have been identified by Dr D. B. Fanshawe, then Chief Scientific Officer to the Northern Rhodesia Department of Forests, who reports as follows:

'None of the species from 13–34 (i.e. 21–44 list B—'Relishes and Fruits') belongs exclusively to *mushitu* (relict evergreen forest, Ed.). *Syzygium guineense* occurs in the drier type of *Parinari mushitu*, as does *Landolphia kirkii*. *Dracaena, Isoberlinia angolensis* and *Vitex doniana* have been observed on the fringes of *mushitu*, especially round Lake Bangweulu. But all these species are more at home in woodland of the plateau or in the evergreen thickets in the woodland. The remaining species are woodland or ant-hill (*Thespesia*) species.'

A. *Medicinal plants and trees*

No.	Botanical name	Native name	Part used	Specific for
1	*Dialiopsis africana*	*mutikalami*	Bark	Pleurisy
2	*Vitex madiensis*	*mufutu*	Root	Toothache
3	*Cissampelos mucronata*	*mwika*	Root	Diarrhoea
6	*Pavetta schumanniana*	*achongalindi*	Root	Stomach pain
8	*Ziziphus* sp.	*chicawasama*	Root	Toothache
9	*Schrebera trichoclada*	*kopandi*	Root	Inflamed eyes
10	*Psorospermum febrifugum*	*katumbi*	Bark	Headache
11	*Solanum* sp.	*tondwa*	Fruit	Sore tongue
12	*Vitex* sp.	*chantua*	Fruit	Fish poison
13	*Kigelia pinnata*	*muzoo*	Pod	Stomach
14	*Polygala persicariifolia*	*muluka*	Root and bark	Coughing
15	*Ochnia angustifolia*	*kampulompombwe*	Root	Chest pains

B. *Relishes and fruits*

No.	Botanical name	Native name	Part eaten
21	*Commelina*	*munwe*	Leaves
23	*Gynandropsis gynandra*	*musunta*	Leaves
25	*Sesamum angolense*	*sumbwe*	Seeds
27	*Dissotis*	*chitukumbe*	Flowers
28	*Liliaceae*	*kaluwa*	Pods
29	*Dracaena reflexa*	*mulenge*	Flowers
30	*Isoberlinia angolensis*	*mwanzia*	Pods
32	*Vitex doniana*	*mufutu*	Fruits
33	*Uvariastrum hexaloboides*	*chizovo*	Fruits
34	*Randia kuhniana*	*musokolowe*	Fruits
35	*Uapaca pilosa*	*mapangwa*	Fruits and leaves
36	*Brachystegia allenii*	*manele*	Fruits and leaves
37	*Landolphia kirkii*	*maungo*	Fruits
38	Not seen—*Uapaca* sp. from the name	*musolalowe*	Fruits
39	*Thespesia garckeana*	*makale*	Fruits
41	*Ziziphus abyssinica*	*kapele*	Fruits and leaves
42	A new genus not yet described	*muliansofu*	Fruits
43	*Syzygium guineense*	*inuga*	Fruits
44	*Parinari curatellifolia*	*moola*	Fruits
	Strychnos sp.	*nakasongole*	Fruits
	Uapaca kirkiana	*musolalowe*	Fruits
	Borassus aethiopium		Fruits

C. *Other useful trees and shrubs*

No.	Botanical name	Native name	Part used	Use
46	*Terminalia sericea*	*nachimpampa*	Bark	String and rope
47	*Cryptosepalum exfoliatum*	*mulenda*	Bark	String and rope
48	?*Dombeya*	*kafunda kaloge*	Bark	String and rope
49	*Brachystegia spicaeformis*	*nachuputu*	Bark	String and rope

APPENDIX H

HEAVY MINERAL ANALYSIS OF SAMPLES FROM SITES A, B AND D, 1956 EXCAVATIONS

By Derek Searle

Excavation A 1, 1956

Sample number	Depositional phase	Identification
A 1/1	F 9. Red Sandy Fill	A brown, iron-stained sand. Iron, 98%; zircon, 2%. A distinct separation without kyanite, garnet, tourmaline and hornblende. Angular quartz iron-stained and angular iron ore.
A 1/2	F 8. Grey, silty clays	A dirty, grey-brown earthy sand; when washed, similar to A 1/4 but finer grained. Iron, 50%; kyanite, 48%; zircon, 2%. A grain of green hornblende; angular and sub-angular kyanite with noticeable twinning.
A 1/3	F 6. Current-bedded sands over Rubble I	A coarse sand similar to A 1/4 but not as coarse. Angular iron ore grains; kyanite ragged and iron-stained; angular limonitic quartz. Iron, 93%, kyanite, 5%; zircon, 2%.
A 1/4	F 6. Sands and clays under Rubble I	A coarse sand, well washed, pale colour, quartz and feldspar. Angular and sub-angular quartz grains, a few subrounded. Kyanite, 70%; iron, 25%; hornblende, 1%; rutile, 1%; zircon, 3%.

Excavation A 3, 1956

A 3/1	F 9. Sand	A dark brown silty sand. Grains highly angular. Iron, 68%; kyanite, 28%; rutile, 1%; zircon, 3%.
A 3/2	F 6. Current-bedded sands over Rubble I	A pale well-washed sand, mainly quartz and feldspar. Nearly all grains angular; a few larger grains more rounded, also a few zircons with purplish tint. Iron, 58%; kyanite, 32%; zircon, 10%.
A 3/3	F 6. Sands and clays under Rubble I	A pale, cream-coloured, loess-like sand; fine-grained. Angular quartz grains. Iron, 38%; kyanite, 38%; rutile, 2%; tourmaline, 5%; zircon, 17%.

Excavation B 1, 1956

Sample number	Depositional phase	Identification
B 1/1	F 8. Grey, silty clays	Grey-brown, loess-like deposit, silty sand. A green hornblende grain noted. Iron, 44%; kyanite, 46%; rutile, 3%; zircon, 7%.
B 1/2	F 6. Current-bedded sands over Rubble I	A well-washed, pale sand similar to A 1/4. Coarse-grained, angular quartz. Iron, 22%; kyanite, 75%; zircon, 2%; garnet and hornblende, 1%.
B 1/3	F 6. Gravel and sand under Rubble I	An orange-brown, limonitic sandstone. Very few detritals recovered; kyanite and iron in equal proportions, two zircons, angular to sub-angular grains.

Excavation D 2, 1956

D 2/1	F 6. Current-bedded sands over Rubble I	A fine-grained, pale cream-coloured sand. Zircons small, kyanite sub-angular, hornblende, rutile worn. Iron, 43%; kyanite, 45%; rutile, 2%; zircon, 10%.
D 2/2	F 6. Grey, sandy clay under Rubble I	A fine-grained, Kaolinized sand. Very few detrital grains and very small in size. Kyanite and iron present. Angular and sub-angular quartz.

Conclusions

A 1/1 is definitely of different age from any other sample with the possible exception of A 1/3, which contains only a little kyanite (5%).

A 1/2, A 1/4, B 1/1, B 1/2 and D 2/1 are regarded as of the same age, a distinctive feature is that they all contain a similar hornblende detrital and kyanite is greater than the iron content. Garnet may also be present, which has not been noted elsewhere.

A 3/1 and A 3/2 appear to be the same horizon, whilst A 3/3 may be slightly younger as a variation towards the top of the horizon containing A 3/1 and /2.

B 1/3 and D 2/2 are too fine-grained for any definite conclusion to be reached but they may themselves be from a similar age horizon since they both contain kyanite and iron and contain also few heavy minerals.

Kyanite has not previously been found as a detrital mineral in the Plateau Series and must be regarded as a distinctive type. Normal Plateau Sandstones give rise to iron and zircon only (cf. A 1/1).

Senga Hill (30 October 1956)

APPENDIX I

SUMMARY OF ANALYSED POLLEN SAMPLES: KALAMBO FALLS

Laboratory sample number	Field register number	Member	Bed(s)	Stratigraphic position Site A	Site B	Climate	Culture	C14 dates B.P.
Zone Z								
764	A 1/56/2	**Mbwilo**		F 6. A 1 1956. Sqr. F/6. Black (peaty) clay; c. 9 ft above river level; c. 3 ft below Rubble Ib	—	Cooler/wetter	Lupemban ?'Magosian'	—
765 2347	A 1/56/3			F 6. A 1 1956. Sqr. F/6. Black (peaty) clay c. 8 ft above river level; c. 4 ft below Rubble Ib	—	Cooler/wetter	Lupemban ?'Magosian'	—
766	A 1/56/4			F 6. A 1 1956. Sqr. F/6. Black (peaty) clay c. 7½ ft above river level; c. 4¼ ft below Rubble Ib, and 1 ft above Rubble Ic	—	Cooler/wetter	Lupemban ?'Magosian'	—
Zone Y		**Mkamba**						
2349	A 4/2		Pits Channel Fill	F 5. A 4 1959. Sqr. B/47. Pit 1. Red-green-grey clay c. 4½ ft above river level; 15½ ft below surface, in top of clay layer under Red Rubble Bed	—	Present day/wetter	Lupemban	—
2351	A 4/4			F 5. A 4 1959. Sqr. B/27. Pit 2. Cream-coloured sandy clay c. 36½ ft above river level; 9½ ft below surface, c. 1½ ft below base of Red Rubble Bed	—	Present day/wetter	Lupemban	—
Zone X								
2365	A 4/13		Ochreous Sands and Grey Clay	F 3. A 4 1959. Sqr. A/16. Grey clay with finely divided charcoal c. 18 ft above river level: 20½ ft below surface and 7 ft 6 in. below datum X	—	Cooler/wetter	Sangoan	> 32,600 (GrN-3668)

Zone W						
2278	B 2/59/3	—	F 3. B 2 1959. Sqr. G/5. Black (peaty) clay in channel fill. c. 6 ft above river level; 4 ft below Rubble Ib, and 13 ft 6 in. below surface	Warmer/present day rainfall?	Sangoan	37,900 ±1,500—−1,200 (GrN-3228)
2281	B 2/59/6	—	F 3. B 2 1959. Sqr. M/6. Black (peaty) clay in channel fill. c. 5½ ft above river level; 4½ ft below Rubble Ib, and 14 ft below surface	Present-day conditions	Sangoan	> 42,500 (L-399B)
2276	B 2/59/1	—	F 3. B 2 1959. Sqr. N/5. Black (peaty) clay in channel fill. c. 5½ ft above river level; 4½ ft below Rubble Ib and 14 ft below surface	Present-day conditions	Sangoan	—
2277	B 2/59/2	—	F 3. B 2 1959. Sqr. N/5. Black (peaty) clay in channel fill with leaves and woody vegetation. c. 5½ ft above river level; 4½ ft below Rubble Ib and 14 ft below surface	Present-day conditions	Sangoan	—
2378	A 4/59/26	White Sands and Dark Clay	F 2. A 4 1959. Sqr. AB/−1. Lump of clay in medium buff sand 6 in. above river level. c. 4½ ft above river level; 21 ft 6 in. below Datum X	Warmer/wetter	Sangoan? Acheulian?	> 49,000 (GrN-3211)
767	A 1/56/5	—	F 2. A 1 1956. Sqr. F/4. Grey/brown clay from Acheulian occupation surface IV. c. 4 ft above river level; 8–12 in. over Acheulian surface V; and 20 ft below surface	?Present-day conditions	Acheulian	—
2286	B 2/59/11	—	F 2. B 2 1959. Sqr. J/4. Brown clay layer in coarse sand c. 4 ft above river level; 16 ft below surface and 9 in. above Acheulian occupation surface V	Cooler/wetter	Acheulian	—
Zone V						
768	A 1/56/6	—	F 2. A 1 1956. Sqr. A/8. Top part black (peaty) clay over white sands and Acheulian occupation surface VI, c. 2 ft above river level	Cooler/wetter	Acheulian	—

Appendix I (*cont.*)

Laboratory sample number	Field register number	Member	Bed(s)	Stratigraphic position Site A	Stratigraphic position Site B	Climate	Culture	C14 dates B.P.
2380	A 4/59/28	**Mkamba**	White Sands and Dark Clay	F 2. A 4 1959. Sqr. B/−4. Upper black clay band of clay Bank (28). c. 4 ft above river level; 21 ft 8 in. below Datum X	—	Cooler/wetter	Acheulian	—
3719	A 6/66/1			F 2. A 6 1966. Upper black clay band of clay bank (28). c. 8 in. above river level and 6 in. below top of bed	—	Cooler and wetter	Acheulian	—
2381	A 4/59/29			F 2. A 4 1959. Sqr. B/−4. Blue-white clay band of clay bank (28). c. 3 ft. 9 in. above river level; 22 ft 2 in. below Datum X	—	Cooler/wetter	Acheulian	—
2382	A 4/59/30			F 2. A 4 1959. Sqr. B/−4. Lower black clay band of clay bank (28), with leaves. c. 3 ft 6 in. above river level; 22 ft 6 in. below Datum X	—	Cooler/wetter	Acheulian	—
3721	A 6/66/3			F 2. A 6 1966. Lower black clay band of clay bank (28) at river level. 1 ft 2 in. below top of bed	—	Cooler and wetter	Acheulian	—
3722	A 6/66/4			F 2. A 6 1966. Lower black clay band of clay bank (28). c. 6 in. below river level and c. 1 ft 10 in. below top of bed	—	Cooler and wetter	Acheulian	—
2342	B 1/56/17			—	F 2. B 1 1956. Sqr. E/1z (ex). 1 ft above base of black banded clay bank over white sands sealing Acheulian occupation surface V c. 1 ft below. c. 4 ft above river level	Cooler/wetter	Acheulian	—
2343	B 1/56/18			—	F 2. B 1 1956. Sqr. E/1z (ex). Base of black banded clay bank over white sands sealing Acheulian occupation surface V 1 ft 9 in. below. c. 3 ft above river level	Cooler/wetter	Acheulian	—
2288	B 2/59/13			—	F 2. B 2 1959. Sqr. M/1. Black clay associated with log on Acheulian occupation surface V c. 3 ft 2 in. above river level	Cooler/wetter	Acheulian	—

No.	Code	Description		Climate	Industry	Date
2383	A 4/59/31	F 2. A 4 1959. Sqr. B/-4. Lower part of lower black clay band of clay bank (28). c. 2 ft 6 in. above river level; 22 ft 11 in. below Datum X	—	Warmer/drier	Acheulian	—
774	A 1/56/13	F 1. A 1 1956. Sqr. A/3. Peaty clay with artifacts (Acheulian) horizon VI. c. 1 ft above river level	—	Warmer/drier	Acheulian	60,300 ±750 (GrN-4644)
780	B 1/56/19	F 1. B 1 1956. Sqr. E/1z (ex). Peaty black clay with artifacts and pebble lines; Acheulian horizon VI. c. 1 ft above river level	—	Warmer/drier	Acheulian	—
781	B 1/56/20	F 1. B 1 1956. Sqr. E/1z (ex). Peaty black clay with artifacts and pebble lines; Acheulian horizon VI. c. 1 ft above river level	—	Warmer/drier	Acheulian	—
2293	B 2/59/18	F 1. B 2 1959. Sqr. M/4. Black clay lens on pebble horizon (Acheulian) VIII in coarse/medium sands. 0 ft above river level	—	Warmer/drier	Acheulian	—
3726	A 6/66/8	F 2. A 6 1966. Grey clay lump in buff sand c. 4 ft below river level and 5 ft 3 in. below top of clay bank (28)	—	Warmer and drier	Acheulian	—
3727	A 6/66/9	F 2. A 6 1966. Brown and black clay bands. Between 4 ft 9 in. and 5 ft 2 in. below river level and between 6 ft and 6 ft 5 in. below top of clay bank (28)	—	Warmer and drier	Acheulian	—
3729	A 6/66/11	F 2. A 6 1966. Black clay band between two brown bands c. 5 ft below river level and 6 ft 3 in. below top of clay bank (28)	—	Warmer and drier	Acheulian	—
3731	A 6/66/13	F 2. A 6 1966. Brown clay band c. 7 ft 11 in. below river level and 9 ft 2 in. below top of clay bank (28)	—	Warmer and drier	Acheulian	—

APPENDIX J
(see folded sheet)

APPENDIX K

(see over)

APPENDIX K

ARCHAEOLOGICAL HORIZONS AND AGGREGATES FROM ARCHAEOLOGICAL HORIZONS, KALAMBO FALLS PREHISTORIC SITE

PROVISIONAL NOMENCLATURE

Industry	Site A Trenches A 1, A 2, A 3, A 4, A 5, A 6 and 1959 River Face	Site B Trenches B 1, B 2	Site C 1963 Trenches	Site D 1956 Trench
Kalambo (Iron Age)	Aggregate from Archaeological Horizon in grey, silty clays of 'Older Channel'	Aggregate from Archaeological Horizon in grey, silty clays of 'Older Channel'	Aggregate from Archaeological Horizon, Cliff Top Trench	Aggregate from Archaeological Horizon, 1963 Cliff Top Trench
Microlithic[1]	Aggregate from Archaeological Horizon, 1966 Camp Trench	—	Aggregate from Archaeological Horizon, Cliff Top Trench	—
'Magosian'	Aggregate from Archaeological Horizon in ferruginous sandy clay and grey sandy clay in Tr. A 4; overlying Rubble Ia in Tr. A 3 Aggregate typologically separated from Archaeological Horizons Rubble I-composite and Ia, Trs. A 1, A 3, A 4 ?in Archaeological Horizon, Tr. A 2	Aggregate from Archaeological Horizon in sands above Rubble Ia, Tr. B 1 Aggregate typologically separated from Archaeological Horizons, Rubble Ia, Ib, and I-composite, Tr. B 1, B 2	—	Aggregate typologically separated from Archaeological Horizon, Rubble I-composite

Lupemban	Aggregate typologically separated from Archaeological Horizon, Red Rubble, Tr. A 4; and from Rubble Ia, Ib, Ic and I-composite, Trs. A 1, A 2, A 3, A 4	Aggregate typologically separated from Archaeological Horizons, Rubble Ia, Ib and I-composite, Trs. B 1, B 2	Aggregate typologically separated from Archaeological Horizons, Rubble Ia, Ib and Ib, composite, Ia and Ib, River Face Trench	Aggregate typologically separated from Archaeological Horizon, Rubble I-composite
?Lupemban	Aggregate typologically separated from Archaeological Horizons, Rubble Ia, Ib, Ic and I-composite, Trs. A 1, A 3, A 4 Aggregate from Archaeological Horizons, Rubble IIa, IIb, II-composite, Trs. A 4, ?A 2	Aggregate typologically separated from Archaeological Horizons, Rubble Ia, Ib, I-composite, Trs. B 1, B 2	Aggregate typologically separated from Archaeological Horizons, Rubble Ia, Ib, composite Ia and Ib, River Face Trench	Aggregate typologically separated from Archaeological Horizon, Rubble I-composite
Sangoan	Aggregate from Archaeological Horizon in basal Ochreous Sands, Trs. A 4, A 5, and 1959 River Face Trench	Aggregate from Archaeological Horizon in Ochreous Sands, Trs. B 1, B 2; and from Archaeological Horizon IV, Trs. B 1, B 2	Aggregate noted in Archaeological Horizon in Ochreous Sands, River Face	Aggregate from Archaeological Horizon in Ochreous Sands
Industry belonging to Acheulian Industrial Complex	Aggregate from: Archaeological Horizon IV, Tr. A 1, A 5 Archaeological Horizon V, Tr. A 1 Archaeological Horizon VI, Tr. A 1 (Below river level) Archaeological Horizon 1, Tr. A 6 Archaeological Horizon 2, Tr. A 6 Archaeological Horizon 3, Tr. A 6	Aggregate from: Archaeological Horizon V, Trs. B 1, B 2 Archaeological Horizon VI, Trs. B 1, B 2 Archaeological Horizon VII, Tr. B 2 Archaeological Horizon VIII, Tr. B 2	(Below river level)	(Below river level)

[1] Other Archaeological Horizons (surface occurrences) are known in the local basin above the Kalambo Falls.

1   The Kalambo Falls from the air at the end of the dry season (October 1966), showing the Spillway Gorge and river meander between Sites A and B, marked by the darker line of trees at top right. Site B is situated immediately to the right of the white sand section near the top right-hand corner of the photograph. (Photo. G. H. Cole.)

2   Air photograph of the western end of the local basin at the Kalambo Falls showing the 1956 and 1959 excavations (Sites A–D) and places mentioned in the text. (Photo. Fairey Air Surveys of Rhodesia, Ltd, 1960.)

3 The local basin at the Kalambo Falls looking east from the top of the 'Tanganyika Cliff' (Mkamba Member). The Mkamba Member and scarp (left), Site B behind tree at extreme right. The modern swamp (right centre) and Chiungu Village (Dominico's) on Chisya Gravel Beds (right centre). Cassava gardens in foreground. Oil palms (*Elaeis guineensis*) extreme left and Borassus palms, right centre.

4   Eroded feature of Chitambala Gravel Beds with soil-covered Chisya Gravel Beds in foreground. East side of Kalambo river near Headman Dominico's (Chiungu) village. (Photo. G. Bond.)

5 The lip of the falls from immediately upstream—end of the dry season, 1959—showing quartzites dipping to the southeast overlain by mudstones with siliceous layers, both important sources of raw material for artifacts in prehistoric times.

6 The landslide between Sites D and B caused by the heavy rains of the 1961–2 season. A 300 foot section of decomposed rock and sediments had slumped into the river half blocking the stream channel.

7   The Kalambo Falls during a period of very low water in October 1959 as seen from the Zambia (Northern Rhodesia) side, looking in a northeasterly direction (compare with Plate 1). The height of the falls is 726 feet. The heavily jointed rock face is composed of thick-bedded, massive, quartzite and sandstone with thin intercalations of sericite schists and sheared, sericitic quartzite. These rocks are overlain by cherty rocks on the hill to the left above the lip of the falls, and in places, on the slope to the right. At the lip of the falls, the quartzite dips at 13° to 110°. The suite of quartzitic rocks is underlain by dark brownish or greenish clay-slates and shales which can be seen above the pool at the bottom of the falls. All these rocks are referred to the Plateau Series. The dense tree growth behind the lip of the falls marks the exit to the Spillway Gorge which controls the outflow from the local basin where the Prehistoric Site is located. The wide valley cross-section, 60–75 feet above the river level in the Spillway Gorge, was formed at the site of an old windgap. (Photo. E. G. Haldemann.)

8   The cliff on the southern side of the Kalambo Gorge as seen from the slope a little to the north
above the Kalambo Falls (September 1959), looking in a southwesterly direction. The position of the
cliff-face is governed by a fracture zone along a fault and related vertical joints which strikes to WSW.
The fault is readily recognizable in the break of the wall in the centre of the picture. In the cliff on the
left the quartzitic rocks dip at low angles to ESE while in the northern flank to the right of the fault the
beds dip to SW. The evidence suggests that vigorous erosion by the Kalambo first led to a cascade in
the fracture zone. Then, after erosion had reached the softer clay-slates which underlie the more
competent quartzitic rocks, the cutting back and the formation of the Kalambo Falls proceeded
comparatively rapidly (Early Pleistocene times). (Photo. E. G. Haldemann.)

9 The Kalambo Gorge as seen from the hill to the north of the Kalambo Falls (August 1963), looking in a westerly direction towards Lake Tanganyika. The sandstones in the higher portion of the slope to the left and in the background to the right, which dip at low angles in a southwesterly direction into the lake, are stratigraphically higher than the quartzitic rocks at the falls. In the fore- and middle-ground, some nickpoints can be seen about half-way up the slopes; they are remnant features of a wide, U-shaped valley interpreted as the end-Pliocene valley. The lower valley section in the foreground is V-shaped and its formation is believed to have coincided with the formation of the Kalambo Falls and the cutting of the Spillway Gorge. In the foreground and further upstream, the Kalambo has cut a narrow inaccessible gorge into the V-shaped valley section. Several smaller falls occur in this inner gorge which is a young feature that can be explained by a late stage of uplift in the area and the increase in the erosional capacity of the Kalambo River after it began to lose a great proportion of its sediment load in the local basin. (Photo. M. R. Kleindienst.)

10 The Kalambo River in the Spillway Gorge during low water conditions (October 1959). The river flows in a westerly direction towards the observer. The debris of the rock-fall is on the north side of the river and at the foot of a steep face masked by dense vegetation. The larger blocks reach about half-way across the river and smaller ones are found in the river bed right across to the south side. This block-fall is impeding the river, which today is only transporting fine sediments through the gorge. The light-coloured outcrop on the south side of the river was included in the surveyed cross-section. Close to this rock the river was 46 feet wide and 6–7 feet deep, and its bed consisted of fine sand. This depth indicates a scouring effect behind the lip of the Kalambo Falls, which is only about 160 yards down-stream. The geological investigations revealed that the direction of the gorge is determined by a fracture zone which strikes to WSW. A second set of joints dips at 65–70° to SW or at about 35° from the north side into the gorge. This explains why rock-falls occur on the north and not on the south side of the Spillway Gorge. (Photo. E. G. Haldemann.)

11 General view of Site A, excavation A 1, 1956, showing the right half of the excavation taken down to the level of the Acheulian V Archaeological Horizon (Mkamba Member). Archaeological Horizon Rubble I c (Mbwilo Member) can be seen in section in the north and east walls, overlain by banded black and grey clays and white sands. The upper half of the excavation is composed of clays and clay sands filling the 'Older' and 'Younger Channel' cuts of the Chiungu Member. (Photo. G. Bond.)

12   A 1, 1956 excavation, northeast wall section showing red and grey clays of 'Younger and Older Channel' cuts (Chiungu Member) with Iron Age remains overlying coarse ferruginous sands, resting on remnant of Rubble I b (Mbwilo Member). The layered white sands and black, organic clays below this (laid down under cooler and wetter climatic conditions than those of the present day), overlie Rubble I c with Lupemban artifacts.

13 A 1, 1956 excavation. General view of Archaeological Horizon Rubble I c of the Mbwilo Member showing the 'form' left by decomposition of tree-trunk formerly intruded from the underlying Ochreous Sands (Mkamba Member). The foot scale is in the centre of one of the 'circles' of larger stones thought to be artificial.

14 A 1, 1956 excavation. Part of the east wall (northeast corner), showing Rubble I b at the top, laminated white sands and black clays, Rubble I c which bifurcates into I c(i) and I c(ii) (Mbwilo Member) at right, resting on the unstratified White Sands, excavated to the level of the Acheulian IV Archaeological Horizon (Mkamba Member). An anvil and flaking area at left; hand-axe groups to right.

19   Trench A 4, 1959, looking north to the Kalambo River, showing Pit 1 and the soil profile overlying the Red Rubble Bed, Pit 2, and the excavated area north of grid line 21. In the right background
is Mkamba Village, on top of the 'Tanganyika Cliff' below Burnt Ridge. (Photo. M. R. Kleindienst).

20 Trench A 4, looking south, cleared to the level of Archaeological Horizon Rubble I-composite, and showing the nature of this deposit (September 1959). The peg in the left foreground marks grid line 2; the 8 foot rod, grid line 7. The thickness of the rubble and its brown sand matrix is about 9 inches in the face in grid squares A and B +5. Rubble I has been removed south of grid line 16, but can be seen in the face at grid line 21. In the west wall, current-bedded ferruginous sand overlies Rubble I-composite; the sand is overlain by light grey sandy clay and grey clay; and these are overlain by brown sandy clay and clay that contain Iron Age remains. (Photo. E. G. Haldemann.)

21 Trench A 4, Pit 1, 1963, south wall. At top, the Red Rubble Bed of the Mbwilo Member, overlying grey-green mottled clay correlated with the upper part of the Pits Channel Fill of the Mkamba
Member in Pit 2. A rubble, thought to belong to the Rubble II complex and marked by the top of the
7 foot rod, occurs in the top of fine cross-bedded sand that becomes medium and current-bedded at
the base where it overlies the main Archaeological Horizon Rubble II (= Rubble Bed of the Mkamba
Member). The dip on the bedding is from 5° to 16° SW. At the base of the section, Rubble II is split
into IIa and IIb lying in a matrix of coarse sand, the latter resting on the eroded top of fine buff-white
clayey sand with clay lenses.

22 Trench A 4, 1959, river end north of grid line 21 (November 1959). In the south wall, sands overlying Archaeological Horizon Rubble II (Rubble Bed of Mkamba Member) and the rubble resting on a banded grey clay bank can be seen at the top. This clay and underlying sands and clays of the Ochreous Sands and Grey Clay Beds have been cleared to the horizon(s) of pebbles and coarse sand which include Sangoan artifacts with cobbles and boulders of quartzites and dolomite. Wood can be seen protruding up into this horizon from below. (Photo. B. Anthony.)

23 The 1959 River Face Cliff clearance (November 1959), looking toward the eroded Trench A 1 from near the mouth of Trench A 4. The 'Younger Channel' Fill (Y.Ch.) and 'Older Channel' Fill (O.Ch.) are marked by dotted lines. The benches follow Archaeological Horizons Rubbles I a, I b, and I c from their junction on the extreme right, or west, side of the photograph. Rubbles I a and I b are cut out by the 'Older Channel', but the base of the 8 foot rod on the east rests on Rubble I c. Below this 'main erosion surface' are truncated deposits of the Ochreous Sands Beds. (Photo. M. R. Kleindienst.)

24 B 1, 1956 excavation, looking west to the river edge showing the Acheulian Archaeological Horizon V underlying the black clay bank and fine White Sands, which in turn are cut out by Ochreous Sands with Sangoan artifacts at the base (top right). The C line of grid squares, removed to drain the remainder of the excavation, has exposed the wood that underlies this occupation surface.

25　B 2, 1959 excavation, south wall excavated to a depth of 7 feet, showing in the floor the spur of Mbwilo Member sediments with the Rubble I Archaeological Horizons projecting into the banked red clays and clay sands of the Chiungu Member with Iron Age remains.

26 B 2, 1959 excavation, west and south walls. The western grid squares excavated to the level of Archaeological Horizon Rubble I b with Lupemban and 'Magosian' artifacts and overlain by sands, clays and fine gravels and Rubble I a seen in section in the west wall. The Rubbles dip down towards the south and join at, or just above, low water level. The gravel bank (Rubble I-composite) exposed in the river bed between Sites A and B can be seen in the top right corner with, beyond the river bank, the A 1 excavation.

27   B 2, 1959 excavation. General view of excavation looking northeast and showing (left) the Mbwilo Member sands and rubble lines unconformable on the Ochreous Sands Beds of the Mkamba Member, both cut through by the channel sediments of the Chiungu Member. Right centre and right—white sands and black and grey clays filling minor channels in the upper part of the Ochreous Sands.

28   B 2, 1959 excavation, western end of north wall. Archaeological Horizons Rubbles I a and I b with Lupemban and 'Magosian' disconformable on Ochreous Sands and pebble stringers with Sangoan, all cut by channelling and overlain by clays and clay sands of the Chiungu Member with Iron Age remains.

29　B 2, 1959 excavation, south wall showing the excavation carried to water level. Red and grey clays and clay sands with Iron Age remains cutting sands of the Mbwilo Member (right), with Rubble lines I a and I b overlying disconformably Ochreous Sands Beds and pebble lines of the Mkamba Member with occasional Sangoan artifacts.

30 B 2, 1959 excavation, east and north walls showing the Acheulian Archaeological Horizon V surface with wood and tools (left), the line of the channel bank cutting out this surface (left centre) and (right and back) the Ochreous Sands Beds that fill this channel.

31 View of Site C facing downstream (1966). The photograph was taken during the course of the excavations. A section had not yet been cleared between excavations 1 and 3. A portion of the wet season channel floor not covered by spoil can be seen in the lower left portion of the photograph. The area of the early Iron Age settlement excavated in 1963 can be seen (upper left) at the top of the terrace. Colluvium over the upper part of the Mkamba Member with mound cultivation for cassava can be seen behind the top of the 30 foot (9 m) terrace. (Photo. G. H. Cole.)

32 Site D in 1956. The river here is flowing northwest (i.e. to the right). At the base, at river level, can be seen Ochreous Sands under brown clay and sand, and white silty clay. (Mkamba Member). These beds are overlain disconformably by Archaeological Horizon Rubble I-composite with Lupemban and 'Magosian' artifacts. Above are buff coloured, bedded sands (Mbwilo Member), dark humic soil and early Iron Age midden deposit.

BIBLIOGRAPHY
INDEX

BIBLIOGRAPHY

Anderson, B. (1957). *A Survey of Soils in the Kongwa and Nachingwea Districts of Tanganyika*. University of Reading and Tanganyika Agricultural Corporation.

Ansell, W. F. H. (1960). *Mammals of Northern Rhodesia*. Government Printer, Lusaka, Zambia.

Atlas of the Federation of Rhodesia and Nyasaland (1961). Federal Department of Trigonometrical and Topographical Surveys, Government Printer, Salisbury, Rhodesia.

Bishop, W. W. & Clark, J. D. (1966). Systematic investigation of the African Later Tertiary and Quaternary. *Curr. Anthrop.* **7**, 2, 253–6.

(1967). *Background to Evolution in Africa*. University of Chicago Press, Chicago.

Brelsford, W. V. (ed.) (1952). Measuring the Kalambo Falls. *Nth Rhod. J.* **1**, 6, p. 73.

Broecker, W. S. & Olson, E. A. (1961). Lamont natural radiocarbon measurements VII. *Radiocarbon*, **3**, 172.

Capart, A. (1949). Sondages et carte bathymétrique. *Inst. Roy. Sci. Nat. Belgique*. Exploration hydrobiologique du Lac Tanganyika (1946–7). *Résultats scientifiques*, **2**, 2.

(1952). Le milieu géographique et géophysique. *Inst. Roy. Sci. Nat. Belgique*. Exploration hydrobiologique du Lac Tanganyika (1946–7). *Résultats scientifiques*, **1**.

Clark, J. D. (1954). An early Upper Pleistocene site at the Kalambo Falls on the Northern Rhodesia/Tanganyika border. *S. Afr. Archaeol. Bull.* **9**, no. 34, pp. 51–6.

(1955). *Northern Rhodesia Excursion Handbook for the Pan-African Congress*. Rhodes-Livingstone Museum, Government Printer, Lusaka.

(1958). Certain industries of notched and strangulated scrapers in Rhodesia, their time range and possible use. *S. Afr. Archaeol. Bull.* **13**, no. 50, pp. 56–66.

(1962). The Kalambo Falls Prehistoric Site: an interim report. In G. Mortelmans and J. Nenquin (eds.), *Actes du IVe Congrès Pan-africain de Préhistoire et de l'Etude du Quaternaire*, Musée royal de l'Afrique centrale, Annales, Série in 8°, Sciences humaines, 40: Section III, pp. 195–201.

(1963). *Prehistoric cultures of northeast Angola and their significance in tropical Africa*. Museu do Dundo, Lisbon, Publicações Culturais, no. 62, p. 18a.

(1965). The influence of environment in inducing culture change at the Kalambo Falls prehistoric site. *S. Afr. Archaeol. Bull.* **20**, no. 75, 93–101.

Clark, J. D. & Zinderen Bakker, E. M. van (1964). Prehistoric culture and Pleistocene vegetation at the Kalambo Falls, Northern Rhodesia. *Nature, Lond.* **201** (4923), 971–5.

Coetzee, J. A. (1964). Evidence for a considerable depression of the vegetation belts during the Upper Pleistocene on the East African Mountains. *Nature, Lond.* **204** (4958), 564–6.

(1967). Pollen analytical studies in east and southern Africa. In E. M. van Zinderen Bakker (ed.), *Palaeoecology of Africa*, III, A. A. Balkema, Cape Town.

Combe, A. D. (1927). Summary of investigations carried out between Entebbe and Cape Town. *Annual Report of the Geological Survey of Uganda* (1926), pp. 28–32. Uganda Protectorate, Government Printer, Entebbe.

16-2

Cooke, C. K. (1963). Report on excavations at Pomongwe and Tshangula Caves, Matopos Hills, Southern Rhodesia. *S. Afr. Archaeol. Bull.* **18**, 146–51.

Cooke, H. B. S. (1958). Observations relating to Quaternary environments in east and southern Africa. *Trans. Proc. geol. Soc. S. Afr.* Annexure to vol. **60** (Alex. du Toit Memorial Lecture, 5).

Cornwall, J. W. (1929). The survey of the Kalambo Gorge. *Geogrl J.* **74**, 33–8.

Dixey, F. (1956). The east African rift system. *Colonial Geol. and Mineral Resources Bull.* Suppl. 1.

Fanshawe, D. B. (1960–1). Evergreen forest relics in Northern Rhodesia. *Kirkia,* **1**, 20–4.

Geochronicle, **5**, 1 (1965). Half life of radiocarbon (C14).

Gilchrist, B. (1952). Vegetation types of southern Tanganyika. In *Report on Central African Rail Link Development Survey*, Part D, 'Tanganyika', vol. **2**, 58–67. U.K. Gov. Col. Office, London.

Gillman, C. (1935). Geomorphological notes. *Annual Report Geological Survey, Tanganyika* (1934), pp. 31–3.

Gordon-Gallien, Mrs Enid (1929). The Kalambo Falls. *Geogrl J.* **74**, no. 1, pp. 28–32.

Haldemann, E. G. (1962). The geology of the Rufiji Basin with reference to proposed dam sites. *Bull. geol. Surv. Tanganyika,* **33**.

(1964). *Mambwe (Mwimbi): brief explanation of the geology.* Geol. Survey Tanganyika, Quarter Degree Sheet 241 (with part of 241 S).

Halligan, R. (1963). The Proterozoic rocks of western Tanganyika. *Bull. geol. Surv. Tanganyika,* **34**.

Haughton, S. H. (1963). *Stratigraphic Geology of Africa South of the Sahara.* Oliver and Boyd, Edinburgh and London.

Hedberg, H. D. (1961). Stratigraphic classification and terminology. *International Geological Congress, report of the 21st Session*, Norden, 1960. Part xxv.

Hore, E. C. (1892). *Tanganyika: Eleven years in Central Africa* (2nd ed.). Edward Stanford, London.

Howell, F. C. & Clark, J. D. (1963). Acheulian hunter-gatherers of sub-Saharan Africa. In F. C. Howell and F. Bourlière (eds.), *African Ecology and Human Evolution.* Aldine, Chicago. Pp. 458–533.

Jackson, S. P. (1961). *Climatological Atlas of Africa.* CCTA/CSA, Government Printer, Pretoria.

James, T. C. (1956). The nature of rift faulting in Tanganyika. *CCTA, East Central Regional Committee for Geology*, 1st meeting, Dar-es-Salaam, pp. 81–94.

King, B. C. (1957). The geomorphology of Africa. *Sci. Progr., Lond.* **15**, 672–81; **16**, 97–107.

King, L. C. (1951). *South African Scenery.* (2nd ed.) Oliver and Boyd, London and Edinburgh.

Kuenen, Ph. H. (1956). Experimental abrasion of pebbles, 2: Rolling by current. *J. Geol.* **64**, 336–63.

Lawton, R. M. (1962–3). Palaeological and ecological studies in the Northern Province of Northern Rhodesia. *Kirkia,* **3** (Jan. 1963), 46–77.

Leopold, L. B., Wolman, M. G. & Miller, J. P. (1964). *Fluvial Processes in Geomorphology.* W. H. Freeman and Co., San Francisco and London.

McConnell, R. B. (1950). Outline of the geology of Ufipa and Ubende. *Bull. geol. Surv. Tanganyika,* **19**.

Moore, J. E. S. (1903). *The Tanganyika Problem*. Hurst and Blackett, Ltd, London.

Mortelmans, G. (1956). Le troisième congrès pan-africain de préhistoire (Livingstone, juillet, 1955). *Académie royale des sciences coloniales*, Classe des sciences naturelles et médicales, *Mémoires in 8°*, nouvelle série, vol. IV, fasc. 3, pp. 1–128.

Olson, E. A. & Broecker, W. S. (1959). Lamont natural radiocarbon measurements V. *Radiocarbon*, **1**, 23–5.

Page, B. G. N. (1959). The Plateau Series and associated formations in the Abercorn district. *Annual Report, Research Inst. Afr. Geol., Univ. of Leeds*, **4**.

—— (1960). The stratigraphical and structural relationship of the Abercorn Sandstones, the Plateau Series and Basement rocks of the Kawimbe area, Abercorn district, Northern Rhodesia. *Annual Report, Research Inst. Afr. Geol., Univ. of Leeds*, **5**.

Pulfrey, W. (1960). Shape of the sub-Miocene erosion bevel in Kenya. *Bull. geol. Surv. Kenya*, **3**.

Quennell, A. M. (1960). Report of the East-Central Regional Committee for Geology, Sub-Committee on Stratigraphical Nomenclature. Joint Meeting, Leopoldville, 1958, *C.C.T.A.* **44**, 11–26.

Rattray, J. M. & Wild, H. (1961–2). Vegetation map of the Federation of Rhodesia and Nyasaland. *Kirkia*, **2**, 94–104.

Reeve, W. H. (1961). Geological map of Northern Rhodesia (scale 1:1,000,000), Geological Survey, Lusaka, Zambia.

Robinson, G. W. (1949). *Soils, an Introduction to Pedology*. Murby, London.

Rose, C. (1929). The geology of the Kalambo Gorge. *Geogrl J.* **74**, no. 1, pp. 38–46.

Sanson, H. W. (1954). The measurement of evaporation in East Africa. *East Afr. Meteorological Dept. Techn. Memorandum*, **5**.

Streel, M. (1963). *La végétation tropophylle des plaines alluviales de la Lufira moyenne*. FULREAC, Université de Liège.

Thompson, J. (1888). *To the Central African Lakes and Back*. Sampson Low, Marston, Searle and Rivington (cheaper edition), London.

Thorenaar, A. (1926). Onderzoek naar bruikbar kermerken ter identificatie van boomen naar hun bast. *Meded. v.h. Proefst. v.h. Boschwezen 16: Wageningen*. English translation: *Investigations on useful characters for the identification of trees from their bark* (of part only), in Botany School, University of Cambridge.

Trapnell, C. G. (1953). *The Soils, Vegetation and Agriculture of Northeastern Rhodesia*. Report of the Ecological Survey. Government Printer, Lusaka.

Van der Hammen, Th. & Gonzalez, E. (1960). Upper Pleistocene and Holocene climate and vegetation of the 'Sabana de Bogota' (Columbia, South America). *Leid. geol. Meded.* **25**, 261–315.

Van Zinderen Bakker, E. M. (1962). A Late-Glacial and Post-Glacial climatic correlation between East Africa and Europe. *Nature, Lond.* **194** (4824), 201–3.

—— (1964). A pollen diagram from Equatorial Africa, Cherangani, Kenya. *Geol. en Mijnboow*, **43**, no. 3, 123–8.

—— (1965) Über Moorvegetation und den Aufbau der Moore in Süd- und Ostafrica. *Bot. Jb.* **84**, no. 2, 215–31.

—— (1967). Upper Pleistocene and Holocene stratigraphy and ecology on the basis of vegetation changes in sub-Saharan Africa. In W. W. Bishop and J. D. Clark (eds.), *Background to Evolution in Africa*, pp. 125–47. University Press, Chicago.

Van Zinderen Bakker, E. M. & Clark, J. D. (1962). Pleistocene climates and cultures in North-Eastern Angola. *Nature, Lond.* **196** (4855), 639–42.

Vogel, J. C. & Waterbolk, H. T. (1964). Groningen radiocarbon dates V. *Radiocarbon*, **6**, 350–2.

(1967). Groningen Radiocarbon Dates VII. *Radiocarbon*, **9**, 144–6.

Wallace, L. A. (1907). Northeastern Rhodesia. *Geogrl J.* **29**, 391.

White, F. (1962). *Forest Flora of Northern Rhodesia*. Oxford Univ. Press, Oxford.

Whitmore, T. C. (1962*a*). Studies in systematic bark morphology, II: General features of bark construction. Bark studies outside Dipterocarpaceae. *New Phytol.* (1962).

(1962*b*). Studies in systematic bark morphology, III: Bark taxonomy in Dipterocarpaceae. *Gdns' Bull.* (1962).

Wissmann, H. von (1891). *My Second Journey through Equatorial Africa from the Congo to the Zambezi in the Years 1886 and 1887*. Chatto and Windus, London.

INDEX

NOTE. *Page numbers in italics refer to pull-out sheets, and give the page number facing the pull-out.*

Abercorn, access to Kalambo Falls from, 1, 20, 197; rainfall at, 3; temperature at, 4; up-warped area round, 31

Acheulian industry
    archaeological horizons of, 239
    artifacts of, from cliff, 10; in Mbwilo Member (derived), 193; in Mkamba Member, 52, 146, 190–1; from Site A, 10, 11, 16, 17, 145, 151, (A 1) 95, 104, 105, 108–9, 145, (A 4) 137, 138, 140, 145, (A 5) 140, 143, 144, (A 6) 120, 121; from Site B, 11, 12, 13, 16, 180, (B 1) 153, 159, (B 2) 172, 174, (B 5) 177
    climate at time of, 191, 233–5
    climatic correlation of, 211, 212, 213
    dating of, 151, 190–1, 236
    occupation floors of, 207–8, 210, 214; at Site A, 16, 86, (A 1) 105–9, (A 5) 144, (A 6) 120; at Site B, 12, 13, 16, (B 1) 159, 160, 179, (B 2) 172, 173, 174, 179

aggradation, phases of, in Kalambo basin, 17

alluvium, in Kalambo basin, 1, 2, 20, 46, 199; *itegi* thicket on, 6

Angola, pollen spectra from, 194; Sangoan in, 192

anvil stones, from Site A, (A 1) 102, 103, 106, (A 4) 127; from Site B, (B 1) 157, (B 2) 167, 168; wedged in sand, 208

axes, 'Later Stone Age', 194; *see also* core-axes, hand-axes

bark, tray of, 173, 222–4

bead, nineteenth-century, 186

blades (artifacts), 148, 167, 181, 185, 188

bones, destruction of, in acid clays of Kalambo basin, 12, 206; vertebrate, in Chiungu Member, 55

'Boulder Beds', 'Older', 54, 194, 204–5 (*see also* Chitambala Gravel Beds); 'Younger', 54, 205 (*see also* Chisya Gravel Beds)

boulders
    bed of, at entrance to Spillway Gorge, 42
    orientation of, in Kalambo River, 40, 127; in Rubble Beds, 41, 127, 134, 135

breccias, in Kalambo basin, 25

burials, pottery possibly associated with, 141, 164, 187

burins (artifacts), 167

Bwinginfumu forests, 61, 63

chalcedony, 'Magosian' artifacts in, 116

'Channel' fills, 48–9, 85
    'Older' and 'Younger', at Site A, (A 1) 92, 93, 97, 99, 147, 149, (A 2) 112, (A 5) 141; at Site B, (B 2) 165
    see also Pits Channel Fill

Channelled Ware, *see under* pottery

charcoals
    from bush fires, in top-soils, 90
    dating of, 104, 115, 124, 133, 135–6, 143–4, 165, 166, *236*
    identification of, 218
    at Site A, (A 1) 90, 92, 93, 101, 104, (A 3) 113, 115, 116, (A 4) 124, 126, 133, 135–6, (A 5) 143, (A 6) 121; at Site B, (B 1) 153, 155, 162, (B 2) 165, 166; at Site C, 17, 185
    taking of samples of, for radiocarbon dating, 12, 17, 88

Chelles-Acheul floors, 207–8; *see also under* Acheulian industry

chert, 23, 148, 198; tools of, 101, 109, 112, 116, 121, 155

chipya woodland, 4

Chisya Gravel Beds (Chiungu Member), 22, 47, 54, 55, 205 n.; *see also* 'Boulder Beds', 'Younger'

Chitambala Gravel Beds (Mbwilo Member), 22, 47, 54, 204 n.; *see also* 'Boulder Beds', 'Older'

chitimene type of agriculture, 4

Chiungu Member of Kalambo Falls Formation, 22, 47, 48, 49, 54–5
    dating of, 55, 165, 166, 194
    geological events during, at Site A, 149; at Site B, 179
    Iron Age artifacts in, 147
    at Site A, (A 1) 101, (A 2) 164, 165, 169, 174, (A 3) 116, (A 4) 50, 124; at Site B, (B 2) 162, 163, 169, 174, (B 4) 176, (B 5) 177
    thickness of, 55
    see also Chisya Gravel Beds

247

choppers, 97, 115, 120, 158

clay, separation of vegetable remains from, 87–8, 162; *see also* Dark Clay Beds, Grey Clay Beds, Red Clays

clay slates, of Kalambo basin, 23, 44

cleavers
  Acheulian, from cliff, 10
  of 'Older Stone Age', 209
  from Site A, (A 1) 102, 106, 107, 108, (A 3) 116, (A 6) 120; from Site B, (B 1) 153, 159, (B 2) 172, 174, (B 5) 177

climate
  affected by topographic changes, 35
  of Kalambo basin, present-day, 3–4; record of changes in, from pollen counts, 5, 18, 70–4
  and vegetation, 58

club, wooden, 172

concrete, pre-cast rings of, as casing for excavation, 17, 85, 117

core-axes, from Site A, (A 1) 101, 102, 104, (A 3) 115, 116, (A 4) 132, 133, 136, 192; from Site B, (B 1) 158, 160, (B 3) 175; from Site C, 181; from Site D, 187

core-scrapers, 120, 181

cores, 93, 129, 136, 175, 181

Cyperaceae, in Pleistocene, 64, 65, 71, 76, 78, 80, 82, 84

daga, fragments of, from Site A, (A 1) 90, 92, 97, 99, (A 2) 112, (A 3) 113, (A 4) 125; from Site B, (B 1) 155, (B 2) 163; from Site D, 186

dambos (swampy valleys), 4–5, 62, 63; deposits in, 101, 130; fauna of, 6; pollen from, 70, 71

Dark Clay Beds (Mkamba Member), 47, 52, 140

dating, *see* radiocarbon dating

deltas, in Kalambo basin, 55, 201, 205

discoid tools, 102, 120, 181

dolerites, in debris in sites A 4 and A 5, 148; intrusions of, in Plateau Series, 1, 2, 22, 25, 198

dry season, at Kalambo Falls, 4

ecotone, between montane and *miombo* forests, 61–2

Ericaceae, above and below montane forest, 63; in pollen samples, 67, 70, 79, 81, 83

erosion, during periods of drier climate, 212

evaporation from Lake Tanganyika, rate of, 33, 35

faults, in rocks of Kalambo basin, 31–2, 43–4

fauna, of Kalambo Falls area, 6, 7, 17, 18; of Lake Tanganyika, 28, 29

feldspars, 23, 148, 198

ferruginization, 129, 158, 204

fires, bush, 19; charcoals from, 90; effects of, 58, 59, 61

flake tools, 102, 136, 171

flakes, from Site A, (A 1) 90, 92, 97, 101, 106, (A 2) 109, (A 4) 127, 128, 131, 132, 136, 138, (A 5) 144–5, (A 6) 120, 121; from Site B, (B 1) 158, (B 2) 169, (B 3) 175; from Site D, 188

floors of occupation, 86
  Acheulian, 12, 16, 86, 105–9, 207–8, 210, 214
  series of, exposed by excavation, 207–8; correlation of, 214
  technique for excavating, 11–12, 85–8

forests, *chipya*, 4; dry conifer, 62; dry evergreen, 59, 63; fringing of lakes, 67, *itegi* (thicket), 6; *miombo* (deciduous), 4, 18, 58; moist tropical, 5; montane (humid evergreen), 5, 59, 60, 62, 63; *mushitu* (swamp evergreen), 5, 6, 7, 62–3, 71; *muulu* (dry semi-deciduous), 58; natural and degraded, 57; Pleistocene, pollen from, 65–83; riparian (evergreen), 7, 62, 67

fruits, from Pleistocene deposits, 67, 216–17

Gamblian climatic episode, 201, 212, 213, 214

gardens, present-day, 18, 163; relics of, 88, 90

geological events, at Site A, 149–51; at Site B, 179–80

geology, of Kalambo Falls area, 20–56, 197–214

geomorphology, of Kalambo basin, 25–33

grasses (Gramineae), pollen of, in Pleistocene deposits, 64, 70, 71, 78, 80, 81, 82, 83, 84

grassland, on mountains, 58, 61; of recent origin, 57, 58; tussock-moor, 62

Grey Clay Beds (Mkamba Member), 22, 47, 48, 52

grey clay sands, chemical composition of, 92

grids, three-dimensional, for excavation sites, (A) 88, 89; (A 4), 122; (B 1), 153, 155; (B 2), 163; (D), 186

grindstones (lower), 93, 141, 155, 168; *see also* rubbers

hammerstones, 138, 168, 175

hand-axes
  Acheulian, from cliff, 10
  of 'Older Stone Age', 209
  from Site A, (A 1), 101, 102, 106, 107, 108, 109, (A 3) 116, (A 6) 120; from Site B, (B 1) 153, 156, 159, (B 2) 169, 172, 173, 174, (B 5) 177, 178; from Site D, 188
  standing on long edges, 87, 173

hearths, 97, 157, 161

Holoholo people, story of island in Lake Tanganyika told by, 35–6

hydrology, of Lake Tanganyika and Kalambo basin, 33–7

Hyparrhenia (elephant grass), 2, 10; charcoals from burning of, 90

Inamwanga people, 7

iron, in samples of sands and clays, 230–1; worked, 163

Iron Age
  artifacts of, from Chiungu Member, 147; from River Face Cliff, 149; from Site A, 205, (A 1) 92, 95, 97, 149, (A 2) 112, (A 3) 113, (A 4), 123, 125, 147, (A 5) 141; from Site B, 205, (B 1) 156, 179, (B 2) 163, 164, 174, 179, (B 3) 176; from Site C, 184, 186; from Site D, 186, 205
  climatic correlation of, 214
  dating of, 149, 194
  Kalambo Industry during, 55
  pottery of, 113, 205
  sediments deposited during, 201, 211
  settlement area of, 11, 16, 86

iron slag, 205, 210; from Site A, (A 1) 90, 92, 93, 97, 99, (A 2) 112, (A 3) 113, (A 4) 125; from Site B, (B 1) 153, 155, 156, (B 2) 163, (B 3) 55, 175, 176; from Site D, 186

ironstone, 204

Kalambo basin, 1–2, 7–8; evolution of, 37–45; origin of, 30–1; sections across, 13, 15, 21, 50

Kalambo Falls, 1, 8–9, 197, 199; date of formation of, 44; height of, 9, 20

Kalambo Falls Formation, 48–50; archaeological horizons from, 238

Kalambo Gorge, 8, 9, 17

Kalambo Industry (Iron Age), 55, 99; pottery from, 55, 93, 155, 165, 186

Kalambo Interstadial period, coeval with Paudorf Interstadial in Europe, 73

Kalambo river, 7, 20, 44, 197, 199; changes in discharge of, 37, 45; comparison between former rates of flow of, and pollen spectra, 64–5, 75; former course of, 28, 30, 42–3, 199–200; longitudinal profile of, 31; orientation of boulders in, 40; Prehistoric Site as crossing place on, 34; present-day deposition of sediments by, 145–6

Kanjeran climatic episode, 213, 124

Kaposwa river, 38, 50, 199, 200, 202

Katanga/Kundelungu system of rocks, 2, 24, 25

Kate Granite, Kate Porphyry, in Kalambo basin, 21, 24, 26

Kawa River, 38, 43, 44, 199, 200, 202

Kipengere range, 3, 58, 62

Lake Beds, 50, 199, 200, 203–4; *see also* Mkamba Member

Lake Sundu fault, 32

lakes, in Kalambo Falls area, 6; temporary, in Quaternary, 200

lanceheads, 115, 167, 168

Levallois technique, 102, 131, 192

Lufira valley, Katanga, *miombo* forest in, 58

Lukuga river, run-off from Lake Tanganyika through, 33, 34, 35

Lungu people, 1, 7, 12, 142; pottery of, 90, 93, 146, 163, 195

Lupemban industry
  archaeological horizons of, 239
  artifacts of, from cliff, 10; from Rubble Beds, 52, 86, 192, 193, 194; from Site A, 11, 13, 150, 151, (A 1) 95, 99, 101, 102, 104, (A 3) 115, 116, (A 4) 128, 129, 131, 133, 135, (A 5) 142; from Site B, (B 1) 179, (B 2) 165, 166, 167, 168, 179; from Site C, 181, 185; from Site D, 187
  climate at time of, 232
  dating of, 150, 192
  final, 102, 109, 112
  lower horizon of, 16
  phases of, 14, 148

'Magosian' industry, 211, 212, 214
  archaeological horizons of, 238
  artifacts of, from Site A, 149, 150, 194, (A 1) 99, (A 2) 109, 112, (A 3) 115, 116, (A 4) 52 n., 125, 126, 127, (A 5) 142; from Site B, (B 1) 157, 179, (B 2) 166, 167, 179; from Site C, 185; from Site D, 187
  climatic correlation of, 212, 214
  dating of, 16, 193, 194

Makalian climatic episode, of increased rainfall in East Africa, 99, 212, 214

Malawi, Lake, 2

Mambwe people, 7, 195

man, effects of interference by, 2, 6, 57, 147

maps and plans
  of area between Lakes Malawi and Mweru, 59
  of Kalambo basin, contour, 14; geological, 22, 197; physiographic, 21
  of Kalambo Falls and surrounding country, 1
  of Site A, 91; of Site B, 154, 155; of Site C, 183

Mbisi forest, 60, 63

mbuga, 31, 32

Mbwilo Member of Kalambo Falls Formation, 22, 47, 48, 50, 53–4, 193
  complicated nature of, 85
  dating of, 54
  deposition of, 147
  geological events during, at Site A, 149–50; at Site B, 179
  pollen analyses from, 232
  at Site A, (A 1) 99, (A 4) 50, 124, 126, 128, 129; at Site B, (B 1) 157, (B 2) 164, 169, 174; at Site C, 50; at Site D, 187
  thickness of, 54
  see also Chitambala Gravel Beds, Rubble Bed I
metal tools, whetstone for, 93
microlithic industry, archaeological horizons of, 238
microliths, 31, 32, 194
  sieving to obtain, 86
  from Site A, (A 1) 90, (A 3) 116; from Site B, (B 1) 156, (B 2) 165; from Site C, 16, 17, 54
minerals, analysis of samples from excavation sites for, 230–1; of Lower Quartzite Series, 23
miombo woodland, 4, 13, 58
Mkamba Member of Kalambo Falls Formation, 22, 47, 48, 49, 50–2, 192
  Acheulian artifacts in, 52, 146, 190–1
  dating of, 52
  deposition of, 147
  geological events during, at Site A, 150–1; at Site B, 180
  pollen analyses from, 233–5
  at Site A, (A 1) 88–9, (A 4) 124, 129, 130, (A 6) 116; at Site B, (B 1) 158, (B 2) 164, 174
  thickness of, 52–3
  vegetable remains in, 87
  see also Lake Beds, Ochreous Sands, Rubble Bed II, Vundwe Gravel Beds, White Sands, etc.
Mount Kenya Hypothermal period, 74
mountains, grassland vegetation of, 6, 57
Muchinga range, 58, 61
mushitu woodland, 5, 7, 62–3, 71; fauna of, 6
muulu woodland, 58
Mwimbi fault, 31

Nakuran climatic episode, 212
Ndumbi forest, Kipengere range, 62
nomenclature, archaeological, 88, 238–9; of rock stratigraphic units at Kalambo Falls, 46–56

Ochreous Sands (Mkamba Member), 47, 48, 52
  complicated nature of, 85
  dating of, 135–6, 143–4, 146, 151, 188, 191
  deposition of, 147
  Sangoan artifacts in, 13, 52, 146, 191

  at Site A, (A 3) 116, (A 4) 135, (A 5) 140, 143, 144; at Site B, (B 1) 158, (B 2) 172, 173, 174; at Site C, 181; at Site D, 189
Odzungere range, 3
oil palm, 5

Pan-African Congress on Prehistory, 11, 153
pH profile, of Kalambo Falls site, 206–7
picks, from Site A, 192, (A 1) 120; from Site B, (B 2) 167, 168, 171
pisolites, iron, 109, 125
Pits Channel Fill, 47, 49, 130–1, 147, 192; Lupemban artifacts from, 52; pollen from, 136, 192
plants, useful, at Kalambo Falls Site, 228–9; see also trees
Plateau Series of Zambia, erosion scarp of, 26; rocks of, in Kalambo basin, 2, 21, 22, 24, 25, 50, 198
Pleistocene geological period, origin of Kalambo Falls during, 44; tectonic activity during, 43; thickness of sediments belonging to, in Kalambo basin, 37–8; vegetation and climate of Kalambo basin during, 57–74
Pliocene geological period, Kalambo basin during, 43
Podostemaceae (water plants), in Pleistocene, 65, 69, 76, 78, 80, 83, 84; pollen of, as percentage of total, 65, 75
points (artifacts), 102, 126, 167
pollen
  analyses of, 63–70, 75–83; conclusions from, 5, 18, 70–4, 191, 192, 193; summary of, 232–5
  from Angola and East Africa, 194
  taking of samples of, 12, 14, 17, 88; from Site A, 53, 93, 101, 191, (A 4) 131, 136, 137, 138, 191, (A 5) 142, 144; from Site B, (B 2) 169
  transport of, by water, 64–5, 75
potsherds
  of 'Middle Stone Age', 210
  at Site A, 90, 92, 97, (A 2) 109, 112, (A 3) 113, (A 4) 125, (A 5) 141; at Site B, (B 1) 153, 156, (B 2) 163–4, (B 3) 55
pottery
  from burials (?), 141, 164, 186–7
  channel-decorated (Channelled Ware), from Site A, 92, 95, 99, (A 5) 141; from Site B, (B 2) 163, 165, (B 3) 175; from Site C, 16
  dimple-based type, 11
  intermediate between channelled and modern Lungu, 17
  Iron Age, 113, 165, 205
  Kalambo Industry, 55, 93, 155, 165, 186
  Lungu (modern), 90, 93, 146, 163, 195

pre-Lungu, 92
undecorated, 97, 186–7, 194–5

quartzite, in debris in Sites A 4 and A 5, 148; flakes of, 90, 97, 106, 132, 158, 169, 188; 'Older Stone Age' tools of, 210; scrapers of, 144, 155
Quartzite Series, of Kalambo basin, 1, 2, 7, 23, 198, 199; gorge through, 8, 17, 38, 40, 201; soils on, 4

radiocarbon dating, 18, *236*; of Acheulian artifacts, 151; of channel fills, 105, 115; of charcoals from surface soil, 124; of Chiungu Member, 55, 165, 166, 194; of Iron Age artifacts, 149, 194; of Kalambo Falls Formation, 50; of Lupemban artifacts, 150, 192; of 'Magosian' artifacts, 16, 149, 193, 194; of Mbwilo Member, 54; of Mkamba Member, 52; of Ochreous Sands, 135–6, 143–4, 146, 151, 188, 191; of Rubble Beds, (I) 53–4, (Ia) 115, 150, (Ic) 104, 130, 150, 194, (II) 52, 130, 133, 136, 151; of sands below Rubble II, 169–70, 171; of Sangoan artifacts, 105, 143, 151, 191, 192; taking of samples for, 12, 14, 17, 88; of White Sands, 109, 137, 144, 146, 151, 191
raffia palm, 7
rainfall in Kalambo basin, 2, 3, 36, 58; in Pleistocene period, 68, 69, 71, 73
Red Clays, 22; chemical composition of, 92
Red Rubble, *see* Rubble Beds
Rhodesia, Sangoan in, 192
River Face Cliff, excavation at, 138; section at, 139
rubbers (upper grindstones), 93, 97, 155, 156, 167, 175
rubble beds
  as lag deposits, 49
  Lupemban artifacts from, 52, 86, 192, 193
  as marking former channels of river, and accumulation from screes, 86
  Red Rubble (colluvial), 16, 49, 53, 124–31 *passim*, 150
  Rubble Bed I (Mbwilo Member), 47, 49, 113, 116, 123, 127–31 *passim*, 150, 157, 181, 184; dating of, 53–4; deposition of, 147; four artifact-bearing horizons of, 17; Lupemban artifacts from, 13, 99, 168; orientation of boulders in, 41, 127; thickness of, 54
  Rubble Bed Ia, 53, 142, 166, 167; dating of, 115, 150
  Rubble Bed Ib, 53, 101, 115, 142, 166, 167, 168
  Rubble Bed Ic, 53, 101, 102, 103, 104, 115, 142; dating of, 105, 130, 150, 194

Rubble Bed II (Mkamba Member), 47, 49, 113, 123, 124, 127–32 *passim*, 150, 239; dating of, 52, 130, 133, 136, 151, 192; Lower Lupemban artifacts from, 52, 133–4, 192; orientation of boulders in, 127 n., 134, 135
Rukwa Lake, 2, 3; Rukwa rift valley, 25, 27
Rungwe mountain, 3, 58
Ruzizi river, rate of discharge of, into Lake Tanganyika, 34

sandstone, tools of, 132
Sandstone Series, Upper, of Kalambo basin, 1, 2, 23; soils on, 4
Sangoan industry
  archaeological horizons of, 239
  artifacts of, from Ochreous Sands, 13, 52, 146, 191; from Site A, 11, 13, 52, 143, (A 1) 95, 102, 104, 105, (A 4) 123, 136, 137, (A 5) 143; from Site B, 13, 52, (B 1) 158, 179, (B 2) 169, 170, 171, 173, 174, 179; from Site C, 52, 181, 182, 185
  climate at time of, 232–3
  climatic correlation of, 213, 214
  dating of, 105, 143, 151, 191, 192
  occupation floors of, 86–7, 158–9, 213, 214
Sansia Falls, 7, 64
schists of Kalambo basin, 23, 38–9
scrapers
  of 'Later Stone Age', 10
  from Site A, (A 1) 109, (A 3) 115, 116, (A 4) 132, 138, (A 5) 142, 144, (A 6) 120, 121; from Site B, (B 1) 155, 162, (B 2) 167
sections
  of cliffs, at Site A (River Face), *140*; at Site C, 51; at Tanganyika Cliff, 52–3
  of excavations, at Site A, 48, 49, (A 1) 94–5, 96, 98, 100, (A 3) 114, (A 4) *124*, (A 5) 139, (A 6) 119; at Site B, (B 1) *164*, (B 2) *172*, (B 3) *172*; at Site D, *186*
  geological, across Kalambo basin, 50, *38*; across Spillway Gorge, 39, 41
  topographic, across Kalambo basin at falls, 13, 15, 21
sediments of Kalambo basin, 17–18, 44–5; fluviatile nature of, 47; present-day deposition of, by Kalambo River, 145–6
seeds, from Pleistocene deposits, 216–17
shales of Kalambo basin, 2, 17, 23
Simwela (Kalindisi) river, 38
Siszya forest, 5, 59; Siszya ridge, 1, 7
Site A, 85–8, 145–8
  deposits at, 54–5
  excavation of, (1953), 10–11; (1956), 11; (1959), 12; (1963), 16; (1966), 17

geological events at, 149–51
plan of, 91
pollen from, 65, 76–7
sections at, 48, 49; showing position of pollen samples, 66
Site A 1, 88–109; analysis of minerals from, 230; pH profile in, 206–7; sections at, 94–5, 96, 98, 100
Site A 2, 109–13; sections at, 110, 111
Site A 3, 113–16; analysis of minerals from 230; section at, 114
Site A 4, 122–38; composition of debris from, 148; pollen from, 88; profile of sediments in auger hole at, 36, 49, 132; sections at, 124; White Clay Band in, 215
Site A 5 and River Cliff Face, 138–45; composition of debris from, 148
Site A 6, 117–22; concrete casing at, 17, 86, 117; section at, 119
Site B, 179–80
deposits at, 54–5
excavation of, (1956), 11, 12; (1959), 12–14; (1963), 16
fruits and seeds from, 216–17
geological events at, 179–80
plans of, 154, 155
pollen from, 65, 76–7
Site B 1, 153–62; analysis of minerals from, 231; section at, 156
Site B 2, 163–74; pollen from, 88; sections at, 164
Site B 3, 175; section at, 172
Site B 4, 176; section at, 172
Site B 5, 177–8
Site C, 181, 182–6
excavation of, (1956), 11; (1963), 16; (1966), 17
Mbwilo Member at, 54
plan of, 183
section at, 51
Site D, 186–9
channel filling at, 52
landslide at, 16
section at, 186
Site D 2, analysis of minerals from 231
sites, archaeological, correlation of, 190–5
slag, see iron slag
soils in Kalambo basin, 4, 6, 198–9; 'creep' of, 37, 38
Spillway Gorge, 10, 38–42, 199, 201–2; blocking and unblocking of, 12, 17, 45, 131, 133, 135, 147, 190, 192, 193, 194; fauna of, 7; geological section across, 39; mapping of, 5; origin of, 44
spores, of fungi and ferns, in pollen from Pleistocene, 77, 79, 81, 83

'Stone Age', artifacts of, ('Later'), 10, 156, 194; ('Middle'), 10, 90, 92, 187, 208, 210, 212, 214; ('Older'), 209, 210
stones, bored, 10, 156, 166–7, 194; circles of, 103; count of, on artifact horizons, Site A 6, 122; semi-circle of, 172
Sumbawanga corridor, 26, 27; Sumbawanga highlands, 7, 26
Sundu, Lake, 32
surfaces, Cretaceous (late), 27, 28; Gondwana, 27, 199; Jurassic (end-), 27, 28; Tertiary (mid-), 27, 28, 42; Tertiary (end-), 28, 30, 37, 43
surveys of Kalambo basin, geological, 12, 13, 47; topographical, 12, 13
swamps, 201; deposits in, 54, 55, 155, 174, 205–6; Pleistocene, pollen from, 65, 76–7, 78, 79; vegetation of, 37; see also dambos

Tanganyika Cliff, 37, deposits in, 49, 52; pollen from, 88; section at, 52, 192
Tanganyika, Lake, 2; bathymetric contours of, 26, 29; changes in level of, 34, 35; forests by, 62; formation of, 28, 30, 32, 43; hydrology of, 33; Kalambo River flows into, 7, 197; rift valley of, 25
Tanganyika/Nyasa corridor, 3
Tanganyika Plateau, 2
temperatures, in Europe and at Kalambo Falls, for last 70,000 years, 72; in Kalambo basin, 4, 36; during Pleistocene, 70–1
Tertiary geological period, Kalambo basin during 42–3
trapeze tool, 102
tree-trunks, 10, 11, 137, 160–1; possible platforms of, 161, 177, 178
trees and shrubs, species of, at Kalambo Falls, 225–7; useful, 228–9
tsetse fly, 6, 7
tuyère, fragments of, 90, 97, 175

Ubendian rocks (Basement Complex, Ruzizi group), 21, 25, 31, 42
Ufipa highlands, 3, 25, 26, 31; grasslands of, 58; Mbisi forest on, 60, 64; origin of, 28; rainfall on, 58; source of Kalambo river in, 7; uplift of, 43

valleys, swampy, section of, 62; see also dambos
varving, 133
vegetation
altitudinal distribution of, 60
in Kalambo basin, 57–63; during Pleistocene, 63–84

method for recovery of samples of, from clays, 87–8, 162

preservation of, in acid clays, 12, 206

record of changes in, from pollen samples, 5, 18, 70–4

from Site A, (A 4) 137, 138, (A 6) 118–19, 121; from Site B, (B 1) 153, 162, (B 2) 169, 173

see also wood

volcanic activity, and levels of Lake Tanganyika, 34; rifting accompanied by, 2–3

volcanic soils, 4, 6

Vundwe Gravel Beds (Mkamba Member), 22, 47, 49, 50

Vundwe river, 49, 204

water table, excavation below level of, 86; and nature of vegetation, 71

whetstone, for metal tools, 93

White Clay Band, at Site A 4, 215

White Sands (Mkamba Member), 47, 52

Acheulian artifacts in, 16, 52, 105–9, 145, 146, 190–1

dating of, 137, 144, 146, 151, 191

fruits and seeds from, 216–17

at Site A, (A 4) 137, (A 5) 144, (A 6) 120; at Site B, (B 1) 159, (B 2) 171, 174; at Site D, 189

winds, in Kalambo basin, 4, 18

wood

carbonized, 10, 121, 162, 173

conditions favouring preservation of, 206

dating of, 105, 109, 143, 144, 170, 171, 188 *236*

identification of specimens of, 67, 68, 87, 174, 218–20, 221–2

implements of, 12, 14, 153, 160, 162, 172, 174

methods for recovery of specimens of, 87, 161

from Site A, 11, (A 1) 103, 104, 108, (A 6) 120–1; from Site B, (B 1) 153, 160–1, 162, (B 2) 172, 174, (B 5) 178

taking of samples of, for radiocarbon dating, 12, 14, 88

see also bark, tree-trunks

woodlands, *see* forests